Economics of the

Property Tax

Studies of Government Finance

TITLES PUBLISHED

Federal Fiscal Policy in the Postwar Recessions
  by Wilfred Lewis, Jr.

Federal Tax Treatment of State and Local Securities
  By David J. Ott and Allan H. Meltzer

Federal Tax Treatment of Income from Oil and Gas
  by Stephen L. McDonald

Federal Tax Treatment of the Family
  by Harold M. Groves

The Role of Direct and Indirect Taxes in the Federal Revenue System
  John F. Due, Editor
  A Report of the National Bureau of Economic Research and the Brookings Institution (Princeton University Press)

The Individual Income Tax
  by Richard Goode

Federal Tax Treatment of Foreign Income
  by Lawrence B. Krause and Kenneth W. Dam

Measuring Benefits of Government Investments
  Robert Dorfman, Editor

Federal Budget Policy
  by David J. Ott and Attiat F. Ott

Financing State and Local Governments
  by James A. Maxwell

Essays in Fiscal Federalism
  Richard A. Musgrave, Editor

Economics of the Property Tax
  by Dick Netzer

Economics of the

Property Tax

DICK NETZER

Studies of Government Finance

THE BROOKINGS INSTITUTION

WASHINGTON, D.C.

ISBN-0-8157-6039-6 (paper)
ISBN-0-8157-6040-X (cloth)
Library of Congress Catalog Card Number 65-28602

THE BROOKINGS INSTITUTION is an independent organization devoted to nonpartisan research, education, and publication in economics, government, foreign policy, and the social sciences generally. Its principal purposes are to aid in the development of sound public policies and to promote public understanding of issues of national importance.

The Institution was founded December 8, 1927, to merge the activities of the Institute for Government Research, founded in 1916, the Institute of Economics, founded in 1922, and the Robert Brookings Graduate School of Economics and Government, founded in 1924.

The general administration of the Institution is the responsibility of a self-perpetuating Board of Trustees. The trustees are likewise charged with maintaining the independence of the staff and fostering the most favorable conditions for creative research and education. The immediate direction of the policies, program, and staff of the Institution is vested in the President, assisted by the division directors and an advisory council, chosen from the professional staff of the Institution.

In publishing a study, the Institution presents it as a competent treatment of a subject worthy of public consideration. The interpretations and conclusions in such publications are those of the author or authors and do not purport to represent the views of the other staff members, officers, or trustees of the Brookings Institution.

Foreword

IN RECENT YEARS, the property tax has accounted for almost nine-tenths of local government tax revenue in the United States and almost one-half of local general revenue from all sources, including grants received from state and local governments. The revenue potential of the property tax, therefore, is a major determinant both of the capacity of local governments to finance public education and other important functions, and of the need for additional state and federal aid. The tax, moreover, may significantly influence the cost of housing, land use, and the economic future of cities and suburbs.

The primary purpose of this study is to investigate the economic effects of the property tax. Dick Netzer's analysis presents a composite picture of the nature of the property tax, its incidence by economic groups and income classes, its effects on residential and industrial properties, future revenue potential, and the advantages and disadvantages of possible modifications. This is the first comprehensive analysis of the property tax to be undertaken since the publication of Jens P. Jensen's *Property Taxation in the United States* in 1931.

The author, who is Professor of Public Finance, Graduate School of Public Administration, New York University, wishes to acknowledge the helpful comments and suggestions made by Richard Goode and Joseph A. Pechman, and by the official reading committee for the volume, which consisted of Jesse Burkhead, George F. Break, and Ronald Welch. The manuscript was edited by Barbara P. Haskins. Helen B. Eisenhart prepared the index.

The study is part of a special program of research and education on taxation and public expenditures, supervised by the National Committee on Government Finance and financed by a special grant from the Ford Foundation.

The views expressed in this study are those of the author and do not purport to represent the views of the National Committee on Government Finance or the advisory committee, or the staff members, officers, or trustees of the Brookings Institution, or the Ford Foundation.

Robert D. Calkins
President

December 1965
Washington, D.C.

Author's Preface

THE MOST RECENT COMPREHENSIVE REVIEW of the economics of the property tax is Jens P. Jensen's *Property Taxation in the United States,* published by the University of Chicago Press in 1931. Although three decades have passed since then, Jensen's book remains the standard work, and with good reason. In many respects, neither property tax institutions nor analytic approaches to the tax have changed very much since 1931, and Jensen's handling leaves little to be desired.

This volume is *not* a latter-day version of Jensen. The reader will find Jensen referred to as one of the basic sources in regard to the history of the tax, property tax incidence theory, and the capitalization process in particular, all of which are treated only briefly here. The book also has little comment on such intricate problems as the application of ad valorem taxation to specialized types of property—public utilities, forest lands, mining property, and the like. A more fundamental restriction is the limited treatment of property tax administration.

The administration problem has been a central one with regard to the American property tax for a century, with general agreement that the tax is frequently, if not usually, very badly administered indeed. There is considerable literature about this, and Jensen devotes many pages to the subject. More recent overviews can be found in works of Frederick Bird and the Advisory Commission on Intergovernmental Relations. Characteristically, writings on administration address themselves to the problem of improving property tax administration, with the implicit or explicit assumption that the property tax has sufficient merits on economic grounds to justify this effort.

The central issue here is: Is this really so? As the property tax actually works in the United States today, what is the state of the economic case for and against it? The reason for making such an inquiry at this point in time is twofold: first, the property tax is most certainly not withering away, despite some earlier indications that this might happen; second, in the years since Jensen wrote, a large body of quantitative information having some bearing on the property tax has been developed. Most of these data are elements of general-purpose statistical programs, such as the national income accounts, national wealth estimates, the economic Censuses, and the Census of Housing. But, in addition, we now have at hand the invaluable data from the 1957 and 1962 Census of Governments and the annual series prepared by the Governments Division of the Census Bureau. A major element of the present study, then, is to appraise the property tax in the light of information and relationships unknown in earlier years.

This is hardly the last word on the economics of the property tax. Although much improved, the data are seldom exactly what one requires to provide clear-cut answers to the principal questions. Moreover, there is enormous geographic variation in property taxation, and generalizations based on nationwide aggregates may prove wide of the mark in many places. Hopefully, the unsatisfactory answers of this study provide some clues for future research.

That the property tax merits enough attention to engage as much as two years of one's life was first suggested to me by George W. Mitchell's penetrating doubts about the institution, which is a bias I share. This book also reflects many hours of discussion with Lynn A. Stiles over the years; some of the most useful ideas here are no more than bowdlerized versions of his original contributions. Another large debt is owed Allen D. Manvel for his continual efforts to provide me with everything the Census of Governments could possibly yield, a debt which I have repaid by making the Census data say a good many indefensible things.

Emanuel Tobier assisted me with the research for this study, and equally important, permitted me to test my ideas against his critical faculties. It is conventional to acknowledge one's secretary in prefaces, but my debt to Marie Muller, who suffered through all the various drafts, is real, not conventional.

Dick Netzer

Studies of Government Finance

Studies of Government Finance is a special program of research and education in taxation and government expenditures at the federal, state, and local levels. These studies are under the supervision of the National Committee on Government Finance appointed by the trustees of the Brookings Institution, and are supported by a special grant from the Ford Foundation.

MEMBERS OF THE ADVISORY COMMITTEE

Contents

Foreword   vii

Author's Preface   ix

  I. The Property Tax in the United States   1
       Critics of the Tax   3
       Property Taxation Today   8
       Property Taxation in Other Countries   11
       Purpose of This Study   16

  II. Sources of Property Tax Revenue   17
       Breakdown by Industry   22
       Standard of Economic Neutrality   26
       Taxes on Housing   29

  III. Who Pays the Property Tax?   32
       Incidence Theory   32
       Evidence on Incidence by Income Class, 1957   40
       Taxes on Nonresidential Property   42
       Taxes on Residential Property   45
       Property Taxes and Expenditure Benefits   59
       Current Versus Permanent Income   62

  IV. Economic Effects   67
       Effect of Income Tax and Property Tax on Housing   69
       Criteria for Neutrality   71
       The Property Tax and the Future of the Big Cities   74

  V. Geographic Differentials in Property Taxation   86
       Interarea Differentials   89
       Differentials Within Urban Areas   116

VI.   The Personal Property Component of the Tax Base   138
      Present Coverage of Personal Property Taxation   140
      Revenue from Taxation of Personal Property   149
      Geographic Differences in the Relative Importance of
          Personal Property in the Tax Base   153
      Incidence of Personal Property Taxation   155

VII. A General Appraisal of the Institution   164
      Alternatives to the Property Tax   166
      Advantages of the Property Tax   170
      Property Tax Administration   173
      Elasticity of the Property Tax   184

VIII. Alternative Forms for the Property Tax   191
      Annual Versus Capital Values   192
      Site Value Taxation   197
      Land Value Increment Taxation   212
      A "Family of User Charges"   214
      Conclusion   217

APPENDIX A.   Derivation of Estimates for Tables 2-1,
              2-2, and 2-3   222

APPENDIX B.   Alternative Estimates of Property Tax
              Impact   238

APPENDIX C.   Nonresidential Property Taxes and
              Expenditure Benefits: Derivation   247

APPENDIX D.   Selected Tables   259

APPENDIX E.   Residential Property Tax Incidence in
              Northern New Jersey, by Emanuel Tobier   265

APPENDIX F.   Evidence from the 1960 Census of
              Housing on Property Tax Rate Differ-
              entials by Type of Property   297

APPENDIX G.   Derivation of Data in Tables to Chapter V   302

APPENDIX H.   Derivation of Table 6-3   310

Index   313

Text Tables

1-1 State and Local Government Property Tax Revenue in the United
States, Selected Years, 1860-1963   2
1-2 The Role of the Property Tax, 1962   9
1-3 Property Taxes in Selected Countries in Recent Years   12
1-4 Property Taxation in Western Europe, 1963   14

2-1 General Property Tax Revenue by Property Use Class, 1957   18
2-2 Total Property Tax Revenue by Property Use Class, 1957   19
2-3 Estimated Distribution of Total Property Tax Revenue by Major
Economic Sector, 1957   20
2-4 Property Tax Payments, Income Originating, and Wealth, Nonfarm Business, 1956-57   24
2-5 Property Tax Payments and Value Added in Manufacturing
Industries, 1957   27
2-6 Property Taxes on Agriculture and Related Magnitudes, 1956-57   28
2-7 Property Taxes on Nonfarm Housing and Related Magnitudes,
1956-57   29
2-8 1960 Census of Housing Evidence on Real Estate Taxes in
Relation to Housing Costs and Property Values   30

3-1 Nonresidential Property Taxes as a Percentage of Money Income
Before Taxes in Various Studies   43
3-2 Estimated Distribution of Nonresidential Property Taxes by
Money Income Class, 1957, Before Federal Tax Offset   44
3-3 Estimated Distribution of Nonresidential Property Taxes for 1957,
by Money Income Class After Federal Tax Offset   45
3-4 Residential Property Taxes as a Percentage of Money Income in
Various Studies   46
3-5 Survey Research Center Findings on Residential Property Tax
and Money Income Relationships, 1959   47
3-6 Real Estate Taxes and Adjusted Gross Income (AGI) on U.S.
Individual Income Tax Returns for 1960   49
3-7 Property Taxes Paid on Owner-Occupied Single-Family Houses,
1959-60, by Income of Owner   50
3-8 Estimated Property Taxes Paid on Renter-Occupied Nonfarm
Housing, 1959-60, by Income of Renter   52
3-9 Estimated Property Taxes on Nonfarm Housing, 1959-60, by
Income Class   54
3-10 Estimated Distribution of Residential Property Taxes, 1957, by
Money Income Class   55
3-11 Estimated Residential Property Taxes as Percentages of Money
Income in Eight Northeastern New Jersey Counties, 1960   58
3-12 Estimated Percentage Distribution of Benefits from Property Tax
Financed Local Expenditures by Money Income Class, 1957   60
3-13 Estimated Benefits from Property Tax Financed Local Expenditures as Percentages of Money Income, 1957   61
3-14 Property Taxes and Expenditure Benefits as Percentages of
Money Income   62

4-1   Assessment Ratios and Assessed Value Composition, Twelve
      Large Cities, 1961   76

5-1   The Property Tax in State-Local Revenue Systems, 1962   90
5-2   Estimated Percentage Distribution of Assessed Value of Property
      Subject to Local General Property Taxation (After Deduction
      of Exemptions), by Type, by States, 1961   98
5-3   Relative Per Capita Economic Base of the Property Tax, by
      States, 1959   100
5-4   Estimated Effective Property Tax Rates, by States, 1957, 1960,
      and 1962   102
5-5   Effective Property Tax Rates and Other Property Tax Charac-
      teristics: Frequency Distributions of 50 States   104
5-6   Regional Differences in Real Estate Taxes on Owner-Occupied
      Single-Family Houses, 1960   106
5-7   Property Tax Differentials, Central Cities versus Suburbs, Se-
      lected Large Metropolitan Areas, Selected Years Between 1957 and
      1961   118
5-8   Extent of Reliance on the Property Tax by Metropolitan Area
      Local Governments, 1957   121
5-9   Relationships Among Tax Rates, Expenditures, and Property
      Values in Selected Areas   126

6-1   Gross Assessed Value of Personal Property Subject to General
      Property Taxation (Excluding Public Utility Property), 1956
      and 1961   142
6-2   Estimated National Wealth in the Form of Privately Owned
      Tangible Personal Property, 1956 and 1958   144
6-3   Estimated National Wealth in the Form of Privately Owned Tan-
      gible Personal Property Legally Subject to General Property
      Taxation, 1956 and 1958   145
6-4   Distribution of Locally Assessed Personal Property Subject to
      Local General Property Taxation, Twenty Selected States, 1961   146
6-5   Estimated Distribution of Assessed Value of Locally Assessed
      Tangible Personal Property, 1961   147
6-6   Estimated Revenue from Taxation of Personal Property (Exclud-
      ing Public Utility Property), 1957   151
6-7   Revenue from Special Property Taxes, 1957, by Type of Property   151
6-8   Estimated Revenue from Taxation of Tangible Personal Property,
      by Type of Property, 1957   152

7-1   Estimated Nationwide Average Tax Rates Required for Alter-
      native Replacements for Local Property Revenue, 1963   167
7-2   Dispersion of Assessment Ratios for Nonfarm Houses in Selected
      Local Areas, 1956 and 1961   177
7-3   Assessment Ratios for Nonfarm Houses and for Locally Assessed
      Realty in General (Partial Coverage), Selected Major Cities,
      1961   178
7-4   Income Elasticity of Privately Owned Components of National
      Wealth, 1900-58 and 1945-58   188
7-5   Evidence on Income Elasticity of the Property Tax in the Post-
      war Period   190

Figures

1 Property Tax Revenue as Percentages of State-Local Revenue and Gross National Product, Selected Years, 1902-50, Annually 1952-63   4

2 Property Tax Revenue as a Percentage of Total General Revenue, by Level of Government, 1962   10

3 Estimated Distribution of Property Tax Revenue by Major Types of Property, 1957   22

4 Property Tax Payments Relative to Income and Wealth, 1957   25

5 Property Taxes and Expenditure Benefits as Percentages of Money Income, 1957   41

6 Relationship of House Value and "Normal Income" in Eight Northeastern New Jersey Counties, 1960   64

7 Intrametropolitan Area Relations Among Tax Rates, Expenditures, and Assessed Values   128

8 Value of Net Stock of Legally Taxable Tangible Assets, 1958, and Total Assessed Value of Tangible Personal Property, 1961   148

Appendix Tables

A-1 Sample of County Areas Used for Estimated Distribution of General Property Tax Revenue by Type of Property, 1957   224

B-1 Two Distributions of Property Tax Revenue by Type of Property Compared   239

B-2 Alternative Estimates of Property Taxes on Nonfarm Housing   242

B-3 Estimated Distribution of Property Tax Revenue Derived from Nonfarm Housing, 1957   244

B-4 Estimated Real Estate Taxes on Nonfarm Housing, 1959-60, Based on 1960 Census of Housing Data   245

D-1 Shifting Assumptions and Allocators for Local Property Taxes on Nonresidential Property, 1957   259

D-2 Distribution of Taxes on Agricultural Property by Income Class, 1957, Under Alternative Shifting Assumptions   260

D-3 Distribution of Taxes on Manufacturing Property by Income Class, 1957, Under Alternative Shifting Assumptions   260

D-4 Marginal Federal Income Tax Rates Used in Computation of Federal Tax Offsets   261

D-5 Estimated Local Government General Expenditure Financed from Property Taxes, 1957   261

D-6 Real Estate Taxes on U.S. Individual Income Tax Returns for 1960   262

D-7 Percentage Distribution of Homeowner Properties by Value, 1960   262

D-8 Income of Households in Owner-Occupied Housing within Standard Metropolitan Statistical Areas, 1959   263

D-9 Income and Rent for Nonfarm Renter-Occupied Housing in the United States, 1960   263

D-10 Income and Value Relationships, Owner-Occupiers of Single-Family Nonfarm Houses, 1960   264

E-1   Population, Number of Households, and Form of Tenure by
      County in Study Area, 1960   283
E-2   Family Income, Property Values, and Property Taxes in Study
      Area, 1960   284
E-3   Actual Real Property Tax Per Occupied Housing Unit by County 284
E-4   Average Sales and Average Assessed Value by Sales Price Interval
      for Residential Properties with Four Housing Units or Less,
      1963   285
E-5   Weighted Assessment-Sales Ratios by Sales Price Interval and
      Type of Residential Property for Counties in the Study Area,
      1963   286
E-6   Estimated Average Gross Monthly Rental by Rental Class for
      Counties in Study Area, 1960   287
E-7   Relationship Between Median Monthly Contract Rent and Median
      Monthly Gross Rent by County in Study Area, 1960   288
E-8   Derivation of Relationship Between Net Rental Receipts and
      Value of Renter-Occupied Housing Units, 1960   289
E-9   Value of Single-Family Owner-Occupied Units and Gross
      Monthly Rents by Income of Household in Bergen County,
      1960   290
E-10 Summary of Estimates of Composite Average Assessed and Average
      Sales Values for All Occupied (Owner and Renter) Housing Units
      by Total Income of Household, 1960   291
E-11 House Value-Income Ratio by Current Income Class for Coun-
      ties in Study Area   292
E-12 Average Adjusted Gross Income by Income Class in Standard
      Metropolitan Statistical Areas Within Study Area, 1961   293
E-13 Income Distribution Among Households in Bergen County by
      Occupation of Head of Household, 1960   294
E-14 Value of Single-Family Owner-Occupied Units and Gross
      Monthly Rentals by Occupation of Head of Household in
      Bergen County, 1960   295
E-15 Weighted Average Value of All Occupied Units, Average Annual
      Lifetime Income, and Value-Income Ratio, by Occupation of
      Head of Household and by County, for Counties in Study
      Area   296
F-1   Composition of Rental and Vacant Nonfarm Residential Proper-
      ties, United States, 1960   298
F-2   Median Values, Rents, and Real Estate Taxes, Mortgaged Rental
      and Vacant Nonfarm Residential Properties, United States,
      1960   300
F-3   Regional Distribution of Mortgaged Rental and Vacant Nonfarm
      Residential Properties, 1960   300

CHAPTER I

The Property Tax in the United States

THE AMERICAN PROPERTY TAX abounds in anomalies. During the past century, no major fiscal institution, here or abroad, has been criticized at such length and with such vigor; yet no major fiscal institution has changed so little in modern times. There is a vast literature on the property tax; yet less is known about its overall impact, incidence, and effects than is known about any other major tax. The demise of the property tax as a major factor in the American fiscal scene has long been heralded; yet it continues to finance more than one-fifth of the civilian general expenditures of federal, state, and local governments. The United States is the citadel of capitalism; yet this tax on wealth is more important in the fiscal system and relative to national income than are comparable taxes in any other advanced country in the world except Canada.

By and large, the keys to the paradoxes lie in the venerability and diversity of the property tax. It is an old institution and it is actually not a single national tax but an incredibly complex collection of taxes with literally thousands of local variations.[1]

---

[1] Until Chap. V, the aggregative behavior of the property tax will be investigated and geographic differences largely ignored.

1

TABLE 1-1. State and Local Government Property Tax Revenue in the United States, Selected Years, 1860–1963

Year[a]	Amount (Millions of dollars)[b]	Per Capita[b]	Total State-Local Tax Revenue	Percentage of Gross National Product[c]	Privately Owned National Wealth[d] Total	Privately Owned National Wealth[d] Excluding Consumer Durables
1860	$ 94	$ 3.00	n.a.	n.a.	n.a.	n.a.
1870	226	5.87	n.a.	3.4%	n.a.	n.a.
1880	314	6.26	n.a.	3.4	0.8%	0.9%
1890	471	7.53	n.a.	3.7	0.7	0.8
1902	706	8.92	82.1%	3.2	0.8	0.8
1913	1,332	13.70	82.8	3.3	0.9	0.9
1922	3,321	30.17	82.7	4.5	1.2	1.3
1927	4,730	39.74	77.7	4.9	1.3	1.5
1934	4,076	32.25	68.9	6.3	1.5	1.7
1940	4,430	33.53	56.7	4.4	1.3	1.5
1946	4,986	35.27	49.4	2.4	0.9	1.0
1950	7,349	48.45	46.2	2.6	0.8	1.0
1952	8,652	55.10	44.8	2.5	0.9	1.0
1953	9,375	58.73	44.8	2.6	0.9	1.1
1954	9,967	61.37	45.2	2.7	0.9	1.1
1955	10,735	64.95	45.7	2.7	0.9	1.1
1956	11,749	70.24	44.6	2.8	0.9	1.1
1957	12,864	75.54	44.6	2.9	1.0	1.1
1958	14,047	81.04	46.2	3.2	1.0	1.2
1959	14,983	84.88	46.3	3.1	n.a.	n.a.
1960	16,405	91.15	46.3	3.3	n.a.	n.a.
1961	18,002	98.35	46.3	3.5	n.a.	n.a.
1962	19,054	102.54	45.9	3.4	n.a.	n.a.
1963	20,089	106.51	45.4	3.4	n.a.	n.a.

n.a. Not available.

[a] Throughout this study, all Census Bureau data on revenues and expenditures apply to the state and local government fiscal years ending during the calendar year indicated. Other data are for calendar years, except where otherwise stated.

[b] Sources: 1860–90, Jens P. Jensen, *Property Taxation in the United States* (University of Chicago Press, 1931), Table 2; 1902–57, U. S. Bureau of the Census, *Census of Governments; 1957*, Vol. IV, No. 3, "Historical Summary of Governmental Finances in the United States" (1959), Table 4; 1958–62, U. S. Bureau of the Census, *Census of Governments; 1962*, Vol. VI, No. 4, "Historical Statistics on Governmental Finances and Employment" (1964), Tables 1 and 2; 1963, U. S. Bureau of the Census, *Governmental Finances in 1963*, Series G-GF63-No. 2 (October 1964), Table 4.

[c] Sources: 1870–1946, U. S. Bureau of the Census, *Historical Statistics of the United States: Colonial Times to 1957*, Series F 1-5 (1960); 1870–1913 data are based on GNP annual averages for five-year periods bracketing the dates indicated; 1950–63, U. S. Department of Commerce, Office of Business Economics, *Survey of Current Business*, July 1964.

[d] Includes privately owned land, structures, producer durables, consumer durables, and inventories, excluding estimated wealth owned by "institutions," presumably exempt from property taxes. Sources: 1880 and 1890, *Historical Statistics of the United States*, Series F 197-221; land value is assumed to be 90 percent of the value of structures, in the aggregate, the relation which obtains in the Goldsmith data for 1900–15; 1902–58, tabulated from various tables in Raymond W. Goldsmith, *The National Wealth of the United States in the Postwar Period* (Princeton University Press for National Bureau of Economic Research, 1962), and *A Study of Saving in the United States* (Princeton University Press, 1956), Vol. III

Property taxation has been the major fiscal resource of American local governments since seventeenth century colonial days. During the first two centuries of its existence, the property tax gradually became a general tax measured by the value of all types of privately owned assets, with all assets taxed at a uniform rate. However, in the last hundred years, it has become less general in coverage, in large part because of the difficulty of administering so universal a tax uniformly in an increasingly complex society.[2] In most of the states the tax is now one chiefly on real estate and business equipment and inventories.[3] Although the property tax is no longer virtually the sole support of state-local government in the United States as it was at the turn of the twentieth century, it remains the single most important factor in state-local finance, by a wide margin (see Table 1-1).

Critics of the Tax

There have been waves of criticism associated in time with the changing fortunes of the property tax: savage across-the-board attacks in the late nineteenth century; a somewhat more moderate tone and a quest for ways to make the institution work more effectively in the 1920's; renewed broadsides in the 1930's; and what can be best described as a "new complacency" regarding the property tax in the last decade. As to the earlier criticisms, Jensen, writing in 1931, had this to say:

If any tax could have been eliminated by adverse criticism, the general property tax should have been eliminated long ago. One searches in vain for one of its friends to defend it intelligently. It is even difficult to find anyone who has given it careful study who can subsequently speak of its failure in temperate language. . . . Should some prosecuting attorney drag the tax as a culprit before a bar of justice, he would be embarrassed by the abundance of expert evidence against it. No writer of repute writing on state and local taxation in the United States has failed to offer his bit of derogatory testimony. No

[2] For an excellent brief history of the property tax in the United States, see Jens P. Jensen, *Property Taxation in the United States* (University of Chicago Press, 1931), Chap. II.

[3] See Chap. VI for a discussion of the present extent of coverage of personal property.

FIGURE 1. Property Tax Revenue as Percentages of State-Local Revenue and Gross National Product, Selected Years, 1902-50, Annually, 1952-63

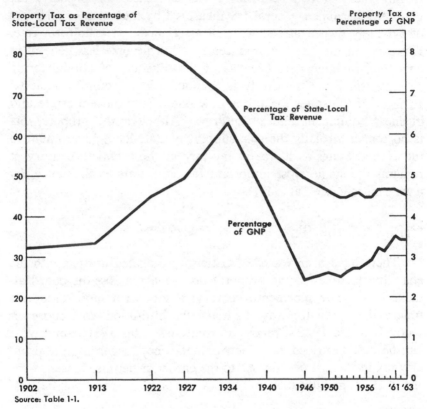

Source: Table 1-1.

commission appointed to investigate any state tax system, which has had time, means, and inclination to secure the evidence, has failed to recommend the abolition of the tax or measures tending toward fundamental modification. Where permanent administrative tax commissions have had time, capacity, and means to busy themselves with what ought to be one of their major tasks, the study and constructive criticism of the state tax system, they have without exception arrived at similar conclusions.

Yet the tax persists.[4]

One strand of the nineteenth century criticism, of course, was the single-tax movement. Taxes on the value of site improvements, structures, and personal property, as well as commodity taxes, were

[4] Jensen, *Property Taxation in the U.S.*, p. 478.

denounced as inequitable and a deterrent to investment.[5] Seligman in his celebrated 1895 essay on "The General Property Tax" summarized the main academic strand of criticism.[6] First, the tax, according to Seligman, was simply not administrable: "Practically, the general property tax as actually administered is beyond all doubt one of the worst taxes known in the civilized world."[7] He classed the administrative defects as inherent rather than correctible. But he also held that, even if the administrative problems could be overcome, the tax was intolerable on theoretical grounds.[8]

The main counts in Seligman's indictment were twofold. First, because of the heterogeneity of property in a modern complex economy and the distinction between rights and claims in property and the physical thing itself, the tax was not one on personal wealth but an erratically double-counting tax on gross assets with virtually no theoretical underpinnings. Second, the tax had almost no relationship to ability to pay, for property had been replaced by product as evidence of such ability. While, over time, asset values do tend to reflect capitalized income, income flows are not necessarily coincident with asset values for particular taxpayers at particular dates. Moreover, property ownership is an incomplete measure of income potentials, since investment in human capital and differences in exertion are not reached by the property tax.

In addition, the property tax worked out in practice to be quite regressive in incidence; that is, the tax as a percentage of the incomes of those who bear the ultimate burden declines as income rises. Other critics supported the regressivity argument with empirical evidence, and found that the incidence of the tax was not only regressive but also poorly related to the benefits received from public expenditure financed by the property tax.[9] Yet another serious shortcoming was considered to be the tax's discouragement of investment in that social necessity, housing.

The early wave of criticism of the tax no doubt contributed to two significant developments: first, the narrowing of the coverage of the tax by constitutional and statutory changes; and second, after 1910, the increasingly widespread adoption by state govern-

---

[5] See Henry George, *Progress and Poverty* (1879), Book VIII, Chap. III.
[6] Edwin R. A. Seligman, *Essays in Taxation* (Macmillan, 1895), Chap. II.
[7] *Ibid.*, p. 61 (1911 edition).
[8] *Ibid.*, pp. 32-36 and 54-60 (1911 edition).
[9] See Jensen, *Property Taxation in the U.S.*, pp. 78-83.

ments of income, consumption, and highway-user taxes, thus reducing state government dependence on the property tax. In the 1920's, however, the property tax seemed to gain a new lease on life. Rapid population increase, growing urbanization, and the lengthening of the period of compulsory school attendance produced a sharp increase in local government spending, and the funds for this were produced by the property tax without apparent difficulty.

This rising productivity of the property tax led to a different line of analysis: the revenues were substantial and no substitute for the tax was in sight; therefore it was unlikely to disappear no matter how deficient. Could anything be done to make it work better? Conventional solutions offered were narrowing the tax base to those classes of property which could be most easily discovered, realty and business personalty (or, alternatively, classifying intangibles and some tangible personalty for taxing at special low rates); improving local assessment administration via larger primary assessment units, better staff at the local level, and more state participation in the form of central assessment, equalization of differences in assessments among counties, and the like; and adopting supplementary state nonproperty taxes to lessen dependence on the property tax.[10]

With the onset of the Great Depression, property values declined sharply; indeed, real estate markets virtually collapsed. This collapse, and the sharp decline in income with which to actually pay property taxes, brought a renewal of the old attack. For, as George Mitchell put it,

. . . the "great defects" had become fatal defects; the "difficulties," frustrating dilemmas. And this economic environment revealed a defect to which no one had theretofore given much attention—the tax could not be collected, at least not with the promptness and certainty required by governments living from hand to mouth or on their short-term credit.[11]

[10] *Ibid.*, pp. 486-92. Two representative expressions of this "conventional answer" are Simeon E. Leland, *The Classified Property Tax* (Houghton Mifflin, 1928), and National Tax Association, "Report of the Committee on a Model System of State and Local Taxation," in *Proceedings of the Twelfth Annual Conference* (1919), pp. 426-70.

[11] George W. Mitchell, "Is This Where We Came In?" *Proceedings of the Forty-Ninth Annual Conference,* National Tax Association (1956), p. 488.

Not without scholarly support, the states were abandoning the property tax, a few were imposing severe overall rate limits on local governments, and one (Florida) came very near abolishing it altogether. The apparent inadequacy of the tax base in a changing economy was added to the old charges of regressivity, lack of correlation with benefits, and poor administration. Scholars urged the adoption of new forms of taxation as well as radical reshaping of the property tax itself.[12]

Just as it did in the 1920's, revenue productivity of the property tax in recent years has softened criticism. By the late 1950's, after years of decline in relative fiscal importance (particularly during World War II), assessments and tax rates were climbing sharply.[13] Moreover, even those investigators who were not well disposed toward the property tax could not deny that its income elasticity appeared to be much higher than they had previously assumed.[14]

Since public expenditures have been increasing and are expected to continue to increase more rapidly at the local level than elsewhere, a major tax producer, the revenues from which appear to be responsive to economic growth, is not without its friends. One group of friendly critics is represented by the Advisory Commission on Intergovernmental Relations: the viewpoint is essentially that the property tax is really not so bad if adequately administered; and reasonably high standards of administration, although infrequently found, are attainable goals.[15] The problem, according

[12] A symposium held in December 1939 by the Tax Policy League (forerunner of the present Tax Institute) provides a good collection of the then-current scholarly opinion. Tax Policy League, *Property Taxes* (1940), especially the papers by Paul Wueller (pp. 21-34), Clarence Heer (pp. 155-64), Edwin H. Spengler (pp. 165-73), Harold M. Groves (pp. 174-86), and C. Lowell Harriss (pp. 218-29).

[13] However, as late as 1956, George Mitchell forecast that, in twenty years, "the property tax will . . . have become an all-but-forgotten relic of an earlier fiscal age," in *Proceedings*, National Tax Association (1956), p. 494.

[14] See Chap. VII. As used here, "income elasticity" refers to the percentage increase in the market value of taxable property associated with a given percentage increase in gross national product.

[15] Advisory Commission on Intergovernmental Relations (ACIR), *The Role of the States in Strengthening the Property Tax*, Vol. 1 (1963). ACIR was established in 1959 as a permanent bipartisan commission with twenty-six members drawn from Congress, the executive branch of the federal government, governors, state legislatures, mayors, elected county officials, and private persons. Its aim is to advance cooperation among levels of government and to improve the effectiveness of the federal system. It has prepared and issued numerous reports dealing with specific intergovernmental problems.

to these critics, is one of "rehabilitation" of the tax, not fundamental reform—language which suggests that there was a Golden
Age in property tax administration in some earlier period. Another
approach has been taken by Jesse Burkhead and other investigators
at Syracuse University. They maintain that the dire economic effects theoretically expected do not seem to be of major consequence
empirically. Their statistical findings also suggest that, "at least in
suburban areas, it is a fairly adequate surrogate for a local income
tax, since a high relationship has been found between property values
and income levels."[16] Thus Burkhead concludes:

> On the whole . . . the property tax is a far better fiscal instrument
> than most of its critics have allowed. There is every reason to believe
> that it will continue to hold its relative fiscal importance in state-local
> public finance structures. . . . Although the property tax has long been
> condemned by students of fiscal affairs, its recent behavior suggests that
> it would be far better to strengthen this levy than to plan for its eradi-
> cation.[17]

Property Taxation Today

Currently, property tax revenues are about the same fraction
of the gross national product (GNP) as they were in the early years
of the century, though well below the percentages in the 1920's
and 1930's. Because of the long historic decline in the ratio of
national wealth to GNP, the property tax is significantly higher in
relation to national wealth than fifty or sixty years ago, but still
below the relationships existing in the 1920's. Perhaps the outstanding feature of the recent behavior of the property tax is the
way in which in the past decade its revenues have kept pace with
increases in state-local expenditure and thus its decline in relative
importance has been arrested. Although the evidence is inconclu-
sive, it does appear that part of the reason for this behavior is that
the economic base of the property tax—the market value of taxable types of property—has been extremely responsive to growth

---

[16] Alan K. Campbell, "Most Dynamic Sector," *National Civic Review,* Vol.
53 (February 1964), p. 9.

[17] Jesse Burkhead, *State and Local Taxes for Public Education* (Syracuse University Press, 1963), pp. 70, 105.

in national output in the postwar period, an apparent interruption to the long decline in capital-output ratios.[18] In any event, property tax *revenues* have exhibited a responsiveness or "GNP elasticity" far higher than earlier expectations.

TABLE 1-2. The Role of the Property Tax, 1962

Level of Government	Amount (Millions of dollars)	Percentage Distribution	Property Tax Revenue As Percentage of—		
			Total Tax Revenue	General Revenue from Own Sources	Total General Revenue
All State and Local Governments	$19,054	100.0	45.9	37.8	32.7
State Governments	640	3.4	3.1	2.7	2.1
Local Governments	18,414	96.6	87.7	69.0	48.0
Counties	3,879	20.4	93.5	74.5	45.7
Municipalities	5,807	30.5	73.2	55.6	44.2
Townships	1,068	5.6	93.3	84.3	67.3
School Districts	7,216	37.9	98.6	86.2	51.0
Special Districts	445	2.3	100.0	31.7	25.0

Sources: U. S. Bureau of the Census, *Census of Governments, 1962*, Vol. IV, No. 4, "Compendium of Government Finances" (1964), Table 3; and *Property Taxation in 1962* (State and Local Government Special Studies No. 47 1964).

For the country as a whole, the property tax is most important for school districts among the tiers of local government (see Table 1-2). School districts, county governments, and townships each receive virtually all their tax revenue and three-fourths or more of all locally raised funds from the property tax. City governments, which are the primary users of local nonproperty taxes and which also rely heavily on charges and miscellaneous nontax revenues,

[18] See the discussion in Chap. VII. "Capital," in the capital-output ratios discussed here, is defined as the capital ordinarily subject to the property tax, including residential real estate. If nonfarm housing is excluded from capital, and the measure confined to privately owned nonresidential realty and business (and farm) personalty, it appears that the long term decline in capital-output ratios (from 1900 to 1958) has been even greater and the interruption in the postwar years even sharper.

The "economic base" of the property tax is not the same thing as the legal base, that is, the assessed values actually appearing on the tax rolls. In general, assessed values are well below market values of taxed assets, and, in addition, there are many types of partial or total exemptions of privately owned assets.

FIGURE 2. Property Tax Revenue as a Percentage of Total General
Revenue, by Level of Government, 1962

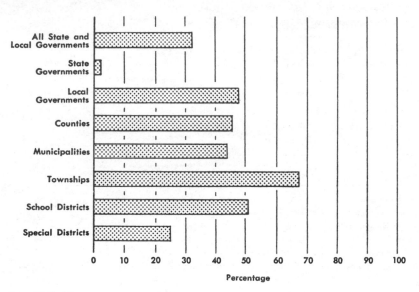

Source: Table 1-2.

are a good deal less dependent on the property tax in the aggregate, although the totals are heavily weighted by the experience of the larger cities. It appears that about 52 percent of local property tax revenue in 1962 was devoted to education, and the property tax financed about 55 percent of school outlays met from current revenues for the country as a whole. Local property tax revenues devoted to nonschool purposes financed about 47 percent of local nonschool general expenditures met from current revenues; somewhat less than 50 percent for highways, health, and hospitals; less than 25 percent for welfare; about two-thirds for sanitation and sewerage; and nearly all for the other common local functions.[19]

[19] These estimates are based on a combination of data from various tables in the 1962 Census of Governments. The basic procedure was to isolate revenues which could be identified with particular programs on the basis of the nature of the revenues and of the level of local government, and to allocate the remainder on the basis of the relative magnitudes of the expenditures not "explained" in the first step.

Property Taxation in Other Countries

Although the American general property tax today has really no counterpart in the rest of the world, it is worthwhile to review briefly here practice in other countries in relation to property taxes defined in the Anglo-Saxon sense: as ad valorem taxes on real and other assets which are a charge against the assets themselves (thus excluding a review of net wealth taxes).

Canada appears to be the only other country in the world in which practice regarding property taxation parallels experience in the United States. The Canadian and United States property taxes are strikingly similar in their relationships to national income, to total tax revenues of governments at all levels, and to total tax revenues at the state and local government level (see Table 1-3). In addition, Canada and Japan are the only two other countries besides the United States in which a general ad valorem tax largely applicable to real property extends also to personal property. But personal property taxation is rather less important in Canada than in the United States since it provides only about 1 percent of property tax revenues in the aggregate, with higher percentages for the Maritime Provinces.[20] Personal property in Japan, on the other hand, provides nearly 40 percent of property tax revenue; this is a much larger share than in the United States.[21]

Ad valorem taxation of real property, on the basis of either annual income or capital value, is widespread. However, among the advanced countries of the world, property taxation as an important source of revenue seems to be largely a product of the English-speaking tradition. In Britain, Ireland, South Africa, and the Antipodes, property taxes provide nearly all local government tax revenues, as in the United States and Canada; and, although not to the same degree as in the latter two countries, they also account for significant fractions of total tax revenues. This phenomenon is clearly related to the much greater role of local government in these countries than in most of the rest of the world, and

[20] Estimated from Dominion of Canada Statistics Bureau, *Financial Statistics of Municipal Governments, 1961* (Ottawa, 1964), Tables 2 and 3.

[21] Based on data for 1963 provided the author by the Statistical Standards Bureau of the Government of Japan.

TABLE 1-3. Property Taxes in Selected Countries in Recent Years[a]

Country and Year	Property Tax Revenue as Percentage of—			
	Total Tax Revenue			National Income
	Local Governments	Local Plus Intermediate Governments[b]	All Governments	
United States, 1962[c]	87.7	45.9	15.4	4.3
Australia, 1961–62	100.0	40.8	6.6	2.0
Canada, 1960–61[d]	90.3	46.3	16.0	5.2
Ireland, 1962–63	100.0	—	13.5	3.8
New Zealand, 1962–63[e]	96.4	—	7.6	2.3
South Africa, 1961–62	84.3	34.3	7.5	1.4
United Kingdom, 1963	100.0	—	11.2	4.2
Austria, 1962	n.a.	n.a.	1.6	0.7
Belgium, 1962	31.8	32.6	4.4	1.2
Denmark, 1961–62[f]	29.7	—	7.9	2.3
France, 1961–62[g]	20.7	—	2.2	0.6
Germany, 1963	17.0	n.a.	2.2	0.6
Iceland, 1961	5.5	—	1.5	0.4
Luxembourg, 1962	22.2	—	2.5	0.8
Netherlands, 1962	60.1	—	2.2	0.6
Norway, 1962	2.1	—	0.6	0.3
Japan, 1963[h]	21.1	—	6.3	1.2

n.a. Not available.

[a] The selected countries include virtually all developed countries in which property taxation appears to be of consequence and for which data can be found. Spain and Switzerland are the principal exclusions on the grounds of data availability. For this purpose, property taxation is defined as ad valorem taxation of tangible assets—usually land and buildings only—either on the basis of capital value or annual rental value; ad valorem taxes on property which form part of broader taxes mainly levied on other bases are excluded. These exclusions include net wealth taxes in a number of European countries, wealth transfer taxes in most of the countries listed, and real property levies which form part of the income tax structure in several countries, notably in Sweden. Except where specific publications are cited, the tax data are based on information supplied by the central statistical offices of the countries listed, whose assistance was most helpful. National income data are from United Nations publications and estimates by United Nations personnel.

[b] Includes local governments plus states and provinces. Shown only for federal countries, and for others in which the data are organized to permit separate treatment of the different tiers of sub-national governments.

[c] Sources: U. S. Bureau of the Census, *Governmental Finances in 1962* (1963); U. S. Department of Commerce, Office of Business Economics, *Survey of Current Business*, July 1963.

[d] Source: Dominion of Canada, Statistics Bureau, *A Consolidation of Public Finance Statistics, 1961* (Ottawa, 1964).

[e] Source: Department of Statistics, New Zealand, *Report on National Income and Expenditure, 1962–63* (Wellington, 1963).

[f] Source: Statistics Department, Denmark, *Statistik Årbog, 1963–64* (Statistical Yearbook), Vol. 68 (Copenhagen, 1964). Final column shows property tax revenue as a percentage of net national product at factor costs.

[g] Property tax and local tax data based on information in O. D. Gorven, *Differential Taxation of Business by Local Authorities* (City Treasurer of Durban, South Africa, May 1964), pp. 92–93.

[h] Sources: Ministry of Finance, Japan, *Quarterly Bulletin of Financial Statistics, 4th Quarter 1963* (Tokyo, March 1964) and *An Outline of Japanese Tax, 1963* (Tax Bureau, Tokyo, 1963).

lends some historical evidence to the proposition that strong local government and reliance on the property tax are inextricably linked.[22]

In other advanced countries, taxation of real property is common but rates are typically very modest and in part based on valuations set years ago—in some instances in the nineteenth century (see Table 1-4). Presumably, where valuations have not been revised for many years, strict implementation of property tax provisions would produce severe and intolerable inequities. In some countries, net wealth taxes appear to have been substituted in place of heavier reliance on the Anglo-Saxon type of property tax. All five of the Nordic countries—Denmark, Finland, Iceland, Norway, and Sweden—use net wealth taxes, which generally produce more revenue than their respective real property taxes. In Germany and the Netherlands, net wealth taxes are also of considerable importance.

Real property is taxed on an ad valorem basis in many developing countries, notably in those exposed to the British tradition.[23] In some cases, only urban real property is taxed, and frequently land and buildings are differently treated. West African countries, for instance, tend to tax only buildings whereas the practice in East Africa is to tax primarily urban land.[24] Because local government is generally of rather minor importance in many of these countries, property taxes are seldom significant. Venezuela is an example of a country where urban real estate taxes, although very poorly administered and equipped with high homestead exemptions, provided about 25 percent of the municipal tax revenues in 1958. This was, however, only 1.2 percent of total tax revenues of all levels of government.[25]

[22] Scandinavian countries, other than Denmark, provide the major exception to this generalization; local government is important in expenditure terms, but they do not rely heavily, if at all, on the property tax. In Denmark, real property taxation is important, by any measure.

[23] See, for example, John F. Due, "Taxation of Property in Developing Economies: The African Experience," *Land Economics*, Vol. 39 (February 1963), pp. 1-14.

[24] *Ibid.*

[25] Carl S. Shoup and others, *The Fiscal System of Venezuela* (The Johns Hopkins Press, 1959), pp. 3-4, 321-23, and 332-36.

TABLE 1-4. Property Taxation in Western Europe, 1963[a]

Country	Property Taxes	Net Wealth Taxes[b]
Austria[c]	Local tax on capital value of real property—0.4%–0.8%, with additional tax of 1.2% on agricultural property.	National tax at 0.75%
Belgium	National and local tax on income from real property, part of income tax system. Base is "cadastral" income, far below actual; rates in total range 20%–25% of base, of which 20% is credited against final income tax liability.	None.
Denmark	National and local land tax. Includes national tax on land values (valued every four years) at 0.6% and national tax on improvements at 1950 values, at 0.45%; local taxes also at 2–4 times national rates, with improvements rates $\frac{3}{4}$ or $\frac{3}{5}$ that on land. Also, national tax on land value increments since 1950 (1950 value+55% or 65%) at 4%.	National tax, 1.2%–2.3%
Finland	None.	National tax, 0.05%–2.0%
France	Local property tax on annual rental value of business land and buildings, at various rates, apparently low.	None.
Germany	Local real estate tax, based on 1935 property values, at rates generally twice the following: agricultural land 0.8%–1.0% other open land 0.5% land prepared for building 2%–3% land used for business 1% buildings—maximum of 1%	National tax, $\frac{3}{4}$% or 1%
Greece	None.	None.

[a] From Federation of British Industries, *Taxation in Western Europe, 1963* (London, October 1963). Does not include taxes on income from property which are part of general income taxes, wealth transfer taxes, stamp taxes, or specific (rather than ad valorem) taxes on particular types of assets.

[b] All net wealth taxes have various deductions, exemptions, and allowances; thus the rates shown are not directly comparable.

[c] In addition to those listed there is a national tax at 1 percent on "cadastral" income of certain vacant real property

TABLE 1-4. Continued

Country	Property Taxes	Net Wealth Taxes[b]
Italy	None.	None.
Luxembourg	Local real property tax, based on extremely low valuations, with rates varying from 15% to 30%.	National tax at 0.5% based on 1935 valuations of some assets, plus local supplement on businesses at 0.4%.
Netherlands	National land tax, based on presumed income at 19th century levels. Rate—land 6%; building 4.86% plus 130% surcharge. Local tax, said to be of small proportions: provincial surcharge of up to 60%; municipal surcharge of up to 60% on buildings, 30% on land.	National tax, 0.5%
Norway	Local property taxes, involving minor revenues. In rural areas based on 1872–75 annual values; in towns 0.2%–0.7% of *annual* values, revalued every 10 years.	National tax, 0.25%–1.75%. Local tax on same base, 0.4%.
Portugal	None.	None.
Spain[d]	National tax at 17.2% and 17.5% of "cadastral" income, with surcharges, plus municipal tax on same basis at 17.2%.	None.
Sweden[e]	None.	National tax, 0.8%–1.8%
Switzerland	Land tax levied by most communes.	Individuals pay cantonal tax on capital, plus surcharges by communes. Companies are taxed on paid-up capital.

[d] In addition to those listed, there are local property value increment charges where the value increments are related to municipal public works.

[e] There is a national tax on separately assessed (under the net wealth tax) forest land, at 1 percent of capital value.

Purpose of This Study

The historic criticisms, recent experience, and recent reapprais-
als of the property tax, then, are the context for this volume. The
following chapters attempt to answer, in the light of the vastly en-
riched supply of economic data available in recent years, the basic
questions raised about the property tax throughout its history:

▪ What sectors of the economy actually bear the initial impact
of the tax, in the aggregate?
▪ Is the incidence of the tax as regressive as traditionally believed?
▪ How significant is the benefit component of the property tax?
▪ Are the effects of the tax on investment and output of consequence, and if so, are they socially undesirable?
▪ Do the geographic differentials in the property tax and the
existence of the tax per se adversely affect the location of economic
activity and the development of the country's urban areas?

In short, what is an appropriate general appraisal of the tax, not
in the abstract, but vis-à-vis other sources of revenue? Should
public policy aim at abolition, fundamental modification, or administrative reform?

CHAPTER II

Sources of Property Tax Revenue

THE BUSINESSES AND INDIVIDUALS that actually make property tax payments, the "sources" of revenue, are not necessarily those that bear the economic burden of the tax. But the first step in appraising the economic burden is to ascertain which economic sectors—households, agriculture, and groups of businesses—make these initial payments and, in conventional public finance terminology, bear the initial impact of the tax. Unlike most other taxes, the distribution of the initial impact of the property tax in the United States by economic sector (and by industry within the business sector) is not readily apparent from conventional data on government finance. In fact, for the country as a whole, the impact of the property tax could not even be crudely approximated during the long period prior to 1957, in which Census of Governments data on taxable property values for the entire country were not available.

In concept, there is no problem about this: the impact of the tax can be ascertained by multiplying the property tax revenue of each of the 82,000-plus taxing units by the percentage distribution of its

TABLE 2-1. General Property Tax Revenue by Property Use Class, 1957

Class of Property	Distribution Based on County Area Sample[a]		Crude Estimate Based on National Assessed Value Data—Percentage[b]
	Millions of Dollars	Percentage	
Total general property tax revenue	$12,443	100.0	100.0
State assessed property	953	7.7	8.2
Locally assessed personal property	2,110	17.0	17.3
Locally assessed real property	9,380	75.4	74.4
Vacant lots	228	1.8	1.7
Acreage and farms	1,015	8.2	10.3
Single-family houses	4,391	35.3	33.8
Apartments	804	6.5	6.5
Commercial property	1,674	13.5	12.3
Industrial property	1,010	8.1	8.0
Other and unallocable	257	2.1	1.6

[a] Results of a special tabulation from 1957 Census of Governments data done by the Governments Division for this study, during 1963. See Appendix A for description.

[b] Percentage distribution of assessed values, United States, 1956, from *Census of Governments: 1957*, Vol. V, "Taxable Property Values in the United States" (1959), Tables 2 and 4.

assessment roll and cumulating these data for all units.[1] This is done regularly in a few states. But the generally poor quality and paucity of available assessment data and the marked extent of inter-state noncomparability (mainly differences in property classification) make this obvious method entirely impracticable. A substitute method, available for 1957 and 1962, is to apply the nationwide distribution of assessed values found by the Census of Governments to total property tax revenues.[2] This approach ignores differences in tax rates and involves some distortion which, however, appears to be minor.

Because of a special tabulation done for this study by the Government Studies Division of the U.S. Bureau of the Census, it has been possible to derive somewhat more refined estimates of the impact of the property tax, based largely on the 1957 Census of Governments data. The first step is illustrated in Table 2-1, in which general property tax revenue, comprising 97 percent of total prop-

[1] Actually, a larger number of taxing units must be used because in many cases there is more than one total tax rate within the boundaries of a single jurisdiction, due to overlapping districts.

[2] U.S. Bureau of the Census, *Census of Governments: 1957*, Vol. V, "Taxable Property Values in the United States" (1959), Tables 2-4; *Census of Governments: 1962*, Vol. II, "Taxable Property Values" (1963), Tables 2-5.

TABLE 2-2. Total Property Tax Revenue by Property Use Class, 1957[a]

(*In millions of dollars*)

Class of Property	General Property Taxes		Special Property Taxes	Total
	State Assessed Property	Locally Assessed Property[b]		
Transportation and public utility property	$858	—[c]	$ 49	$ 907[c]
Personal property, total[d]	51	$2,110	373	2,534
Tangibles	34	2,043	202	2,279
Intangibles	17	67	171	255
Real property, total[d]	44	9,380	—	9,424
Vacant lots	—	228	—	228
Acreage and farms	—	1,015	—	1,015
Single-family houses	—	4,391	—	4,391
Apartments	—	804	—	804
Commercial property	—	1,674	—	1,674
Industrial property	44[e]	1,010[f]	—	1,054[f]
Other and unallocable	—	257	—	257
Total	953	11,490	422	12,864

Note: Because of rounding, detail may not add to totals.
 [a] For derivation of these estimates, see Appendix A.
 [b] From Table 2-1, above.
 [c] Substantial revenues are derived from locally assessed utility property, classified within the Census of Governments' "industrial" category. It is difficult to estimate this amount; it appears to have been over $200 million in 1957.
 [d] Excludes identifiable transportation and public utility property.
 [e] Includes both mining and manufacturing properties.
 [f] Includes substantial revenues from locally assessed public utility property; see note([e]) above.

erty tax revenue in 1957, is distributed among the property use classes defined for the Census of Governments. This distribution was built up from data for a sample of counties and county areas and it reflects intercounty differences in tax rates.[3] Property classes which are especially urban in character—notably housing and commercial realty, such as stores and office buildings—appear to produce more revenue than their shares of assessed values would suggest. This is to be expected since property tax rates are higher in urban areas than in rural areas; the farm realty share of tax revenue is appreciably lower than its share of assessed values.

Table 2-2 represents a second step toward a classification of property tax payments by intelligible economic sectors. Here, special as well as general property tax revenues are included, and some attempt is made to subdivide the two large heterogeneous cate-

[3] See Appendix A for a description of this tabulation.

TABLE 2-3. Estimated Distribution of Total Property Tax Revenue by Major Economic Sector, 1957[a]

Sector and Type of Property[b]	Millions of Dollars	Percentage Distribution
Nonfarm households:		
Nonfarm residential realty	$5,195	40.4
Household personalty	114	0.9
Nonfarm personal motor vehicles	287	2.2
Nonfarm residential realty listed on tax rolls as acreage	77	0.6
Total	5,673	44.1
Agriculture:[c]		
Farm realty	914	7.1
Farm equipment and inventories	205	1.6
Farm motor vehicles	45	0.3
Total	1,164	9.0
Nonfarm business:[d]		
Locally assessed realty—		
Commercial	1,674	13.0
Industrial	1,010	7.8
Other and unallocable	257	2.0
State assessed property—		
Transportation and public utility	858	6.7
Industrial and mining realty	44	0.3
Commercial, industrial, and mining tangible personalty	34	0.3
Other commercial and industrial tangible personalty	1,471	11.4
Nonfarm business motor vehicles	123	1.0
Special property taxes on utility property	49	0.4
Nonfarm business realty listed on tax rolls as acreage	24	0.2
Total	5,544	43.1
Property not allocated by sector:		
Vacant lots	228	1.8
Intangibles	255	2.0
Total	483	3.8
Total property tax revenue	12,864	100.0

Note: Because of rounding, detail may not add to totals.

[a] Based on Tables 2-1 and 2-2 and material in Chapter VI, on personal property taxation. See Appendix A for derivation of the estimates.

[b] This distribution is designed to be on the basis of property use, not ownership or incidence, to the extent possible. For example, "manufacturing" represents estimated taxes on property used by manufacturing industries, regardless of ownership and incidence.

[c] Includes farm residences and personal motor vehicles, as well as farm "business" property.

[d] The breakdown of nonfarm business property tax revenue by major industry group, as follows:

Industry Group	Millions of Dollars	Percentage Distribution
Common carrier transportation and other public utilities	$1,541	12.6
Manufacturing	1,620	12.0
All other	2,383	18.5
	5,544	43.1

gories at the top of Table 2-1: state assessed property and locally assessed personalty. The net effect of these additions and refinements is to increase the importance of personal property in the overall picture to nearly 20 percent of total revenue, and to break out a large segment of the property tax which is in a class of its own; namely, taxes on transportation and public utility property.[4]

Table 2-3 is the final step in this process of economic sectoring: the distribution is by major economic sector rather than by property use class; it is based on estimates of the composition of personal property taxes and on the refinement of one major realty category: acreage and farms.[5] According to this distribution, slightly less than a tenth of all property tax revenues in 1957 was derived from agriculture and the rest was about equally divided between nonfarm households and nonfarm businesses.[6] Nonfarm residential realty alone accounted for 41 percent of all property tax revenues.

Since 1957, housing has increased substantially as a proportion of assessed values for general property taxation, while acreage and farm property have declined; so have state assessed property and locally assessed personalty. Meanwhile, both nominal and effective property tax rates have risen; quite evidently this rise has been largest in urban areas and therefore on urban-type properties.[7] In all probability, therefore, very close to 50 percent of total property tax revenues is now collected from nonfarm households, about 40 per-

[4] The railroad and utility category can be regarded "as rather widely representing a family of nominally ad valorem levies imposed in lieu of 'the' property tax, rather than as a component of the property tax base in the more usual sense" because of the distinctive methods of assessing and taxing this property and because of the economic characteristics of taxes on regulated utilities ("Taxable Property Values," p. 4).

[5] This category includes all real property described on local tax rolls as acreage rather than lots, thus comprehending significant amounts of "exurban" nonfarm residential property as well as timber, mineral, and waste lands. See Appendix A for a description of the derivation of Table 2-3.

[6] Taxes on vacant lots and on intangibles are not allocated by sector in Table 2-3. Virtually none of these can be ascribed to agriculture; on balance, it would appear that somewhat more than half of these amounts could be allocated to businesses rather than households, but this is an educated guess, not a reasoned estimate.

[7] The Census data show that property tax revenues rose by 48.1 percent from 1957 to 1962, while assessed values subject to tax rose by 30.8 percent; the estimated market value of locally assessed real property (before partial exemptions) rose by 40.8 percent.

FIGURE 3. Estimated Distribution of Property Tax Revenue by Major Types of Property, 1957

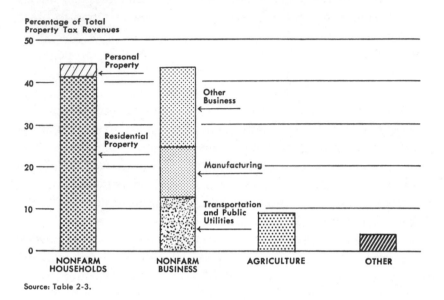

Source: Table 2-3.

cent from nonfarm businesses, and less than 8 percent from agriculture.

Breakdown by Industry

Census of Governments data do not provide a basis for an industry breakdown of property tax payments within the nonfarm business sector, a breakdown which is of some importance for an economic appraisal of business property taxes. However, there are a large number of fragmentary indicators, and a reasonably reliable gross breakdown appears in Footnote *d* of Table 2-3, separating nonfarm business property taxes into manufacturing, utilities, and all other.[8]

[8] As Appendix A indicates, the utility figure (which is based on industry sources in the main) appears to be 20 to 25 percent higher than can be supported on the basis of Census of Governments data; this difference remains an unreconciled one.

Differences among types of nonfarm business in the amount of property tax payments relative to measures of output, income, and wealth are related to three principal factors. First, capital-output ratios do differ considerably by industry; property taxes—taxes on capital—should be high relative to output and income measures for capital-intensive industries. As Table 2-4 shows, the 1957 capital-output ratio (ratio of value of tangible assets at current prices to national income originating) for all nonfarm business was roughly 2:1, but nearly 5:1 for the utility group and less than 3:2 for manufacturing. Consequently, property tax payments in 1957 were equal to 2.1 percent of net output (national income originating) for all nonfarm business, but 6.3 percent for utilities and 1.4 percent for manufacturing.

However, differences in capital-output ratios are not the entire story, for property tax payments as a proportion of capital (or wealth) also differ among industries. One obvious factor behind this is the location of investment in the light of geographic differences in tax rates: activities which tend to be concentrated in urban centers where tax rates are high will surely bear heavier taxes on the average than activities like mining and logging, which are located in inherently low tax rate areas. For example, real estate owned by banks, insurance companies, and hotels, which are notably urban in character, appears to be taxed at average rates well above even those which apply to utility property overall.[9]

Another variable comprises the methods and coverage which actually govern the property tax treatment of different industries. The principal reason that utilities exhibit such high ratios of taxes to property values lies in the method of taxation. Typically, assessment by a state agency is at a relatively high proportion of estimated "full value" of the property, while locally assessed properties are assessed at low fractions of "full value"; the divergent state-

---

[9] Life insurance company real estate taxes in recent years have been about 1.8 percent of the value of real estate owned, according to the *Life Insurance Fact Book, 1962* (Institute of Life Insurance). Federal Reserve member banks in 1961 paid taxes on bank premises and leasehold improvements equal to more than 3 percent of the balance sheet values of these assets, which are, however, in many cases very much understated (*Federal Reserve Bulletin,* Vol. 48, May 1962). According to Horwath & Horwath, the hotel industry accounting firm, property taxes on hotels average about 2.5 percent of market value (letter to author, March 1, 1963).

TABLE 2-4. Property Tax Payments, Income Originating, and Wealth, Nonfarm Business, 1956–57

(Amounts in millions of dollars)

Tax, Income, and Wealth Items	Total Nonfarm Business[a]	Selected Utilities and Transport[b]	Manufacturing	Other
1. Estimated property tax payments, Fiscal 1956	$ 5,544	$ 1,541	$ 1,620	$ 2,383
2. National income originating, Calender 1957	269,383[c]	24,549	112,476	132,358
3. (1) as percentage of (2)	2.06%	6.28%	1.44%	1.80%
Value of tangible assets in current prices, year-end 1956				
4. Structures	$150,486	$ 79,073	$ 32,237	$ 39,176
5. Underground mining construction	26,774	—	—	26,774
6. Land	40,580	8,777	5,674	26,129
7. Forests	14,690	—	—	14,690
8. Subsoil assets	19,000	—	—	19,000
9. Producer durable goods[d]	154,705	30,308	71,608	52,789
10. Inventories	97,051	[e]	52,295	44,756
Subtotals				
11. Land and structures (4)+(5)+(6)	$217,840	$ 87,850	$ 37,911	$ 92,079
12. All realty (11)+(7)+(8)	251,530	87,850	37,911	125,769
13. Land and structures plus personalty (11)+(9)+(10)	469,596	118,158	161,814	189,624
14. All realty and personalty (12)+(9)+(10)	503,286	118,158	161,814	223,314
15. (1) as percentage of (11)	2.54%	1.75%	4.27%	2.59%
16. (1) as percentage of (12)	2.20	1.75	4.27	1.89
17. (1) as percentage of (13)	1.18	1.30	1.00	1.26
18. (1) as percentage of (14)	1.10	1.30	1.00	1.07

Sources: Property Tax Payments—Table 2-3, above, Income Originating—U. S. Department of Commerce, Office of Business Economics; Survey of Current Business, July 1962; Value of Tangible Assets—Raymond W. Goldsmith, The National Wealth of the United States in the Postwar Period (Princeton University Press for National Bureau of Economic Research, 1962), especially Tables B-123, B-124, B-125, B-126, B-129, B-130, B-132, and B-135; inventories (manufacturing)—U. S. Bureau of the Census, Historical Statistics of the United States: Colonial Times to 1957 (1960).

[a] Excludes the residential real estate "business," whether owner-occupied or tenant-occupied housing. Industry groups distinguished on an activity or establishment basis, not on the basis of ownership. For example, forests and mineral resources owned by manufacturing firms are classed as "other."

[b] Property tax and national income data include only utilities and transportation activities commonly subject to special treatment under the property tax. Wealth data cover Goldsmith's "public utility" category.

[c] Total national income originating in business less income originating in government enterprises, farms, and residential real estate. The latter figure is estimated: personal consumption expenditures for nonfarm housing less the deduction items used to reconcile income and gross product, in this case estimated depreciation charges on nonfarm housing and estimated property tax payments ("indirect business tax liability").

[d] Allocated among the industry groups on the basis of the estimated 1954 distribution of particular types of producer durables. For example, the utilities group is assumed to own half the value of the stock of electrical machinery, 20 percent of trucks and buses, 90 percent of aircraft, and all the railroad equipment, to mention just a few of the categories.

[e] Inventories owned by utilities are assumed to be minor in amount (mostly stocks of fuel, which are probably low at December 31), and the amounts are included in "other" industries.

FIGURE 4. Property Tax Payments Relative to Income and Wealth, 1957

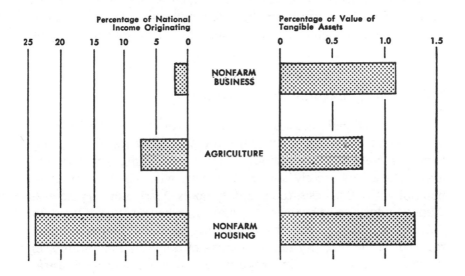

Sources: Tables 2-4, 2-6, and 2-7.

local assessments are incompletely equalized. This will produce assessments which are higher relative to the Goldsmith estimate of wealth in this sector than is the case for other sectors of the economy.[10] In contrast, assessors' values of underground mining construction and subsoil assets are likely to be rather low proportions of depreciated replacement costs, leading to low tax-to-capital ratios for mining. Similarly, personal property is usually taxed at lower effective rates than real property—in part because much of it is exempted from tax legally or extralegally and because some personal property in classes not exempted is simply not discovered by the assessor. Industries with a substantial personal property component are likely to enjoy lower overall effective rates than industries with a much larger proportion of assets in the form of real property; for example, manufacturing property is probably taxed at a lower overall effective rate than tangible property used in office activities. Indeed, in 1957, just about one-half of the property taxes

[10] Raymond W. Goldsmith, *The National Wealth of the United States in the Postwar Period* (Princeton University Press for the National Bureau of Economic Research, 1962).

ascribed to manufacturing is estimated to represent taxes on personal property rather than real estate. Comparing this estimate to the data in Table 2-4 suggests an effective rate for manufacturing realty of 2.1 percent and an effective rate for manufacturing personalty of 0.7 percent.

Standard of Economic Neutrality

A conventional yardstick for appraisal of taxes is the standard of economic neutrality—neutrality among industries, inputs, and locations. Net output, or national income originating, is perhaps the most satisfactory readily available statistic with which to measure neutrality. On this basis, the property tax is clearly not very neutral among industries, whatever the reason: whether it is related to differences in capital-output ratios, in the profitability of investment reached by the property tax (which is not quite the same thing), in geographic location, or in property tax coverage and administration. Even within the utility group, differences are substantial, as these estimates for 1957 show:[11]

	Property Taxes as Percentage of National Income Originating
Electric and gas utilities	11.6
Pipelines	7.0
Telephone and telegraph	5.8
Railroads	4.9
Air transportation	0.04

The proportions for manufacturing industries are not only lower overall, but differences among individual industries appear to be somewhat less than among utilities. Property taxes paid in 1957 by manufacturing industries (excluding taxes paid indirectly, through rents) were clustered around 1 percent of adjusted value added, according to the Census of Manufactures evidence in Table 2-5.

Evidence on industry differences within the heterogeneous "other" category (shown in the last column of Table 2-4) is limited. The category principally covers trade, services, finance, and mining.

[11] Tax payment data based largely on industry sources. See Appendix A.

TABLE 2-5. Property Tax Payments and Value Added in Manufacturing Industries, 1957[a]

(Amounts in millions of dollars)

Industry[b]	Property Taxes Paid	Adjusted Value Added	Property Taxes as Percentage of Adjusted Value Added
All manufacturing	$1,450	$147,929	0.98
20 Food and kindred products	176	16,349	1.07
21 Tobacco manufactures	10	1,246	0.80
22 Textile mill products	39	5,197	0.76
23 Apparel and related products	19	6,067	0.32
24 Lumber and wood products	50	3,285	1.53
25 Furniture and fixtures	21	2,514	0.85
26 Pulp, paper, and products	74	5,724	1.30
27 Printing and publishing	47	7,922	0.60
28 Chemicals and products	120	12,474	0.96
29 Petroleum and coal products	83	3,249	2.56
30 Rubber products	26	2,462	1.04
31 Leather and leather goods	9	1,892	0.38
32 Stone, clay, and glass products	50	4,980	1.00
33 Primary metal industries	171	13,320	1.29
34 Fabricated metal products	101	9,544	1.05
35 Machinery, except electrical	160	15,978	1.00
36 Electrical machinery	65	9,620	0.67
37 Transportation equipment	178	18,486	0.96
38 Instruments and related products	20	2,872	0.69
39 Miscellaneous manufactures	31	4,748	0.65

[a] From U. S. Bureau of the Census, *Census of Manufactures: 1958*, "Supplementary Employee Costs, Costs of Maintenance and Repairs, Insurance, Rent, Taxes, and Depreciation and Book Value of Depreciable Assets: 1957," Subject Report MC58(1)-9 (1961). Excludes taxes paid indirectly on manufacturing property through rents, estimated (in Appendix A)at $170 million .

[b] Initial digits indicate Standard Industrial Classification number.

As noted earlier, property taxes paid by banks, insurance carriers, and hotels seem to equal relatively large proportions of net product. The proportions appear relatively low for trade and most services, and variable for mining: high for metal mining (perhaps because of heavy taxation via state assessment in most western states) and low for oil, gas, and coal mining.[12]

[12] In part, this conclusion is based on background data provided by Professor J. Fred Weston, for his article, "The Measurement of Comparative Tax Burdens of Firms in Different Industries," *National Tax Journal*, Vol. 16 (September 1963), pp. 230-37. These data, based on corporate income tax returns for 1958-59, compare all nonincome taxes paid with various indicators. Nonincome taxes include payroll taxes, excise and other consumption taxes paid by businesses essentially as

**TABLE 2-6. Property Taxes on Agriculture and
Related Magnitudes, 1956–57**

Tax, Income, and Wealth Items	Millions of Dollars	Property Tax Payments as Percentage of Column 1
Estimated property tax payments, 1957[a]	$ 1,164	—
Gross farm income, 1957[b]	34,389	3.4
Net farm income, 1957[c]	13,505	8.6
National income originating in agriculture, 1957[d]	15,397	7.6
Value of tangible assets in current prices, year-end 1956:[e]		
Farm land	73,966 ⎱	
Farm structures	34,368 ⎰	0.84
Farm producer durables[f]	15,565 ⎫	
Inventories and livestock	18,234 ⎬	0.61
Motor vehicles	6,984 ⎭	
Total	149,117	0.78

[a] From Table 2-3, above.
[b] Realized gross income, from U. S. Bureau of the Census, *Statistical Abstract of the United States, 1962*, Table 871.
[c] Net income to persons on farms from farming, from *Statistical Abstract of the United States, 1962*, Table 871.
[d] From *Survey of Current Business*, July 1962.
[e] Wealth data from Raymond W. Goldsmith, *The National Wealth of the United States in the Postwar Period* (Princeton University Press for National Bureau of Economic Research, 1962), Tables A-54 and B-82. Percentages shown are for farm realty and farm personalty taxes in Table 2-3, above.
[f] Excluding farm trucks, included in motor vehicles.

As is often claimed, farmers do pay substantial property taxes relative to farm income and farm net product (see Table 2-6). However, farm property taxes are low in relation to the value of the capital employed in agriculture. Moreover, in nearly all states, the overall effective rates on farm real estate are well below the rates on nonagricultural real property.[13] The disparity between the tax/income and the tax/wealth relationships is, of course, a reflection of the markedly lower rate of return in recent years on investment in farm property relative to nonagricultural investment.[14]

---

intermediaries, and certain nonproperty business taxes, as well as business property taxes. Nonetheless, exclusion of the glaring excise tax cases—such as taxes on tobacco, petroleum, and motor vehicles—probably yields an array which is dominated by property tax differences.

[13] See Chap. V.

[14] This disparity is more fully discussed in Chap. V.

TABLE 2-7. Property Taxes on Nonfarm Housing and Related Magnitudes, 1956–57

Tax, Income, and Wealth Items	Millions of Dollars	Property Tax Payments as Percentage of Column 1
Estimated property tax payments, 1957[a]	$ 5,195	—
Personal consumption expenditures for private nonfarm housing, 1957[b]	32,028	16.22
National income originating in nonfarm housing, 1957[c]	21,434	24.24
Value of assets in current prices, year-end 1956:[d]		
Private residential land	55,400	—
Private nonfarm residential structures	351,380	—
Total value of assets	406,780	1.28

[a] From Table 2-1, above.

[b] From *Survey of Current Business*, July 1962; excludes expenditures for public and tax-exempt housing (estimated at 1 percent of the total, based on Goldsmith's data).

[c] Personal consumption expenditures for private nonfarm housing less indirect business tax liability—i.e., property taxes; and less depreciation (partly estimated).

[d] From Raymond W. Goldsmith, *The National Wealth of the United States in the Postwar Period* (Princeton University Press for National Bureau of Economic Research, 1962), Tables A-35 and A-40

Taxes on Housing

The housing component of the property tax is, in many ways, quite distinct from the business component, and it is hardly surprising that property taxes amount to large fractions of expenditures for housing and of housing net product. For one thing, the ubiquity of housing relative to business property suggests that taxes on housing could amount to large percentages of current account flows (expenditures; income; product), since migration to flee high tax rates will affect only a small part of the housing tax base. Moreover, the tax-benefit nexus is far more readily perceived for housing taxes than business taxes, since so much of the property tax is devoted to financing local public services enjoyed by consumers as individuals, especially education. Thus, high taxes relative to housing outlays are more acceptable to consumer-voters.

In addition, acceptability is heightened by the ability-to-pay aspect of the property tax on housing: occupants of more valuable housing are indeed likely to have greater ability to pay taxes than

TABLE 2-8. 1960 Census of Housing Evidence on Real Estate Taxes in Relation to Housing Costs and Property Values[a]

Type of Property	Median Real Estate Taxes as Percentage of—	
	Property Values	Rental Receipts or Annual Housing Costs[b]
Rental and vacant properties:		
All properties	1.5	n.a.
Single-family houses	1.4	17
1–4 Unit properties	1.4	17
5–49 Unit properties	2.0	17
50 or More unit properties	2.7	20
Homeowner properties (single-family houses):		
All	1.3	17
Mortgaged	1.4	15
Not mortgaged	1.3	27

n.a.—Not available.

[a] From U. S. Bureau of the Census, *Census of Housing: 1960*, Vol. V, "Residential Finance," Parts 1 and 2 (1963). Covers only properties acquired before 1959.

[b] Percentage of rental receipts for rental properties; the figures shown are for mortgaged properties only, but both real estate tax as a percentage of value and rental receipts as a percentage of value are substantially the same for mortgaged properties and for all properties, within each class. For homeowner properties, the figures shown are median real estate tax divided by median monthly housing costs times twelve.

occupants of less valuable housing. This is especially true of relatively small and homogeneous taxing units, such as residential suburbs; it is no accident that the highest and most rapidly rising property tax rates in the country in recent years have been found mainly in dormitory suburbs of the largest metropolitan areas.

Although understandable, it is nonetheless noteworthy that the property tax on housing, viewed as an excise tax and leaving aside all benefit considerations, is higher in rate than any other generally used American consumption tax, except taxes on liquor, tobacco, and gasoline. As Table 2-7 shows, housing property taxes in 1957 were equal to nearly one-fourth of national income originating in private nonfarm housing and nearly one-sixth of personal consumption expenditures (Department of Commerce concept) for private nonfarm housing. Property taxes are also sizeable proportions of money outlays for housing—monthly expenditures of homeowners and rental receipts of tenant-occupied properties (see Table 2-8). In most large metropolitan areas outside the South, property tax payments in 1959-60 averaged over 20 percent of money expenditures for housing by owner occupiers of single-family houses, and nearly 30 percent in the New York, Boston, and Buffalo areas.[15] Relative to value, however, property taxes on housing are little higher, in the aggregate, than those on nonfarm business assets.

Measurement of the initial impact of the property tax is in part merely a prerequisite to the quantitative appraisal of the incidence of the tax nationwide presented in the following chapter. The impact of the tax has some additional importance since, whether or not the tax is shifted, an unneutral tax will affect investment, output, and the allocation of resources generally. These more general effects will be considered in Chapter IV.

[15] See Table 5-6.

CHAPTER III

Who Pays the Property Tax?

IN THE PAST FORTY YEARS, there has been little theoretical controversy over the incidence of the American property tax. By and large, the "conventional wisdom" is accepted. There is less agreement, however, about the empirical shape of the distribution of the tax burden by income class because of uncertainty over which of the alternative assumptions possible in incidence theory is empirically valid. In addition, definitions of income and evidence of income, consumption, and wealth provide ample scope for debate.

Incidence Theory

The accepted body of doctrine stems from Ricardian rent theory as restated by neoclassical economists, with important corrections by F. Y. Edgeworth and, more recently, H. G. Brown.[1]

---

[1] These statements and the summary of incidence theory immediately below are based on Jens P. Jensen, *Property Taxation in the United States* (University of Chicago Press, 1931), pp. 53-75, and Herbert A. Simon, "The Incidence of a Tax on Urban Real Property," in American Economic Association, *Readings in the Economics of Taxation*, Richard A. Musgrave and Carl S. Shoup, eds. (Irwin, 1959), pp. 416-35. Perhaps the most important classical contributions relevant to local property taxation (especially in an urban setting) are Edwin Cannan's testimony in "Minutes of Royal Commission on Local Taxation, 1899," *Readings in*

Property tax incidence theory, like most incidence theory, utilizes partial equilibrium analysis, rather than a more general and comprehensive analysis of the economic cosmos. Initial price and output changes in response to the imposition of new and higher property taxes are appraised, largely by holding everything else constant. A general analysis then goes on to deal with the subsequent effects of these changes in relative prices—effects on substitution among factors of production and objects of consumer expenditure as well as on incentives to work and invest. In the literature, a few efforts have been made to generalize the analysis used in regard to the property tax by dealing, for example, with the benefits from property-tax-financed expenditures and by considering the impact of the tax on the rate of return on capital. Nonetheless, it remains essentially a partial equilibrium treatment.

It is generally agreed that taxes on the value of bare land—the sites themselves exclusive of applications of reproducible capital in the form of grading, fertilizer, and the like—rest on the owners of the sites at the time the tax is initially levied or increased. The tax cannot be shifted, because shifting is possible, under reasonably competitive conditions, only if the supply of sites is reduced. But the supply of land is, for all practical purposes, perfectly inelastic. Individual landowners will not respond to an increase in land taxes by withdrawing their sites from the market, since doing so will not affect their tax liability. Indeed, their only chance of reducing the burdensomeness of the tax relative to their income streams is to seek to raise the latter by encouraging more intensive use of the sites they own. Collectively, landowners cannot reduce the stock of land: if individual landowners wish to liquidate in the face of higher taxes, they must sell the sites to other owners.

Thus, increased taxes on bare land values will reduce the attractiveness of investing in land vis-à-vis other assets but will not destroy the land itself. Therefore, land prices will fall: the taxes will be capitalized. Land rents before taxes are unchanged, but because of higher taxes, after-tax returns are lower, and investors offer less for land. High land taxes, at the extreme, can appropriate most of the value of land but, as long as value remains the measure they can

---

the Economics of Taxation, and Alfred Marshall's *Memorandum on Imperial and Local Taxes,* which appears in slightly different form as Appendix G of his *Principles of Economics,* 9th edition (Macmillan, 1961).

never reduce the value to zero, since the amount of tax liability will shrink as land values decline. For example, if the rent of a parcel of land before taxes is $1,000 and the market rate of interest used for capitalization is 5 percent, then the value of the site is $20,000 with a zero tax rate ($1,000 ÷ .05). Suppose a site value tax of 10 percent is now applied. The value of the site will equal $1,000 divided by the interest rate plus the tax rate (.05 + .10), or $6,667. A 100 percent tax rate would reduce the value to $952. A 200 percent tax rate would reduce the value to $487; a 500 percent tax rate to $198.[2]

Unshifted taxes on capital assets of any type, not only land, will be capitalized in prices paid for the assets, but the impact of ad valorem tax rates (in the usual range) on values will be relatively modest for short-lived assets, since the capitalization periods are short and the present values of future taxes are thus low relative to initial capital values.

Evidence on Capitalization

The simple statement that unshifted property taxes will be capitalized into lower asset prices masks a variety of analytical and empirical problems, as the literature points out.[3] One important consideration is the use of the proceeds of the tax. If they are devoted to public services which enhance the value of the property taxed, it is conceivable that property values may rise rather than fall after a tax increase. Thus, empirical evidence on capitalization is most unsatisfactory. Jensen, on the one hand, found strong evidence of capitalization for farm land values in the period of rising property tax rates between 1919 and 1924.[4] But Daicoff, on the other hand, in a more recent study, found little such evidence.[5] Daicoff used regression analysis with data for farm land values over a long time series, data for taxing jurisdictions in Washtenaw County, Michigan between 1951 and 1957, and data on individual parcels of land in that county and the city of Ann Arbor during the same period. In

[2] Jensen, *Property Taxation,* pp. 63-75, has a very lucid discussion of the mechanics of capitalization.

[3] See Carl S. Shoup, "Capitalization and Shifting of the Property Tax," in *Property Taxes,* Tax Policy League (1940), pp. 187-201.

[4] Jensen, *Property Taxation,* pp. 69-75.

[5] Darwin W. Daicoff, "Capitalization of the Property Tax" (doctoral thesis, University of Michigan, 1961).

most cases, increases in property values and increases in tax rates were positively rather than negatively associated. He concluded that:

. . . all the tests of the usually accepted doctrine produced results which are inconsistent with the doctrine. The most relevant explanation for the results of the aggregate models seems to be in terms of service differentials between jurisdictions. Within a jurisdiction this did not prove to be an adequate explanation; here the meaning of assessed values to the purchaser and the assessor may be the best explanation.[6]

There is room for more empirical research here. As noted in Chapter V, within a single urban area, low tax, high expenditure jurisdictions with high property values can exist side by side with high tax, low expenditure jurisdictions with low property values. Even more common are areas with jurisdictions providing similar levels of service, but at different tax rates. This suggests the presence of capitalization.

Although there is general agreement that taxes on bare land are not shifted but capitalized, some observers have felt that it is both theoretically and practically impossible to separate the land and improvements components of improved sites. This general argument is discussed in Chapter VIII. There is one form of the argument directly applicable to incidence theory. This was advanced by Edgeworth and elegantly synthesized with the more conventional approach by Simon.[7] Essentially, Edgeworth's thesis is that differences in urban ground rent are due more to differences in the productivity of capital applied to different sites than to differences in accessibility and similar factors. That is, building a house in a centrally located site results in more house (in value terms) than building the same house on a peripheral site. The conventional attitude is to assume that the landowner bears that portion of the tax that is applicable to the land value share of the total property value. The Edgeworth approach maintains, however, that since the different sites yield differences in value in a reproducible form (improvements), the incidence of the entire tax is the same as that of any tax on reproducible assets—on the occupier or final user of the property, in all probability, rather than on the site owner.

[6] *Ibid.,* p. 112.
[7] Simon in *Readings in the Economics of Taxation,* pp. 422-28.

Simon's contribution is to point out that either approach may be valid, depending on the empirical evidence, which is not readily available. However, there is some evidence which suggests that changes in accessibility (particularly transport improvements) have a major bearing on changes in land values. This indicates that the conventional wisdom may approximate the truth in American cities today.

Shifting of Property Taxes

In theory, property taxes on improvements and on tangible personal property used in business (mainly producer durables) can be expected to be shifted forward to final consumers of business services and occupants of housing. Such taxes will discourage new investment. The reduced supply of capital assets, over time, will raise the prices of business services produced by investment in these types of assets. In the theoretical model for this incidence analysis, it is assumed that the combinations of inputs used by business are already the most efficient possible. Therefore, unit costs of production will rise even if the higher price of capital assets leads to substitution of labor for capital. Owner occupants of housing, on the other hand, may very well not be deterred by higher property taxes; there is in any case no mechanism available for them to shift their taxes.

This general statement immediately stimulates a host of qualifications. These relate to the differences between general and partial equilibrium analysis, between long- and short-term consequences, and between taxes which are equal and general in application and those which are unequal and/or limited in application. For example, in a general equilibrium analysis, the effects of shifts of resources to nontaxed sectors of the economy would have to be considered: output of these sectors would be expected to rise. This would benefit consumers in general, offsetting to some extent losses caused by forward shifting of taxes on improvements and business personalty.

Moreover, a general equilibrium analysis questions the effect on interest rates of taxes on capital. In effect, the reasoning would be along the following lines. The initial shifting of these taxes, via reduced new investment and higher prices for the remaining supply of capital assets, results in a reduced demand for capital in general. If the rate of saving—the supply of investment funds—is not affected by the resulting lowered rate of return on investment funds, then an important element of the incidence of the tax is on suppliers of investment funds. This will hold true so long as the supply of investment funds is interest inelastic, even if the initial tax is only on some types of assets (the case with the American property tax). Prices of taxed assets will rise, but prices of most untaxed assets will fall; there will be lower returns to capital in general. The impact on the rate of interest is likely to be small; it would be spread over the whole stock of capital.

The test of this analysis, then, is the actual interest elasticity of saving. Although examination of the evidence on this point is not a matter for discussion here, it should be pointed out there is no general agreement as to how responsive saving in the aggregate is to changes in interest rates.

There is yet another consequence of the more general analytic approach. Earl R. Rolph argues at some length that traditional theory on the incidence of commodity taxes (to which the American property tax bears a strong resemblance) is incorrect in neglecting the extent to which these taxes can be shifted backwards. They can be shifted to the owners of resources, engaged in producing the taxed commodities, whose output has declined as a result of the tax. Rolph and George F. Break, in extending this analysis to the property tax, consider an important consequence of the tax to be "the reductions in money income suffered not only by the owners of resources originally located in the construction industry but also by owners of resources that compete with them for jobs."[8]

Obstacles to the Shifting of Taxes

Incidence analysis generally compares equilibrium conditions both before and after the tax and its consequences have been worked out. For structures, the period elapsing between the old and the new equilibria can be long indeed because the annual increment to the supply of structures is a small fraction of the supply. Moreover, there are some special obstacles to adjustment of the tax incidence. One such obstacle results from the number of rented single-family houses not held for investment purposes, the owners of which are not particularly sensitive to changes in tax rates. For ex-

[8] Earl R. Rolph and George F. Break, *Public Finance* (Ronald Press, 1961), p. 345; see also the entire section on property tax incidence, pp. 342-47.

ample, according to the 1960 Census of Housing data given in Appendix Table B-2, it appears that, in 1959, nearly one-seventh of the property tax revenue came from taxes on rented residential property; 30 percent of this proportion was from rented single-family houses. This type of house is very frequently offered for rent on a more or less temporary basis, perhaps by owners awaiting a buyer or by owner occupants who are temporarily absent. Increased property taxes on such houses will not affect the supply and hence not affect the rent paid.

Another barrier to adjustment may be created by the huge supply of sparsely occupied industrial rental property that appears characteristic of many older cities. Although little new space of this type has been constructed for years, demand for it is so low that rents are also extremely low. Shifting of higher property taxes on such realty may very well take place only in that ultimate long run in which we are all dead.

The partial and unequal nature of the property tax itself is a further impediment to the shifting of taxes on buildings and producer durables. Incidence analysis starts with a closed national economy and examines taxes which are generally applicable at uniform rates. But the real-world property tax is a local institution with widespread variation in both rates and coverage. Firms competing in national markets are able to shift a certain proportion of their property taxes on structures, equipment, and inventories. But they can shift them only to the extent, in the first place, that these taxes are common to most of their competitors; and, in the second place, that they reflect the value of publicly provided services—services which in other locations would have to be provided by the firms themselves. As the discussion in Chapter V suggests, these two provisions are by no means insignificant and would appear to lead to a substantial shifting of the tax burden, especially when considered in relation to a very important third factor—the large number of firms that compete mainly in local markets. Within these local markets, of course, tax rates on business property show much less variation than rates across the country.

As for the portion which is not shifted: in the long run, differentially high local taxes on reproducible capital should have an adverse effect on local economic activity and the taxes will consequently be shifted backwards to local landowners by reducing local land values.

In general, a significant portion of taxes on buildings in cities may be shifted backwards to landowners, partly because of the competition of sites in nearby jurisdictions or other cities with lower tax rates. But there is another important reason. If the owner of a particular site has little choice of land use, he may be better off absorbing all or part of increased building taxes than if unabsorbed taxes lead in time (for example, after expiration of ground leases) to less profitable use of his site. Zoning and building code regulations, together with gross differences in accessibility within larger cities, greatly restrict the use of individual sites. In extreme cases, the existing use, antedating zoning ordinance or building code, may be the most profitable lawful use. To the extent that this holds true, increased taxes on existing structures will tend to be shifted backwards to landowners, and a large part of the taxes on new structures also will be shifted backwards.[9]

Taxes on household personalty—consumer durables—are usually considered to rest on the owners rather than shifted backward to producers of these goods. It is usually assumed, explicitly or implicitly, that consumers do not readily substitute services or nondurables for durables as taxes on the latter are marginally increased. Since the effective rates of property taxes on housing are likely to be higher than taxes on household personalty, the argument surely holds for housing vis-à-vis consumer durables. Property taxes on consumer-owned automobiles may be a somewhat different case, since these taxes, if used, are frequently high (see Chapter VI); however, the demand for automobiles is thought to be relatively price inelastic.[10]

It is possible, as Jensen suggests, to develop a full-blown analysis of the shifting of taxes on intangibles, but this would be entirely an

[9] This argument is more fully developed by Raymond L. Richman in "The Theory and Practice of Site-Value Taxation in Pittsburgh"; a paper presented at the 57th Annual Conference on Taxation, September 1964.

[10] This statement is based on Gregory C. Chow, "Statistical Demand Functions for Automobiles and Their Use for Forecasting," in *The Demand for Durable Goods,* Arnold C. Harberger, ed. (University of Chicago Press, 1960), pp. 149-78. Chow found price elasticity coefficients, in his model allowing for time lags, of about −0.7.

academic exercise.[11] Intangibles are so infrequently and so erratically taxed that incidence in practice must be very obscure. The
safest assumption seems to be that this minor element of the property tax rests on the owners of the assets.

Evidence on Incidence by
Income Class, 1957

In the following sections of this chapter, the empirical findings
of earlier studies on the incidence of the tax by income class are
noted, and an across-the-board analysis for the United States in
terms of money income before taxes is developed for 1957. In general, the results conform with the conventional wisdom: the property tax is on balance somewhat regressive when compared to current money income. Because a substantial part of business property
taxes, notably those on utilities and most trade and service activities, is undoubtedly shifted forward to consumers, the nonresidential property tax is in part a general consumption tax and, like any
general consumption tax, regressive through much of the income
range. Because some of the tax is not shifted, however, the incidence curve turns upward for the highest income class (see Figure 5).

Rather good evidence on incidence by income class of property
taxes on owner-occupied houses strongly indicates that this component of the tax is even more regressive than the nonresidential
component.[12] Somewhat less direct evidence indicates that the tax
on rented housing is still more regressive. However, because renters
tend to be both poorer and decidedly smaller consumers of housing
(and hence pay less property tax, via rents), when the two series are
combined, the picture is less clear. Residential property tax payments decline sharply as a percentage of aggregate income as income
rises in each class in the lower half of the income distribution but
the percentage climbs again in the middle income range up to the
$10,000–$15,000 level. For the income class over $15,000, the
percentage again drops.

Residential and nonresidential property taxes combined are

[11] Jensen, *Property Taxation*, pp. 54-55.
[12] The evidence is obtained from U.S. Treasury Department publications on
Statistics of Income and U.S. Bureau of the Census *Census of Housing* publications.

FIGURE 5. Property Taxes and Expenditure Benefits as Percentages of Money Income, 1957

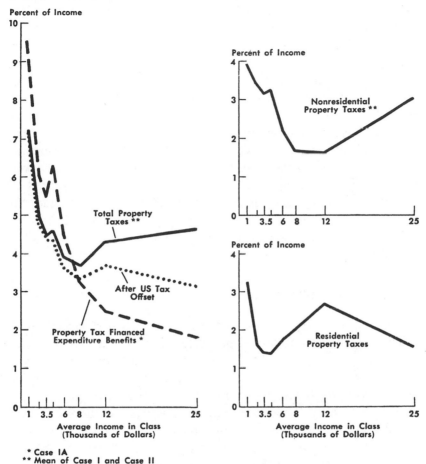

Percent of Income

Total Property Taxes **

After US Tax Offset

Property Tax Financed Expenditure Benefits *

Average Income in Class (Thousands of Dollars)

Percent of Income

Nonresidential Property Taxes **

Percent of Income

Residential Property Taxes

Average Income in Class (Thousands of Dollars)

* Case IA
** Mean of Case I and Case II

Sources: Tables 3-2, 3-10, and 3-14. Approximate mean income in each income class is used. Average incomes for two classes not designated are $2,500 and $4,500.

thus markedly regressive in the lowest income brackets, but only mildly regressive in the middle ranges. Before any allowance for savings in federal income tax liability due to the deductibility of the property tax, the overall tax becomes progressive above $10,000. Federal income tax offsets eliminate this progressivity for the top income groups, converting the property tax into one which is better described as proportional than as regressive for incomes above $3,000.

In contrast, the benefits from expenditures financed from the property tax are distinctly regressive in their incidence, amounting to a steadily declining percentage of income as income rises. On balance and considered in the aggregate, therefore, the property tax as an institution is no mean contributor to income redistribution from the richer to the poorer income groups. However, in view of the wide dispersion around the means within income classes, especially in regard to the housing expenditure/income relationship, the redistributive effects for individual households are highly uneven.

The above discussion is based on current money income. Indications are that, when considered on the basis of a broader income definition and/or on the basis of income after federal income taxes, the property tax is substantially less regressive. When measured by "normal" or "permanent" income, rather than current income, the tax similarly becomes less regressive, since the dispersion in income shrinks and housing expenditures may be quite elastic with respect to permanent income.[13]

Taxes on Nonresidential Property

It is both convenient and conventional to deal separately with residential and nonresidential property taxes. There is a considerable body of data from the Census of Housing and from Internal Revenue Service materials on the incidence by income class of residential property taxes; but there are no such data for nonresidential property taxes. Therefore, empirical analyses of nonresidential property tax incidence have been forced to rely on sets of shifting assumptions plus series of proxy allocators to distribute the tax amounts assigned to particular sectors among income classes.

The major studies of this type have followed similar, and essentially rather simple, methods. Nonresidential property taxes assumed to be shifted forward are distributed among income classes in proportion to consumer expenditures, either for all goods and services or for particular items of consumption. Business property taxes not shifted are distributed in proportion to business, farm, or property income. Personal property taxes on consumer-owned property

[13] "Normal" or "permanent" income is the income an individual expects to receive over some longer period of time. The broadest definition is lifetime income expressed in terms of annual averages.

are distributed on the basis of selected types of consumer expenditure.

The results of four major studies are shown in Table 3-1. Where there are alternative sets of shifting assumptions which affect property tax incidence, the table presents the results on the basis of that set of assumptions treated by the relevant study as most probable. The studies differ in their treatment of federal income tax de-

TABLE 3-1. Nonresidential Property Taxes as a Percentage of Money Income Before Taxes in Various Studies

Income Class	United States 1948[a]	Minnesota 1954[b]	Michigan 1956[c]	Wisconsin 1956[d]
Less than $1,000	3.2%	4.3%	—[e]	4.6%
$1,000–$2,000	1.8	5.3	3.7%	3.5
2,000– 3,000	1.6	3.2	2.3	2.8
3,000– 4,000	1.5	2.1	1.9	2.4
4,000– 5,000	1.4	2.0	1.5	1.8
5,000– 6,000	—	2.4	—	1.7
5,000– 7,000	—	—	1.4	—
5,000– 7,500	1.5	—	—	—
6,000– 7,500	—	2.4	—	1.6
7,000–10,000	—	—	1.2	—
7,500–10,000	1.8	3.2	—	1.6
Over $10,000	—[f]	5.2	1.7	2.4
All classes	1.7	3.3	1.6	2.0

[a] Richard A. Musgrave and others, "Distribution of Tax Payments by Income Groups: A Case Study for 1948,' *National Tax Journal*, Vol. 4 (March 1951), p. 37; standard case.

[b] O. H. Brownlee, *Estimated Distribution of Minnesota Taxes and Public Expenditure Benefits* (University of Minnesota, 1960), computed from Tables 5, 6, and 1; allows for federal tax offset only for taxes paid by corporations.

[c] Richard A. Musgrave and Darwin W. Daicoff, "Who Pays the Michigan Taxes?" *Michigan Tax Study Staff Papers*, Harvey E. Brazer, ed. (Lansing, 1958), Table 5, p. 138; property tax burdens after federal tax offsets.

[d] University of Wisconsin Tax Study Committee, *Wisconsin's State and Local Tax Burden* (University of Wisconsin School of Commerce, 1959), Table 10, p. 58; property tax burdens after federal tax offsets.

[e] Computed only for 0–$2,000 bracket.

[f] Computed only for $7,500-and-over bracket.

ductibility of state-local taxes which has led to differences in both the level and the shape of the distribution of property taxes by income class. The findings of the four studies, however, generally agree: nonresidential property taxes as a percentage of income trace a U-shaped curve, initially falling as income rises, but rising once again for the highest income groups.

In the Minnesota study, the rise begins quite soon, at the $5,000 income level. Because the Minnesota study assumes very little forward shifting of business property taxes, business and prop-

TABLE 3-2. Estimated Distribution of Nonresidential Property Taxes by Money Income Class, 1957, Before Federal Tax Offset[a]

Income Class	Percentage Distribution		Percentage of Money Income	
	Case I	Case II	Case I	Case II
Less than $2,000	7.7	8.2	3.8	4.1
$ 2,000–$3,000	8.8	9.3	3.3	3.5
3,000– 4,000	11.4	12.5	3.0	3.3
4,000– 5,000	14.7	17.2	3.0	3.5
5,000– 7,000	19.2	21.3	2.1	2.3
7,000–10,000	12.5	13.1	1.7	1.7
10,000–15,000	6.6	5.4	1.8	1.5
Over $15,000	19.1	13.0	3.6	2.5
All classes	100.0	100.0	2.6	2.6

[a] See Appendix A for derivation. Case I involves less forward shifting of taxes on agricultural and manufacturing property.

erty income is more unequally distributed than consumption spending, and taxes which fall heavily on business property tend to be progressive in character. In the other studies, in contrast, considerable forward shifting is assumed, and thus the rise in nonresidential property taxes as a percentage of income occurs only in the top, open-ended income class.

The approach used in this study to allocate 1957 property taxes by income class is summarized in Appendix Table D-1. Alternative assumptions as to shifting have been made for agricultural and manufacturing property taxes, with substantially less shifting in Case I than in Case II.[14] Taxes on utilities and other business property are assumed to be largely shifted. It is assumed that taxes on the various nonbusiness personalty categories will not be shifted.

The results are given in Tables 3-2 and 3-3. As expected, they correspond in general with those of earlier studies. Nonresidential property tax incidence is regressive in the lower parts of the income range under both sets of shifting assumptions and income concepts. The tax rises as a percentage of income for the top income class in all cases, however. Federal income tax deductibility—of business

[14] See Appendix A for a detailed discussion of the basis for Appendix Table D-1. On balance, it seems likely that Case I is the more likely for agriculture and Case II the more likely for manufacturing, and that something like a mean figure for the two cases, in Tables 3-2 and 3-3, is the most likely situation.

TABLE 3-3. Estimated Distribution of Nonresidential Property Taxes for 1957, by Money Income Class after Federal Tax Offset[a]

Income Class	Percentage Distribution		Percentage of Money Income	
	Case I	Case II	Case I	Case II
Less than $2,000	8.6	8.7	3.7	4.0
$ 2,000–$3,000	9.4	9.6	3.0	3.4
3,000– 4,000	12.3	13.1	2.8	3.2
4,000– 5,000	16.2	18.1	2.8	3.4
5,000– 7,000	20.7	22.3	1.9	2.2
7,000–10,000	12.9	13.3	1.5	1.6
10,000–15,000	6.1	5.1	1.5	1.3
Over $15,000	13.9	9.8	2.3	1.7
All classes	100.0	100.0	2.2	2.4

[a] See Appendix A for derivation. Case I involves less forward shifting of taxes on agricultural and manufacturing property. Detail may not add to totals because of rounding.

taxes and of personal property taxes paid by consumers—increases the regressivity of the property tax, mainly by substantially reducing the net burden of the tax in the very highest bracket.

Taxes on Residential Property

The earlier discussion of incidence theory has suggested that, in a partial equilibrium analysis, taxes on housing (other than the land component) are borne by the occupants of the property, whether owners or tenants. Owner occupants at the time the tax is imposed or increased will suffer a capital loss, which will be realized when they sell. Owners of rental property confronting an inelastic demand (for example, under rents controlled at low levels, as in New York City) will raise rents and pass on the tax promptly; other landlords will suffer reduced net earnings and, over time, the deterrent to new investment will shrink the supply of rented housing and raise its price.

There are, of course, obstacles to complete and rapid shifting; for instance, the noninvestment character of many rented single-family houses. But, by and large, it seems reasonable to conclude that occupants bear the brunt of the tax other than the land component. The latter, however, is usually a small fraction of total property value; and most empirical studies of property tax incidence by

TABLE 3-4. Residential Property Taxes as a Percentage of Money Income in Various Studies

Income Class	All Residential Property Taxes			Taxes on Owner-Occupied Houses	
	Minnesota 1954[a]	Michigan 1956[b]	Wisconsin 1956[c]	Lansing, Mich. 1955[d]	Wichita, Kans. 1958[e]
Less than $1,000	5.11%	—[f]	14.47%	—[f]	—[f]
$ 1,000–$2,000	2.16	5.05%	5.42	8.83%	16.1%
2,000– 3,000	1.38	2.71	3.39	—[g]	8.4
3,000– 4,000	1.07	2.02	2.75	5.00	4.8
4,000– 5,000	0.89	1.63	2.53	3.53[h]	3.8
5,000– 6,000⎫	0.77	—	2.21	—	3.5
5,000– 7,000⎭	—	1.51	—	2.86[i]	—
6,000– 7,500⎫	0.67	—	2.18	—	3.1
7,000–10,000⎬	—	1.21	—	2.25	—
7,500–10,000⎭	0.57	—	1.97	—	2.8
10,000 and over	0.64	1.01	1.48	2.12	2.5
All classes	0.88	1.49	2.49	n.a.	n.a.

n.a. Not available.

[a] O. H. Brownlee, *Estimated Distribution of Minnesota Taxes and Public Expenditure Benefits* (1960), computed from Appendix tables. Income concept: money income before taxes. No allowance for federal tax offset.

[b] Richard A. Musgrave and Darwin W. Daicoff, "Who Pays the Michigan Taxes?" *Michigan Tax Study Staff Papers* (Lansing, 1958), p. 138. Income concept: money income before taxes. Percentages shown are net of federal income tax offsets.

[c] University of Wisconsin Tax Study Committee, *Wisconsin's State and Local Tax Burden* (University of Wisconsin, Department of Commerce, 1959), pp. 57–58. Income concept: "revised adjusted gross income." Property taxes net of federal tax offsets.

[d] Robert H. Pealey and others, "The General Property Tax," *Michigan Tax Study Staff Papers*, p. 187. Income concept: family income after payment of federal income taxes. Based on sample survey of 827 Lansing homeowners.

[e] Jack E. Robertson, "Comparative Tax Burdens for a Midwestern City," *National Tax Journal*, September 1962, p. 311. Income concept: adjusted gross income on state income tax returns plus social security and public assistance receipts. Based on sample survey of 396 Wichita homeowners.

[f] Computed only for 0–$2,000 bracket.

[g] Computed only for $2,000–$4,000 bracket.

[h] $4,000–$5,400 class limits.

[i] $5,400–$7,000 class limits.

income class have assumed that residential property taxes rest on the occupants.

Regressive Nature of Tax in Relation to Money Income

On this assumption, taxes on residential property have been found, without exception, to be markedly regressive when compared to money income before taxes; when federal income tax deductibility of state-local taxes (on owner-occupied properties) is taken into account, the regressiveness is even greater. In Table 3-4, the results of five Midwest studies for periods in the mid-1950's all

TABLE 3-5. Survey Research Center Findings on Residential Property Tax and Money Income Relationships, 1959[a]

(*In percentages*)

Money Income Class	Ratio of Mean Tax to Mean Money Income		
	All Families	Owners	Renters
Under $1,000	5.7%	9.7%	4.2%
$1,000–$1,999	4.0	6.4	2.1
2,000– 2,999	3.6	5.9	1.6
3,000– 4,999	2.3	3.4	1.3
5,000– 7,499	1.8	2.4	0.9
7,500– 9,999	2.0	2.5	0.7
10,000 and over	1.8	2.0	1.7
All classes	2.1	2.6	1.0

[a] From James N. Morgan, Martin H. David, Wilbur J. Cohen, and Harvey E. Brazer, *Income and Welfare in the United States* (McGraw-Hill, 1962), Chap. 19, Tables 19-1 and 19-6. Families whose heads are either farmers or self-employed businessmen are not included.

show this pronounced regressivity. The three state-wide studies cover both rented and owner-occupied housing; the two individual city studies cover only owner-occupied housing, but exhibit similar degrees of regressivity. A 1959 nationwide study, based on a sample survey of approximately 2,400 families by the Survey Research Center of the University of Michigan, also found pronounced regressivity—for owners, for renters, and for both categories combined (Table 3-5).[15]

Yet another source of evidence is in agreement, and this time it is one which does not depend on indirect allocators of tax payment amounts among income classes. Beginning with tax returns for 1960, federal individual income taxpayers itemizing their personal deductions have been asked to specify the amount of real estate taxes within the state-local tax category.[16] In 1960, real estate taxes

[15] Walter Morton's book, *Housing Taxation* (University of Wisconsin Press, 1955), is designed to explore the empirical evidence on the relationship of income to property taxes on housing. Morton subjects the evidence on Wisconsin owner occupiers in the 1930's to detailed scrutiny and produces results showing even more regressivity than appears in Tables 3-4 and 3-5 (Chap. 8, pp. 144-76).

[16] The returns call for real estate taxes, state income taxes, state and local sales taxes, and other taxes (specify). It is suggested in Appendix B that these data are not entirely unambiguous since reported deductions for real estate taxes may include taxes on personal property or business property, or they may exclude some relevant tax payments.

were reported on 16.4 million of the 24.1 million returns with itemized deductions, which in turn represented two-fifths of all returns.[17] The real estate taxes claimed as deductions aggregated $4.1 billion. If this amount can be said to comprise only taxes on owner-occupied residential property, the deductions claimed are estimated to equal about 80 percent of total taxes paid on these properties and to involve about 60 percent of owner-occupied properties.[18]

No doubt the real estate tax deductions claimed in some cases do cover property other than owner-occupied residential property: small business, farm, empty lots, and the like. However, this is not likely to be large in amount, since the regulations and instructions require that taxes on income-producing property be charged against gross income as business expenses rather than as personal expenses. It would often be advantageous for the taxpayer to do this, and to use the standard deduction in lieu of itemized personal deductions. By and large, the *Statistics of Income* data are probably reasonably good reflections of actual residential property tax/income relationships for owner occupiers in the income classes above the very bottom of the distribution. For the lowest income classes, the proportion of itemizers is very small.[19]

Table 3-6 and Appendix Table D-6 present the *Statistics of Income* data for taxpayers with adjusted gross income of $3,000 or more, a level at which a third or more of all taxpayers itemize deductions. These taxpayers claimed $3.9 billion in real estate tax deductions of the $4.1 billion paid in such taxes in 1960. When aggregate real estate tax deductions are divided by adjusted gross income on all itemized deduction returns, the real estate tax appears to be roughly proportional within each bracket for income classes between $3,000 and $20,000. This, however, is not an adequate comparison for, as Appendix Table D-6 shows, the proportion of itemizers claiming real estate tax deductions is quite a bit lower for the lowest income groups covered, and thus this comparison understates regressivity.

[17] U.S. Treasury Department, *Statistics of Income, Individual Income Tax Returns, 1960,* Table O.

[18] See Appendix B.

[19] In addition, there are some familiar reasons for not trusting data for persons at the lower end of the income distribution, such as the temporary status of many in that group and the relatively large gap between adjusted gross income and other measures of economic welfare for lower income people.

TABLE 3-6. Real Estate Taxes and Adjusted Gross Income (AGI) on U.S. Individual Income Tax Returns for 1960[a]

Adjusted Gross Income Class	Average Adjusted Gross Income within Class, Returns with Itemized Deductions[b] (1)	Average Amount of Real Estate Taxes Deducted on Returns Claiming Deductions[c] (2)	Column (2) ÷ Column (1) (3)	Column (3) Adjusted to Reflect U.S. Income Tax Savings[d] (4)
$3,000–$4,000	$3,523	$157	4.46%	3.57%
4,000– 5,000	4,516	168	3.72	2.98
5,000– 6,000	5,504	184	3.34	2.67
6,000– 7,000	6,483	204	3.15	2.52
7,000– 8,000	7,481	230	3.07	2.46
8,000– 9,000	8,470	251	2.96	2.31
9,000–10,000	9,472	274	2.89	2.25
10,000–15,000	11,835	330	2.79	2.18
15,000–20,000	17,087	463	2.71	1.90
20,000–25,000	22,256	560	2.52	1.70
25,000–50,000	33,541	716	2.13	1.21
50,000 and over	92,418	1,371	1.48	.52
All taxable returns:				
$3,000 and over	8,473	259	3.06	2.39
$3,000–$5,000	4,091	164	4.01	3.21
5,000– 7,000	5,973	194	3.25	2.60
7,000–10,000	8,256	247	2.99	2.33
10,000 and over	18,200	436	2.40	1.68

[a] U. S. Treasury Department, *Statistics of Income, Individual Income Tax Returns, 1960.* Taxable returns only.
[b] Total adjusted gross income, within AGI class, divided by number of returns, for taxable returns with itemized deductions.
[c] Total amount of real estate taxes deducted, within AGI class, divided by number of returns claiming deduction for real estate taxes.
[d] Column (3)×marginal U. S. income tax rate, for each AGI class; the marginal rates applied here are those for married taxpayers filing joint returns with itemized deductions, and were computed by comparing the tax rate schedule with mean taxable income, for these taxpayers, for each AGI class (total taxable income, within AGI class, divided by number of returns, Table 13, Part III, SOI); where mean taxable income less real estate taxes deducted (Column 2) straddles the bracket limits (for only the $20,000–$25,000 AGI class) a weighted marginal rate was computed.

In an effort to restrict the analysis to those taxpayers actually reporting deductions for real estate taxes, and thus to remove the obvious distortion for incomes below $7,000, some less direct comparisons have been made and are shown in Table 3-6. The procedure here has been to compute, within each income class, both the average adjusted income on all returns with itemized deductions and the average amount of real estate taxes deducted on those returns actually claiming the deduction. The latter was then divided by the former to produce the set of tax/income ratios shown, on the

TABLE 3-7. Property Taxes Paid on Owner-Occupied Single-Family Houses, 1959–60, by Income of Owner

(Number of properties in thousands; dollar amounts in millions)

Item	Less than $2,000	$2,000–$3,000	$3,000–$4,000	$4,000–$5,000	$5,000–$7,000	$7,000–$10,000	$10,000–$15,000	Over $15,000	All Classes
Number of properties: real estate tax as percentage of income (in thousands)									
Less than 1.0	520	308	355	438	896	517	320	220	3,573
1.0–1.9	252	205	291	484	1,111	1,255	682	312	4,592
2.0–2.9	203	146	284	453	1,090	1,123	691	250	4,239
3.0–3.9	167	133	192	322	932	778	383	136	3,044
4.0–4.9	173	125	160	215	567	535	187	66	2,028
5.0–7.4	372	255	284	326	681	392	122	35	2,466
7.5–9.9	277	146	126	132	157	46	23	6	914
10.0 or more	1,187	191	89	45	79	15	11	11	1,629
All properties[a]	3,151	1,509	1,781	2,415	5,513	4,662	2,418	1,037	22,485
Estimated real estate taxes paid[b]	198	171	230	353	1,018	1,081	726	665	4,442
Mean income in class[c]	977	2,503	3,495	4,497	5,935	8,242	11,753	27,999	6,784[f]
Estimated total income in class[d]	3,078	3,777	6,224	10,861	32,720	38,424	28,419	29,035	152,538
Estimated effective rate of real estate tax[e]	6.43%	4.53%	3.70%	3.25%	3.11%	2.81%	2.55%	2.29%	2.91%

Note: Because of rounding, detail may not add to totals.

a Covers only properties acquired before 1959; based on a special tabulation by the Housing Division of the Census Bureau from Residential Finance Survey data, Census of Housing: 1960.

b Number of units in each cell above times mean income in the relevant class times the midpoint of the percentage class interval in the stub. The multiplier for the bottom class was 0.5 percent; that for the top class was 11.0 percent.

c Adjusted gross income on U. S. individual income tax returns in class, divided by number of taxable and nontaxable returns, from U. S. Treasury Department, Statistics of Income, Individual Income Tax Returns, 1960. Figures are to nearest dollar.

d Mean income times total number of properties (or households).

e Real estate tax divided by aggregate income in class.

f Computed mean for this universe.

assumption that, within each income class, the average income of real estate taxpayers is no different from the average income of those not claiming the deduction. This is likely to be a reasonably good assumption, at least for the narrower income classes at the bottom of the income scale (probably all the way up to $25,000).

The evidence in Table 3-6 is in line with that of other studies. This portion of the property tax is regressive throughout the income range: significantly regressive up to about $6,000-$7,000, mildly regressive or proportional from there to $20,000, and steeply regressive for higher incomes. The burden of the real estate tax adjusted for federal income tax savings (the final column of Table 3-6) is even more regressive but only to a marked degree for adjusted gross income classes above $8,000 as the marginal federal rates begin to climb.

Property Taxes per Housing Unit and Income

In the 1960 Census of Housing Residential Finance Survey, data were collected on real estate tax payments in absolute dollars per housing unit and as a percentage of property value; also, data were tabulated on real estate tax payments relative to income for single-family, owner-occupied properties and relative to rental receipts for rental properties. These data and tabulations provide direct evidence on the income distribution of property taxes on owner-occupied houses and, combined with other Census of Housing data, indirect evidence as to taxes and rental housing.

Table 3-7 shows the relationship between income and real estate taxes as a percentage of income for owner-occupied, single-family houses acquired before 1959. Substantial proportions of the properties in each income class are in the low burden categories—say, less than 2 percent of income. But there are also large numbers of the poorer homeowners in the high burden categories; indeed, over 70 percent of all homeowners paying real estate taxes equal to 10 percent or more of income had 1959 incomes of less than $2,000. In contrast, very few rich homeowners are in the high burden categories. Thus, despite all the dispersion, the results are a substantial degree of regressivity (the bottom line of Table 3-7): results which compare quite closely with the *Statistics of Income* data for 1960.

In these estimates, real estate taxes on the land component of the value of owner-occupied houses have not been distinguished from taxes on the structure. A distinction would require a separation of taxes on land into three components. The first is taxes in existence at the time present owners purchased the sites, which would have been capitalized into the value of the land and borne by the previous owners. The second is the portion of tax increase in earlier years, but after the present owners took title. This too would have been capitalized, with present owners taking capital losses. The third is the current year's increase, presumably the smallest part of the total. Since the second and third components both involve the same owners, it does not seem worthwhile making the heroic efforts necessary to isolate these elements of the present tax liability. Moreover, distinguishing taxes on the land component might lower the present burden of the tax on current income somewhat, but would change its distribution among income groups very little, if at all.

In Table 3-8, an estimate has been developed of the distribution

TABLE 3-8. Estimated Property Taxes Paid on Renter-Occupied Nonfarm Housing, 1959–60, By Income of Renter[a]

(Dollar amounts in millions)

Income Class	Number of Renter-Occupied Units (In thousands)	Estimated Gross Annual Rent[b]	Estimated Real Estate Tax[c]	Mean Income in Class[d]	Estimated Total Income in Class[e]	Estimated Effective Rate of Real Estate Tax[f]
Less than $2,000	4,523	$ 2,658	$ 375	$ 977	$ 4,419	8.49%
$ 2,000–$3,000	2,202	1,534	216	2,503	5,512	3.92
3,000– 4,000	2,412	1,878	249	3,495	8,430	2.95
4,000– 5,000	2,460	2,080	273	4,497	11,063	2.47
5,000– 7,000	3,869	3,621	472	5,935	22,963	2.06
7,000–10,000	2,493	2,640	359	8,242	20,547	1.75
10,000–15,000	1,003	1,210	191	11,753	11,788	1.62
Over $15,000	331	467	125	27,999	9,268	1.35
All classes[g]	19,294	16,088	2,258	4,871	93,990	2.40

[a] Based largely on data in U. S. Bureau of the Census, *Census of Housing: 1960,* "Metropolitan Housing," Final Report HC(2)-1 (1963), Table A-2.

[b] Number of units in each gross rent class times midpoint of gross rent class interval, times twelve.

[c] Total from Appendix Table B-4; it is estimated that $406 million represented the land tax component, distributed on the basis of rental income in adjusted gross income. The remainder equals 10.6 percent of aggregate gross annual rent; this percentage is applied to each gross rent figure.

[d] Adjusted gross income on U. S. individual income tax returns in class, divided by number of taxable and nontaxable returns, from U. S. Treasury Department, *Statistics of Income, Individual Income Tax Returns, 1960.* Figures are to nearest dollar.

[e] Mean income times total number of renter-occupied housing units.

[f] Real estate tax divided by aggregate income in class.

[g] Detail may not add to totals because of rounding.

of taxes on renter-occupied housing. Here it has been assumed that real estate taxes on structures are a uniform percentage of aggregate gross rents paid by people in each income class, the gross rent estimate based on the Census cross-classification of monthly rents and income. The assumption of a uniform rent/real estate tax relationship among income classes is perhaps a doubtful one, but there is little basis for any other assumption. According to the Census Bureau's Residential Finance Survey, real estate taxes absorb about the same fraction of rental receipts as size of structure rises, until buildings with fifty or more apartments are reached. Here, the tax proportion is somewhat higher. On balance, both rents and income are probably above average in the largest buildings, since these are concentrated in the biggest cities and tend to be of relatively recent vintage. Therefore, the uniformity assumption may understate the real estate tax burden of the highest income classes. Nevertheless, the tax on renters appears to be at least as regressive as that on owner occupiers.

The regressivity is slightly modified, in Table 3-8, by the allocation of estimated taxes on the land component of rental property value on the basis of income from rents; this assumes that this element of the tax is borne by landlords. Evidence from the Federal Housing Administration suggests that, in the late 1950's, land values equalled nearly 20 percent of the value of one-to-four-family structures, or one-sixth of the total property value; Goldsmith estimates that land equalled 25 percent of the value of multi-family structures in the postwar period, or one-fifth of total property values.[20] These seem reasonable estimates; assessed value data are notoriously poor indicators of the distinction between land and building value, but nevertheless roughly confirm the Goldsmith estimates.[21] Therefore, 16.7 percent of taxes on rented one-to-four-family houses and 20 percent of taxes on rented multi-family housing, as estimated in Appendix Table B-4, have been assigned to landlords.

[20] Raymond W. Goldsmith, *The National Wealth of the United States in the Postwar Period* (Princeton University Press for National Bureau of Economic Research, 1962), Tables B-10, B-11, B-12, B-16. The FHA data appear in Table B-11.

[21] For example, assessed values for residential land in Wisconsin have averaged 17 percent of total residential property values in recent years (Department of Taxation, State of Wisconsin, *Property Tax 1956*, Bulletin No. 456; *Property Tax 1961*, Bulletin No. 461).

Table 3-9 combines the tax payment distributions shown for owners and renters in the preceding tables, plus an estimated distribution for owner occupants of units in two-to-four-family houses (assumed to be similar to that for renters, on the basis of the evidence in Appendix Tables D-7 and D-8). The result is an estimated distribution by income class of all taxes estimated, in Chapter II, to have been on nonfarm housing in 1959-60. In Table 3-10, this percentage distribution is used to compute burden estimates for 1957, to match the nonresidential tax burden estimates in Tables 3-2 and 3-3.

The combined results indicate regressivity over all, but it is by no means a smooth regression. The effective rate (on income) falls to about the $5,000 income level, then rises steeply to $15,000, and then falls once again. The explanation for this is an obvious one. Renters consume considerably less housing than homeowners at the same income level, therefore paying substantially less in property taxes. At the same time, renters tend to be concentrated at lower income levels than owners. Consequently, combining the two separate regressive distributions can produce progressivity in some ranges. For example, the income classes between $2,000 and $5,000 are dominated by renters, in terms of

TABLE 3-9. Estimated Property Taxes on Nonfarm Housing, 1959–60, by Income Class

(Dollar amounts in millions)

Income Class	Owner-Occupied Housing		Renter-Occupied Housing[c]	Total	Percentage Distribution
	Single-Family Houses[a]	In Multi-Family Structures[b]			
Less than $2,000	$ 200	$ 61	$ 375	$ 636	9.0
$ 2,000–$3,000	172	34	216	422	5.9
3,000– 4,000	232	43	249	524	7.4
4,000– 5,000	356	47	273	676	9.5
5,000– 7,000	1,027	81	472	1,580	22.2
7,000–10,000	1,090	61	359	1,510	21.3
10,000–15,000	732	28	191	951	13.4
Over $15,000	671	10	123	804	11.3
All classes	4,480	365	2,258	7,103	100.0

[a] Total from Appendix Table B-4; percentage distribution from Table 3-7.
[b] Total from Appendix Table B-4; percentage distribution assumed to be the same as that for the building component for renters, in view of the generally low value of such units and low income of their occupants. See Appendix Tables D-7 and D-8.
[c] From Table 3-8.

TABLE 3-10. Estimated Distribution of Residential Property Taxes, 1957, By Money Income Class

(*Dollar amounts in millions*)

Income Class	Percentage Distribution of Tax Payments[a]	1957 Tax Amounts[b]		Tax as Percentage of Income[d]	
		Before U.S. Tax Offset	After U.S. Tax Offset[c]	Before U.S. Tax Offset	After U.S. Tax Offset
Less than $2,000	9.0	$ 468	$ 468	3.27	3.27
$ 2,000–$3,000	5.9	307	300	1.61	1.57
3,000– 4,000	7.4	385	372	1.41	1.37
4,000– 5,000	9.5	494	470	1.40	1.33
5,000– 7,000	22.2	1,154	1,062	1.74	1.60
7,000–10,000	21.3	1,108	986	2.04	1.82
10,000–15,000	13.4	697	608	2.68	2.34
Over $15,000	11.3	587	433	1.57	1.15
All classes	100.0	5,200	4,700	1.86	1.68

Note: Because of rounding, detail may not add to totals.
[a] From last column of Table 3-9. Assumes that 1957 and 1959–60 percentage distributions were identical.
[b] Estimated local government property tax collections from residential property. Adapted from Table 2-3.
[c] Amounts in preceding column less percentages shown in Appendix Table D-4, column 3.
[d] 1957 adjusted gross income is the denominator here.

numbers of households, resulting in relatively low aggregate property tax liability for these classes. In contrast, nearly two-thirds of the families in the $7,000-$10,000 bracket are homeowners whose aggregate property tax liability is high, resulting in a high burden figure for the income class as a whole. Similar results also appear in the Survey Research Center results in Table 3-5, although in not quite so marked a form.[22]

Comparable to analysis of the incidence of any tax, the extent of regressivity is in part a consequence of the income concept employed. Use of a broader income concept—one which includes transfer as well as factor payments—tends to reduce regressivity, since it adds proportionately more to the income of people at the lower end of the scale. Additional elements are the inclusion as income of both imputed rent on owner-occupied houses and imputed personal interest income. The first also tends to reduce regressivity, largely because many low-income retired people have large net equities in their houses; but the second has an offsetting effect.

[22] See the discussion in James N. Morgan, Martin H. David, Wilbur J. Cohen, and Harvey E. Brazer, *Income and Welfare in the United States* (McGraw-Hill, 1962), pp. 297-99.

Another measure which reduces regressivity is the use of income after, rather than before, deduction of federal income taxes. Federal income taxes are larger proportionate subtractions from the incomes of richer people. Thus, in an after-tax income comparison, property tax payments by upper income groups are divided by relatively smaller income aggregates, resulting in higher effective rates for the rich. The Survey Research Center study combines these various adjustments into a measure of "gross disposable income," held to be a "more adequate measure of ability to pay"; on this basis, the property tax appears to be a proportional, not a regressive tax, for incomes of $1,000 or more.[23]

Reasons for Property Tax Regressivity

There are two explanations traditional in the literature for the regressivity of the property tax on residential property. The first is that assessors tend to value higher priced houses at lower figures, relative to market value, than is the case with cheaper houses. The presumed rationale for this is the greater ease of accurately assessing the more numerous cheap properties, which are frequently sold; in the absence of good market evidence for the more expensive properties, assessors minimize litigation by erring on the low side. Clearly, this tendency would have to be a very powerful one to explain, by itself the marked degree of regressivity within owner and renter classes.

In point of fact, the Morgan survey found no perceptible regressivity in assessments.[24] The 1957 and 1962 Censuses of Governments do suggest some degree of regressivity in the assessment of single-family nonfarm houses for the country as a whole.[25] That is, of the large number of assessment areas analyzed, a substantial majority seem to assess expensive houses at lower proportions of market value. However, this regressive tendency is very mild for urban areas in general, and is barely perceptible in some of the largest cities, such as New York, Los Angeles, Washington, Chicago, St. Louis, Cleveland, and Milwaukee. Since population, income, prop-

[23] *Ibid.*, pp. 294-96.
[24] *Ibid.*, pp. 293-94.
[25] U.S. Bureau of the Census, *Census of Governments: 1957,* Vol. V, "Taxable Property Values in the United States" (1959), Tables 17 and 20; *Census of Governments: 1962,* Vol. II, "Taxable Property Values" (1963), Tables 17 and 20; Frederick L. Bird, *The General Property Tax: Findings of the 1957 Census of Governments* (Public Administration Service, 1960), pp. 59-60.

erty values, and tax revenues (in increasing order) are concentrated in areas with low assessment regressivity, assessment practices are not likely to be a consequential explanation for the demonstrated regressivity of the residential property tax.

A more adequate explanation is found in the second traditional argument: expenditures on housing exhibit a relatively low order of income elasticity in the sense that, at any one time, richer families spend less proportionately for housing than poorer families. One-time cross-sectional observations rather consistently support this argument, when the income measure used is actual income in the given year of observation. In 1960, for example, as Appendix Table D-9 shows, the median renter family with an income between $10,000 and $15,000 was spending less than twice as much for rent as the median family with an income below $2,000. The median family spending less than 10 percent of its income for rent had an income of $8,500; the median family spending between 25 and 35 percent of its income for rent had an income of $3,200. For homeowners, as Appendix Table D-10 indicates, there was somewhat more dispersion in the income/house value relationship but, even so, house values rose less rapidly than incomes, according to the first column of the table.

It is not at all surprising that this should be the case. For one thing, additional expenditures for housing can buy either more space or better quality (including location), or both combined. It is likely that the demand for space alone is less sensitive to income status than to family composition and the like, above, say, the median income level within a large metropolitan housing market. More important, housing choices are not made continuously by every household, but relatively infrequently. Therefore, for many families, present housing consumption patterns are determined not by current income levels but by income levels or expectations some years earlier. In general, this averaging of income, or lagging in other cases, might be expected to result in low income elasticity of demand observations for families with rapidly rising incomes, consuming less housing than present incomes warrant, and also for older people, consuming much more housing than would be expected on the basis of low retirement incomes.

In any event, the property tax on housing can be expected to be less regressive when the income measure or the time period spans a number of years. The consequences of treatment of both residential

TABLE 3-11. Estimated Residential Property Taxes as Percentages of Money Income in Eight Northeastern New Jersey Counties, 1960ᵃ

County	Income Class						
	Under $3,000	$3,000– $5,000	$5,000– $7,000	$7,000– $10,000	$10,000– $15,000	$15,000– $25,000	Over $25,000
Bergen	17.6%	6.2%	4.7%	3.7%	2.9%	2.3%	1.1%
Essex	15.6	6.0	4.5	3.8	3.3	2.8	1.3
Hudson	10.5	4.4	3.1	2.5	1.9	1.3	0.6
Middlesex	12.3	4.8	3.6	2.9	2.2	1.6	0.7
Morris	17.2	6.5	4.8	3.8	3.4	2.6	1.3
Passaic	13.4	5.1	3.9	3.3	2.6	2.1	1.0
Somerset	13.5	5.4	3.8	3.1	2.3	1.8	0.9
Union	15.4	5.8	4.3	3.6	3.0	2.4	1.2

ᵃ Based on unpublished tabulations from the 1960 Census of Population and Housing, and New Jersey Division of Local Governments data on assessment ratios. The results shown here are weighted combinations of renters and owner occupiers, with rental data translated into property values on the basis of nationwide relationships of rental receipts and property values. See Appendix E for further description.

and nonresidential property taxes, and of expenditure benefits as well, on the basis of permanent or lifetime income, are analyzed in a section below.

An Empirical Investigation in Northern New Jersey

To some extent, at least, the progressive nature of taxes on residential property for the $5,000 to $15,000 current income range may be no more than a result of geographic differentials in property tax rates and in income distributions. In general, the highest effective tax rates on housing are found in the suburbs of the nation's larger metropolitan areas, especially those in the Northeast. These jurisdictions tend to be inhabited by families in the upper middle income ranges. Thus, a significant proportion of upper middle income families reside in high tax communities, perhaps explaining much of the apparent progressivity.

An examination of individual metropolitan areas can avoid some of the complications stemming from these factors. The data in Table 3-11 are the result of an intensive analysis of residential property taxes in eight counties in northeastern New Jersey.[26] These

[26] This analysis, developed by Emanuel Tobier, is discussed more fully in Appendix E.

counties are highly urbanized and have effective property tax rates which are among the highest in the nation. As Table 3-11 shows, the residential property tax is markedly regressive in all eight counties. Regressivity is continuous and by no means inconsiderable, even if the suspect results for the lowest income groups are ignored because renters in these groups mainly reside in older central cities with exceedingly high effective rates for rental property, most of which no doubt has been capitalized into low land values. Indeed, the degree of regressivity is probably greater than that for any other major tax in use in the United States.

Property Taxes and Expenditure Benefits

Often, studies of the incidence of state and local taxes by income class are concerned primarily with the distributional effects of alternative state tax policies. In such cases, the distribution of expenditure benefits can be ignored: they are invariant, and the variable is the choice of the tax measure or measures to finance these benefits. In this study, focusing on the property tax per se, it seems worthwhile—at least at this point—to compare the incidence of the property tax directly with that of the expenditures it finances rather than with that of other taxes. One reason for doing this is that the property tax is so important in the finances of local governments. The adoption of alternative taxes by local governments or by state governments, together with greater state aid, does not displace the property tax but only marginally reduces its importance. Moreover, as seen in Chapter I, alternative taxes in recent years have not reduced the importance of the property tax in the aggregate.

To the extent that the property tax is in fact a good user charge —a revenue device for the support of particular services under which individuals' tax liabilities accord rather well with their consumption of the specific services—it would be best to subtract both revenues and expenditures for these services before beginning the analysis. These revenues and expenditures would not affect the final results; moreover, the notion of the incidence of a price, rather than a tax, is conceptually somewhat peculiar. However, although in some taxing jurisdictions property tax liabilities may closely parallel the use of some public services, there are widespread geographic differences in this regard. In general, the existing American prop-

TABLE 3-12. Estimated Percentage Distribution of Benefits from Property Tax Financed Local Expenditures by Money Income Class, 1957[a]

Income Class	Case I			Case II		
	A	B	C	A	B	C
Less than $2,000	11.1%	11.6%	14.3%	8.9%	9.9%	15.9%
$ 2,000–$3,000	9.4	8.9	11.2	8.4	7.3	12.3
3,000– 4,000	12.2	10.8	13.5	11.3	8.3	14.0
4,000– 5,000	18.0	15.9	19.6	15.9	11.4	19.3
5,000– 7,000	24.1	20.2	23.2	23.9	15.6	21.9
7,000–10,000	14.6	12.2	12.1	16.4	11.1	10.8
10,000–15,000	5.2	5.6	3.7	6.8	7.6	3.4
Over $15,000	5.4	14.8	2.5	8.4	28.8	2.2
All classes	100.0	100.0	100.0	100.0	100.0	100.0

[a] See Appendix A for derivation. In Case I, a large proportion of expenditures is assumed to provide specific rather than general benefits; in Case II, the opposite assumption is made. General benefits are distributed on the basis of (A) family income; (B) property income; and (C) number of families. Detail may not add to totals because of rounding.

erty tax does not appear to measure up well as a user charge for any important public service.[27]

Therefore, in this section, it is assumed that the incidence of the property tax and of the expenditures it finances are separate and distinct. Appendix Table D-5 presents estimates by major function of local government general expenditure financed by the property tax in 1957. On the basis of assumptions as to incidence of the benefits of each of these functions (explained in Appendix A), over-all expenditure incidence results have been computed under alternative assumptions and are presented in Tables 3-12 and 3-13.

In all cases, the impact is markedly progressive: the benefits are substantially larger percentages of the income of lower income groups than of higher income groups. For the most part, the pattern is more progressive in the Case I examples. In this case it is assumed that most of the expenditures provide benefits to specific groups rather than to the population at large.[28] This assumption results in more progressivity for two reasons: first, certain expendi-

[27] See the discussion in Chap. VIII.

[28] In Case I, all outlays for education, highways, health and hospitals, sanitation, and welfare are assigned to specific beneficiaries. Also, 20 percent of all other expenditures are assumed to be specific benefit expenditures, in that they are provided to business. In Case II, one-third of all expenditures for education, highways, health and hospitals, sanitation, and welfare are treated as general benefit outlays, as are all other expenditures.

TABLE 3-13. Estimated Benefits from Property Tax Financed Local Expenditures as Percentages of Money Income, 1957[a]

Income Class	Case I			Case II		
	A	B	C	A	B	C
Less than $2,000	9.6%	10.0%	12.4%	7.7%	8.6%	13.8%
$ 2,000–$3,000	6.1	5.7	7.2	5.4	4.7	7.9
3,000– 4,000	5.5	4.9	6.1	5.1	3.8	6.4
4,000– 5,000	6.3	5.6	6.9	5.6	4.0	6.8
5,000– 7,000	4.5	3.8	4.3	4.5	2.9	4.1
7,000–10,000	3.3	2.8	2.8	3.7	2.5	2.5
10,000–15,000	2.5	2.7	1.8	3.2	3.6	1.6
Over $15,000	1.8	4.9	0.8	2.8	9.5	0.7
All classes	4.4	4.4	4.4	4.4	4.4	4.4

[a] See Appendix A for derivation. In Case I, a large proportion of expenditures is assumed to provide specific rather than general benefits; in Case II, the opposite assumption is made. General benefits are distributed on the basis of (A) family income; (B) property income; and (C) number of families.

ture categories, like welfare and health, are concentrated on benefits to the lowest income groups; and second, expenditures benefiting businesses rather than individuals are treated as, in effect, a negative sales tax.

Cases I and II differ in proportion to benefits assumed to be general in character. Cases A, B, and C allocate the general benefit component of expenditures in three different ways. The sensible choice appears to be between (A) family income and (C) number of families.

In Table 3-14, residential and nonresidential property taxes are combined and compared with expenditure benefits, all on the basis of money income concepts. The overall property tax burden traces a rather definite U-shaped curve before any allowance is made for federal tax offset. In Case I, in fact, the burden is higher on the top income class than on any other class except the bottom one. When federal income tax saving is taken into account, the net property tax burden is more clearly regressive over the entire income distribution. However, in all four cases, the degree of regression or progression is relatively mild for all incomes above $2,000.

This broad characterization disguises many local variations; in fact, it is quite possible for the tax to be distinctly regressive within most taxing jurisdictions (or for those containing the bulk of the country's population), but roughly proportional for the country as a whole because of the mix of income levels and property tax rates

**TABLE 3-14. Property Taxes and Expenditure Benefits
as Percentages of Money Income**

| Income Class | Total Local Government Property Taxes | | | | Property Tax | |
| | Before U.S. Tax Offset[a] | | After U.S. Tax Offset[b] | | Financed Expenditures[c] | |
	Case I	Case II	Case I	Case II	Case IA	Case IIC
Less than $2,000	7.1%	7.4%	7.0%	7.3%	9.6%	13.8%
$ 2,000–$3,000	4.9	5.1	4.6	5.0	6.1	7.9
3,000– 4,000	4.4	4.7	4.2	4.6	5.5	6.4
4,000– 5,000	4.4	4.9	4.1	4.7	6.3	6.8
5,000– 7,000	3.8	4.0	3.5	3.8	4.5	4.1
7,000–10,000	3.7	3.7	3.3	3.4	3.3	2.5
10,000–15,000	4.5	4.2	3.8	3.6	2.5	1.6
Over $15,000	5.2	4.1	3.4	2.9	1.8	0.7
All classes	4.4	4.4	3.9	4.1	4.4	4.4

[a] From Tables 3-2 and 3-10.
[b] From Tables 3-3 and 3-10.
[c] From Table 3-13.

among jurisdictions. The New Jersey evidence presented above indicates one regional example.

In addition to this roughly proportionate nature of the tax considered by itself, Table 3-14 shows that benefits from expenditures
financed by the tax more than offset the tax burden for some income
classes below $7,000. For the lowest income class, expenditure
benefits are estimated to be one and a half to two times the tax burden. For the $15,000-and-over class, the tax burden is estimated to
be anywhere from two to seven times expenditure benefits accruing
to people in this income group. In short, if the existence of the property tax and the relative ease of squeezing more revenue from it actually have contributed to the rapid rise in local expenditure in recent years, then the institution has redistributed real income from
rich to poor, on balance, and in fairly large dollar amounts.

Current Versus Permanent Income

Recent discussion of the concept of permanent income in the
economic literature is essentially concerned with explanation of
consumer behavior.[29] But two observations have been made of im-

[29] Among the primary contributions relevant here are Milton Friedman, *A*

portance to an analysis of property tax incidence. First, it appears that expenditures for housing and other consumer durable goods with long service lives seem to be governed more by expectations as to levels of normal or "permanent" income than by current, more transitory income levels, an observation which seems likely enough. Second, lifetime incomes exhibit much less variation than current incomes. For a variety of reasons, many households at both the top and bottom ends of the current income distribution are in those positions only temporarily.

The first of these observations is relevant to the incidence of the residential property tax, since it concludes that housing expenditures increase considerably more rapidly than income, and thus there may be a significant degree of progressivity in the tax. This is in contrast to the time-honored view that, as family income increases, the proportion spent for housing declines, a view supported by the 1960 data in Appendix Tables D-9 and D-10, as well as by numerous earlier empirical studies. Muth's permanent income analysis, using both time-series and cross-section data among cities, found that housing/income ratios rise markedly with income.[30] Margaret Reid's very elaborate empirical work produced a number of different income elasticity coefficients for housing demand in different comparisons, but most of them were high; her "findings imply an elasticity of housing with respect to normal income of around 2.0."[31]

Another set of data testing the permanent income hypothesis was developed in the course of the northern New Jersey investigation discussed above.[32] In this analysis, it was assumed that a reasonable approximation of permanent, or "normal," income is the average income levels of the major occupational classes in each of the eight counties. The rationale is that occupation is the major determinant of lifetime earnings (within reasonably small areas) and that age is the principal determinant of the ratio of current to normal income. The more refined the occupational classes and the

---

Theory of the Consumption Function (Princeton University Press for National Bureau of Economic Research, 1957); Arnold C. Harberger and others, *The Demand for Durable Goods* (University of Chicago Press, 1960); and Margaret G. Reid, *Housing and Income* (University of Chicago Press, 1962).

[30] Richard Muth, "The Demand for Non-Farm Housing," in Harberger, *The Demand for Durable Goods*, pp. 29-98.

[31] Reid, *Housing and Income*, p. 388.

[32] See also Appendix E.

FIGURE 6. Relationship of House Value and "Normal Income" in Eight Northeastern New Jersey Counties, 1960

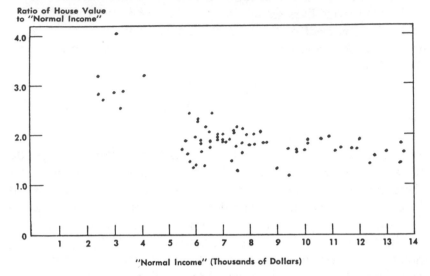

Ratio of House Value
to "Normal Income"

"Normal Income" (Thousands of Dollars)

Source: Appendix C. Note that each observation is for one of nine occupational groups in one of the eight counties

smaller the geographic unit of observations, the more likely this is to be valid.

Figure 6 is a scatter of the relationships between normal income (defined in this way) and house value/income ratios for the nine major occupational groups in the eight counties. The cluster of dots with low incomes and high housing/income ratios in the upper left part of the figure are for private household workers. This group is the only exception to a general profile suggesting an elasticity of demand for housing with respect to normal income of something like unity. Within each of the eight counties, the occupational groups in the very highest income bracket—the professional and managerial categories—tend to have slightly lower house value/income ratios, but this is only a mild tendency.

Both the conceptual argument for the permanent income hypothesis and the empirical evidence presented in support of it have been challenged.[33] Consumers may very well consider more than current income in making housing choices, but there is no convinc-

[33] Notably by Robert Ferber in his review of Miss Reid's book in the *American Economic Review*, Vol. 54 (March 1964), pp. 212-16.

ing evidence that they actually do so, or that they are freely able to act on these considerations, in light of income constraints at the time the decisions are made, racial barriers, uncertainty, and the like. Moreover, the data used to approximate permanent income are shaky and the methods used to relate housing to income data complicated.

Ferber, in his criticism, concludes that the income elasticity of demand for housing may very well be substantially higher than is indicated by the obvious data on housing-income relationships (such as in Appendix Tables D-9 and D-10), but largely because incomes tend to be understated in consumer surveys and the extent of understatement rises with income.[34] If this is so, then the residential property tax may be even less regressive with respect to "true" current income than is indicated in Table 3-14; resort to a permanent income hypothesis or analysis would be unnecessary to counter the traditional charge of regressivity.

The observation that lifetime incomes are more evenly distributed than current incomes is relevant to a property tax incidence analysis in view of the observed U-shaped curve of the current income tax burden distribution. If smaller proportions of households have average annual lifetime incomes at either end of the income scale than is suggested by current income data, then the burden of the property tax is likely to be more nearly proportional than the conclusions above suggest.

But, similarly, the distribution of benefits from expenditures financed by the property tax is likely to be more nearly proportional from the standpoint of lifetime income, at least in the lower half of the income distribution. This is especially so in view of the relatively large number of older people in the lowest current income classes paying substantial property taxes, but not directly benefiting from current school expenditures. Over their lifetimes, however, their average incomes are on balance higher, and many did benefit in earlier years from school expenditures, when their children were in school.

It should be noted that the degree of equity in property tax incidence suggested by findings of proportionality, or even progressivity, in a permanent income analysis refers to "statistical equity," not interpersonal equity. For any tax not directly on income, the stand-

[34] *Ibid.,* pp. 215-16.

ard empirical incidence analysis is faulty on this score since, within income classes, there are wide individual variations in spending patterns which affect the individual family's tax burden. This is perhaps especially true of the property tax, in view of variations in housing choice relative to income. However, it does appear that people who consume a large amount of housing relative to income tend also to have a larger number of schoolchildren than families with similar incomes but lower housing expenditures. Thus, to some extent, the degree of interpersonal equity may be considerable in practice. And, despite the conceptual inadequacy of a "statistical equity" notion, the evidence on balance suggests that regressivity of the property tax with respect to income is hardly the most impressive charge that can be laid against the property tax.

CHAPTER IV

Economic Effects

LIKE MOST OTHER TAXES, aside from poll taxes and taxes confined to true economic surpluses, the effects of the American property tax on resource allocation stem from its economic unneutrality. The property tax does affect incentives to work, to save, and to invest; it has a bearing on choices among types of consumption expenditure, business inputs, and spatial location.[1] It therefore tends to lead to patterns of resource allocation which differ from those which would obtain in its absence, either if other taxes were used to finance the identical level and composition of public expenditure or if both the property tax and the expenditure it finances were to disappear.

Some broad-scale effects are obvious. About one-half of property tax revenues are devoted to education, and perhaps another 20 percent to health, welfare, and other "human services."[2] The remainder is used to finance what can be characterized as services to property (street maintenance, sanitation, fire protection, and the like) and general local government overheads. The great bulk of property tax revenues is derived from housing, business structures, and business equipment, a significant share of the taxes on utility property being indirectly related to the scale of investment in housing.[3] Thus, to the extent that investment in buildings and equipment

[1] Locational effects of the property tax are largely reserved for discussion in the following chapter.
[2] See Appendix Table D-5.
[3] See Table 2-3.

67

is not price inelastic, the property tax can be said to shift resources from these types of private physical investment to investment in human development.

On balance, this shift seems to be a beneficial one. The large and growing body of literature concerned with the economic value of education and of investment in human capital in general contains two findings which support this proposition.[4] First, the social rate of return on investment in education and human development is at least as high as that on investment in physical capital, and probably higher. Second, during the last three decades, education has been a more important source of national economic growth than investment in material capital.[5] Both of these conditions seem to apply with more force to underdeveloped than to advanced economies. Moreover, the evidence suggests that the net advantage to be gained from shifting resources from investment in material capital to investment in human capital may diminish in the United States in coming years. But it will be a long time, if ever, before investment in human development becomes actually less advantageous relative to other investment. Other taxes can and do have this broad effect, as well. But, on a less aggregative scale, the effects of the property tax are distinctive.

As for private production of goods and services, the property tax is unneutral among inputs. It encourages the substitution of other inputs for real property and, to a more limited degree, for producer durables. To the extent that firms and industries are limited in their opportunities to effect such substitutions without raising costs of production above those of their direct and indirect competitors, the tax will tend to divert resources away from particular firms and industries.

As for the disposition of personal income, property taxes on housing amount to an average rate of excise tax which is far higher than those applying to most other uses of personal income (see Chapter II). This tends to discourage consumption of housing relative to consumption of almost anything else, aside from liquor and tobacco. Offsetting this, conventional American consumption taxes

[4] Summarized in Theodore W. Schultz, *The Economic Value of Education* (Columbia University Press, 1963), pp. 38-63.
[5] *Ibid.*, p. 44.

largely exempt housing outlays; American personal income taxes provide a positive inducement to invest in owner-occupied housing, through the failure to tax imputed rent on housing combined with the deductibility of interest expenditures which help produce this untaxed imputed income.

The unneutrality of the property tax is, of course, far less objectionable to the degree that it offsets other unneutralities in the tax system. This is apparent in a number of respects. In regard to business inputs, for instance, it can be considered as a counterpart to the existing taxes on payrolls levied for social insurance purposes. In regard to investment decisions, the property tax to some extent offsets the favorable income tax treatment of capital gains, for which investment in real estate provides especially good opportunities. In regard to consumption decisions, as noted above, the unneutrality of the property tax exists alongside the favored treatment of housing under American consumption taxes and the income tax.

Effect of Income Tax and Property Tax on Housing

It is worthwhile comparing somewhat more closely the effects of the offsetting unneutralities of the income tax and the property tax with respect to housing. Richard Goode has estimated that in 1958 the exclusion of imputed rent from federal income taxation combined with the deductibility of mortgage interest and housing property taxes reduced federal revenues by $3.2 billion.[6] This equalled an estimated one-eighth of the gross rental value of owner-occupied housing and about 8.7 percent of the gross rent of all housing. Assuming unitary price elasticity of the demand for housing, this tax treatment can be said to have increased housing consumption in the same proportions. Three-fourths of the impact of the favorable income tax treatment stemmed from the imputed rent exclusion and interest deductibility, the rest from property tax deductibility.[7]

Property taxes on owner-occupied nonfarm housing probably

[6] "Imputed Rent of Owner-Occupied Dwellings Under the Income Tax," *Journal of Finance*, Vol. 15 (December 1960), pp. 504-30.

[7] For the present purposes, some of Goode's estimates were revised on the basis of the property tax sources estimates in Chaps. II and III above. These estimates assign lower amounts to housing than those of the Office of Business Economics used by Goode.

amounted to about $4.0 billion in 1958, of which perhaps one-fifth was offset by federal income tax deductibility. Thus, a net burden of $3.2 billion in property taxes on housing compares with an income tax saving of $2.4 billion through favorable treatment of owner-occupied housing. If both the housing property tax and the favorable income tax features were abolished, consumer expenditure for owner-occupied housing in the aggregate would be encouraged. Rising property tax rates and lowered federal income tax rates since 1958 have increased this net effect.

However, there is a marked disparity among income groups in the balance between property tax deterrents and income tax encouragement to home ownership. Property tax payments are probably roughly proportional to gross rental value of housing among the various income classes.[8] The income tax advantages are zero for homeowners with no taxable income; under the pre-1964 rates, they were equal to about one-eighth of gross rental value for first bracket homeowners and one-third of gross rental value for a married couple with income of about $40,000.[9] On balance, therefore, the combined property tax/income tax system discourages expenditure for owner-occupied housing at the lower end of the scale and encourages it for better off families. Moreover, it surely discourages consumption of rental housing, which has no income tax advantage, relative to owner-occupied housing and to other forms of consumption. Since tenants tend to be lower income people, the overall system is decidedly unneutral with respect to housing consumption in the lower income groups.

The unneutrality of the property tax is also mitigated to the extent that it is, in part, really a charge for the use of certain types of public facilities or consumption of specific public services. If a tax does no more than replace private expenditure for particular services which would be made in the absence of public provision, or if the amount of tax paid by individual taxpayers is offset by the benefits those taxpayers derive from the public services, then the tax is in no sense unneutral. It is, rather, akin to the prices paid for privately produced goods and services; in a competitive equilibrium,

[8] There may be a small upward bias due to geographic tax rate differentials: effective property tax rates, incomes, and rental values all tend to be higher in urban areas.

[9] Goode, *Journal of Finance*, p. 514.

higher prices for one set of inputs than for another cannot be said to "distort" the allocation of resources.

Criteria for Neutrality

The property tax does finance some service to property. However, by and large, a tax based on the value of taxable property does not closely resemble, in its distribution of payments among individual users of the service, a price-like user charge, even for local government services to property. Consider, for example, sewers and sewage disposal. A firm with substantial taxable property may be a relatively modest user of water and contributor to sewerage costs—a telephone company, to cite an extreme case—while a run-down low value industrial plant may impose heavy sewerage costs. If sewer service is financed from the property tax, the telephone company will pay far more heavily than if the conventional sewerage charges tied to water consumption (which are hardly ideal as a user charge, either), are employed.[10]

The user charge component aside, a tax can be neutral among industries and inputs only under one of two conditions. First, if it is levied on some type of surplus, it will not affect the supply of the taxed factor, but will reduce the surplus. This applies to the land component of the property tax or to location rents in general. Second, if a tax is completely general on all inputs and industries, it will have effects on the aggregate level of economic activity and, since the composition of output is sensitive to changes in aggregate demand, indirect effects on resource allocation. However, it will not directly lead to changes in the price or quantity of individual inputs and products. A tax which meets this description would be a value-added tax with no exemptions whatsoever and with all activities and all factors of production subject to the same rate of taxation.

The property tax, like other real-world taxes, does not satisfy these criteria for neutrality. It applies to all industries, but not to all inputs. And property taxes on nonfarm business property are not an inconsequential share of the total tax payments by businesses which might affect the composition of inputs. In 1957, property taxes on nonfarm business property amounted to $5.5 billion. In contrast,

[10] See Chap. VIII for more extensive treatment of this point.

the employers' share of payroll taxes, which have an impact on input composition directly opposite to that of the property tax, amounted to $4.8 billion; taxes on intermediate purchases of goods and services by business, such as utility services, motor fuel, and the like, were less than $3 billion; and general business taxes—primarily on corporate profits—were $22.5 billion.[11]

Thus, other things being equal, the property tax would tend to encourage the substitution of labor for taxable physical capital and, where personalty is not taxed or is taxed more lightly than realty, substitution among the forms of physical capital. It would, moreover, tend to encourage labor-intensive industries to locate in areas with high property tax rates and capital-intensive industries to locate where property tax rates are low, if other taxes are similar in the various locations or if nonproperty taxes work in the same direction.

However, other things are not equal, by any means. Historically, the advantages of substituting capital for labor have been so large as to overwhelm any property tax disadvantages. When property taxes equal only 1.4 percent of net output, as in manufacturing in 1957 (see Table 2-4), and payrolls amount to 80 percent of net output, substitutions of capital for labor which reduce average unit costs by, say, 10 percent will be clearly advantageous. Even where property tax burdens are relatively much larger, as in the case of utilities, they are unlikely to deter substitution appreciably. Moreover, payrolls themselves are subject to high rates of taxation in the United States, mainly for social insurance purposes, which hardly enhances the competitiveness of labor as a factor input. Nevertheless, to the extent that capital intensity is associated with relative profitability, the combination of high taxes on business profits and high taxes on physical capital tends to make the American tax system "anti-capitalist" in this sense.

The unneutrality of the property tax among inputs may not encourage substitution, but it does produce unneutrality among industries. This is significant only to the extent that it involves industries which compete with one another. Perhaps the only major example of this in the real world is the case of the railroads. No

[11] Derived or estimated from U.S. Bureau of the Census, *Census of Governments: 1957*, Vol. III, No. 5, "Compendium of Government Finances" (1959), Tables 2 and 13.

doubt the competitive decline of the railroads has been inevitable in the face of new transportation technology which eliminated their monopoly position of the late nineteenth century; but the property tax may have hastened this decline. Railroads are inherently real property intensive and thus subject to heavier property taxation than their air, water, and road competitors. In 1957, for example, property taxes absorbed nearly 3.5 percent of rail operating revenues, but only 0.4 percent for motor carriers and 0.2 percent for air carriers.[12] Rising property tax rates in the postwar years imposed costs on the railroads far in excess of any parallel general tax increases confronting their competitors, and contributed to increases in railroad rates, hardly a good competitive strategy for a hard-pressed industry.

The extent to which the relatively high property tax burden on housing discourages housing consumption vis-à-vis other types of consumption depends in part on the price elasticity of the demand for housing. Some investigators have found this to be quite low, but more recent studies have concluded that the elasticity is near unity: that is, housing demand declines by approximately 1 percent for each 1 percent increase in price.[13] Margaret Reid has given a reasonable explanation for this: the demand for housing space per se is quite unresponsive to price, depending much more on family composition and similar exogenous factors, but the demand for better or less *quality* in housing has a lot to do with price.

Perhaps the biggest single type of quality upgrading which occurs in the housing market is the shift from rented to owner-occupied housing. Since high property taxes on housing are far more apparent to present or prospective owner occupants than to renters, the short-term deterrent effects of increased property taxes should be particularly important in this regard. However, there has clearly been a vast amount of this type of upgrading in the past twenty years in the face of high and rising property taxes. One explanation of this apparent anomaly lies in the many offsetting factors at work in this same period: the liberalization of mortgage terms; the

[12] Based on property tax estimates in Appendix A.
[13] Richard Muth, "The Demand for Non-Farm Housing," in *The Demand for Durable Goods*, Arnold C. Harberger, ed. (University of Chicago Press, 1960), p. 49; and Margaret Reid, *Housing and Income* (University of Chicago Press, 1962), p. 381.

inflation hedge aspect of investment in housing (or in other real property); the advantageous income tax treatment of home ownership for better off families; and, for apartment housing and non-residential construction, the favorable depreciation/capital gains treatment of real estate investment under the federal income tax, especially since 1954.

Another and perhaps equally important explanation lies in the nature of the property tax on housing in suburban communities, in which most of the new housing built in the past twenty years has been located. Property taxes are frequently very high in dormitory suburbs, whether measured by house value or by personal income. However, the tax is directly tied to school and other expenditure benefits realized by householders; it therefore comes close to being a true benefit tax, neutral by definition. Moreover, in dormitory suburbs the tax may approximate a proportional personal income tax; local income or sales taxes financing the same benefits might have less effect on housing consumption choices, but the differences are likely to be small ones in this type of environment.

In large cities, however, the tie to expenditure benefits is tenuous for many housing consumers, and property taxes amounting to large fractions of gross rental receipts—25 percent or more in large northeastern cities—are likely to inhibit the construction of new rental housing and rebuilding of the older cities. This warrants examination at greater length.

The Property Tax and the Future of the Big Cities

Although large central city governments rely more heavily on nonproperty taxes than other local governments, in 1962 about $4.8 billion in property tax revenue—one-fourth of total property revenue—was collected from property located in the forty-three largest cities (with a population of over 300,000 in 1960).[14] The

[14] Nearly $2.8 billion of this amount constitutes revenue of the central city governments themselves, according to the Census Bureau's *Compendium of City Government Finances in 1962* (Series G-CF 62- No. 2, 1963). Property taxes paid by central city taxpayers to jurisdictions other than the city itself were estimated from revenue data in the Bureau's *Tax Revenue of State and Local Governments in Calendar 1962* (State and Local Government Special Studies No. 46, 1963),

older large cities—in the Northeast and Midwest—generally operate with higher effective property tax rates than their suburbs.[15]
Moreover, the level of effective rates in these cities is high in absolute
terms. For example, in 1962, almost all northern central cities had
effective rates in excess of 2 percent, and in some, like Boston, Newark, and Milwaukee, effective rates exceeded 3 percent.[16]

Thus, there is a prima facie case that the property tax at the
margin may be a deterrent to investment in real property in the
large old central cities. Other things being equal, it clearly provides
an incentive to locate investment in suburban areas in most large
metropolitan areas, thus marginally deterring renewal of the big
cities' physical plant on a private, unsubsidized basis. Moreover, the
high absolute level of big city tax rates may marginally discourage
investment in urban real property relative to investment in other
assets. Investors in real estate generally require high rates of net return because of risk and illiquidity; high property taxes further increase the gross receipts required to make the investment attractive,
and it appears that real estate taxes frequently exceed 20 percent of
gross rentals for apartment buildings and 15 percent of gross rentals of retail-use structures.[17] The disincentive effects of the property
tax on investment in real estate may very well be overwhelmed by
special factors in particular cases—for example, extremely high location rents for central office activities in downtown areas—and by
federal income tax provisions in general, but the property tax per se
is not a negligible factor.

The Lack of Uniformity

The impact of the property tax within the big cities is complicated by the fact that it is not a uniform tax on all real property

---

mainly on the basis of the distribution of assessed values in *Census of Governments: 1957*, Vol. II, "Taxable Property Values" (1963), Table 21, and the effective rate relatives in Table 5-7 below.

[15] See Table 5-7, below.

[16] These estimates are based on the revenue and assessed value estimates referred to in the preceding footnote, combined with the Census "partial-coverage"
assessment ratios.

[17] National Association of Real Estate Boards, "Apartment Building Experience
Exchange of Rental Income and Operating Expense Data, 1963," *Journal of
Property Management* (special issue, 1963); Urban Land Institute, *The Dollars and
Cents of Shopping Centers, 1963*.

TABLE 4-1. Assessment Ratios and Assessed Value Composition, Twelve Large Cities, 1961[a]

City	Single-Family House Average Assessment Ratio[b] (1)	All Locally Assessed Realty, Partial-Coverage Assessment Ratio[c] (2)	Size Cut-Off for Column (2)[d] (3)	Percentage of Locally Assessed Realty Covered by Column (2) (4)	Percentage Distribution of Gross Assessed Value of Locally Assessed Realty			
					Single-Family Houses (5)	Other Residential Property (6)	Commercial and Industrial (7)	Other[e] (8)
A. Cities with Partial-Coverage Ratio Significantly Above Single-Family House Ratio								
Chicago	35.5	44.2	$300,000	71.8	21.7	35.8	39.5	3.1
Cleveland	35.4	38.0	50,000	57.5	40.8	1.4	56.5	1.3
New York	47.6	58.0	300,000	48.2	10.7	44.9	31.9	12.5
Pittsburgh	35.8	40.7	300,000	68.4	44.8	6.9	45.9	2.6
San Francisco	11.8	15.9	300,000	75.4	33.7	20.5	44.3	1.5
Seattle	13.9	15.2	300,000	86.6	48.3	10.1	38.4	3.2
B. Cities with Partial-Coverage Ratio Significantly Below Single-Family House Ratio								
Atlanta[f]	18.1	15.5	20,000	56.3	41.0	11.0	46.0	2.0
Dallas	18.7	17.5	15,000	63.2	56.8	4.2	36.8	2.2
Kansas City[g]	26.1	23.5	20,000	58.6	47.8	9.0	40.3	2.9
Los Angeles	20.4	17.3	300,000	90.0	54.5	15.0	26.7	3.8
St. Louis	35.6	27.9	300,000	78.0	43.3	7.2	43.2	6.2
San Diego[h]	21.1	18.0	300,000	96.1	65.1	7.6	18.1	9.2

Note: Detail in Columns 5 to 8 may not add to 100.0, due to rounding.

Sources: Columns 1 and 5–8, U. S. Bureau of the Census, Census of Governments: 1962, Vol. II, "Taxable Property Values" (1963), Table 22. Columns 2–4, special tabulation from the 1962 Census of Governments, September 1963.

a Includes twelve of the twenty-three cities which are primary centers of an SMSA with a 1960 population of one million or more; only those cities for which the partial-coverage ratio differs substantially from the average assessment ratio for single-family houses are included in the table.

b Sales-based average assessment ratio, based on measurable sales.

c Size-weighted average assessment ratio, based on measurable sales, for all classes of locally assessed realty assessed at less than the cut-off indicated in Column 3.

d The value-size cut-off is $300,000, plus any size classes of less valuable property with fewer than five sample transfers in the 1962 Census of Governments.

e Includes vacant lots, acreage and farms in a few cases, and "other and unallocable."

f Includes only Fulton County portion.

g Includes only Jackson County portion.

h Includes entire county, not just the central city.

within the city at an effective rate of, say, 2 or 3 percent, but one which has many variations among and within different types of properties. Because of the inherent difficulty of valuing property in the absence of actual market transactions and because of the extremely varied nature of properties within a large city, it is hardly likely that assessors could achieve a high degree of uniformity, even if they attempted to do so. And, of course, the attempt is not always made.

There is some limited evidence on this. First, the biggest of the older cities do not achieve a high degree of uniformity even in assessing single-family houses. This is not altogether surprising since the stock of single-family houses within a large city is heterogeneous with respect to age, neighborhood, and other market characteristics. In the 1962 Census of Governments (1961 assessed values), the coefficient of dispersion around the median assessed value to sales price ratio was 20 percent or more in two-thirds of the cities with a population over 300,000. The performance was least adequate, in general, in the oldest cities—those that lost population between 1950 and 1960, for example. A third of these had coefficients of 30 percent or more.[18]

Second, in some large cities, there appear to be systematic differences in assessment ratios among broad classes of property. The Government Division of the Census Bureau has prepared a special tabulation from the 1962 Census of Goverments sales data, covering assessment ratios for all use classes of locally assessed realty within the twenty-three central cities which are primary centers of a Standard Metropolitan Statistical Area (SMSA) with a 1960 population of more than one million. This tabulation has an upper cut-off that excludes high assessed value properties for which bona fide sales are scarce. The size cut-off varies among the cities, but is never higher than $300,000. Thus, most locally assessed utility property is excluded, along with a sizeable proportion of industrial plant, central business district store, hotel, and office buildings, and probably close to half of all apartment houses with fifty units or more.

A comparison of these partial-coverage assessment ratios for all realty classes with the published ratios for single-family houses con-

[18] From "Taxable Property Values," Table 22.

sequently is an indicator of relative assessment practices for single-family houses vis-à-vis those for small multi-family residential buildings, small commercial and industrial properties, and vacant lots (where these are significant portions of the assessment rolls).

What do the data show? In eleven of the twenty-three cities, the partial-coverage ratios are very close to those for single-family houses; in seven cases the ratio is within 2 percent (percentage, not percentage points). This does not prove uniformity among use classes, but it affords no evidence to suggest significant nonuniformity—at least, that is, systematic nonuniformity by use classes. However, for the twelve cities examined in Table 4-1, the partial-coverage ratios differ significantly from the ratios for single-family houses. In six cases, the partial-coverage ratios are higher; in New York, Chicago, and San Francisco, they are substantially higher. In these three cities, there is a substantial volume of two-to-four-family housing which is likely to be treated rather like single-family housing; this suggests that larger multi-family housing and commercial and industrial property are much more heavily taxed than single-family housing. The indications are that average assessment ratios for realty other than single-family housing, which is valued at less than $300,000, are more than 50 percent higher than the average for single-family housing in Chicago and San Francisco, and more than 25 percent higher in New York.

In the other six cases, the partial-coverage ratios are significantly lower. They are substantially lower in St. Louis where the average assessment ratio for realty other than single-family housing, which is valued at less than $300,000, is little more than half the average for single-family housing. The advantage here, in view of the distribution of assessed values, appears to accrue heavily to commercial and industrial properties.

Some data from the 1960 Census of Housing, discussed at length in Appendix F, suggest that, in general, effective property tax rates in large American cities tend to be a good deal higher on large apartment buildings than on single-family houses. The basic data, expressed as median annual real estate taxes per $1,000 of property value (owners' estimates) for the year preceding the survey date, are:[19]

[19] From U.S. Bureau of the Census, *Census of Housing: 1960,* Vol. V, "Residential Finance," Parts 1 and 2 (1963).

Type of Property	Tax rate per $1,000 value
1-family homeowner properties	$13
1-family rental and vacant properties	14
1–4 unit rental and vacant	14
5–49 unit rental and vacant	20
50 unit and over rental and vacant	27

Crude adjustment of these data to account for differences in urbanization and regional differences in tax rates indicates that effective rates on the larger buildings may average about 50 percent more than those on single-family houses.

To some extent, systematic differentials among property classes or subclasses are an inadvertent consequence of the techniques assessors employ that are designed to produce uniformity. A conscientious assessing agency will try to utilize the best evidence on property market values available; the difficulty is that, for different types of property, the best available evidence varies considerably. For example, for single-family houses in relatively new subdivisions in the outer parts of the city, the best evidence of value is likely to be recent sales price. For older, small residential structures which are partly or wholly owner-occupied, sales may be so infrequent that reproduction cost less depreciation (on the basis of some standardized formulas and tables) is the best indicator of value. For "income property" (rental residential, office, and commercial buildings), capitalized net income or a multiple of gross income is likely to be an important indicator. However, the end result of using the best possible evidence for each type of property may be significant nonuniformity between classes.

The application of any single standard, such as depreciated reproduction costs, will produce substantial nonuniformity, unless the tables and formulas—for costs and for depreciation, in this case—are extremely refined and frequently revised to coincide as closely as possible with the market's evaluation. This is hardly easy to achieve in large cities. The characteristic practice is infrequent revision of the construction cost tables and use of rather gross bases for handling depreciation. For example, St. Louis assesses on the basis of 1942 cost data and assumes depreciation at a flat 2 percent (declining balance method) for both residential and commercial

properties.[20] The Cuyahoga County 1955 reappraisal involved re-
valuing all properties on the basis of 100 percent of 1941-42 construction costs (in other Ohio counties, the basis at that time was 50
percent of 1950 costs), but applying a slower depreciation schedule
than had been used previously. It was estimated that the overall results were average values equal to 50 percent of 1946-52 sales
prices and 42 percent of 1955 reproduction costs, but average
assessment sales ratios differed considerably among property
classes: 36 percent for residential property, 55 percent for commercial, and 43 percent for industrial.[21]

Deliberate differentials among classes are common, in addition.
Washington, D.C., uses very refined and reasonably current cost
tables and depreciation schedules, as well as other aids; this results
in a considerable degree of uniformity, according to Census data.
There is an explicit attempt, however, to assess residential properties at 50 percent of market value and commercial properties at 65
percent.[22]

Long-standing practices in Massachusetts cities gained national
attention a few years ago when the highest Massachusetts court
struck down a comprehensive revaluation in Springfield, based on
an explicit decision to assess single-family houses at 55 percent,
two-family houses at 60 percent, multiple dwellings at 70 percent,
and business property at 90 percent of market value.[23] In New
York City, the differences among the five boroughs in the state-es-
tablished equalization rates in recent years have correlated strongly
with the composition of assessed values by property class; in fact,
the variation in percentages represented by one- and two-family
houses in the boroughs' tax bases "explains" a large part of the difference in equalization rates, suggesting that there are deliberate
interclass differentials of large magnitude.[24]

[20] Joseph P. Sestric, Assessor for the City of St. Louis, letter to the author, Nov.
12, 1963.

[21] Seymour Sacks and William F. Hellmuth, Jr., *Financing Government in a
Metropolitan Area* (The Free Press, 1961), pp. 229-33.

[22] Kenneth Back, Finance Officer for the District of Columbia, letter to author,
Nov. 5, 1963; see also District of Columbia Real Property Assessment Manual
(1958).

[23] *New York Times,* Nov. 25, 1961.

[24] Based on data from New York City Tax Commission and Tax Department,
Annual Report as of June 30, 1962, and earlier years. These interclass differentials
are not officially admitted.

The motives from which such deliberately differential taxation of different classes of big city property stems are obvious enough, although the consequences may not always be as beneficent as local officials hope. Business property can be heavily taxed in particular places without fear of stimulating migration away from the area over the long pull to the extent that particular types of business activities (such as local utilities, newspapers, and banks) are essentially captive to the area, and where particular sites confer extremely high location rents for certain business activities (such as central business district locations for central offices). These opportunities for heavy taxation of business property are especially significant for large central cities; hence, downtown commercial properties in places like New York, Chicago, Cleveland, and San Francisco are heavily taxed. In such cases, the city fathers, with some justification, may worry little about long-term mobility and may hope that a significant portion of the business property tax burden is exported to the rest of the country and the world at large.

It is all too easy to extend heavy taxation of business property to situations in which eventual migration to lower tax jurisdictions is not only possible but also probable; this applies especially to industrial property. The motivation here, however shortsighted, is the fact that less adverse voter reaction is encountered when business property is discriminated against in favor of residential property. The relative "invisibility" of indirect taxes applies in another way, too. Even if business property taxes will not be exported from the city, but instead shifted forward to residents, the general case for taxes on local service activities, such as utilities and retailers, as well as on apartment property, is that voter reaction is likely to be more muted than in the case of the highly visible taxes on owner-occupied housing. Moreover, there is at least a reasonable hope that the tax may not be entirely shifted forward to consumers since it is not a completely general and uniform tax. In the short run, apartment house owners, for example, may have to absorb some of their differentially heavier property taxes rather than risk vacancies, since their housing units are competitive with smaller structures bearing lower taxes.

There is another somewhat more subtle and yet conceivable motivation for heavier taxation of multi-family housing. The property tax on housing might be considered in part to be a benefits tax.

A large part of the local expenditures it finances involves benefits to persons rather than to property and thus numbers of households or persons may be a better allocator of public costs than property value. But the value per housing unit of apartments is considerably less than that of one- and two-family houses. In 1960, the median value of owner-occupied units in metropolitan areas, almost all of which were in one- and two-family houses (the majority single-family), was $13,500; the median value of units in large apartment houses was less than half as much, $6,200.[25] Thus, if number of households is to be the allocator, and if the property tax is to be the primary local tax, apartment houses would have to be taxed much more heavily on an ad valorem basis.[26]

Yet another motivation for differentially favorable treatment of smaller residential properties may be connected with the middle-class migration from central cities to the suburbs. Most big city officials publicly express concern at the rapid rate at which white middle-class families with children have been leaving the big cities in the past ten or fifteen years. Deliberately favorable treatment of the housing which such families might choose within the city limits may serve the real purpose of enhancing the city's competitive position vis-à-vis the suburbs, by affording a tax advantage to offset other disadvantages.[27] If this is the goal, then the favorable treatment should systematically be directed at that portion of the city's housing supply which is most competitive with suburban housing. This is not always the case; in some cities, the favored housing seems to be the old houses in downtown areas, rather than the newer houses in the outer parts of the city. Moreover, even if the differential treatment is well designed for this purpose, the tax ad-

[25] U.S. Bureau of the Census, *Census of Housing: 1960,* Vol. II, "Metropolitan Housing," Final Report HC (2)-1 (1963); and Vol. V, "Residential Finance," Part 2, for properties of fifty units or more. Much of the difference in value is related to size, of course: the median number of rooms in the former case was 5.6, while it was 3.0 for apartment houses with twenty or more units.

[26] This may sound a fanciful argument, but it actually has been used to justify a formal legal system of discrimination against apartment property in connection with a proposed revision of the property tax system in the city of Durban, South Africa (O. D. Gorven, City Treasurer, City of Durban, letter to author, April 10, 1964).

[27] The Mayor's Budget Message in New York City in recent years has included a comparison of taxes on "similar one-family houses" located on either side of the city line. In the 1964 comparison, the suburban taxes were 72 percent higher for example. *Message of the Mayor Submitting the Executive Budget for the Fiscal Year 1964-1965,* New York City, April 15, 1964, pp. 8-9.

vantage could be dissipated if capitalized in higher land values (which seems to be the New York City experience).

The Property Tax and Its Effect on Renewal

In the big cities, most of which have little vacant land within their boundaries, a prospective investor in real property or a present property owner can own and operate existing properties more or less "as is"; he can replace the existing improvements with a new structure; or he can follow an intermediate course by remodelling or otherwise improving the existing structure. Systematic differences in the tax treatment of different types of property surely will affect this choice. Moreover, if these differences are of long standing and are expected to continue, there may be some capitalization of them, which may or may not be advantageous from the city's overall standpoint.

For example, the data for Chicago in Table 4-1 suggest that replacement of four old frame single-family houses purchased for a total of $50,000, with a low-rise apartment structure representing a total investment of $250,000 might involve a tenfold increase in property tax liability.[28] It would take bright rental prospects to overcome this tax deterrent. Moreover, as nominal property tax rates rise over time, the market price of the old deteriorated, but tax-favored, property should rise relative to that of the after-renewal property, thus adding to the redevelopers' difficulties. If, in addition, assessors give little credence to expenditures for remodelling older properties, which seems to be the case in most cities,[29] the owner's best choice may be to remodel rather than rebuild.

The evidence thus appears to suggest that the American property tax is no help in the process of rebuilding the big cities. Investment in substantial improvements on central city sites will generate stiff increases in tax liability (in the absence of tax abatement arrangements, a form of subsidy). In most places, the percentage increase in tax liability will be greater than the percentage increase in

[28] In the author's actual experience in Chicago, admittedly a tiny sample, the increase has been far greater than this.

[29] This is entirely logical; appraisal of the market value of remodelling individual properties which do not change hands is extraordinarily difficult, and assessors therefore should be expected to err on the side of underassessment, assuming often that much of the expenditure represents the owners' unmarketable personal preferences.

the market value of the property if the characteristic assessment practices are followed; whether this deters the new investment will depend on the income prospects in each case, but there will be some effect at the margin. The general effect of high city property taxes in deterring investment in real estate relative to other forms of investment similarly depends on how close to the margin each decision is. It does seem, however, that part of the renewal problem is simply the lack of significant prospects for adequate returns on investment in big city real estate improvements. Such returns are often not adequate compared to nonrealty investments, to investments beyond the central cities, and to the returns that accrue from the present uses of sites, which may be high even if they bear heavy property taxes.

The situation is often barely marginal when the problem is not complete rebuilding on sites, but rehabilitation and remodelling of existing structures. For one thing, financing is often a major obstacle. Then, too, rehabilitation of residential property occupied by lower income people (many of whom are owner occupiers) has to be limited because the occupants, whether they are owner occupiers or not, cannot support large increases in costs of any kind, including taxes.[30]

A fair number of private urban renewal decisions are barely marginal, or even submarginal, made on the basis of nonmarket considerations unique to the parties involved. For example, owner occupants may place a very high value on continuing to live in a certain neighborhood; life insurance companies may put a high public relations value on investing in a renewal project which is a questionable commercial proposition. In such cases, the pre-renewal acquisition price plus the new investment may exceed any reasonable market value of the after-renewal assets. Property taxes imposed on the latter basis may present no problem, but if imposed on the basis of the former measure of value, they are in effect taxes on public spiritedness—or on folly. And such taxes may be discouragingly high in relation to those on blighted properties, even if the latter are in no way underassessed as measured by city-wide assessment sales ratios.

If the property tax is, in fact, in particular situations *the* critical

---

[30] In this particular situation, the fact that assessors frequently discount rehabilitation expenditures heavily may be helpful, and rigorous pursuit of uniformity in assessments might be harmful.

deterrent to desired private rebuilding of the urban physical plant, tax exemption or abatement for particular projects is one strategy to use to overcome the obstacle.[31] It is not the only possible strategy; ideally, there should be a form of cost-benefit analysis applied to all the various alternatives. Nevertheless, it is a popular one, first used by New York City in 1921.[32] Although other states and cities have adopted abatement provisions, New York State is still the primary user. Under a variety of laws providing either freezing of the pre-improvement taxes or partial abatement of post-improvement taxes for periods of 25-30 years, over $750 million in assessed values of multi-family housing—5.5 percent of the total—was exempt from taxation in 1961.[33] Most of this is in New York City.

The tax abatement weapon in New York can be a powerful one. For new apartment houses built without any public aid in New York, property tax payments currently equal about 25 percent of gross rents. For projects built with a 50 percent tax abatement, the tax savings can reduce monthly rents by more than $6 per room. In one example cited by the City agency responsible for the program, rents were $30 per room per month, a figure made possible by a combination of subsidies: tax abatement, mortgage financing at below-market rates, and land write-down under the federal urban renewal program. A project of similar cost without subsidy would have rented for more than $50 per room per month.[34]

Such programs as these are essentially ad hoc responses to the difficulty of encouraging rebuilding of the large cities. This is one of many areas connected with the property tax in which far more knowledge is needed, on a highly disaggregated basis. Just how serious is the property tax per se as an obstacle to urban renewal in particular places and particular forms? Are differentials systematic or erratic? What are their effects? If differentials are systematic and deliberate, do they achieve their goals? Are they an efficient means of doing so? The problems are complex, and the future research agenda is a long one.

[31] For a generally hostile reaction to this strategy, see Mabel L. Walker, "Property Tax Expedients in Urban Renewal," *Proceedings of the Fifty-Third Annual Conference,* National Tax Association (1960), pp. 44-51.

[32] *Ibid.,* p. 49.

[33] "Taxable Property Values," pp. 6-7, Tables 4, 21, and 22, as corrected in August 1964.

[34] Based on material supplied by the New York City Housing and Redevelopment Board, April 1964.

CHAPTER V

Geographic Differentials in Property Taxation

THE APPRAISAL OF THE ECONOMIC CONSEQUENCES of the property tax in the United States in the preceding chapters is a highly incomplete picture for, in truth, there is no such thing as "the" property tax. Instead, there are more than 82,000 local governments relying, often heavily, on a tax with a distinctive tax base and a distinctive tax rate. And while these 82,000 different taxes are set within a framework of fifty-one state (and District of Columbia) tax laws, the problem is further compounded by the enormous intrastate dispersion in both rates and tax bases within many states.

In part, geographic differentiation is a consequence of age. Any tax of such long standing which is not imposed on a uniform national basis will produce, in time, considerable local variation. The evolution of the property tax—from one on all classes of private property and virtually the sole support of state and local government to one with many classes of property exempt and supplemented by a variety of nonproperty taxes—has proceeded at very different rates among the states and within each state. Moreover, the measurement of the tax base, however defined, is a highly subjective

86

enterprise, and the measurement process itself—the assessment—will differ considerably from place to place.

But geographic variation in property taxation is not simply a result of historical accident reinforced by the harsh facts of economic life. There is an element of variation which can be attributed to deliberate choice; and no doubt there are other elements which can be attributed largely to ignorance of the economic consequences of tax differentials: ignorance more to be expected in connection with the property tax than with any other tax in view of its complexity and the scarcity of good comparative data. Differentials stemming from deliberate choice relate to two kinds of preferences: relative preferences for public versus private goods and preferences in connection with the income distribution characteristics of state and local tax systems.

As to the first kind of choice, consider the following evidence: in 1962, property tax revenue was a somewhat smaller proportion of total state-local tax revenue in New York State than in the country as a whole (44 percent versus 46 percent), and local *nonproperty* taxes were about twice as important as a share of local tax revenue (23 percent versus 12 percent). Yet property tax revenues in New York were one-third above the national average on a per capita basis, nearly one-tenth higher as a proportion of personal income, and more than 75 percent higher relative to the estimated market value of taxable property.[1] This appears to reflect a clear preference of New York State residents for public goods, relative to Americans living in other states. Clear-cut examples of differences in taste in regard to the distributional effects of state-local taxes are harder to find, since states with relatively low ratios of property taxes to personal income tend to have high consumption taxes (not income taxes) which presumably have similar distributional consequences. Nonetheless, the existence of high property tax states like New Jersey and Oregon immediately adjacent to very low property tax states like Pennsylvania and Washington is suggestive of this kind of deliberate choice.

Even if property tax rates and bases were a good deal more uniform than they are, there would be reason to look into the spatial aspects of the tax. The property tax is largely a tax on investment in

[1] See Tables 5-1 and 5-4.

land and buildings, principally in urban areas. Only if it were confined to site or location rents would it be neutral in its impact on the spatial distribution of economic activity. Since the diverse 82,000 property taxes in the United States cannot meet this test of neutrality, concern with the economic efficiency aspects of the tax must include attention to its locational effects.

Geographic differentials are analyzed in the following pages at two levels, each with distinctive classes of effects and policy issues. The first level is the more conventional one, the one which is no doubt synonymous with the title of this chapter to most readers—differentials among states and sections of the country. The issues here include interstate and interregional competition for income- and wealth-creating activities, the place of the property tax in over-all state-local tax systems, and comparative performance of the property tax institutions themselves.

The second level deals with property tax differentials within rather than among subnational economies. Within regions which constitute meaningful economic entities—typically metropolitan areas—there are wide disparities in property tax rates, expenditure levels, income, and wealth among individual taxing jurisdictions. These differences are both a consequence of and contribute to the location pattern of economic activity in metropolitan areas. The nation's population and economy are concentrating in urban complexes and it can be argued that the larger metropolitan areas are becoming more similar in their economic characteristics. If this is the case, then intrametropolitan location characteristics will be an increasingly important efficiency consideration for the nation. Moreover, from the standpoint of tax policy, the most significant competition for the location of economic activity is not among widely separated regions, but among adjacent urban locations where market access and costs of production and transportation are generally comparable and where, therefore, tax considerations can loom large at the margin.

Still another reason for concern with intrametropolitan differentials is that they do bear on equity: the income distribution effects of a state-local fiscal system in which services are provided by a large number of small local units from their own very different fiscal resource endowments will be very different from one in which public services are financed largely from area-wide taxes which transfer income in kind from the residents of high income (or high property value) subdivisions to the residents of poorer communities.

The large central cities of metropolitan areas, which constitute single taxing jurisdictions, raise another set of geographic issues. The problem is not simply the central city versus the suburbs, but the structure of the property tax within the central cities themselves, since there are differences in effective tax rates, related mostly to different property types, within a single large city. The major economic policy issue here relates to the effects of the property tax on the large older city's capacity to provide adequate levels of public services—especially to its many lower income residents—while not deterring, even encouraging, private investment which renews the city's physical plant.

Interarea Differentials

The state—the state government itself and all local governments within the state—is the logical unit for observation of variations in property tax importance. This is not only because property tax institutions and property tax substitutes are governed by state law but also because the nature of state tax resources and state aid arrangements seem to be the major determinant of the role of the property tax.

The Property Tax in State-Local Revenue Systems

In 1962, property tax revenues ranged from 16 percent of state-local tax revenue in Hawaii to 70 percent in Nebraska, with median and average values in the neighborhood of 45 percent. There is, as Table 5-1 indicates, a pronounced regional character to the variation. This is perhaps to be expected, for the economic, cultural, and historic backdrop for tax policy is more similar among adjacent states than for the country as a whole. Moreover, to the extent that states emulate one another in instituting and adapting tax measures, they are more likely to emulate nearby states rather than distant states.

At any rate, region seems to be the principal variable: reliance on the property tax is relatively high in New England, uniformly high in the Great Lakes states, and even higher in the northern

TABLE 5-1. The Property Tax in State-Local Revenue Systems, 1962

Region and State	Property Tax Revenue* ($ million)	As a Proportion of Total State-Local Tax Revenue		Per Capita	Per $1,000 of Personal Income
		Percentage	Rank		
Northeast	$5,748.0	47.9%	—	$125.19	$46.22
New England	1,544.0	57.0	—	144.60	54.26
New Hampshire	79.8	63.6	3	128.34	57.27
Massachusetts	861.7	60.6	4	166.09	60.30
Maine	104.2	52.8	15	106.51	54.40
Connecticut	366.5	53.6	12	139.61	45.68
Rhode Island	90.3	47.8	21	102.84	44.00
Vermont	41.6	45.2	26	107.52	53.21
Middle Atlantic	4,204.0	45.2	—	119.31	43.84
New Jersey	975.6	64.7	2	153.47	54.11
New York	2,418.1	44.4	27	138.19	47.43
Pennsylvania	810.4	34.7	34	71.20	30.14
North Central	6,179.4	53.0	—	117.90	48.23
West North Central	1,828.3	53.7	—	117.45	51.67
Nebraska	190.9	70.5	1	132.02	55.66
South Dakota	88.8	58.4	5	123.22	59.67
Iowa	360.9	56.6	7	130.12	59.39
Kansas	290.8	56.1	9	131.28	59.87
Minnesota	476.7	54.9	11	137.72	61.35
North Dakota	71.3	52.8	15	112.63	48.86
Missouri	348.9	42.6	29	80.83	33.67
East North Central	4,351.1	52.7	—	118.09	46.92
Indiana	534.8	56.2	8	114.69	48.32
Wisconsin	541.9	55.6	10	134.84	58.02
Illinois	1,315.6	53.4	13	130.28	45.59
Ohio	1,023.7	51.7	17	101.98	42.38
Michigan	935.1	49.3	19	116.47	48.44
West	3,806.3	46.3	—	126.06	47.80
Mountain	754.4	45.1	—	101.76	46.09
Montana	92.0	56.8	6	132.06	58.81
Wyoming	43.8	53.4	13	131.81	55.39
Arizona	156.6	47.7	22	105.36	49.49

Source: U. S. Bureau of the Census, *Property Taxation in 1962* (November 1964), Tables 1, 3, and 5.
* U. S. total property tax revenues.

TABLE 5-1. Continued

Region and State	Property Tax Revenue[a] ($ million)	As a Proportion of Total State-Local Tax Revenue		Per Capita	Per $1,000 of Personal Income
		Percentage	Rank		
Mountain (continued)					
Colorado	$226.9	47.7%	22	$119.88	$50.21
Idaho	66.2	48.6	20	94.61	48.88
Utah	90.5	44.1	28	94.50	44.93
Nevada	31.1	32.7	36	88.99	28.37
New Mexico	47.1	25.2	45	47.28	25.34
Pacific	3,052.0	46.6	—	133.97	48.25
California	2,579.6	50.2	18	151.48	52.45
Oregon	198.2	47.4	24	109.68	45.47
Washington	234.4	30.9	39	77.87	31.37
Alaska	12.0	22.9	47	49.58	18.29
Hawaii	27.8	16.0	51	40.11	17.45
South	3,320.6	34.4	—	57.95	30.87
West South Central	1,201.8	37.3	—	67.58	35.93
Texas	838.8	45.3	25	82.87	41.20
Oklahoma	142.9	31.2	38	58.38	30.64
Arkansas	72.0	28.3	42	39.11	26.27
Louisiana	148.1	22.6	48	43.93	26.08
East South Central	500.3	28.6	—	40.63	25.51
Tennessee	175.8	33.3	35	48.13	28.42
Kentucky	141.4	30.3	40	45.85	26.80
Mississippi	94.6	29.9	41	41.84	32.74
Alabama	88.6	20.3	50	26.70	16.84
South Atlantic	1,618.4	34.5	—	59.50	29.69
Florida	436.8	41.2	31	80.38	39.14
Maryland	297.5	41.7	30	92.02	34.75
District of Columbia	67.8	37.0	32	85.87	26.84
Virginia	223.9	35.9	33	52.72	26.57
Georgia	199.7	31.8	37	48.91	27.69
North Carolina	206.0	27.9	43	43.78	25.13
West Virginia	83.4	27.2	44	46.43	25.98
South Carolina	80.4	24.3	46	32.84	21.36
Delaware	23.0	20.5	49	49.27	15.81
United States Average	19,054.3	45.9	—	102.54	43.33
Median State	—	45.2	26	94.61	44.00

Plains states. In the Middle Atlantic states the picture is mixed, as it is in the northern Mountain states and in the Far West, but in most of these the property tax percentage is on the high side. The southeastern quadrant of the country includes nearly all the states where the property tax is relatively unimportant. A three-dimensional map of the country, in which property tax revenue as a proportion of total state-local tax revenue represents height, would show a remarkably smooth gradient overall, despite a few sports.

Within broad regions, the richer and more urbanized states tend to depend more on the property tax than their neighbors, but this is by no means uniform. Moreover, differences in wealth and the extent of urbanization do not coincide with the broad regional differences. For example, the northern Plains states are among the country's least urbanized and are far from its richest, but lead in dependence on the property tax. The final two columns of Table 5-1 bear this out. The fifteen states which rank highest in dependence on the property tax in 1962 had revenues equal to $114, or more, per capita, compared to $95 in the median state; eleven of these fifteen had revenues above $125. In twelve of them, property tax revenues were more than 5.5 percent of personal income, compared to 4.4 percent in the median state.

It is quite clear that the low extent of reliance on the property tax in the South is not a direct consequence of low incomes. Indeed, in most southern states, property tax revenues in 1962 were well below 3 percent of personal income. Conceivably, there may be a more subtle indirect relationship between markedly low incomes and low utilization of the property tax. This could take a number of forms. One is the possibility that the *willingness* to utilize a direct tax largely on housing has a high degree of income elasticity. A second is that the ratio of privately owned capital, especially realty, to income increases as income levels rise, and thus high income states have disproportionately higher amounts of taxable property. The evidence on effective tax rates below suggests that this is not a viable explanation; moreover, the southern states tend to exempt large proportions of privately owned wealth from the tax base (mostly via homestead exemptions), and this would suggest that the low property tax/personal income ratios are partly optional rather than a consequence of external economic forces. A third possibility is that low reliance on the property tax stems from a largely inarticulate recognition that it is a good development strategy for capital-short regions. This strategy would work best if the property tax burden in such states were especially low on business property; this possibility will be examined below, but the homestead exemption practice would tend to dilute the advantage by shifting the tax load from residential to nonresidential property.

The counterpart to relatively high dependence on the property tax is relatively low dependence on taxes collected by the state government, and vice versa, as this frequency distribution for the fifty states in 1962 shows:

Property Tax as a Percentage of Total Tax Revenue	*State Government Percentage of Total Tax Revenue*			
	Less than 40	*40–50*	*50–60*	*Over 60*
Less than 35	—	—	1	15
35–50	—	5	11	—
50–60	1	12	1	—
Over 60	4	—	—	—

The role of local nonproperty taxes in this is rather small since, for all local governments in 1962, nonproperty taxes provided only 12 percent of tax revenue. Even in the very large cities where there is inherently more scope for nonproperty taxes, the property tax in 1962 provided two-thirds of tax revenue. Moreover, the role of the property tax in a given state is not greatly affected by the existence of one or a few large cities which are heavy users of nonproperty tax sources, for the large cities' nonproperty taxes are far overshadowed by the state government's nonproperty tax revenue. For example, in New York State in 1962, state nonproperty tax revenue was $2.3 billion, compared to $626 million for New York City.[2]

[2] The following tabulation for three large states indicates the impact of the large city in 1962:

	Percentage of State-Local Tax Revenue from the Property Tax
New York State	43.9
excluding New York City	40.2
Illinois	53.2
excluding Chicago	53.0
California	50.4
excluding five largest cities	49.8

In this computation, to obtain the denominator, state aid to these cities (other than estimated federal aid channelled through the state government) was sub-

The character of state tax institutions appears to affect the relative role of state-levied taxes and, through this, the relative role of the property tax. The three states which levy no broad-based tax on either sales or income—Nebraska, New Jersey, and New Hampshire —are those in which the property tax is most important. There appears to be some tendency for states which are mainly income tax states to rely on the property tax more heavily than those which are mainly sales tax states. Compare, for example, the seven states in which the individual income tax provides more than 30 percent of state tax revenue and the twenty-four states in which a general sales tax provides a similar share of state tax revenue. In five of these income tax states, the property tax percentage is well above the national median, and it is very close to it in a sixth state. In fourteen of the twenty-four sales tax states, on the other hand, the property tax role is well below the median.

As Table 5-1 shows, moreover, the property tax in relation to personal income appears to be a good deal higher in the income tax states than in their sales tax neighbors: Massachusetts versus Connecticut; Minnesota versus the other Plains states; Wisconsin versus the other Great Lakes states; Oregon versus Washington. This is difficult to explain. It may be that sales tax rates can be altered with relative ease to meet changing revenue needs. The converse may be true of those states depending on the income tax. There is usually strong resistance to any rise in rate and consequently greater reliance has to be placed on the property tax as revenue demand rises. Again, the difference in emphasis on the property tax among states may also be due to differences in attitude with regard to public as opposed to private goods. Some states with both high income taxes and high property taxes tend to spend more, both per capita and relative to personal income, than their neighbors. Constituencies

---

tracted. The denominator thus equals total state-local tax revenue in the state excluding the tax revenue of the indicated cities and estimated tax revenue which reflects state aid (from its own resources) to the indicated cities.

Sources for this computation and the figures in the above paragraph: U.S. Bureau of the Census, *Census of Governments: 1962,* Vol. VI, No. 2, *"State Payments to Local Governments"* (1963); *Compendium of State Government Finances in 1962* (Series G-SF 62-No. 2, 1963); *Compendium of City Government Finances in 1962* (Series G-CF 61-No. 2, 1963); *Government Finances in 1962* (Series G-GF 62-No. 2, October 1963).

which have a taste for public goods (which tend to be redistributive on the state-local level) may have a preference for redistributive taxes as well.

The Character of the Tax Base

Interstate and interregional differences in the composition of the property tax base—meaning here not the market value of privately owned wealth but rather assessed values actually subject to taxation—appear to stem as much from tax policy choices as from economic differences among the states. These choices take a number of major forms. One is the decision on the extent to which personal property is included in the tax base. Since, as is pointed out in Chapter VI, the personal property tax is largely one on business equipment and inventories, comprehensive exemption of personalty tends to reduce the share of the tax base attributable to business-owned property. On the other hand, when only specified classes of personalty are legally exempted, or when a high degree of informal exemption of personalty (via marked underassessment or incomplete assessment) is tolerated, it is nonbusiness personalty which is nearly always the beneficiary, and business property is likely to end up comprising a larger share of the total tax rolls.

Another tax policy choice which affects tax base composition is the decision to provide for state assessment of certain classes of business property. Whatever the administrative rationale for this, state assessment of business property (other than that of public utilities and railroads) is very likely and appears in practice to yield much higher assessed values than does local assessment. It is a fair bet that this is a conscious goal of the system: to achieve higher assessed values by overcoming the limited competence, greater susceptibility to improper influences, and promotional zeal of local assessors. At any rate, the five states with a sizeable proportion of state-assessed nonutility property (15 percent or more of the total) turn out to have a very large proportion of their tax base in the form of business property, from 57 percent to over 70 percent.[3]

Yet another policy choice concerns partial exemptions—the practice of exempting specified dollar amounts of the assessed value of otherwise taxable property. Half the states provide such exemp-

[3] The five states are Arizona, New Mexico, South Carolina, Utah, and Wyoming.

tions, most frequently for veterans and/or for household goods and similar personalty. For the most part, these involve small fractions of the gross tax base. In six states, there are homestead exemptions, and these account for large fractions of assessed values before exemptions—one-fifth or more in four southern states. Indications are that the great bulk of the dollar amount of these partial exemptions serves to reduce the taxable assessments of nonfarm residential property (including some exemptions applying to consumer-owned personalty), and a lesser proportion applies to farm realty; hardly any applies to business property. Thus, in four of the homestead exemption states, exemptions appear to reduce the value of residential realty by 45 percent or more, thereby in effect increasing the business proportion of the tax base significantly.

In Table 5-2, an estimated distribution of assessed values after deduction of partial exemptions among residential, farm, and other property, is presented. The "other" category is a catchall but very largely consists of nonfarm business holdings. On balance, the more urbanized a state is, the higher the proportion of the tax base accounted for by residential property. The coefficient of correlation between the proportion of assessed values located within standard metropolitan statistical areas[4] and the residential percentages in Table 5-2 is a highly significant $+ .64$.

The farm share is high (a fourth or more of the tax base) almost entirely in the Plains states which have two characteristics in common: high value agricultural activity and limited urbanization. In general, states which have high value agriculture but also extensive urban populations (California and the Great Lakes states) or in which the farm population is a large share of the total but relatively poor (the South, for the most part) do not depend heavily on agricultural property. And, as noted earlier, the importance of business property seems to relate as much to tax policy as to the presence or absence of extensive industrial and commercial development. Business property appears to account for more than half the tax base in fourteen states. Only one of these—Ohio—is in the country's main industrial belt. Six are nonindustrial Mountain states, and five are very low income southern states.

Up to this point, the discussion has been in terms of the legal,

[4] From "Taxable Property Values" (1963), Table 3.

rather than the economic, tax base—the market value of privately owned property which is actually taxed in a given state or which is characteristically subject to property taxation in most states. Table 5-3 presents data on the relative per capita economic tax base in the economic sense of the term. These data are taken from calculations made by the Advisory Commission on Intergovernmental Relations.[5] The purpose of the Advisory Commission's analysis was to develop interstate comparisons of the productivity of a "representative" tax system. Thus, the tax base is not the estimated market value of property on the assessment rolls in a state, but rather the estimated market value of the classes of property which are generally subject to tax in more than half the states: privately owned realty (except for tax-exempt organizations) and agricultural and business tangible personalty, except motor vehicles. These estimates thus ignore partial exemptions, actual legal provisions for taxing or exempting personalty, and differences in assessors' ability or determination to discover taxable personalty.

Within most regions—with the Plains states a signal exception—states with high per capita personal income rank high in per capita property value as well. The interregional differences, however, are much more impressive, notably the high values of the West compared to the low values of the Northeast. Seventeen of the twenty-five states with per capita property values above the national average are west of the Mississippi, including all those with values 25 percent or more above the national average. On the other hand, although nine of the twelve eastern states north of the Potomac have had per capita personal income in excess of the national average in recent years, only four of these have above-average property values in Table 5-3. In 1959, estimated property values were three to five times personal income in the West and only about twice personal income in the Northeast.

The Advisory Commission's report deals with this apparent paradox at some length.[6] By and large, the explanation cannot be found in regional differences in tastes for housing (two-fifths of the tax base nationwide) relative to personal income. Californians and Floridians seem to have pronounced tastes for housing, as would be

[5] *Measures of State and Local Fiscal Capacity and Tax Effort* (1962), Table 17.
[6] *Ibid.*, pp. 56-67.

TABLE 5-2. Estimated Percentage Distribution of Assessed Value of Property Subject to Local General Property Taxation (After Deduction of Exemptions), by Type, by States, 1961[a]

Region and State	State Assessed Property and Locally Assessed Realty			Locally Assessed Personalty	All Types		
	Nonfarm Residential	Acreage and Farms	Other		Resi-dential	Farm	Other
Northeast							
New England							
New Hampshire	58.6	3.5	29.7	8.2			
Massachusetts	61.2	1.3	28.6	8.9	61.2	1.3	37.5
Maine	47.0	5.0	30.4	17.6	47.0	5.8	47.1
Connecticut	52.7	3.9	20.7	22.7			
Rhode Island	54.8	0.9	23.5	20.9			
Vermont	43.4	12.7	29.2	14.6			
Middle Atlantic							
New Jersey	58.5	1.6	28.4	11.5	60.4	1.7	37.9
New York	54.8	1.8	43.5	—	54.8	1.8	43.5
Pennsylvania	63.8	4.9	31.2	—	63.8	4.9	31.2
North Central							
West North Central							
Nebraska	25.1	36.4	12.2	26.3	29.3	47.9	22.8
South Dakota	18.1	42.6	14.2	25.0	22.2	57.7	20.1
Iowa	23.3	40.2	22.0	14.5			
Kansas	20.4	27.0	27.0	25.5			
Minnesota	33.4	22.4	25.3	18.9	33.9	26.0	40.0
North Dakota	14.1	43.4	21.5	20.9	17.0	54.3	28.6
Missouri	36.7	13.7	28.6	20.9	43.1	20.7	36.0
East North Central							
Indiana	27.8	12.0	27.9	32.3			
Wisconsin	45.9	12.8	26.1	15.3	45.9	16.0	38.2
Illinois	43.3	12.9	26.0	17.8	46.8	13.9	39.3
Ohio	38.5	6.6	31.3	23.6	38.5	8.0	53.5
Michigan	44.3	6.8	21.9	27.1			
West							
Mountain							
Montana	16.9	16.9	35.7	30.4			
Wyoming	13.1	10.9	59.1	16.9			
Arizona	33.8	4.6	44.6	16.9			
Colorado	40.0	10.1	32.7	17.1	40.2	13.1	46.7
Idaho	17.0	29.6	37.7	15.7	17.0	35.3	47.6
Utah	27.9	7.3	47.2	17.5	32.2	9.6	58.2
Nevada	28.3	10.9	42.2	18.6			
New Mexico	24.0	8.8	57.1	10.0			

TABLE 5-2. Continued

Region and State	State Assessed Property and Locally Assessed Realty			Locally Assessed Personalty	All Types		
	Nonfarm Residential	Acreage and Farms	Other		Residential	Farm	Other
Pacific							
California	44.6	7.3	33.6	14.5			
Oregon	36.8	18.1	31.3	13.7	36.8	20.1	43.0
Washington	40.8	13.6	27.4	18.3			
Alaska	43.8	0.6	37.2	18.3			
Hawaii	57.2	8.4	34.4	—	57.2	8.4	34.4
South							
West South Central							
Texas	25.1	9.6	40.8	24.5			
Oklahoma	29.2	15.2	35.7	20.0			
Arkansas	29.1	17.2	31.9	21.8	36.7	21.6	41.6
Louisiana	19.6	4.4	47.5	28.5	21.4	4.4	74.2
East South Central							
Tennessee	43.0	12.5	35.9	8.6			
Kentucky	33.1	15.1	38.8	12.8	37.7	16.1	46.0
Mississippi	13.5	11.2	43.2	32.2	23.6	13.2	63.3
Alabama	32.3	8.2	35.0	24.6			
South Atlantic							
Florida	43.0	8.2	32.0	16.9			
Maryland	54.8	5.2	37.8	2.1	54.9	5.9	39.2
District of Columbia	52.2	—	32.8	15.0	52.2	—	47.8
Virginia	46.1	6.8	27.9	19.3			
Georgia	27.0	6.2	32.2	34.5			
North Carolina	33.5	12.0	24.6	29.7	41.1	14.3	44.4
West Virginia	26.0	5.9	38.0	30.2	41.2	6.2	52.7
South Carolina	25.0	7.2	54.6	13.2	33.3	9.4	57.2
Delaware	60.8	6.1	33.2	—	60.8	6.1	33.2

Note: Because of rounding, detail may not add to totals.
a For derivation of these estimates, see Appendix G.

expected, but there is little difference between the Northeast and the trans-Mississippi states taken as a group. Absentee ownership of income-producing property in the West seems to be part of the explanation. The fact that some portion of the income produced in the West shows up in the personal income of people residing in the Northeast can be seen by the somewhat smaller interregional variation in the ratio of income produced to nonresidential property than in the ratio of personal income to nonresidential property value.

TABLE 5-3. Relative Per Capita Economic Base of the Property Tax, by States, 1959[a]

Region and State	Index, U.S. Average = 100	Region and State	Index, U.S. Average = 100
Northeast		Colorado	120
New England		Idaho	120
New Hampshire	94	Utah	113
Massachusetts	89	Nevada	143
Maine	70	New Mexico	98
Connecticut	107		
Rhode Island	78	Pacific	
Vermont	82	California	135
		Oregon	101
Middle Atlantic		Washington	102
New Jersey	100	Alaska	50
New York	97	Hawaii	74
Pennsylvania	87		
		South	
North Central		West South Central	
West North Central		Texas	130
Nebraska	141	Oklahoma	83
South Dakota	127	Arkansas	67
Iowa	137	Louisiana	76
Kansas	122		
Minnesota	108	East South Central	
North Dakota	122	Tennessee	66
Missouri	95	Kentucky	71
		Mississippi	52
East North Central		Alabama	62
Indiana	107		
Wisconsin	99	South Atlantic	
Illinois	121	Florida	101
Ohio	105	Maryland	92
Michigan	98	District of Columbia	110
		Virginia	78
West		Georgia	60
Mountain		North Carolina	69
Montana	153	West Virginia	68
Wyoming	172	South Carolina	52
Arizona	109	Delaware	103

[a] Based on estimates for all classes of property taxed in more than half the states. See Appendix G.

The major explanation seems to be, however, that there is a lower rate of return on investment in farm property relative to investment in other physical assets. In the postwar period, farm land values have been rising rapidly and nearly continuously in much of the country, while farm income has shown no such buoyancy; there are a number of reasons for *this* paradox, which need not be explored here. In the Advisory Commission's data, farm property is less than 30 percent of the total value of nonresidential property nationally. However, in the states with per capita property values above the national average and per capita personal incomes below the national average, farm property tends to be far more important —nearly 70 percent in Iowa, Nebraska, Montana, and Idaho, and over 80 percent in the Dakotas. As is evident from the data in Table 5-1 on property tax revenues as a proportion of personal income, voters in these states do tend to regard the existence of high per capita property values as an indicator of taxpaying capacity which is independent of personal income: property taxes absorb a relatively large proportion of income.

Effective Tax Rates

It can be argued that the notion of a market value of taxable property for use in comparing effective property tax rates among states and regions is so slippery in concept that overall tax rate comparisons either ought not to be made at all, or should be confined to those that are conceptually less difficult; that is, to comparisons of property tax revenues as ratios of personal income or income produced. A third alternative is to confine the comparison to selected types of property—single-family houses, farm real estate—whose character is unambiguous and for which exceptionally good data are at hand. Nevertheless, it does appear, as in the case of the Plains states, that property value is treated as a separate and distinct base from which revenue can be had, which suggests that interstate comparisons of effective rates are worthy of attention.

Some effective rate estimates are shown in Table 5-4. The first three columns are the Advisory Commission's estimates for its "representative tax base" at market value; that is, estimates which ignore differences in coverage and exemptions in individual states. The rates in the last two columns apply to the market value of locally assessed realty. Despite the differences in concept (and in timing), the results are similar from the standpoint of interstate comparisons. Effective tax rates are very much above the national average in the Northeast and well below in the South. Rates in the central and western parts of the country tend to cluster around the national average, but there are some marked differences among

TABLE 5-4. Estimated Effective Property Tax Rates, by States, 1957, 1960, and 1962[a]

(In percentages)

Region and State	Advisory Commission on Intergovernmental Relations Estimates[b]			Census Bureau, Locally Assessed Realty[c]	
	All Taxable Property, 1960	Farm Real Estate, 1957	Single-Family Dwellings, 1957	1962	1957
Northeast					
New England					
New Hampshire	1.9	2.0	1.9	2.3	2.0
Massachusetts	2.4	1.9	2.3	2.7	2.8
Maine	2.4	2.3	1.9	2.1	2.0
Connecticut	1.6	1.5	1.5	1.9	1.6
Rhode Island	1.9	1.0	1.7	2.2	1.9
Vermont	2.1	1.8	1.9	2.2	2.0
Middle Atlantic					
New Jersey	2.3	1.5.	1.9	2.6	2.3
New York	2.1	1.9	1.8	2.5	2.7
Pennsylvania	1.3	1.1	1.4	1.7	1.6
North Central					
West North Central					
Nebraska	1.4	1.3	1.4	1.4	1.3
South Dakota	1.4	1.4	1.3	1.7	1.5
Iowa	1.2	1.1	1.1	1.5	1.1
Kansas	1.4	1.1	1.0	1.2	1.2
Minnesota	1.9	1.4	1.5	1.9	1.9
North Dakota	1.3	1.1	1.2	1.4	1.3
Missouri	1.1	0.8	0.5	1.1	1.0
East North Central					
Indiana	1.2	0.8	1.0	1.2	0.9
Wisconsin	1.9	1.8	1.8	2.1	1.9
Illinois	1.5	1.3	1.3	1.7	1.4
Ohio	1.4	0.8	1.0	1.0	1.0
Michigan	1.8	1.0	1.3	1.7	1.3
West					
Mountain					
Montana	1.1	0.9	1.0	0.8	0.9
Wyoming	1.0	0.9	0.8	0.8	0.6

n.a. Not available

[a] Effective tax rates equal estimated state-local general property tax revenue (from the classes of property indicated) in the year designated divided by estimated market value of the classes of property indicated in the preceding year.

[b] From *Measures of State and Local Fiscal Capacity and Tax Effort* (1962), Tables 37 and 41.

[c] From U. S. Bureau of the Census, *Property Taxation in 1962* (November 1964), Table 7.

TABLE 5-4. Continued

Region and State	Advisory Commission on Intergovernmental Relations Estimates[b]			Census Bureau, Locally Assessed Realty[c]	
	All Taxable Property, 1960	Farm Real Estate, 1957	Single-Family Dwellings, 1957	1962	1957
Mountain (continued)					
Arizona	1.0	0.7	1.1	1.0	1.0
Colorado	1.4	1.2	1.4	1.3	1.2
Idaho	1.0	1.0	0.9	1.0	0.8
Utah	1.1	1.0	0.8	1.0	0.7
Nevada	0.9	0.5	0.8	0.8	0.8
New Mexico	0.6	0.3	0.6	0.5	0.5
Pacific					
California	1.4	0.9	1.3	1.3	1.2
Oregon	1.6	1.0	1.4	1.4	1.3
Washington	0.9	0.6	0.8	0.8	0.8
Alaska	1.1	n.a.	n.a.	n.a.	n.a.
Hawaii	0.7	n.a.	n.a.	0.6	n.a.
South					
West South Central					
Texas	1.0	0.5	1.0	1.0	0.8
Oklahoma	0.9	0.6	0.7	0.8	0.7
Arkansas	0.6	0.5	0.6	0.6	0.5
Louisiana	0.8	0.4	0.5	0.5	0.6
East South Central					
Tennessee	1.0	0.5	1.1	1.2	1.1
Kentucky	0.8	0.7	0.8	0.7	0.9
Mississippi	0.7	0.5	0.5	0.5	0.6
Alabama	0.5	0.4	0.6	0.6	0.5
South Atlantic					
Florida	1.1	0.5	0.8	1.1	0.9
Maryland	1.5	0.7	1.5	1.4	1.3
District of Columbia	1.3	—	1.0	1.3	1.2
Virginia	0.9	0.6	0.8	0.9	0.7
Georgia	0.9	0.5	0.7	0.8	0.8
North Carolina	0.8	0.4	0.7	0.7	0.6
West Virginia	0.9	0.4	0.4	0.6	0.5
South Carolina	0.8	0.4	0.4	0.5	0.6
Delaware	0.7	0.5	0.8	1.0	0.7
United States Average	1.4	0.9	1.3	1.4	1.3

TABLE 5-5. Effective Property Tax Rates and Other Property Tax Characteristics: Frequency Distributions of 50 States[a]

Item	Estimated Effective Property Tax Rates, 1962[b]					Total
	0.6–0.8	0.9–1.0	1.1–1.4	1.5–1.9	20 and Over	
Relative per capita economic base, 1959[c]						
50–74	7	1	2	—	1	11
75–94	—	3	1	1	4	9
95–104	2	2	1	2	3	10
105–124	—	3	5	3	1	12
125 and over	2	2	2	2	—	8
Total	11	11	11	8	9	50
Property tax as percentage of total state-local tax revenue, 1962[d]						
Less than 30	7	3	—	—	—	10
30–39	3	2	3	1	—	9
40–47	—	4	2	1	2	9
48–55	1	1	3	4	2	11
55 and over	—	1	3	2	5	11
Total	11	11	11	8	9	50
Property tax revenue as percentage of personal income, 1962[e]						
Less than 2.7	7	3	1	—	—	11
2.7–3.9	3	3	3	1	—	10
4.0–4.9	—	4	2	2	2	10
5.0–5.5	1	—	4	3	2	10
5.6 and over	—	1	1	2	5	9
Total	11	11	11	8	9	50

[a] Excludes Alaska but includes District of Columbia.
[b] From Table 5-4, column 4, based on locally assessed realty.
[c] U. S. average = 100. From Table 5-3.
[d] From Table 5-1, column 2.
[e] From Table 5-1, column 5.

individual states within these regions: Washington vs. Oregon, Colorado vs. Wyoming, Michigan vs. Ohio, Minnesota vs. Nebraska, for example.

The data from several earlier tables are combined in Table 5-5. They indicate that there is no clear-cut connection between the relative magnitude of the potential property tax base and the height of effective rates. The states with relatively high taxable (market) values per capita are mostly in the middle tax ranges, perhaps due to their characteristically limited extent of urbanization. The states with very low rates have limited wealth, but so do some of the high rate states in the Northeast.

If income differences were a major influence on property tax rates, there would be little association between the level of rates and the percentages of personal income absorbed by the property tax. But low rates are associated with property tax revenues which absorb small fractions of personal income, while high rates exist in states where the property tax accounts for relatively large proportions of personal income. The really important determinant of rate differentials seems to be public policy regarding reliance on the property tax as a source of tax revenue. The states with low property tax rates generally obtain a third or less of their tax revenues from the property tax. The high rate states typically get half or more of their tax revenues from this source.

EFFECT OF URBANIZATION. In part, of course, differences in effective tax rates are linked to the extent of urbanization. Local governments even in urban areas are heavily dependent on the property tax, and urban local governments do appear to spend relatively more than their rural counterparts, whatever the standard of measurement, whether it is population, income, or wealth. To some extent this is inherent in densely built-up areas where certain services provided privately by households themselves or not consumed at all in a rural environment must be provided collectively. Examples are police and fire protection, parks and recreation, and waste disposal. The need for other public services, notably those that are poverty-oriented, is also more visible in urban surroundings; and finally, there is evidence that certain services such as education have a highly income elastic demand, costing urban governments more than their rural counterparts.

Whatever the explanation, effective property tax rates are highest in the most highly urbanized regions of the country—New England and the Middle Atlantic states. This shows up to some extent within regions as well. Florida, the most highly urbanized state in the Southeast, and Colorado and Arizona, the most urbanized of the Mountain states, exhibit the highest tax rates within their respective regions. But urbanization is by no means the entire explanation for the differences. In the 1960 Census of Housing, data

TABLE 5-6. Regional Differences in Real Estate Taxes on Owner-Occupied Single-Family Houses, 1960[a]

Area	Median Annual Real Estate Taxes		
	Per $1,000 of Property Value	As Percentage of Median Family Income of Owners[b]	As Percentage of Median Annual Housing Costs[b]
United States	$13	2.5	17.4
Inside SMSA's	15	3.0	18.8
Outside SMSA's	11	n.a.	n.a.
Northeast[c]	19	3.8	23.6
Boston SMSA	24	5.3	28.6
Buffalo SMSA	19	4.3	27.2
New York SCA	22	5.1	28.2
Philadelphia SMSA	18	3.0	22.6
Pittsburgh SMSA	15	2.8	23.6
North Central[c]	14	2.7	19.8
Chicago SCA	15	3.3	20.2
Cleveland SMSA	14	3.3	20.3
Detroit SMSA	16	3.1	20.0
Minneapolis SMSA	17	3.7	21.0
St. Louis SMSA	14	2.7	18.7
South[c]	8	1.4	10.3
Atlanta SMSA	10	1.9	12.8
Baltimore SMSA	20	3.4	21.3
Dallas SMSA	12	1.9	13.6
Washington, D.C., SMSA	13	2.6	16.4
West[c]	13	2.8	17.5
Los Angeles SMSA	15	3.3	20.7
San Francisco SMSA	15	3.2	21.5

SMSA = Standard Metropolitan Statistical Area.
SCA = Standard Consolidated Area.
n.a. = Not available.

[a] Data from U. S. Bureau of the Census, *Census of Housing: 1960*, Vol. V, "Residential Finances," Part 1, "Homeowner Properties." Data apply to both mortgaged and nonmortgaged properties. Separate data are shown in the Census volume for the two classes, but, although the levels differ considerably, the interregional comparisons are substantially similar. The data on real estate taxes and housing costs apply only to properties acquired before 1959 (approximately 90 percent of the number of properties nationwide).

[b] These figures are median values divided by median values rather than true medians of the percentages for individual properties.

[c] Data for regions include the SMSA's indicated plus all other single-family owner-occupied houses within the region.

were tabulated on real estate taxes on owner-occupied single-family houses in the seventeen largest urban concentrations in the country; these are shown in Table 5-6. Among these urban areas, effective rates are substantially higher in the Northeast than elsewhere and substantially lower in the South. Moreover, this is *not* an income phenomenon. The same relationships obtain when real estate taxes on these properties are compared to the owners' incomes and to actual cash outlays for housing by owners. Chicago area homeowners with mortgaged properties spend more for housing currently than homeowners in any other of these areas, and they have higher incomes than homeowners in any other area except Washington. Yet their median real estate tax payments were only $275, compared to approximately $400 in the Boston and New York areas. Dallas and Atlanta homeowners with mortgaged properties have incomes and current housing costs equivalent to those in the Philadelphia area, but they made median tax payments of approximately $140, compared to $215 in the Philadelphia area. Again, the explanation for the differences seems to relate to differences in both the relative preferences for public services and the relative reliance on the property tax to support the levels of public services provided.

Other available estimates of effective rates for particular classes of property are consistent with these findings on regional differentials. The Advisory Commission 1957 estimates for single-family dwellings, shown in Table 5-4, suggest that single-family houses often bear somewhat lower rates than all taxable property in a state, but these are parallel to the overall regional patterns.

RATES ON FARM REALTY. The farm real estate estimates in Table 5-4 indicate that farm property often is taxed at substantially lower rates than other property (the Plains states, where farm property is a large proportion of the total, are notable exceptions) but that it also exhibits a similar regional pattern.

U.S. Department of Agriculture (USDA) estimates for 1962 are in agreement. Taxes levied on farm real estate averaged about 1 percent of "full value" and about 9 percent of net farm income. In the southern regional groupings, however, the rates were only about 0.5 percent of value and 4 percent of farm income. In the Northeast, the figures were 1.7 percent and 17 percent, respectively, and were also above the national average in the Great Lakes and northern Plains states. Interestingly, there were only three states in which the effective tax rate estimate for farm realty was higher than the overall estimate for locally assessed realty in the fourth column of Table 5-4, which also applies to 1962. In forty-two states, the USDA figure is lower; in twenty-six of them, more than 20 percent lower. Despite low overall effective rates, the spread between rates on farm property and overall rates is widest in the South.[7]

RATES ON BUSINESS PROPERTY. The 1958 Census of Manufactures affords some limited evidence on regional differentials in property taxes paid by manufacturers.[8] These data do not include property tax payments on rented property used in manufacturing, which are important in states like New York where much manufacturing activity is carried on in rented quarters. But there are some clues. In the South, property tax payments are very low proportions of both net book value of depreciable assets and value added, despite the fact that there seems to be little utilization of rented assets. On the other hand, in both the Pacific Coast states and New England, property tax payments are high by these measures, in the face of rather heavy reliance on rented assets. In the Middle Atlantic states, property tax payments appear to be low, but rented property is especially important in these states, and, moreover, equipment and inventories are not taxed in New York and Pennsylvania.

A 1963 survey based on a sample of nearly 29,000 apartments in over 500 (mostly large) buildings is similarly in line with the findings above.[9] In northeastern metropolitan areas, real estate taxes were generally between 20 and 25 percent of gross possible rental income. In midwestern areas, the figures were generally in the 15 to 20 percent range, while they were 12 to 15 percent in the West, and less than 10 percent in southern cities.

It has been suggested earlier that low reliance on the property tax in the South might stem from the recognition (perhaps not articulated, however) that this is a good strategy for fostering development in capital-short regions. Indeed, effective rates appear to be markedly lower on business property in the South than in the rest of the country, a situation made possible apparently by lower levels of

---

[7] The source for this paragraph is U.S. Department of Agriculture, Economic Research Service, *Farm Real Estate Taxes, Recent Trends and Developments* (September 1963).

[8] U.S. Bureau of the Census, *Census of Manufactures: 1958*, "Supplementary Employee Costs, Costs of Maintenance and Repair, Insurance, Rent, Taxes, and Depreciation and Book Value of Depreciable Assets: 1957," Subject Report MC 58(1)-9 (1961).

[9] National Association of Real Estate Boards, "Apartment Building Experience Exchange of Rental Income and Operating Expense Data, 1963," *Journal of Property Management* (special issue, 1963).

public expenditure combined with greater reliance on state-imposed consumption taxes and on federal aid.

But some of the potential advantage seems to be dissipated by providing even more favorable treatment to nonbusiness property. In five states, this is done by means of homestead exemptions, a situation noted earlier. According to the 1962 Census of Governments, three of these states provide partial offsets by assessing commercial and industrial property at lower proportions of market value than apply to nonfarm residences. Of the other eight southern states with low effective rates, commercial and industrial property is relatively favorably treated by assessors in only one case (Arkansas); in four cases (Texas, Kentucky, Virginia, and North Carolina), business property is assessed at significantly *higher* rates than residential property, while in the remaining cases, the assessment ratios are similar. Moreover, all these thirteen southern states achieve differentially lower effective rates for farm property by assessing farm realty at significantly lower percentages of market value than either residential or business property.[10] This would hardly seem to be an effective developmental strategy; southern assessors and legislators seem as prone as their counterparts elsewhere to temper long-run strategy to the short-run fact that homeowners and farmers outvote business by a wide margin.

Locational Effects of Interarea Differentials

In recent years, increasing state-local tax rates and increasing concern with regional differentials in rates of economic growth have combined to produce a considerable literature dealing with the influence of state-local taxation on the location of economic activity.[11] Not surprisingly, some of the most careful work has been done in particular states which appear to have relatively high state-local tax burdens and in which the rate of economic growth has been especially disappointing. The three northern Great Lakes states—Michigan, Minnesota, and Wisconsin—are notable cases in point.[12]

[10] "Taxable Property Values" (1963), Tables 8-11, 13-14.

[11] A good review of much of this literature is John F. Due, "Studies of State-Local Tax Influences on Location of Industry," *National Tax Journal*, Vol. 14 (June 1961), pp. 163-73.

[12] See, for example, Wolfgang F. Stolper, "Economic Development, Taxation,

The impact of property tax differentials on location cannot be ignored, in view of the relatively large magnitude of the rate differentials discussed above, with effective rates on locally assessed realty in 1962 varying from as little as 0.5-0.6 percent in eight states to 2.5 percent or more in three states (Table 5-4). To be sure, the largest differentials are among different parts of the country, which are not always direct competitors for specific types of economic activity, but even within regions some states which do compete with one another show large variations. Moreover, the property tax is a major component of total state-local tax payments by business in the high tax states—for example, it amounted to 58 percent of state-local business taxes in Michigan in 1956.[13]

Regardless of the size of property tax differentials and their relation to measures of economic activity, it is clear a priori that there are some forms of economic activity whose location can be little affected by local tax differentials. Differentials in the height of taxation on residential property may have some bearing on choice of residential location within an urban area but surely have little to do with personal decisions to migrate relatively large distances; moreover, households, to a much greater extent than businesses, are likely to find the tax differentials tied to differentials in public spending benefits.

The probability that property tax differentials for business property will affect locational decisions depends very much on the competitive conditions in particular types of industry.

AGRICULTURE. Competition in national and world markets among individual producers within regions characterized by similar soils and climate is considerable, but there is much less competition among regions, although there is also some substitutability among agricultural products of different regions. By and large, however, low taxes on farm property in the South would not be expected,

and Industrial Location in Michigan," Chap. 2 of *Michigan Tax Study Staff Papers,* Harvey E. Brazer, ed., (Lansing, 1958); *Report of the Governor's Minnesota Tax Study* (University of Minnesota, 1956), Chap. IV; Ronald J. Wonnacott, *Manufacturing Costs and the Comparative Advantage of United States Regions,* Upper Midwest Economic Study (Minneapolis, 1963), Chap. 4; University of Wisconsin Tax Study Committee, *Wisconsin's State and Local Tax Burden* (University of Wisconsin School of Commerce, 1959).

[13] Stolper, *Michigan Tax Study,* p. 86.

even in a world with much greater mobility of labor and capital, to induce additional investment in production of, say, wheat in the South rather than in the Plains states with higher tax rates.

Within regions producing similar farm products for sale on world markets, higher taxes on farm property should be reflected in reduced net returns for farmers in those locations, since the higher taxes will not be passed on to consumers. However, even in these cases of big differentials among adjacent states, the adverse impact of higher tax rates on investment and output in agriculture is limited by the relative immobility of farm entrepreneurs. Farmers in the high tax states are likely to stay put and suffer lower incomes, perhaps capitalizing their farms even more heavily to offset the income loss. By lowering farm income, higher taxes would have some toxic side effects on the scale of operation of activities serving farmers in the area, and no doubt lower net income over the long run may reduce the farm population even more rapidly than it is reduced in the adjacent low-tax states. To some extent, the differentially high taxes will be capitalized in the form of lower prices for land, a consequence which should not affect investment and output in agriculture, except insofar as lowered farm land prices may impede mobility. On the whole, property tax differentials would be expected to have a minor locational impact on agriculture.

NONFARM BUSINESSES. The likely locational impact is mixed.[14] Local tax differentials will not affect the locational decisions of businesses serving local markets and populations, since they are not competitive for the most part with producers of similar goods and services in other areas. The classical "space-less" argument on the incidence of indirect taxes applies here, with the property tax likely to be passed on to consumers and consequent changes in output determined largely by the elasticities of demand for particular goods and services. The insulation from the rest of the world is not perfect; local production is in part a substitution for imports. Higher local taxes thus can narrow the area in which local firms have a cost advantage over outside producers. But quantitatively this is likely to be a small effect, since local producers of services are rather well insulated (in the case of public utility services, by

---

[14] Stolper, *ibid.*, has an excellent treatment of this.

regulation as well as by transport costs); so also is the distribution function for goods.

In contrast, local firms which produce for sale in competitive national and regional markets are vulnerable to higher local taxation. These higher costs cannot be exported to consumers, and thus, other things being equal, the profitability of a location in a high property tax area will be lower than elsewhere. When other things are in fact equal, substantial property tax differentials will affect location over time.

On the other hand, the locational decisions of local firms producing for a national market—a market in which the local firms' position is dominant like the automobile manufacturers in Michigan—may not be affected by higher local taxes, since the local firms can pass these costs on to consumers. This is not the whole story, however. The demand for the output of the local industry may be highly price elastic, in which case local output may suffer from an effort to pass on high local taxes. If the local industry instead absorbs the high taxes, the inducement to shift its activities to other areas with lower taxes, or to expand only in these other places, may prove irresistible in time. The point is that even where monopoly elements exist, high local taxes may be imposed with impunity only when they are exceeded by other advantages of operation in that location. Thus, for example, rather high property taxes (and other state-local taxes as well) on office activities in New York City appear to be of very much less consequence than the advantages of a Manhattan location.

Recent studies of the influence of state-local taxes on location generally have used the state as the unit for observation, considering the total height of state-local taxes on businesses but emphasizing state tax devices since these are more readily varied as acts of deliberate policy by state governments. Thus their conclusions are not necessarily directly applicable to property tax differentials per se, which the studies themselves frequently point out. In general, however, their conclusions should be relevant to the property tax. The most important conclusion is that "relatively high business tax levels do not have the disastrous effects often claimed for them."[15] This finding stems from interviews with businessmen designed to

[15] John F. Due in *National Tax Journal,* p. 171.

elicit ratings of the factors involved in locational choice, from comparisons of the historical record of long-term economic growth and the relative height of business taxes, and from evidence which shows that taxes are minor elements in business costs and thus tax differentials are likely to be overwhelmed by differentials in other costs.[16]

Even though taxes are small fractions of total business costs, tax differentials can be significant for locational decisions. For one thing, tax differentials may not offset but may instead *reinforce* other cost differentials. Thus, Wonnacott found that Minnesota's business tax burden appears to be substantially higher, in general, than in nearly all other states, but that on the average differences for specific industries in tax costs are only about one-tenth the differences in labor and transport costs.[17] However, for many types of industry, the differences are cumulative, not offsetting. Moreover, however small the tax differentials may be relative to other costs, governments can do something about tax differentials, but little about other cost factors. Finally, there are surely cases in which other cost factors are similar at alternative sites for new or expanded business operations, with tax differentials exercising considerable leverage at the margin. During the expansion period in the first postwar decade (say, 1947-57), sites in central Illinois, Indiana, and Ohio were frequently considered close competitors. Tax differentials of the order suggested by Table 5-4 could have made the difference in the final choice, if the state-wide averages were

[16] An extraordinary fallacy recurs frequently in analyses of state-local taxes as business costs: it is asserted that state-local taxes are even less significant than they appear to be, since businesses are concerned with after-tax profits and state-local taxes are deductible expenses in determining federal corporate income tax liability. As Wonnacott points out, this is also true of locational differences in other costs: "A reduction of all of these costs by one-half does not change their relative significance. The only effect is to reduce cost influences compared to noncost influences, such as local amenities and the attractiveness of climate or geography." (*Manufacturing Costs and the Comparative Advantages of U.S. Regions*, p. 46). These noncost factors are indeed important in some locational decisions. Moreover, net after-tax cost differentials are important when the decision involves abandoning existing plant in order to construct new plant in another place, with recovery of capital costs over a long period of time. Federal tax deductibility may therefore effectively reduce the importance of local tax differentials in some cases, but not for the superficial reasons presented in some analyses.

[17] *Manufacturing Costs*, Tables 8, 9, and 10.

applicable to the specific cities under review. A dissenter from the conclusions of the Wisconsin tax study held that this marginal situation obtains for Wisconsin because it is located on the fringe of the nation's major manufacturing belt and it has few nontax advantages to offset its tax disadvantages.[18]

Property tax differentials might have a lesser or greater impact than that found by these studies for state-local taxes in the aggregate. Higher property taxes on business property conceivably might be offset by lower taxation of business in other forms. However, more often than not, the high property tax states have relatively high corporate income tax rates as well, and/or tax business relatively heavily in other ways. Moreover, property tax differentials can be especially serious for particular types of business, either because these types have especially high capital/output or capital/profits ratios, or because they involve heavy investment in assets which assessors in one state are particularly effective in reaching, notably tangible business personalty. Erratic but frequently high assessment of business personalty is perhaps an even more serious locational deterrent.

In appraising the locational impact of interarea property tax differentials, it is well to keep in mind that effective property tax rates have been climbing in the last decade. It appears that the effective rate on locally assessed realty rose from roughly 1.3 percent in 1957 to over 1.4 percent in 1962; a similar rate of increase appears to apply to the 1952-57 period as well. If effective rates continue to rise, it seems logical to assume that an increasing number of marginal location decisions will be uncovered: in situations, that is, in which tax differentials are large enough to make the difference in the final decision to shift location.

EFFECT ON USE OF NATIONAL RESOURCES. Finally, there is the question of the effect that locational decisions induced by tax differentials have on allocative efficiency for the national economy as a whole. As Due puts it:

To the extent that firms are influenced by tax factors, a species of Gresham's Law operates: these firms will tend to gravitate to the low tax cost areas. If these low taxes arise from actual economies in the provision of public services, the tax factor reflects a real economic factor and its

[18] *Wisconsin's State and Local Tax Burden,* p. 35.

influence does not distort location from the sites which are most economic. But if this is not the case, tax influences do exercise an undesirable influence, by leading firms to locate in places other than those which involve maximum efficiency in the use of resources.[19]

In a world with complete factor mobility and perfectly competitive markets, there are only a limited number of ways in which business enterprises can be taxed differentially by state and local governments without inducing inefficient locational shifts over time.[20] If prices throughout the economy are to reflect the full costs of production at particular sites, then businesses must pay, through user charges or through taxes which have a user charge element, the costs of the public services they consume. In addition, businesses must also reimburse the community for any external diseconomies they create—public and private nonbusiness costs relating to air and water pollution, for example.

Beyond this, location rents can be taxed in full without affecting locational choice. Location rents are the rents that "arise whenever the advantages of location at a particular site are sufficient to yield a return to the firm in excess of the return obtainable, all other things being equal, at alternative available sites.[21] Now, if all or most jurisdictions tax business in excess of amounts related to use of public services, external diseconomies, and location rents, there is further scope for business taxation by any given jurisdiction, without harming allocative efficiency. Indeed, the locational effects of the property tax will be improved if low tax rate areas raise their taxes on business, and more or less equalize the overall impact. Such equalization is, of course, unlikely to occur in reality. Moreover, if factors are immobile (for example, farmers), business taxation will not cause locational shifts (but may be objectionable on distributional grounds).

It is not possible to quantify the extent to which the real-world property tax on business property contains these elements. It is a reasonable guess that the user charge component—for business property—is small since so much of the tax revenue is used to finance education and other personally consumed services, rather

[19] Due, in *National Tax Journal*, p. 171.

[20] This discussion rests largely on an elegant exposition by Harvey E. Brazer, "The Value of Industrial Property as a Subject of Taxation," *Canadian Public Administration*, Vol. 55 (June 1961), pp. 137-47.

[21] *Ibid.*, p. 139.

than police and fire protection, sewage disposal, and other services to property. The active bidding for industry by small suburban jurisdictions, in order to alleviate their fiscal positions, strongly suggests that the user charge component is small indeed.

Thus the bulk of the business property tax in high tax rate areas is likely to consist of: (1) a locationally neutral element made possible by the fact that business property is subject to taxation above and beyond the costs it imposes nearly everywhere; (2) an element which does not exceed location rents; and (3) some "excess burden" which adversely affects allocative efficiency. Since the high rate areas have effective tax rates which are three or four or more times those in the low rate areas, elements (2) and (3) are likely to comprise the bulk of the tax. But since economic growth has not been systematically related to the height of business property taxes—for example, very high tax New Jersey has grown much more rapidly than moderate tax Pennsylvania; office buildings continue to flourish in high tax Manhattan—it is likely that the location rent element is far from small. The tentative conclusion offered here is that property tax differentials among states and regions of the country probably have had a relatively limited impact on allocative efficiency overall, but the problem may be a much more real one within particularly large urban areas.

Differentials Within Urban Areas

For many years—in fact, ever since there have been suburban populations living beyond central city boundaries but economically tied to the city—central city governments have been faced with problems arising from the concentration of needs for public services within their jurisdictions. They have, throughout this period, provided a variety of services on behalf of their entire urbanized areas. The poor and the disadvantaged tend to cluster downtown, giving rise to high welfare, health, educational, and similar expenditures. Moreover, many specialized services have been provided only by central city governments simply because only the central city had the size necessary to support activities with markedly increasing returns to scale, many of them "natural monopolies," ranging from water supply to zoos.

Central Cities versus Suburbs

Although complaints are not new that suburbanites enjoy a free ride and that they have the benefits of central city public services without paying for them in taxes, until fairly recently the heavy concentration of business activity within central city boundaries provided a substantial offset to higher central city governmental burdens. Nearly all high value taxable business property fell within the net of central city tax collectors. As recently as 1953, it could be asserted with some confidence that "those who work and shop in the central cities and live in the suburbs impose few costs on the cities which are not recouped indirectly through taxes levied on their places of employment or on the retail shops with which they deal."[22]

But even in 1953, this must have been less true than it had been in earlier years, and it is surely a much less accurate observation today. The concentration of property values in central cities of metropolitan areas has been substantially reduced both by the powerful forces leading to dispersal of economic activity from central cities to outlying sections and by the decentralization of population; the suburban in-migrants tend to be in the upper half of the income distribution and thus bring to the suburbs the higher value residential properties and, in the wake of this, much high value commercial property. The facts on dispersal of economic activity are clear: in thirteen large metropolitan areas, the central cities' share of manufacturing employment declined from 66.5 percent in 1929 to 57.5 percent in 1954; their share of employment in wholesale trade declined from 93.1 percent to 81.7 percent; and their share of employment in retail trade declined from 78.0 percent to 62.7 percent.[23]

The recent evidence on taxable property values per capita for thirty-two of the nation's forty-three largest urban areas is presented in Table 5-7 (in which the per capita values for the outlying portions of the areas are expressed as percentages of the central city values). In most cases, taxable capacity (as indicated by this measure) appears to be higher in suburban territory than in central

---

[22] "Unbalanced Cities," *The Economist* (London), March 28, 1953, p. 873.
[23] Raymond Vernon, *The Changing Economic Function of the Central City* (Committee for Economic Development, 1959), Appendix Tables 2, 3, and 4.

TABLE 5-7. Property Tax Differentials, Central Cities versus Suburbs, Selected Large Metropolitan Areas, Selected Years Between 1957 and 1961[a]

(Values shown = outlying portions of area as percentage of central city)

Region and Metropolitan Area	Estimated Per Capita Taxable Property Values	Estimated Per Capita Property Tax Revenue	Approximate Effective Tax Rate Relationship[b]
Northeast:			
New York City and rest of SMSA	131	134	102 (100)
Philadelphia and rest of SMSA	146	94	64
Buffalo and rest of Erie County	112	96	86 (92)
Newark and rest of Essex County	158	91	58 (51)
Rochester and rest of Monroe County	100	58	58 (75)
North Central:			
Chicago and rest of Cook County	123	93	76
Detroit and rest of Wayne County	102	87	85
Cleveland and rest of Cuyahoga County	106	88	83 (97)
St. Louis and rest of SMSA	96	105	109
Milwaukee and rest of Milwaukee County	138	91	66 (81)
Cincinnati and rest of Hamilton County	122	66	54
Kansas City and rest of Jackson County	52	62	119
Columbus and rest of Franklin County	117	137	117
Toledo and rest of Lucas County	122	107	88
Omaha and rest of Douglas County	148	65	44
West:			
Los Angeles and rest of Los Angeles County	102	68	67
San Francisco and rest of SMSA	85	89	105
San Diego and rest of San Diego County	100	90	90
Seattle and rest of King County	91	66	73
Denver and rest of SMSA	90	58	64
Phoenix and rest of Maricopa County	116	163	141
Portland and rest of Multnomah County	77	47	61
Oakland and rest of Alameda County	90	78	87
South:			
Baltimore and rest of SMSA	110	58	53 (55)
Washington, D.C., and rest of SMSA	95	96	101
San Antonio and rest of Bexar County	203	17	8
Memphis and rest of Shelby County	108	4	4
Atlanta and rest of Fulton County	82	71	87
Louisville and rest of Jefferson County	145	98	68
Fort Worth and rest of Tarrant County	88	32	36
Birmingham and rest of Jefferson County	87	102	117
Oklahoma City and rest of Oklahoma County	97	48	49

SMSA—Standard Metropolitan Statistical Area.
[a] See Appendix G for derivation.
[b] Figures in parentheses are based on direct computations of effective rate differentials from various local sources. The other figures are derived by dividing the data in Column 1 by those in Column 2. See text.

cities.[24] This is especially true of the older metropolitan areas, particularly those in the Northeast and Midwest such as New York, Philadelphia, Newark, Chicago, Milwaukee, Cincinnati, and Toledo. In newer areas, the central cities' position is generally more favorable, in some cases no doubt because much of the area beyond the frequently extensive central city boundaries is still largely rural.

RELATIVE CHANGES IN PROPERTY VALUES. Historical evidence on trends in the relative position of central cities and suburbs in regard to taxable values per capita is hard to come by (partly because effective equalization by state or county agencies is a relatively recent phenomenon in many places).

The fragmentary data support the reasonable hypothesis that the central cities' relative position has deteriorated. In the Baltimore area, for example, suburban property values per capita were only 81 percent of those in the central city in 1950, but had risen to 110 percent by 1960.[25] In the nine counties of northeastern New Jersey, 22 of the 279 municipalities have central city characteristics; in 1951, real property values per capita in the 257 outlying places averaged 169 percent of those in the 22 core communities; and by 1960, the figure had risen to 186 percent.[26] In suburban Cook County, real property values per capita were 119 percent of those in Chicago in the 1928 reassessment completed in 1930; but, in 1961, they were 136 percent.[27] And in Milwaukee County, suburban property values per capita were 105 percent of those in the central city in 1935, 120 percent by 1940, and 138 percent by 1960.[28] The Milwaukee data suggest what probably has been generally true: from the earliest years in this period, residential property values per capita were higher in the suburbs than in the central

[24] The data are assessed values where the central city and its suburbs are in a single assessment jurisdiction and equalized values elsewhere.

[25] Baltimore Metropolitan Area Study Commission, *Final Report to the Governor of Maryland* (September 1963), Table 1.

[26] Computed from various tables in Morris Beck, *Property Taxation and Urban Land Use in Northeastern New Jersey,* Urban Land Institute (1963).

[27] Herbert D. Simpson, *Tax Racket and Tax Reform in Chicago,* Institute for Economic Research (Chicago, 1930), pp. 164-65; "Taxable Property Values" (1963), Table 21. These figures apply to real property only. Those in Table 5-7 apply to total real and personal property.

[28] Donald J. Curran, S.J., "The Metropolitan Problem: Solution from Within?" *National Tax Journal,* Vol. 16 (September 1963), p. 219. Father Curran very kindly provided his worksheets, based on Wisconsin Department of Taxation data.

city, but this differential was partly offset by substantially higher nonresidential property values in the city. In the postwar period, however, while the spread in residential values widened somewhat, there was a reversal in the business property relationship; in 1960, per capita business property values were significantly higher in the suburbs.

Whatever the relationship of per capita *levels* of business property values, business property tends to be a substantially larger *fraction* of assessed values in central cities than in suburbs. At least this is the case for twenty-four of the large cities covered in Table 5-7, cities located within a larger county for which 1961 Census data permit a comparison of the composition of assessed values in the central city and in the county as a whole.[29] Personal property, which is largely business-owned, is a larger fraction of the central city tax base in nearly all northern cities in which personalty is taxable. In the West and South there are generally no appreciable differences between central cities and suburbs on this score, but nowhere is personalty significantly *less* important in the central city. Confining the analysis to locally assessed realty, commercial and industrial property is an appreciably larger fraction of the total for the central city in twenty-one of the twenty-four cities; in the other three cases, central city and suburban proportions are similar.

The other side of the coin is the greater importance of residential property, especially single-family houses, in suburban territory. This is true in twenty-one of the twenty-four cases.[30] Apartment property is more important, of course, in all central cities than in their suburbs; where the differences are small ones, it is because apartment property is of little consequence throughout the county.[31]

Clearly, as the data on tax base per capita in Table 5-7 indicate, the concentration of business property in central cities is insufficient to make the older cities in the Northeast and Midwest at least as well off from the standpoint of fiscal capacity as their suburbs. Clearly, too, if overall property values per capita are higher in

[29] From "Taxable Property Values," Tables 21 and 22.

[30] The exceptions for both business and residential property are Milwaukee and Omaha (where there seem to be only minor differences between the central city and the suburbs) and Oklahoma City, which is an unexplained sport.

[31] Newark and Essex County provide the notable exception here; much of Essex County outside Newark is highly citified.

TABLE 5-8. Extent of Reliance on the Property Tax by Metropolitan Area Local Governments, 1957

Metropolitan Area	Property Tax Revenue as Percentage of		
	General Revenue	General Revenue From Own Sources	Tax Revenue
232 city governments, in cities with 1950 populations of 50,000 or more[a]	46.2	57.4	71.3
41 city governments, in cities with 1950 populations of 250,000 or more[b]	44.0	55.1	67.8
9,706 local governments in central portions of 174 Standard Metropolitan Areas (as defined in 1957)[c]	49.2	65.7	82.1
5,952 local governments in outlying portions of 63 Standard Metropolitan Areas (as defined in 1957)[d]	58.7	78.6	92.8

[a] From U. S. Bureau of the Census, *Compendium of City Government Finances in 1957* (1958), Table 5. A few of these cities are suburban in character, but the great majority are central cities of metropolitan areas. In the 1960 Census, for example, 225 of the 310 cities over 50,000 were central cities of SMSA's.
[b] *Ibid.*
[c] From U. S. Bureau of the Census, *Census of Governments: 1957*, Vol. III, No. 6, "Local Government Finances in Standard Metropolitan Areas" (1959), Table 1. "Central portions" comprise the counties or equivalent areas that include the central city or cities of each area. For the 111 single-county areas, the entire SMA is included here.
[d] *Ibid.* "Outlying portions" consist of the outlying counties or their equivalent in the 63 multi-county SMA's.

the suburbs with larger proportions of these values in the form of residential property than in the central cities, residential values per capita must be very low indeed in older central cities, relative to their suburbs. Low-value housing tends to be occupied by poorer people, and concentrations of poorer people in an urban environment tend to be associated with high levels of public expenditure for welfare and health services, for law enforcement and correction, and for other "human services."

Low property values and high expenditure requirements, in combination, should lead to relatively high effective tax rates in central cities, unless offset by greater central city reliance on state aid and on local nonproperty tax revenues. As the 1957 data in Table 5-8 show, central cities do rely much less heavily on the property tax than suburban areas. In general, state and federal aids are at least as important for suburban area local governments as for central cities, but central cities can and do rely more heavily on local nonproperty revenues, both local nonproperty taxes and charges for services. However, as the second column in Table 5-7 indicates, the offset is far from complete: for the most part, per capita property tax revenues are appreciably higher in central cities than in their suburbs. The exceptions are cases in which central city governments rely quite heavily on local nonproperty taxes, such as New York, St. Louis, Columbus, and Toledo.

EFFECTIVE RATE RELATIONSHIPS. Direct evidence on the consequence of low values and high tax revenues—high effective rates—is scarce, for central cities/suburbs comparisons. A few such cases are shown in parentheses in the final column of Table 5-7. More generally, the figures in this column represent the results of dividing the per capita revenue relative by the per capita property value relative, yielding a rough approximation of the probable effective rate relationship in the thirty-two selected areas. In most of these metropolitan areas effective tax rates are higher in the central city than in the suburbs—nearly twice as high in Baltimore and in northeastern New Jersey (two cases in which the data are dependable). Fragmentary data—for New York, New Jersey, Cleveland, and Milwaukee—suggest that effective school tax rates are indeed higher in suburban areas, suggesting a highly income-elastic demand for education.[32] However, for the most part, the school tax differential is overwhelmed by an even larger differential in the opposite direction with regard to taxes levied for municipal nonschool purposes.

These relatively high tax rates in central cities have consequences which reinforce the central cities' plight. Relatively high tax rates on a tax base in which business property is a major component—property which is hardly likely to benefit proportionately from increases in property-tax-financed expenditures—can help speed the dispersal of economic activity from central cities to outlying areas. Relatively high tax rates on the limited proportion of the tax base consisting of high value housing can help speed this dispersal as well. The occupants of such housing have some measure of

[32] Part of the explanation for this no doubt lies in the characteristically smaller proportion of school-age children in central city populations and the characteristically larger proportion of these children attending nonpublic schools. However, there is something to the income elasticity thesis, at least in the New York metropolitan area where school expenditures per pupil are substantially higher in the suburbs and where local school taxes, adjusted for differences in the proportion of public school pupils in the population, absorb significantly higher percentages of personal income in the suburban counties. (New York State Department of Audit and Control, *Comparison of Revenues, Expenditures and Debt: 1949-1959*, Comptroller's Studies in Local Finance, No. 1 (1961, Tables 8 and 10).

choice as to residential location and are, moreover, likely to consider high public outlays for the poor somewhat less favorably than high public outlays for schools—the suburban situation.

This does not mean that property tax differentials have been major contributors to the decentralization of metropolitan areas in the past few decades, or that they are currently of major consequence. The forces making for decentralization are so potent that it can be confidently asserted that the tide would not have been stemmed even had there been large property tax differentials *in favor of* the central cities. In fact, the decentralization process seems to have proceeded no less rapidly in those few areas in which the central city does appear to have an advantage in effective tax rates. Nevertheless, if tax differentials against the central city are widening, which may be the case at the present time and is, in any event, a distinct possibility, the chances become greater that local fiscal arrangements will have an unneutral locational effect: that businesses and residents who otherwise might have preferred a central city location will choose instead a location in outer portions of the metropolitan area. And if, on balance, the migrants contribute more to tax revenues than the public service costs they occasion, the situation of the central cities is further worsened.

The conventional wisdom about the economic future of large cities holds that the central business districts of at least the very largest cities will continue to have strong attractions for a wide variety of office activities.[33] Location rents for these activities are likely to exceed any conceivable property tax differentials by wide margins. But the vast "graying" expanses of the large cities extending from the central business districts out toward the cities' fringes are occupied by uses for which the central cities' location rents frequently appear to be negative: extensive goods-handling activities (manufacturing, warehousing, railroad yards), aging housing, and population serving trade and service establishments. The possibilities for reuse and rebuilding of these areas, without massive public intervention and subsidy, are commonly thought to be limited indeed.[34] Property tax differentials which further limit these possibilities are surely worthy of concern, if for no other reason than the fact that

[33] Vernon, *The Changing Economic Function*, pp. 55-60.
[34] *Ibid.*, pp. 61-62.

governments can revise their own fiscal systems more readily than they can reverse economic and sociological forces. And while local tax differentials may be of small consequence for interregional and interstate location decisions, they surely have far more scope for influence within a single urban area where so many other factors affecting location are subject to rather modest differentiation.

Beyond the Central Cities

The portions of metropolitan areas outside the central city are by no means homogeneous with respect to the property tax. In 1962, there were more than 16,000 local governments with property taxing power in standard metropolitan statistical areas; in the areas covered by Table 5-7—parts or all of thirty-two metropolitan areas—there were approximately 4,000 property taxing units.[35] Most of these thirty-two areas have more than fifty taxing units, and some of the largest—New York, Chicago, Philadelphia, Los Angeles, and San Francisco—have several hundred. These large numbers imply, of course, that the size of most metropolitan area property taxing units is small; small size alone makes it probable that there will be wide disparities among the individual jurisdictions in a single urban area in regard to the level and composition of the tax base and the height of tax rates. If governmental fragmentation is sufficiently extreme, as in parts of the New York and Chicago areas, the location of individual plants can have major effects on intrametropolitan differentials.

The differentials are in fact large, even if the extreme cases such as industrial enclaves and resort communities are ignored. In the Chicago area in 1957, per capita assessed values exhibited a 15:1 range for ninety-one municipalities, and municipal tax rates had a 7:1 range.[36] Among the 164 cities, towns, and villages in the New York Standard Metropolitan Statistical Area in 1959, per capita property values had a 10:1 range and overall tax rates a 3:1 range.[37] In Cuyahoga County in 1955-56, the range of per capita

[35] U.S. Bureau of the Census, *Census of Governments: 1962*, Vol. I, "Governmental Organization" (1963), Tables 14 and 15.

[36] Northeastern Illinois Metropolitan Area Planning Commission, *Suburban Factbook, 1950-1960* June 1960), Table 10. Data have been equalized among counties on the basis of the county-wide equalization ratios.

[37] New York State Department of Audit and Control, *Comparison of Revenues,*

assessed values for municipalities was 18:1 and that of municipal tax rates was 5:1; school districts had somewhat lesser, but still considerable, variation in values per pupil and in tax rates.[38] In the nine counties of northeastern New Jersey, the range of equalized values per capita in 1960 was 32:1 and the range of overall tax rates 7:1.[39] Some but not all of the variation in tax base per capita is attributable to the extreme variability in business property; in northeastern New Jersey, even with the exclusion of the principal industrial enclave, the range of commercial and industrial property per capita was 169:1. However, there was also a substantial range in the value of residential property per capita—26:1. In Cuyahoga County, the comparable residential value range for 1955-56 was 14:1.

RELATIONSHIP OF TAX BASE TO TAX RATES. Such wide variation in *tax base* among the communities of the larger urban areas has a major impact on intrametropolitan *tax rates*. These rates do exhibit considerable variation within urban areas. The available evidence suggests that differences in tax base are, in fact, a major determinant of rate differentials. Table 5-9 includes scattered pieces of evidence, mostly from the high tax areas of the country (New York, New Jersey, and New England); the data are those developed in the course of particular studies, mostly done for other reasons, plus some computations made for the present study. In most of these places, tax rates are negatively related to per capita or per pupil property values, to a powerful degree for school districts in Cuyahoga and Bergen counties and for Connecticut communities.

This is entirely understandable. Property values per pupil or per capita typically seem to vary more widely among the taxing jurisdictions within a metropolitan area than expenditures per pupil or per capita. Thus, the most potent factor in explaining tax rates is the relative abundance of property values in the different jurisdic-

Comptroller's Studies in Local Finance, No. 1; also the same agency's *1959 Tax Atlas of New York State*, Comptroller's Studies in Local Finance, No. 2 (1961). Resort extremes have been excluded.

[38] Seymour Sacks and William F. Hellmuth, Jr., *Financing Government in a Metropolitan Area: The Cleveland Experience* (The Free Press, 1961), Tables VI-7(a) and VI-9. Industrial enclaves have been excluded.

[39] Beck, *Property Taxation and Urban Land Use*, Appendix C. One extreme case at each end of the scale has been excluded for each comparison.

TABLE 5-9. Relationships Among Tax Rates, Expenditures, and Property Values in Selected Areas[a]
(Simple correlation coefficients)

Area	Expenditures (Per Pupil or Per Capita) and Tax Rates	Expenditures and Property Values (Per Pupil or Per Capita)	Tax Rates and Property Values
Chicago area, 1957:			
26 Upper income suburban municipalities	+.663	+.661	+.188*
New York State, 1959:			
Cities	—	+.64	—.26
Villages	—	+.54	—.35
Towns	—	+.82	—.14*
Westchester County, New York, 1959:			
Villages	+.103*	—	—
Cuyahoga County, Ohio, 1956:			
School Districts	—.364	—	—.738
Cities and Villages	—	—	—.167*
Cities	+.755	—	—
Villages	+.421	—	—
Bergen County, New Jersey, 1960–61:			
School Districts	—.531	+.725	—.707
	(—.153*)	(+.705)	
Hartford, Connecticut, area, 1960:			
Municipal	+.690	+.523	—.216
School	—.374*	—	—
Municipal plus School	+.324*	+.228*	—.607
Connecticut and Massachusetts, 1960:			
Connecticut Cities and Towns	—	+.704	—.479
Massachusetts Cities and Towns	—	+.392	—.152

Note: Blanks represent coefficients not computed in source document or difficult to compute from available data.
* Coefficient not significant at the 5 percent level.
[a] See Appendix G for sources and derivation. Figures in parentheses indicate correlations using school tax levy per pupil (an indicator of total school expenditures financed from local revenues) instead of total expenditures per pupil (including state-aided expenditures).

tions. Tastes may differ, and the high income communities spend more per capita or per pupil than the low income communities, as shown in Table 5-9. But richer communities in property value terms can indulge their tastes for more and better public goods at lower, not higher, tax rates, since tax rates decline rapidly as property values rise. Thus, among school districts in the Cleveland area, in the Hartford area, and in Bergen County, New Jersey (a rather high income, relatively homogeneous suburban area), higher expenditures are associated with *lower* tax rates, because of the strong influence of widely ranging property values. Similarly, in the cities and towns of Connecticut and Massachusetts it appears that higher personal incomes are associated with higher property values; higher property values are associated with higher expenditures, but lower tax rates.[40]

Richer communities, in this sense, are not only high income suburbs but also those jurisdictions blessed with large chunks of business property, places which can offer high quality services at very low tax rates. In the extreme cases, such as industrial enclaves, tax rates are so low that sizeable amounts of the metropolitan area's business property tax base can enjoy, in effect, partial tax exemption.

THE TIEBOUT HYPOTHESIS. There is an alternative explanation of intrametropolitan tax rate differentials which indicates that the property tax need not have unneutral locational consequences. This is the now celebrated Tiebout hypothesis.[41]

It is Charles M. Tiebout's contention that one factor in the choice of a residential location is the quality and quantity of public services provided in different governmental jurisdictions. Some communities in a given part of a metropolitan area offer high quality public services, but at a high tax rate. Others offer lower quality services with lower tax costs. Individuals choose among these alternatives on the basis of their relative preferences for public and private expenditures. Thus, disparities in tax rates are based on differences in public expenditures. Tax rates may rise or fall with income and wealth. To the extent that the Tiebout hypothesis holds, there is no a priori expectation of a significant correlation between tax rates and per capita or per pupil property values.

The Tiebout hypothesis is based on a theoretical model at a fairly high level of abstraction. To work out in practice, it would require a number of conditions no*t* commonly found. First, since these are *personal* decisions linked to residential location, all revenue to support public services should be derived from taxes imposed on residents: there should be no nonresidential property tax

[40] See "The Property Tax and Local Spending," *New England Business Review*, Federal Reserve Bank of Boston, December 1962. Negative associations between tax rates and per capita expenditures are implicit in the underlying data.

[41] Charles M. Tiebout, "A Pure Theory of Local Expenditure," *Journal of Political Economy*, Vol. 64 (October 1956), pp. 416-24.

FIGURE 7. Intrametropolitan Area Relations among Tax Rates, Expenditures, and Assessed Values

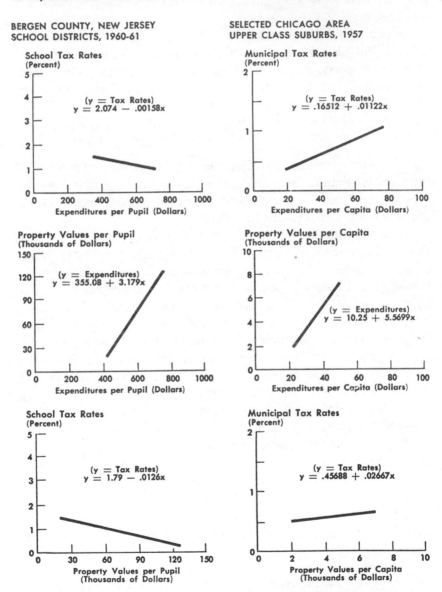

BERGEN COUNTY, NEW JERSEY
SCHOOL DISTRICTS, 1960-61

School Tax Rates
(Percent)

(y = Tax Rates)
y = 2.074 − .00158x

Expenditures per Pupil (Dollars)

Property Values per Pupil
(Thousands of Dollars)

(y = Expenditures)
y = 355.08 + 3.179x

Expenditures per Pupil (Dollars)

School Tax Rates
(Percent)

(y = Tax Rates)
y = 1.79 − .0126x

Property Values per Pupil
(Thousands of Dollars)

SELECTED CHICAGO AREA
UPPER CLASS SUBURBS, 1957

Municipal Tax Rates
(Percent)

(y = Tax Rates)
y = .16512 + .01122x

Expenditures per Capita (Dollars)

Property Values per Capita
(Thousands of Dollars)

(y = Expenditures)
y = 10.25 + 5.5699x

Expenditures per Capita (Dollars)

Municipal Tax Rates
(Percent)

(y = Tax Rates)
y = .45688 + .02667x

Property Values per Capita
(Thousands of Dollars)

Source: Table 5-9. The tax rate and property value data are not directly comparable in thet wo columns but
direction of the slopes is significant.

128

base, no aid from higher levels of government, and no nonproperty revenues except those collected from local residents. Second, these personal taxes on residents should be as broadly based as is conceivable; residential property taxes are not ideal from this standpoint, since differing tastes with regard to the proportions of income devoted to housing can obscure differences in tastes for public versus all private goods combined. Third, a certain degree of socioeconomic homogeneity among the competitive residential jurisdictions and among the persons making the choices is necessary, for the following reasons: (a) if the rival communities differ widely in other regards than tax rates and public services, the role of the public sector is far from clear; (b) if the income elasticity of demand for public goods is less than unity, as is likely on a cross-section basis at any point in time, richer communities will not spend enough more than poorer ones to keep tax rates from being lower; and (c) more generally, only relatively well-off people are in a position to choose effectively on the basis of this particular set of preferences.

EMPIRICAL SUPPORT FOR THESIS. In view of these requirements, it is not surprising that most of the evidence does not unequivocally support this hypothesis. However, the set of correlation coefficients for twenty-six upper-class Chicago suburbs in Table 5-9 (developed because superficial examination suggested that the Tiebout thesis might be borne out here) *does* lend weight to the thesis. The level of per capita municipal expenditures seems to be the most powerful explanation of variations in municipal tax rates: high levels of expenditures and high tax rates are associated, and differences in property values seem to have no significant connection with tax rates.

In all the cases presented in Table 5-9, local public spending levels rise with property values, and in a few cases, in addition to the Chicago one, tax rates rise with levels of public spending—notably, Hartford-area municipal taxes and spending and Cleveland-area cities. But in these cases, tax rates appear also to *decline* as property values rise. That is, the simple Tiebout explanation in which tastes for public goods determine tax rate variation is complicated by tax base disparities; it is not simply a matter of consumer choice but partly a consequence of luck or historical accident in regard to the distribution of tax base among taxing jurisdictions. The contrast between this situation and the working of the Tiebout hypothesis in two high income areas—Bergen County and Chicago suburbs—is highlighted by the simple regression equations plotted in Figure 7.

It is not hard to see why property value differentials should overwhelm differences in tastes for public goods in the typical suburban situation with large numbers of taxing jurisdictions. First, as noted earlier, there is the simple fact of geographic size: the location of one or a few large business establishments (plants, laboratories, suburban office centers, shopping centers) in a small taxing unit can make a sizeable impact on the tax base of that jurisdiction and, moreover, will preempt a good deal of the jurisdiction's land area, preventing development in the form of less valuable property. Further, an entirely different ratio of tax revenues to public service costs applies for nonresidential property; this is obviously so for schools, which serves to explain the nature of the results for school districts reported in Table 5-9.

The extreme consequences of this are seen in the industrial enclaves—taxing jurisdictions in which the bulk of the land area is occupied by industrial property, often with the property owners supplying on a private basis a major portion of what are public services elsewhere. Such enclaves, moreover, have few schoolchildren to educate. The result is often a negligible tax rate; where this is capitalized into land values, there is little likelihood of residential development of vacant land within the enclave, and thus the "tax colony" nature of the place is further reinforced.[42]

Nonresidential property is not the entire explanation, however. Suburban communities with high residential property values, high incomes, high quality public services, and low effective tax rates are almost certain to reflect this favorable situation in high prices for residential properties. Moreover, this is typically reinforced by zoning. As indicated in my earlier study:

[42] Ordinarily, capitalization should make no difference in land use: the equilibrium situation is one in which the marginal prospective developer or homeowner is indifferent as between the high price for the land with a low annual tax, and land at a lower price with a higher annual tax. In the industrial enclave situation, the negligible tax rate for *both* land *and* improvements—available only in the enclave—is likely to be capitalized into land prices. However, since the ratio of improvements to land value is generally much higher for industrial than for residential development (especially where personal property is part of the tax base), industrial developers are likely to be willing to pay more for the tax advantage than residential property owners.

Deliberate public decisions on land use, principally through zoning, have all but eliminated the free workings of the "Tiebout effect": one cannot choose to get the benefit of high services and low taxes in a high price community by building an unusually inexpensive house on an unusually small lot, for that community. And quite generally, governmental intervention in the market determination of land use has tended to reinforce the wide disparities in the ratios between taxable values and local government service needs.[43]

FISCAL MERCANTILISM. Locational unneutrality inherent in tax rate differentials stemming from tax base differentials is in practice strengthened by the fiscal incentive to zone land use on a basis which is hardly optimal from the standpoint of either an individual metropolitan area or the country as a whole. The examples of the industrial tax colonies and the high income/low tax rate enclaves have encouraged large numbers of communities to zone to attract tax base and repel consumers of public services.[44] From a fiscal standpoint, the best of all possible worlds appears, to many suburban decision-makers, to be development of the community's vacant land by campus-type offices and laboratories and by housing expensive enough to assure that there will be few schoolchildren (because of the anticipated age levels of the owners).

The popularity of this "fiscal mercantilism"—efforts to export service costs and import tax base—has generated a good deal of argument about the extent to which the various forms of land development "pay for themselves."[45] There are, of course, endless possibilities for local variations in cost-revenue situations for particular classes of property. The presence of factories and shopping centers can increase some costs disproportionately, under certain circumstances, and have adverse rather than favorable effects on

[43] Dick Netzer, "The Property Tax and Alternatives in Urban Development," *Papers and Proceedings,* Regional Science Association, Vol. 9 (1962), p. 193.

[44] There is an extensive literature on this, in addition to the paper cited in the preceding note. The best treatment is found in a number of papers by Lynn A. Stiles, including "Financing Government in the Suburbs—The Role of the Property Tax," *Proceedings of the Fifty-Third Annual Conference,* National Tax Association (1960), pp. 52-57; and "Restructuring Local Taxation," a paper presented at the 17th Regional Plan Conference and printed in *Urban Land,* Vol. 22 (January 1963).

[45] The best overall review of this literature is Ruth L. Mace, *Municipal Cost-Revenue Research in the United States* (Institute of Government, University of North Carolina, 1961).

property tax rates. In some places, more expensive residential property is associated more with larger numbers of schoolchildren per family than with less expensive residential development. But by and large, the intuitive judgments of local policy-makers are likely to be right since, in suburban areas, the school levy is usually more than half the total property tax levy; business property, that is, produces a school tax "profit," and much residential property produces a school tax "deficit."[46] And if the latter is the case, the best way to minimize the "problem" is to have as few "deficit-producing" houses as possible, for example, by requiring very large minimum lot sizes for single-family houses. Thus, in the New York area as of 1960, nearly half the vacant land in the twenty-two county region was zoned to require single-family houses on lots of one acre or more.[47]

This is not the place to comment in depth on the adverse consequences of land use decisions made on the basis of property tax considerations. It should suffice to say that efficient patterns of land use in metropolitan areas, in the broadest sense, are not necessarily those that maximize the current fiscal position of governments in the area. There is more to urban society than the contemporary public sector and governments are seldom in business to maximize their *own* welfare. Even if maximization of the public fisc were the overriding criterion for land use planning, the property tax is far from the whole story (see Table 5-8); moreover, a multiplicity of taxing jurisdictions, each striving to maximize its own cost-revenue combination, is highly unlikely to maximize for the area as a whole.

TREND TOWARD UNIFORMITY. The adverse consequences of intra-metropolitan property tax differentials would be of much less concern if the differentials themselves appeared to be diminishing, particularly if property tax rates tended toward homogeneity as a metropolitan area grew. Recent empirical studies have devoted a good deal of attention to this possibility.

The Sacks-Hellmuth study, for example, found increasing uniformity of tax rates among Cuyahoga County taxing units between

[46] If the average (market) value of single-family houses in a jurisdiction is $20,000 and there are 1.5 schoolchildren per single-family house, then even a relatively high effective tax rate of 2 percent will yield less than $300 per pupil.

[47] Regional Plan Association, *Spread City*, Bulletin No. 100 (September 1962), Tables 10-12.

1940 and 1959.[48] Burkhead intensively analyzed the Sacks-Hellmuth data from the standpoint of fiscal homogeneity, that is, homogeneity of per capita and per pupil expenditures and assessed values (and, inferentially, tax rates); he found that:

. . . the increased economic specialization within the metropolitan area is accompanied by an increased fiscal homogeneity. Both government expenditure patterns and taxable resources come to be more uniformly distributed among municipalities within the metropolitan area. There is a pronounced tendency, although with some prominent exceptions, for increased clustering around average values, for both expenditures and resources. However, and of almost equal significance, is the finding that this increased fiscal homogeneity, measured in terms of central tendency, is frequently accompanied by a persistent skewness. High expenditure and high resource communities persist, but tax havens among the municipalities, where high resource values and low expenditures are combined, tend to disappear.[49]

In northeastern New Jersey, as in Cuyahoga County, the evidence seems to suggest that property tax rates tend toward homogeneity as a metropolitan area grows. Beck's study covering the 279 local governments in nine counties for the period 1950-60 concludes that this has been the case.[50] Both tax rates and property values per capita rose a good deal more in the outer parts of the region (which had the lower values in 1950) than in the inner parts. An analysis of trends between 1940 and 1960 among Connecticut municipalities, grouped within planning regions, suggests that regional dispersion in per capita and per pupil expenditures decreased (if central cities are excluded) as did dispersion in per capita property tax revenue.[51] Investigators in the New York metropolitan regional study of 1956-59 projected increased fiscal homogeneity with regard to both tax rates and expenditures.[52]

[48] Sacks and Hellmuth, *Financing Government in a Metropolitan Area,* pp. 209-10.
[49] Jesse Burkhead, "Uniformity in Governmental Expenditures and Resources in a Metropolitan Area: Cuyahoga County," *National Tax Journal,* Vol. 14 (December 1961), p. 347.
[50] Beck, *Property Taxation and Urban Land Use,* p. 32.
[51] Connecticut Development Commission, *Public Finance* (Connecticut Interregional Planning Program, Technical Report 157, 1963), pp. 118-20, Appendix Tables 9a, 9b, 11a, 11b, 12a, and 12b.
[52] Alan K. Campbell, "Taxes and Industrial Location in the New York

However, the evidence is not as unequivocal as it may seem at first blush. Riew, in commenting on Burkhead's Cleveland data, points out that the trend toward uniformity was pronounced between 1940 and 1950, but reversed, according to most measures, between 1950 and 1956. By 1950, virtually all of Cuyahoga County had become urbanized. Thus, much of the credit for the convergence seems to be due to the conversion, in the earlier decade, of the outer areas from nonurban to urban status, with attendant rapid increases in both local government expenditures and property values.[53] This raises the important question: is there any tendency toward uniformity within the already developed parts of metropolitan areas? Or do the differentials tend to be perpetuated, as might be expected, in the light of the many barriers to intrametropolitan mobility which might otherwise eliminate the differentials?

In Beck's study of northeastern New Jersey, 123 of the 279 taxing units were places which had reached a population density of 2,000 per square mile by 1930 or 3,000 per square mile by 1950, and thus were urbanized prior to the study period. (These standards are consistent with development with residential lots as large as one-half acre.) The median effective tax rate for these 123 places rose from 1.835 percent to 2.49 percent between 1950 and 1960. The coefficient of variation (Q3-Q1/median) declined barely perceptibly, from .367 to .325, while the Bowley measure of skewness rose sharply, from .08 to .43.[54] This indicates that the tendency toward uniformity is weak and that, at the extremes, the most favored places improved their positions relatively, or the least favored became even worse off. Visual inspection of the data indicates that the latter is the case: the larger, older central cities during the 1950's became increasingly cities of the disadvantaged with high service costs; they participated to a very limited extent in the economic growth of the area. Indeed, their relatively high tax rates at the beginning of the period very likely were a substantial deterrent to

Metropolitan Region," *National Tax Journal*, Vol. 11 (September 1958), pp. 205-08; see also, Jesse Burkhead, "Metropolitan Area Budget Structures and Their Significance for Expenditures," in *Proceedings of the Fifty-Second Annual Conference*, National Tax Association (1959), p. 289.

[53] John Riew, "Uniformity in Governmental Expenditures and Resources in a Metropolitan Area: A Comment," *National Tax Journal*, Vol. 15 (June 1962), p. 218.

[54] Based on data in Beck, *Property Taxation and Urban Land Use*, Appendix B.

expansion of business investment within their boundaries, and even to the maintenance of the earlier levels.

In contrast to the New Jersey evidence, some data for the Philadelphia area indicate that there has been a bona fide tendency toward uniformity of per capita property *values,* quite apart from the effect of the transition from nonurban status.[55] It should be noted that this evidence concerns only values and not tax rates, in contrast to both the New Jersey data and Burkhead's analysis which includes both expenditure and property value data. It is entirely possible that per capita values became more uniform, without leading to greater uniformity in tax rates since trends in expenditure are not presented in the Philadelphia data.

Father Curran's study of Milwaukee County municipalities produced conclusions which are as pessimistic as those which apply to the already developed sections of northeastern New Jersey. Per capita expenditures seem to be tending toward uniformity, but taxable resources do not; nonschool tax rates have become much *less* uniform since the days before World War II, while school tax rates and total tax rates are more uniform. On the basis of detailed scrutiny of the actual cases, the movement in tax rates appears to result from a highly income elastic demand for education in previously low tax rate, wealthy suburbs combined with a resistance to tax rate increases in previously high tax rate, poorer communities.[56]

This last point suggests that intrametropolitan differentials in property taxation not only may produce inefficiency in resource allocation via their effects on location and on land use controls, but also may have important adverse effects on interpersonal equity, as long as barriers to intraurban mobility (via zoning, racial discrimination, etc.) exist.[57] On balance, a uniform area-wide property tax might be a reasonably close surrogate for a proportional income tax without exemptions in some circumstances, at least for all but the

[55] Charles S. Liebman, Harold Herman, Oliver P. Williams, and Thomas R. Dye, "Social Status, Tax Resources and Metropolitan Cooperation," *National Tax Journal,* Vol. 16 (March 1963), pp. 57-59.

[56] Donald J. Curran in *National Tax Journal,* pp. 216-21.

[57] For an excellent treatment of the efficiency argument, which is much more complete than the analysis in earlier pages, see Harvey E. Brazer, "Some Fiscal Implications of Metropolitanism," in *Metropolitan Issues: Social, Governmental, Fiscal,* Guthrie S. Birkhead, ed. (Maxwell Graduate School of Citizenship and Public Affairs, Syracuse University, 1962; Brookings Institution Reprint 61, July 1962), pp. 71-78.

bottom layer of the income distribution. But if significant numbers of higher income families enjoy more and better public services at lower tax rates than low income families in other jurisdictions in the same metropolitan area, the property tax becomes a highly regressive instrument with respect to income distribution within that metropolitan area. Essentially, in this situation, governmental fragmentation, together with barriers to mobility, frustrates the degree of income redistribution that occurs, via the property tax and services it supports, within the boundaries of the large central cities: within the big city, the somewhat regressive property tax is probably more than offset, in its distributional effects, by the highly progressive incidence of local public services.[58]

REFORM PROPOSALS. Since at least some of the adverse effects of intrametropolitan differentials on efficiency and equity stem from the combination of fragmented tax bases and fragmented local government services and powers, one partial remedy—within a framework which retains the property tax as the bulwark of local finance—is to enlarge the area within which single local government units function. An example of this is the transferring of land use controls to county or larger units.

Another remedy is to homogenize, in part, the tax base of the metropolitan area: to support some public expenditures by tapping the taxpaying capacity of the whole metropolitan economy (or a major component, in the larger areas), rather than by dividing the metropolitan tax base into disparate and highly uneven fragments. Fiscal federation is one such device:

Under this plan, the local units accounting for a major share of the local property tax dollar—generally the schools—would share in the proceeds of a uniform area-wide property tax imposed by the county, the state or some new public body created for the purpose. The area tax levy would be great enough to supplant locally-levied taxes for the same general purpose. Individual communities desiring to offer more than the basic program could then levy supplementally at their discretion.[59]

[58] The larger the central city population relative to the metropolitan area total and the more homogeneous the suburban jurisdictions, the less regressive will the property tax be on balance. In many metropolitan areas, this is perhaps not a real problem as yet.

[59] Stiles, "Restructuring Local Taxation," *Regional Plan Conference,* p. 4.

A less drastic version of this is suggested by Sacks and Hell-muth for Cuyahoga County school districts. They propose a 10-mill county-wide school tax distributed back to the school districts on a per pupil basis, with optional local school taxes to provide a program beyond that supported by the 10-mill levy. Had this been in effect in 1956, when the average school tax rate was 14.2 mills, the average deviation in school tax rates would have been reduced by more than one-third.[60] A similar procedure applied to Bergen County school districts in 1959 would have reduced the variation in school tax rates by one-half.[61] Analogous computations have been made in a study of the twenty-six cities and towns in the Hartford, Connecticut, area for 1961. Here, two forms of fiscal federation were examined: (1) a region-wide tax designed to provide $200 per pupil—in essence a regional school "foundation program"—with optional local supplements; and (2) the regional school tax plus region-wide taxation to meet local welfare costs. With 1961 tax rates averaging 20.6 mills (on "full value"), these were the results:[62]

	Range of Rates (in mills)	*Average Deviation from Mean*
Present system	15.1–36.2	3.7
$200 per pupil tax	12.4–27.3	3.0
$200 per pupil tax plus regional welfare tax	12.9–27.8	2.8

All sorts of other combinations are possible including, of course, replacement of the property tax per se. The point here is that, if intrametropolitan variations in property tax rates are not simply a product of consumer choice and if they result in adverse consequences which are considered serious—both of which conditions seem to obtain in many places—then it is not hard to devise means of reducing the dimensions of the problem.

[60] Sacks and Hellmuth, *Financing Government in a Metropolitan Area*, Table VIII-14 and p. 360.

[61] Dick Netzer in *Papers and Proceedings, Regional Science Association*, p. 196.

[62] Capitol Region Planning Agency, *Municipal Taxation and Regional Development* (East Hartford, Connecticut, 1963), pp. 24-26.

CHAPTER VI

The Personal Property
Component of the Tax Base

ANY COMPREHENSIVE APPRAISAL of the American property tax must come to terms with the disparate nature of the major elements of the tax base. Of these elements, public utility property, agricultural property in urbanizing areas, natural resource property (notably mining and timber properties), and personalty have generated a good deal of special attention in the past. In revenue terms, personal property is by far the most important of these special elements of the tax base. It is, moreover, the most American of property tax institutions.[1] It has been singled out for special treatment here, however, because of the opportunity to utilize recently available data to shed further light on the quantitative aspects of this form of taxation.

A very considerable proportion of the voluminous literature on the property tax in the United States is addressed to the conceptual and administrative difficulties stemming from the effort to apply a universal and uniform system of ad valorem taxation to the various types of personal property. These difficulties became painfully

[1] As noted in Chap. I, personal property is not taxed at all under the property tax in most other countries, and only in Japan is personal property more important in revenue terms.

138

apparent almost as soon as the property tax had reached its apogee of universality in coverage about the time of the Civil War, and legal and extralegal exemptions of personal property spread rapidly.[2] By the 1890's, when Seligman and others were thundering that a universal property tax was neither administrable nor equitable, the high-water mark had passed: from the 1870's on, personal property assessments were a declining share of total assessed values. Between the 1870 and 1890 Census, realty assessments increased by $9 billion, or 91 percent, while personalty assessments increased by only $2.3 billion, or 53 percent. In the larger states, the relative decline in personalty assessments was even sharper.[3]

The relative importance of personal property assessments continued to decline moderately until the 1930's. In the 1932 Census of Governments, personal property accounted for about 19 percent of total assessments. By 1937, the assessed value of personal property had shrunk to less than 16 percent of the total, and in the five-year period between 1932 and 1937, personalty assessments declined by 28 percent, while realty assessments went down only 12 percent.[4] Since the late thirties, as Table 6-1 indicates, the decline in the relative importance of personalty in the property tax base has been arrested, and personalty is estimated to have accounted for 16-17 percent of the tax base in recent years.

It is clear that the explanation of the reduction in the relative importance of personalty is to be found in legal and extralegal exemptions, not in the lesser secular growth rate of wealth in the form of privately owned equipment and inventories vis-à-vis privately owned real estate. Quite the contrary, for Goldsmith's data indicate that the value of privately owned tangible personal property has consistently increased more rapidly, and by a significant margin. Over the entire period 1900-58, the growth rate of tangible personalty value was half again as rapid as that of realty—an increase of 2,100 percent compared to one of 1,400 percent. Similar disparities

---

[2] For concise reviews of the ancient and more recent history of personal property taxation, see: Edwin R. A. Seligman, *Essays in Taxation,* Chap. II, "The General Property Tax" (Macmillan, 1895); Alfred G. Buehler, "Personal Property Taxation," Chap. VIII in *Property Taxes,* Tax Policy League (1940); Frederick L. Bird, *The General Property Tax: Findings of the 1957 Census of Governments,* Chaps. 1 and 3 (Public Administration Service, 1960).

[3] Figures cited in Seligman, *Essays in Taxation,* seventh edition (1911), p. 27; also, U. S. Bureau of the Census, *Compendium of the Ninth Census* (1870), p. 638.

[4] Figures cited in Buehler, *Personal Property Taxation,* p. 118.

in rates of increase occurred between 1900 and 1929 and in the postwar period.[5] Moreover, both the evidence and reason indicate that the total value of intangibles—financial assets—has increased more rapidly than that of real assets over time, since economies in the use of demand deposits have not been sufficient to offset increases in the dollar volume of securities which do not reflect directly underlying real assets,[6] and increases in the liabilities of financial intermediaries, which in effect double-count real assets.

Present Coverage of Personal Property Taxation[7]

The progressive withdrawal of particular classes of personal property from the scope of the general property tax represents a surrender to reality. The process of exemption has gone furthest for those classes which pose the greatest difficulties in regard to discovery and valuation of the assets and in regard to the economic consequences of uniform valuation and taxation even where these are possible.

Intangible Personalty

Intangibles present the extreme case, for they are either readily concealed or highly mobile (or both) and thus hard to locate on assessment day; moreover, the incentive to evade or avoid the asses-

[5] Based on various tables, especially Table A-5, in Raymond W. Goldsmith, *The National Wealth of the United States in the Postwar Period* (Princeton University Press for National Bureau of Economic Research, 1962).

[6] These would include, for example, business equities reflecting the capitalized future earning power of going concerns.

[7] In the remainder of this discussion and in the accompanying tables, personal property is defined as excluding that owned by railroads and other public utility companies. This is done for a number of reasons. For some types of utilities—such as electric power and telephone utilities—the distinction between equipment (personalty) and structures (realty) is particularly ephemeral, although not necessarily more so than for some types of industrial and mining property, for which the definitions applicable in state laws are relied upon. Moreover, the widespread assessment of utilities on a unit basis (that is, systemwide rather than by cumulating figures for individual chunks of physical assets) makes the separation impossible. Thus, the Census of Governments does not separate state assessed utility property between realty and personalty. In general, as the Census Bureau suggests, taxation of utility property is in a class of its own, and represents "a family of nominally ad valorem levies imposed in lieu of 'the' property tax, rather than as a component of the property tax base in the more usual sense." *Census of Governments: 1962*, Vol. II, "Taxable Property Values" (1963), p. 4.

sor is substantial, since investment in the form of intangibles frequently yields considerably lower rates of return than comparable investment in tangible assets. Hence a uniform area-wide property tax rate is likely to absorb a substantially larger part of the (realized or imputed) return from intangibles than of the return from other assets, especially when one considers that the assessor cannot as readily underassess fixed value claims, such as bank deposits, as he can other types of assets. Thus, where bank deposits have been subject to the general property tax at the area-wide rate, very large annual shifts of deposits to other states and into nontaxable U. S. Treasury securities have occurred regularly on the assessment date. The shift is so large in Cook County, Illinois, that it has a discernible impact on Treasury bill yields. Chicago banks, in behalf of their customers, bid aggressively for Treasury bills maturing shortly after the April 1 assessment date. These bills usually are sold at lower yields (higher prices) than are adjacent weekly issues.[8]

Consequently, all intangible property is part of the legal base for local general property taxation in only nine states (plus Alaska, at local option). An additional five states legally subject certain types of intangibles to local general property taxation.[9] Even in these fifteen states, in practice, as is to be expected, coverage is far from complete; only in West Virginia are intangibles a really significant element of the tax base. As Table 6-1 indicates, intangibles represent about 4 percent of total personalty assessments for

[8] The net decline in deposits (except those of banks) at the large Chicago "money market" banks during the week ending April 1 ranged from $649 million to $1,011 million between 1956 and 1962 and averaged $868 million, which is close to 20 percent of their privately owned deposit total. One additional indicator of the impact of these transactions on the Treasury bill market is found in the rate of decline in the market yields of particular issues of Treasury bills. All Treasury bills tend to decline in yield as they approach maturity and become more nearly money-like. As the April 1 Illinois assessment date approaches, the shifting of bank deposits into nontaxable Treasury bills maturing right after the assessment date produces an intensified demand for these particular bills, and a very rapid decline in their yields in the market. Thus, between 1956 and 1960, the market yields of Treasury bills maturing during the first week in April consistently declined considerably more rapidly during the first three months of the year than did the yields of bills maturing immediately prior to April 1—on the average, the decline in yield for the early April bills was 40 basis points (0.4 percentage points) greater. This yield relationship is obviously related to the Chicago deposit shifts. (Information based on studies done at the Federal Reserve Bank of Chicago, by Dorothy M. Nichols in 1960 and Neva Van Peski in 1962.)

[9] "Taxable Property Values," p. 6.

TABLE 6-1. Gross Assessed Value of Personal Property Subject to General Property Taxation (Excluding Public Utility Property), 1956 and 1961

(In millions of dollars)

Type of Property	1956[a]	1961[b]
Locally assessed personalty	$47,978	$57,614
Estimated state assessed personalty		
(excluding that owned by utilities)	1,406	1,855
Total	49,384	59,469
Percentage of all property subject to local general property taxation (before exemptions)	17.6%	16.2%
Composition:		
Intangibles—		
Identifiable locally assessed[c]	$ 1,415	$ 1,631
Estimated locally assessed in other states[d]	100	175
Identifiable state assessed[e]	484	601
Subtotal, intangibles	1,999	2,407
Tangibles—		
Locally assessed[f]	46,463	55,808
Identifiable state assessed[g]	782	1,104
Estimated state assessed in other states[h]	140	150
Subtotal, tangibles	47,385	57,062

[a] Based on data in U. S. Bureau of the Census, *Census of Governments: 1957*, Vol. V, "Taxable Property Values in the United States" (1959), Table 2. 1956 data are adjusted to take account of corrected figures for South Carolina shown in *Census of Governments: 1962*, Vol. II, p. 19.
[b] Based on data in U. S. Bureau of the Census, *Census of Governments: 1962*, Vol. II, "Taxable Property Values" (1963), Table 2.
[c] For 6 states in 1956 and 8 states in 1961. 1956 data are adjusted to take account of an error in reporting for Texas, for 1956.
[d] For 7 states in each year, but not the identical states.
[e] For 4 states in 1956 and 3 states in 1961.
[f] Amounts shown in first line less intangibles shown above.
[g] For 2 states in 1956 and 3 states in 1961.
[h] For 7 states in 1956 and 8 states in 1961.

the nation as a whole, and about 0.6 percent of total general property tax assessments. The $2.4 billion of estimated intangible assessments in 1961 compares to a total of perhaps $1,100 billion worth of deposits, corporate stocks and bonds, and mortgages owned by individuals and businesses subject to the property tax.[10]

In fifteen other states, intangibles have been completely exempted from the property tax. In the remaining twenty states, intangibles are partly or wholly subject to special types of property taxes,

[10] Estimated on the basis of various tables in U. S. Bureau of the Census, *Statistical Abstract of the United States, 1962*.

usually low flat rates of less than one-half of one percent, thus in effect offering taxpayers a chance to be honest at a relatively modest price. In all, revenue from these special taxes in 1962 appears to have been no more than $180 million.[11] Revenue from general property taxation of intangibles—that is, on the assessments reflected in Table 6-1—was probably no more than $120 million. Thus, in all, intangibles probably yielded only about $300 million in revenues in 1962, about 1.5 percent of total property tax revenues, and only about 0.03 percent of the $1,100 billion figure cited above. Comparable figures for 1957 are shown in Table 6-6.

Tangible Personalty

While taxation of tangible personal property is considerably more widespread than taxation of intangibles, substantially general coverage exists in only sixteen states with 31 percent of the country's population (and a significantly smaller share of economic activity). There is complete exemption in four states, including New York and Pennsylvania, and partial coverage in thirty states and the District of Columbia.[12] Evidence of the limited extent of legal coverage—and legal fractional assessment or extralegal underassessment where covered—is found in the fact that the 1956 total of tangible personalty shown in Table 6-1 is only about 10 percent of estimated total national wealth (in current dollars) in the form of privately owned producer and consumer durables and inventories in that year.[13]

The relative difficulty of assessment, plus, apparently, the relative number of voters involved, has governed the extent of legal coverage of the major classes of tangible personalty.[14] Commercial and industrial personal property (nonfarm business equipment and inventories) is generally subject to tax in forty-six states (counting the District of Columbia as a state for these purposes). Agricultural equipment and inventories are generally taxed in forty-two states, although permissive local exemptions of particular types of agricultural property are widespread, more so than in the case of nonfarm

[11] Estimated from "Taxable Property Values," Table 25.
[12] "Taxable Property Values," p. 5.
[13] Goldsmith, *The National Wealth of the U. S.*, Table A-5. See also Table 6-2, below.
[14] The following information is based on "Taxable Property Values," pp. 5-6.

business personalty. Household effects are completely exempted in eighteen states, virtually completely exempted via local option in another three states, and subject to special partial exemptions or local option provisions in another eighteen states. Legally, house-

TABLE 6-2. Estimated National Wealth in the Form of Privately Owned Tangible Personal Property, 1956 and 1958

(In billions of current dollars)

Type of Property	Net Stock of Tangible Assets			
	1956		1958	
Commercial and industrial personalty (non-farm business inventories and equipment, excluding motor vehicles and all public utility property)				
Inventories	$ 97.1		$ 95.7	
Equipment	153.0		173.3	
Less: motor vehicles	−11.9		−12.8	
Less: portion of equipment estimated to be owned by public utilities[a]	−33.2	$205.0	−37.7	$218.5
Agricultural personalty (inventories, livestock, and equipment, excluding motor vehicles)		33.8		42.5
Household personalty (consumer durables except automobiles and accessories)				
Nonfarm individuals	97.9		106.5	
Farm	8.8	106.7	8.4	114.9
Motor vehicles and accessories[b]				
Nonfarm individuals	48.0		54.3	
Farm autos and trucks	6.6		7.1	
Business passenger cars	5.3		5.8	
Business trucks, trailers and buses[c]	6.6	66.5	7.0	74.1
Total		412.1		450.0

Source: Raymond W. Goldsmith, *The National Wealth of the United States in the Postwar Period* (Princeton University Press for National Bureau of Economic Research, 1962): Commercial and industrial—Tables A-52 and A-54; Agriculture—Table A-53; Household—Tables B-36 and B-86; Motor vehicles—Tables B-36, B-82, B-86, B-119, and B-129.

Note: Because of rounding, detail may not add to totals.

[a] Utilities accounted for an estimated 23.5 percent of purchases of private producers' durables between 1956 and 1961, deducted from equipment net of motor vehicles.

[b] Dealers' margins on used cars are deducted where practicable.

[c] Estimated; the Goldsmith data extend only through 1954 in this category.

TABLE 6-3. Estimated National Wealth in the Form of Privately Owned Tangible Personal Property Legally Subject to General Property Taxation, 1956 and 1958[a]

(In billions of current dollars)

Type of Property	Net Stock of Tangible Assets	
	1956	1958
Commercial and industrial personalty	$159.1	$170.0
Agricultural personalty	27.0	34.0
Household personalty	37.3	40.2
Motor vehicles	23.3	25.9
Total	246.7	270.1

Sources: Table 6-2 and U. S. Bureau of the Census, *Statistical Abstract of the United States*, 1962.
[a] See Appendix H for derivation.

hold effects are fully subject to the tax in only twelve states. Motor vehicles are generally taxed in twenty states, and at local option in three others, although special property taxes at state-wide rates are collected by state and/or local governments in eight other states.

Goldsmith's national wealth estimates permit some quantitative evaluation of the extent to which legal exemption has reduced the theoretical base for personal property taxation, and the extent to which extralegal exemption and both legal and extralegal assessment at fractions of estimated market value—in this case, depreciated replacement cost in current dollars—have further reduced the tax base. Data are presented in Tables 6-2 and 6-3 for 1956 and 1958: for 1956 to permit direct comparison with 1956 assessment data, and for 1958 to facilitate extrapolation forward for comparison with 1961 assessment data. Table 6-2 organizes Goldsmith's data into the four categories most closely related to conventional assessment categories: commercial and industrial, agricultural, household, and motor vehicles—with public utilities excluded from all data to the extent possible. In all, national wealth in the form of tangible personalty of the types taxable under the most general form of the general property tax amounted in 1956 to $412 billion, compared to total assessed values for tangible personalty of $47 billion.

In Table 6-3, an effort is made to account for legal exemptions. That is, on the basis of various proxy allocators, estimates have been made of the proportions of national wealth in each of the four major categories which are located in the states which do not tax personal property in those forms. In addition, some rather rough adjustments have been made to account for partial rather than total exemption. About 60 percent of estimated national wealth in these forms is estimated to have been legally taxable in 1956-58. As Table 6-1 shows, tangible personalty assessments were only about 19 percent of the amount estimated to have been legally taxable in 1956. If the Goldsmith data are updated to 1961 (using essentially his methodology), tangible personalty assessments in that year appear to have been a slightly smaller proportion of the amounts estimated to be legally taxable—about 17.5 percent. The final column of Table 6-5 shows a more comprehensive comparison, including assessments for special as well as general property taxes.

The 1962 Census of Governments data of assessments for 1961 offer, for twenty of the states, a somewhat closer look at the com-

TABLE 6-4. Distribution of Locally Assessed Personal Property Subject to Local General Property Taxation, Twenty Selected States, 1961

(Amounts in millions of dollars)

Type of Property	Amount	Percentage Distribution of Tangibles
Total locally assessed personal property subject to tax (after exemptions), U. S.	$56,456	
Total for twenty selected states	26,136ᵃ	
Intangiblesᵇ	498	
Tangibles	25,677	100.0
Commercial and industrialᶜ	17,420	67.8
Agriculturalᵈ	2,803	10.9
Householdᵉ	1,196	4.7
Motor vehiclesᶠ	2,913	11.3
Other and unallocableᵍ	1,350	5.3

Source: U. S. Bureau of the Census, *Census of Governments: 1962*, Vol. II, "Taxable Property Values" (1963), Table 23.

Note: Because of rounding, detail will not necessarily add to totals.

ᵃ Total is $39 million less than the sum of the detail, because of unallocable partial exemptions in Maine, New Jersey, and Oregon.

ᵇ Subject to tax in only 2 of the 20 states.

ᶜ Subject to tax in all 20 states, but only minor amounts (less than $10 million) in one of these.

ᵈ Subject to tax in 19 of the 20 states, but only minor amounts in one of these 19.

ᵉ Subject to tax in 12 of the 20 states, but only minor amounts in 4 of these 12.

ᶠ Subject to tax in 8 of the 20 states.

ᵍ Significant amounts for 10 states, and minor amounts for 6 states.

TABLE 6-5. Estimated Distribution of Assessed Value of Locally Assessed Tangible Personal Property, 1961

(Amounts in billions of dollars)

Type of Property	Locally Assessed for General Property Taxation		Total, Including State Assessed and Special Property Taxes[c]	Estimated Percentage of National Wealth Legally Subject to General Property Taxation[d]
	Percentage Distribution[a]	Amount[b]		
Commercial and industrial	64.5	$36.0	$37.9	20
Agricultural	11.6	6.5	6.7	18
Household	5.4	3.0	3.0	6
Motor vehicles	13.2	7.4	16.9	42
Other and unallocable	5.4	3.0	3.0	n.a.
Total	100.0	55.8	67.4	21

Sources: Tables 6-1, 6-3, and 6-4; U. S. Bureau of the Census, *Statistical Abstract of the United States,* 1962.
Note: Because of rounding, detail will not necessarily add to totals.
n.a. Not available.
[a] States covered in Table 6-4 are estimated to account for the following percentages of the total legal tax base:

          Commercial and industrial   49%
          Agricultural   44
          Household   41
          Motor vehicles   40
          Other and unallocable   46

These estimates are based on state data on income, output, and inventories in manufacturing, trade, and agriculture, personal income, and motor vehicle registrations. The "other and unallocable" estimate is the relationship of the first two lines of Table 6-4.
[b] Gross assessed value, before exemptions.
[c] Amounts shown in Table 6-1 for state assessed tangible personalty are entirely in the commercial and industrial category; the bulk of tangibles assessed for special property taxes consists of motor vehicles ($9.5 out of $10.3 billion), with the remainder farm and business property in Kentucky.
[d] Exhibit based on a rough extrapolation of the 1958 data shown in Table 6-3, using methods essentially the same as those employed by Goldsmith.

position of that part of the stock of tangible personal property which actually is caught by the coarse net of the assessment process.[15] In the minority of states which subject motor vehicles to

[15] The data appear in "Taxable Property Values," Table 23. The twenty states covered in the treatment are those which tax some forms of personal property under the general property tax, provide the data needed for a state-wide disaggregation of personal property by major class, and do *not* have partial exemptions involving large dollar amounts which cannot be allocated by property class. All twenty states do not tax all forms of personalty or even all forms of tangible personalty: farm and nonfarm business personalty is quite generally subject to tax, but other types of personalty are subject to tax in half or fewer of the twenty states. Thus, the selected states are in no sense representative of the nationwide personal property tax base, but instead are an almost accidental grouping.

FIGURE 8. Value of Net Stock of Legally Taxable Tangible Assets, 1958, and Total Assessed Value of Tangible Personal Property, 1961

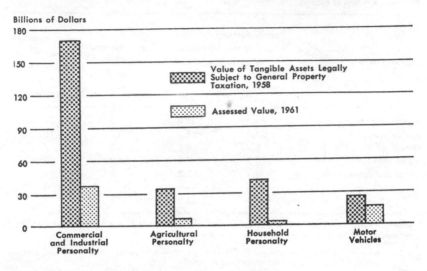

Sources: Tables 6-3 and 6-5, excluding data on public utility property.

the general property tax, motor vehicles tend to be a considerably larger proportion of the personal property tax base than one would expect on the basis of the Goldsmith estimates. On the other hand, even in the few states that contain significant amounts of household personalty assessments—Illinois, Missouri, New Jersey, North Carolina—household personalty nonetheless is far less important than Goldsmith would suggest.

Although these states are not representative, a summary of their experience is presented in Table 6-4, largely as a step toward a national estimate of the distribution of the tax base. Table 6-5 presents the estimates for the country as a whole. The procedure followed first produced an estimate, on the basis of various state economic series and of legal exemption provisions, of the proportion of the total legal tax base accounted for by the states included in Table 6-4, for each of the major categories. For example, in 1960, total motor vehicle registrations in the twenty-one states which subject motor vehicles to the general property tax were 27.6 million; registrations in the eight states included in Table 6-4 which tax motor vehicles in this manner were 11.1 million, or 40 percent of the relevant national total. To avoid the problem of partial exemptions (important for states other than those covered by Table 6-4), the weights were applied to the percentages in the final column of Table 6-4.

With respect to tangible personalty which is locally assessed for general property taxation, commercial and industrial personalty seems markedly heavily represented relative to its share of national wealth, and farm personalty somewhat overrepresented. However, when state assessed personalty and assessments for special property taxes—largely for motor vehicles—are added, the picture changes sharply.

Business equipment and inventories, both farm and nonfarm, are a fraction of total assessments more or less consistent with their share of national wealth, and assessments equal about one-fifth of legally taxable national wealth in this form. Household durables, which amount to roughly one-fourth of national wealth in the form of privately owned tangible personalty, are less than 5 percent of total personalty assessments, and only about 6 percent of the value of legally taxable national wealth in this form. Motor vehicles, in sharp contrast, are strikingly overassessed in relative terms: they amount to one-fourth of total tangible personalty assessments, and over 40 percent of the estimated value of legally taxable vehicles does in fact appear on the assessment rolls, an extraordinarily high proportion.[16]

Revenue from Taxation of Personal Property

Because of geographic differences in tax rates and the complex pattern of special property tax provisions, composition of the tax base and the sources of tax revenue are not identical. One reasonably reliable set of estimates is available with which to begin an analysis of personal property tax revenues. In early 1963, the Census

---

[16] Although relatively overassessed, motor vehicles may be actually taxed at special low rates, as is the case in California.

Bureau made special tabulations for this study of data from the 1957 Census of Governments, designed to produce estimates of general property tax revenues in 1957 from each of the property use classes employed in the 1957 Census.[17] Operating under the implicit assumption that variation in property tax rates within counties (and independent cities) is less significant than the variation in rates among county areas (counties and independent cities), the Bureau estimated the distribution of general property tax revenues by use class for each of 516 of the nation's 3,096 county areas, a size-stratified sample developed for nationwide tax collection estimation purposes. Within each county area, the distribution of revenues was assumed to mirror the distribution of net taxable assessed values. The county area estimates were then cumulated and blown up to national totals.

Two of the resulting estimates are relevant here and form the basis for the first two lines of Table 6-6:

	Estimated Revenue ($ million)	Percentage of Total	Percentage of Total Taxable Assessments
State assessed property	$ 953	7.7%	8.2%
Locally assessed personal property	2,110	17.0	17.3

The figures in Table 6-6, distinguishing tangible and intangible personalty and separating out state assessed realty and personalty, are based on the author's estimates (supported by some Census data) of the composition of assessments of these two Census categories, shown in Table 6-1. The distribution of revenue from special, as distinct from general, property taxes is based on the Census of Governments data shown in Table 6-7. The overall estimate, then, is that personal property taxes yielded $2.5 billion in 1957, 19.7 percent of total property tax revenues of $12.9 billion. Of the 19.7 percent, 17.7 percent was from tangible personal property, and 2.0 percent, or about $250 million, was from intangibles. As noted earlier, a comparable estimate for intangibles for 1961 is about $300 million, or 1.5 percent of total property tax collections.

In Table 6-8, there is a further disaggregation of revenue from taxation of tangible personalty. Figures shown for locally assessed

[17] The findings of these tabulations are discussed more fully in Chap. II.

TABLE 6-6. Estimated Revenue from Taxation of Personal Property (Excluding Public Utility Property), 1957

(In millions of dollars)

Type of Tax	Tangibles	Intangibles	Total
General property taxes[a]			
State assessed property	$ 34	$ 17	$ 51
Locally assessed property	2,043	67	2,110
Subtotal	2,077	84	2,161
Special property taxes[b]	202	171	373
Total	2,279	255	2,534

[a] Based on a special tabulation done by the Census Bureau using data from the 1957 Census of Governments, with total revenue from state assessed property allocated by the author on the basis of the assessed valuation data shown in Table 1, and total revenue from locally assessed personal property similarly allocated between tangibles and intangibles.

[b] Based on *Census of Governments: 1957*, Vol. V, "Taxable Property Values in the United States" (1959), Tables 1 and 23 (see Table 6-7, below).

general property taxation are simply an extension of the assessment distribution presented in the first column of Table 6-5. As such, revenues from agricultural personalty are probably overstated, since

TABLE 6-7. Revenue from Special Property Taxes, 1957, by Type of Property

Level of Government and Type of Property	Number of States Involved	Revenues, 1957 ($ million)[a]	Percentage of Total
Total state-local revenue from special property taxes	35	$421.6	100.0%
State revenue	33	267.6	63.5
Local revenue	20	153.9	36.5
Intangibles—total	20	170.5	40.4
state	14	92.1	21.8
local	14	78.4	18.6
Motor vehicles—total	8	200.3	47.5
state	6	124.8	29.6
local	6	75.5	17.9
Transportation and public utility property (state)	22	48.6	11.5
Machinery and inventories (state)	1	2.1[b]	0.5
Other (state)	1	*	*

Source: U. S. Bureau of the Census, *Census of Governments: 1957*, Vol. V, "Taxable Property Values in the United States" (1959), Tables 1 and 23.

* Less than $50,000 or 0.05 percent.

[a] Distribution of approximately $5 million of revenue for 2 states is estimated.

[b] Includes about $500,000 of farm products and livestock, and $1.6 million of machinery, largely manufacturing.

TABLE 6-8. Estimated Revenue from Taxation of Tangible Personal Property, by Type of Property, 1957

(In millions of dollars)

Type of Property	General Property Taxes		Special Property Taxes[b]	Total
	State Assessed	Locally Assessed[a]		
Commercial and industrial	$34[c]	$1,318	$ 2	$1,354
Agricultural	—	235	—	235
Household	—	110	—	110
Motor vehicles	—	270	200	470
Other and unallocable	—	110	—	110
Total[d]	34	2,043	202	2,279

Sources: Tables 6-5, 6-6, and 6-7.

[a] Taxes on locally assessed properties allocated on the basis of the percentage distribution shown in the first column of Table 6-5; this assumes implicitly that geographic rate differences are of small consequence. There is some likelihood that the results overstate the revenues from agricultural properties on this score. The "other and unallocable" category also appears to be overstated, and moreover, undoubtedly largely comprises business property (other than motor vehicles). Thus, a rough guess is that commercial and industrial personalty probably accounts for more than 70 percent of the total in this column, instead of 64.5 percent.

[b] From Table 6-7.

[c] Includes property used in mining.

[d] Totals from Table 6-6.

property tax rates tend to be markedly lower in nonurban areas (because of the lesser demand for public services), and revenues from business personalty understated.[18] It is also likely that general property tax revenues from motor vehicles are overstated, since half of the twenty-one states taxing motor vehicles in this manner are in the South where nominal property tax rates tend to be below the national average.

If the "other and unallocable" is distributed among the other categories (with a heavy share to commercial and industrial), a rough guess is that the actual distribution looks something like this:

Commercial and industrial	66%
Agricultural	9
Household	5
Motor vehicles	20

Thus, in the aggregate, it appears that the existence of personal property taxation amounts mainly to a substantial increase in the

[18] The Department of Agriculture estimates personal property taxes paid by farmers in 1957 at $233 million, including property taxes on farm motor vehicles. It is likely that 10 to 15 percent of this amount applies to motor vehicles.

share of the property tax borne by business property above that which would be indicated by consideration of the tax on real property only.

Geographic Differences in the Relative Importance of Personal Property in the Tax Base

As the above discussion of the extensive interstate differences in the legal and administrative treatment of personal property would suggest, the geographic differences in the relative importance of personalty in the tax base are considerable. In five states, approximately one-third of assessed value subject to general property taxation is in the form of locally assessed personalty.[19] In four others, at the other extreme, the percentage is zero. In the median state in 1961, the percentage was nearly 19.

There are some broad regional differences, although the differences are not pronounced. In the Northeast, personalty tends to be a smaller share of the tax base than for the country as a whole, while in the South and Midwest, personalty frequently comprises a sizeable portion of the tax base, as the following tabulation, by number of states, shows:

	Personalty as Percentage of Assessed Value Subject to Tax, 1961[20]		
	0–14	*15–24*	*25–34*
Northeast	8	4	0
South	2	7	5
Great Lakes and Plains	0	7	5
Mountain and Pacific	4	8	1
All states	14	26	11

Differences in the composition of the stock of privately owned wealth do not appear to explain very much of the interstate difference in reliance on personal property taxation. Similarly, differences in levels of income or in the basic nature of state-local

[19] Data in this section are from "Taxable Property Values."
[20] Percentages have been adjusted for Illinois, Kentucky, and Maryland to account for large amounts of state assessed personalty. For this comparison, the southern border of the Northeast region has been set at the Potomac.

fiscal systems (for example, the extent of reliance on the property tax overall) do not provide useful explanatory variables. Rank order correlation coefficients were computed for state data for personalty as a percentage of the tax base against each of the following variables:

- Commercial and industrial realty as a percent of total locally assessed realty
- Residential realty as a percent of total locally assessed realty
- State and local expenditures per $1,000 of personal income
- Property taxes per $1,000 of personal income and
- Property taxes as a percent of total state and local general revenue.

In all cases, there was a small (and insignificant) negative correlation.

Interstate differences thus appear to be largely the consequence of almost random differences in the legal coverage of the property tax. This is to be expected in the light of the historical evolution of the tax: a long-term trend toward a tax confined to real property. All sorts of institutional differences among the states would make this trend an inherently uneven one. For example, the long tradition of rigid constitutional interpretation and a difficult constitution-amending process explain the persistence of the all-inclusive legal nature of the property tax in Illinois, whereas in the District of Columbia, in contrast, there are no constitutional obstacles to exempting forms of personalty from taxation.

Furthermore, this explanation is consistent with some regional similarities. One would expect neighboring states to emulate one another in the process of progressively exempting personalty, partly, of course, because legislators and governors are more aware of developments in states nearby than in those at a distance. Equally significant, states within the same region are typically direct competitors economically and taxpayers are likely to exert greater pressure for exemption when their nearby competitors in an adjacent state enjoy exemption.

Within a single legal and institutional framework (that is, within a single state), differences in the composition of the stock of wealth should explain the differences in the importance of personalty in the property tax base. Thus, within a single state, since commercial and industrial personalty is so large a component of the personal property tax base and since nonfarm business property tends to be concentrated in urban areas, personalty should be more important in urban than in nonurban areas. In fact, there are forty-five standard metropolitan statistical areas with a 1960 population of 500,000 or more located in states which do *not* completely exempt personalty. In two-thirds of these large urban complexes personalty looms larger in the tax base, either for the metropolitan area as a whole or for the central city, than for the less populous districts of their respective states.[21] Moreover, within individual metropolitan areas, personalty is distinctly more important in the tax base in the central cities than in outlying suburbs. For the country as a whole, however, personalty is relatively more important in the less populous counties (see Appendix A), primarily because state property tax systems as a whole rely less heavily on personalty in the urban states (see Table 5-2).

Incidence of Personal Property Taxation

Any meaningful analysis of the incidence and effects of a given type of tax attempts to differentiate between the consequences of the particular tax and the effects of alternative courses of action. The alternatives may be other types of taxes, or a reduction in expenditures by the amount of the tax; in the latter case, the incidence and effects of the foregone expenditures must enter the analysis.[22] The evidence suggests that the existence of the personal property tax does not produce higher levels of state-local expenditure; at the very least, as indicated above, there is no correlation between the importance of personal property as a subject of taxation among the states and state expenditure levels.

A more reasonable hypothesis is that the personal property tax is in practice a substitute for other forms of state and local taxation. The alternatives to personal property taxation relevant to an analysis of incidence appear to be some combination of heavier state taxation of consumption, business activity, or personal income and/or

[21] A number of the exceptions are in states where motor vehicles—more important in nonurban areas—are a major source of personal property taxation.

[22] In dealing with subnational governments, borrowing can be ignored, since it is for the most part only a short-run alternative to tax increases or expenditure reductions.

heavier local taxation of real property. Investigators dealing with the tax in particular states or jurisdictions will choose different alternatives, based on the institutional environment. Thus, in the only recent discussion of the subject—for Minnesota in 1958—the comparison was with four variants of a proposed new state sales tax.[23]

Personalty Tax vs. Heavier Realty Taxes

In this study, it seems most useful to begin by considering the personal property tax as a substitute for heavier property taxes on real property. On a nationwide basis, the personal property tax has a sharp impact on nonfarm business, with householders largely excluded from its net, but with motor vehicle owners (both businesses and households) hard hit in some states. Where motor vehicles are taxed, most of the impact of this element of the tax is on households, because business-owned vehicles are a relatively small share of the total (see Table 6-2). The incidence of the property tax on household vehicles is likely to be on the owners, for the most part; the tax is not general enough in its application, nor applied at high enough rates, to dampen purchases of motor vehicles sufficiently (in the light of a probably low price elasticity for automobiles) to produce significant backward shifting to suppliers of automobiles.[24]

In the majority of states in which motor vehicles are not taxed, elimination of the personal property tax and heavier taxation of realty would on balance mean lighter taxation of business property and heavier taxation of residential realty, since residential property is so large a share of realty in most of the country. Whether this is good or bad public policy depends, of course, on the incidence of the two schemes of taxation, not merely their nominal impact. From the standpoint of one particular state, the relevant groupings of ultimate tax burden bearers might be: (1) resident consumers and householders; (2) within-state businesses, their local suppliers, and their locally purchased factors of production; (3) out-of-state purchasers of local output; and (4) out-of-state suppliers and factors of production.

Consider states such as Minnesota, Ohio, Wisconsin, New Jer-

---

[23] Thomas F. Hady, "The Incidence of the Personal Property Tax," *National Tax Journal*, Vol. 15 (December 1962), pp. 368-84, especially pp. 381-83.

[24] This ignores, as does the subsequent discussion, the shifting which stems from federal income tax deductibility of state and local tax payments; this applies to alternative state-local taxes as well.

sey, and Oregon, where well over 80 percent of the personal property tax base is composed of business property (farm as well as non-farm). In such states, the tax on household goods can be ignored, and thus the part of the personal property tax which comes to rest on residents as consumers will stem mainly from the forward shifting of personal property taxes paid by local businesses. Backward shifting to out-of-state suppliers and factors (group 4) is likely to be small, consisting mainly of the burden on out-of-state owners of local corporations unable to shift the tax; a Wisconsin survey suggests that two-thirds of the income of Wisconsin corporations is assignable to Wisconsin residents.[25]

In general, producers of goods and services which are largely sold in national (or broad regional) markets will be unable to shift the tax forward to out-of-state purchasers, because of the existence of competitors in other states who do not face the same personal property tax situation. The tax burden might be exported in this case, if the product does not face such competition, either because the state in question produces a very large proportion of total output (such as iron ore in Minnesota), or because similar tax provisions apply in the states which account for most of the output. For example, the five leading wheat producing states which account for more than half the nation's output are all states which have relatively heavy dependence on personal property taxation and tax agricultural personalty; in years when market considerations govern wheat prices and farm income, personal property taxes on wheat growers are likely to be shifted forward and exported from the state.

But the more usual situation for national market activities will involve competition precluding forward shifting. The tax will be borne by owners of local businesses, or by other factor inputs, to the extent that these cannot transfer to activities in which personal property taxation is less of a problem (because less inventory and equipment are required per dollar of output), notably landowners in the case of agriculture.

[25] University of Wisconsin Tax Study Committee, *Wisconsin's State and Local Tax Burden* (University of Wisconsin School of Commerce, 1959), p. 44. This was based on a questionnaire survey of Wisconsin corporations. There is some evidence that the percentage of local ownership of Wisconsin industry is unusually large, at least in the Milwaukee area. (See Federal Reserve Bank of Chicago, *Annual Report 1956*, pp. 22-23.) However, the proportion of resident ownership is probably high in older industrial states in general.

Producers of goods and services sold largely within the state will be able to shift the tax forward to consumers unless they face heavy competition from out-of-state producers or unless they confront a high degree of price elasticity of demand. The most significant intrastate producers from the standpoint of the personal property tax are wholesalers and retailers who face taxes on their inventories. The Minnesota study cited above suggests that inventory taxes relative to sales are heaviest for hardware, drug, and furniture stores, which are not those confronting very high price elasticities.[26] Thus, a fair amount of forward shifting seems likely.

Hady, for Minnesota in 1958, concludes that about one-tenth of the personal property tax burden (other than that shifted to the federal government via income tax deductions) was borne by out-of-state residents, about 50 percent by local consumers, and 40 percent by local business owners and other factor inputs, including farmers and farm landowners.[27] This adds up to a fairly regressive tax, little of which is exported to other states.[28] More elaborate and refined assumptions, based on examination of industry data, probably would produce the conclusion that a somewhat larger share of the burden falls on local businesses and factor inputs, at least in industrialized states, but the change in proportions should not be a large one.

Substitution of heavier taxation of realty for the personal property tax would shift the burden on balance in the direction of consumers, as noted earlier. In New Jersey, for example, 1962 property tax revenues were distributed as follows:[29]

Nonfarm residential realty		58.7%
Nonresidential subtotal		41.3
Farm and business realty	28.5%	
Farm and business personalty	9.7	
Vacant lots	3.1	

[26] Hady, in *National Tax Journal*, pp. 380-81. The evidence used here is a combination of assessment to book value ratios (for inventories) and sales to inventory ratios.

[27] *Ibid.*, pp. 374-76.

[28] Alternative shifting assumptions do not appreciably change the degree of regressivity.

[29] Based on New Jersey Commission on State Tax Policy, *Tenth Report* (1963), pp. 91-93. Data adjusted to take account of estimated distribution of veterans exemptions.

Hady's conclusions on the incidence of taxes on business personal property seem roughly applicable to New Jersey.[30] That is, assume that one-tenth of the business property tax burden is exported to out-of-state purchasers and suppliers and that the rest is equally divided in its incidence between local consumers and local businesses and factor inputs. This, then, would be the incidence of the property tax in 1962 in New Jersey:

Sector of Incidence	*Class of Property*		
	Residential	*Business*	*All Classes*
Consumers	58.7%	18.6%	77.3%
Business and farm (including factors)	—	18.6	18.6
Out of state	—	4.1	4.1
All sectors	58.7	41.3	100.0

Suppose, however, that New Jersey did *not* tax personalty, but raised the same property tax revenues from the existing realty tax base. In 1962, taxes on real property were distributed in this manner:

Nonfarm residential realty	65.0%
Farm and business realty	31.6
Vacant lots	3.4

Applying the incidence findings of the preceding paragraph to this distribution of tax revenues, the results are:

Sector of Incidence	*Class of Property*		
	Residential	*Business*	*All Classes*
Consumers	65.00%	15.75%	80.75%
Business and farm (including factors)	—	15.75	15.75
Out of state	—	3.50	3.50
All sectors	65.00	35.00	100.00

Thus, the share of local consumers rises, in this example, from 77 percent to 81 percent of total property tax liability, a small but significant redistribution.

[30] With allocation of vacant lots to the business sector, in this comparison.

The New Jersey data can also be used to compare business property tax payments with economic activity within the state and to compare New Jersey with an adjacent state—Pennsylvania—which does *not* tax personalty. In 1961, New Jersey property taxes on commercial and industrial property (excluding utility property) amounted to an estimated $301 million: $230 million on realty and $71 million on personal property.[31] If the personal property tax had been eliminated and replaced by increased realty taxes, commercial and industrial property owners would have paid $258 million, or almost one-sixth less. Property taxes on commercial and industrial property in New Jersey in 1961 amounted to 2.9 percent of the estimated net product of the industries relevant to this comparison—manufacturing, construction, mining, trade, finance (excluding real estate), and services (excluding private households, education, and nonprofit organizations).[32] This is the comparison of the two tax systems in New Jersey and the existing system in Pennsylvania:

	New Jersey		Pennsylvania
	Actual	Personalty Exempt	Actual
Commercial and industrial realty	2.2%	2.4%	1.2%
Commercial and industrial personalty	0.7	—	—
Total percentage of net product	2.9	2.4	1.2

For firms in the two states which compete in national markets, the contrast is a striking one. Were all other business taxes similar in the two states (which is clearly not the case), New Jersey firms which compete in national markets would have considerably lower net earnings or, to the extent they employ relatively immobile factors, factor returns would be lower. In this example, the height of

[31] 1961 data are used for comparability with subsequent materials; 1962 proportions have been applied to 1961 tax collections, with an adjustment for household personalty which was not tax exempt in the earlier year.

[32] The state's share of national income originating in these industries in 1961, derived on the basis of various allocators—wage and salary payments, value of output, and value added—for 1959, 1960, and 1961—from the Census Bureau's *Statistical Abstract of the United States, 1962,* and from the July 1962 issue of the *Survey of Current Business,* Office of Business Economics, Department of Commerce.

the real property tax makes even more of a difference than the existence of the personal property tax; if New Jersey were compared with New York, where effective property tax rates are also very high but where personalty is not taxed, the comparison would be more satisfying.[33]

Campbell's analysis of tax burdens for selected types of manufacturing firms in the New York Metropolitan Region, at various locations, permits a limited comparison of this type.[34] It indicates that the typical manufacturing firm in northern New Jersey pays real property taxes which are only slightly more than those paid by its counterpart in southern New York State, but in addition pays a personal property tax bill equal to half its realty tax bill. Again, were other business taxes the same in the two states, New Jersey competitors would be hard hit. But to the extent that they were able to shift their tax burdens backward to their employees, there would be some offset. This is because residential property taxpayers are substantially more heavily burdened in New York than in New Jersey, largely due to the absence of the personal property tax on business personalty. Thus, holding other things constant, housing costs to employees would be lower in New Jersey.

Tax on Business Personalty vs. Corporation Income Tax

Since other business taxes are not the same among the states, it is worthwhile comparing the major alternative business tax—the corporation income tax—with taxation of business personalty. A state corporation income tax is a partial tax[35] measured by business profits, and as such is probably less easily shifted than the tax on business personalty, but the more significant difference between the tax forms is their differential impact among industries. The issue here is the relation between profitability and requirements for equipment and inventory per dollar of output or, more appropriately, value added.[36] While it is reasonable to assume a strong posi-

---

[33] This comparison was not made above because the New York data for industrial property include a considerable amount of utility property.

[34] Alan K. Campbell, "Taxes and Industrial Location in the New York Metropolitan Region," *National Tax Journal,* Vol. 11 (September 1958), pp. 195-218.

[35] Partial both geographically and in regard to forms of business organization.

[36] Both profits and personalty requirements should be measured against value added if concern is not with the firm as such but with the volume of economic activity within the taxing jurisdiction.

tive relationship between profits per dollar of output and investment in plant and equipment per dollar of output by industry, there is much less reason to expect the relationship to be nearly as good for investment in equipment alone. Moreover, inventory requirements per dollar of output vary widely among industries. For example, on a seasonally adjusted basis in recent years, inventories have been running about 40 percent of national income originating for manufacturing industries as a group, about 50 percent for wholesale trade, and nearly 60 percent for retail trade.[37] Making for even more variation is the fact that, in some states, inventories are not assessed for tax purposes on a seasonally adjusted basis but as of assessment day. (Other states provide for averaging.)

In the absence of far more data on the relationships among equipment, inventories as of the dates of assessment, profits, and output, little can be said other than the bare statement that there are wide industry differentials in the impact of the two tax forms. It does seem likely, however, that trade activities, because of relatively greater inventory requirements, lower profitability, and lower proportion of business done in the corporate form, are more heavily burdened by a personal property tax than by a corporate income tax raising the same total revenues within the state. Manufacturers are likely to be in the converse position. Since trade firms can probably shift the taxes they pay more easily than can manufacturing firms (within a single state), the burden of personal property taxation thus is likely to fall more heavily on consumers within the state than would the burden of a state corporate income tax.

Summary

In current policy discussions at the state-local government level, concern with the incidence and effects of taxation centers on two issues: the distribution of the tax burden among individuals by income group and the impact of taxation on the location of economic activity that is relatively mobile. To some extent, these are competing considerations. A tax that is rather regressive, because it is largely paid by local consumers in proportion to consumption outlays, is likely to have minimal competitive effects on the location of economic activity. With this in mind, the characteristic personal

---

[37] *Statistical Abstract of the United States, 1962, passim.*

property tax can be compared, in summary, with other taxes raising the same total revenues:

1.   Compared to increased real property taxation, it probably has a greater impact on location, but is probably less regressive on the average.[38]

2.   Compared to a state corporate income tax, it probably has a lesser impact on location, but should be more regressive.

3.   Compared to a sales tax of the usual type, it has far more impact on location; it is apt to be somewhat less regressive if the sales tax has very few exemptions, but perhaps more regressive as exemptions and personal credits are added to the sales tax.[39] This conclusion is based on the assumption that retail sales taxes are largely shifted forward to consumers, in part because retailers in one state do not face significant competition from untaxed out-of-state businesses. Thus, the sales tax has little impact on location, and very little of the sales tax falls on either local firms or out-of-state residents, in contrast to the personal property tax.

4.   Comparison with a state personal income tax is difficult on the score of location, for there is at least some doubt that state personal income taxes at high rates are entirely harmless, as much of the literature avers. There is, of course, no question on the score of regressivity, by definition.

[38] Permanent income analyses suggest that there is little regressivity in housing expenditures; see, for example, Margaret G. Reid, *Housing and Income* (University of Chicago Press, 1962). Shifting the net tax impact from business personalty to residential realty might not appreciably increase regressivity, when regressivity is expressed in terms of permanent income.

[39] See Hady, in *National Tax Journal*, pp. 381-82, for a Minnesota comparison.

CHAPTER VII

A General Appraisal
of the Institution

CONSIDERED BY ITSELF and relative to the expenditures it finances, the American property tax has so far been found by this study to be defective on a number of economic counts, but by no means on all counts. It remains to appraise the economic merits of the existing institution vis-à-vis conceivable alternative sources of local government finance; to come to terms with the most widely discussed aspect of the property tax, the quality of its administration; and to examine the probable cause of its persistence in the face of nearly a century of hostile criticism: its capacity to produce revenues pure and simple.

The strongest part of the case for the property tax developed in preceding chapters emerges when it is considered in the aggregate and its revenue producing capabilities are held to have been at least partly responsible for the rapid growth in local public expenditure. So considered, the tax has positive advantages on both distributional and efficiency grounds. In aggregate terms, it contains a large measure of "vertical equity": that is, on balance, it redistributes income from the rich to the poor. This comes about because the tax itself is more or less proportional in its incidence among income groups, but the expenditures it finances are very heavily "pro-poor" in their incidence. The property tax in the aggregate also tends to increase the application of resources to high return human investment and may deter somewhat lower return investment in physical capital.

On a less global scale, the preceding chapters suggest that some charges leveled against the property tax are wide of the mark in practice. For example, the tax does not seem to be significant in inducing inefficient shifts in the spatial distribution of economic activity among regions of the country. Also, its deterrent effect on housing construction in general has been of small consequence in recent years, no doubt because of the link between property taxation and school expenditures in the suburban areas in which much postwar American housing has been built.

On the other hand, some obvious and frequent criticisms of the property tax have been sustained in earlier chapters. The tax may redistribute income in a desired direction, but it does this with great unevenness, both among and within tax jurisdictions. It is, in many metropolitan areas, regressive as between high income and low income government units.

Another frequent criticism leveled against the tax: that it is defective from the standpoint of horizontal equity, "equal treatment of equals," has been validated on two counts. First, gross inequalities in assessments relative to property value are the rule rather than the exception. (This aspect is discussed in greater detail below.) Second, either because of tastes or circumstances, consumption patterns vary widely among individuals with similar incomes. This affects taxes on both housing and nonresidential property. Within narrow income groups, housing consumption is quite variable; for example, in metropolitan areas in 1960, the coefficient of variation of house values for single-family homeowners with incomes of $6,000-$7,000 (the median range) was over .50.[1] As a consequence of this, plus geographic differentials and assessment practices, real estate taxes as a proportion of income vary widely within income classes; in the 1960 Census of Housing, for homeowners in the $3,000-$5,000 range, 37 percent paid real estate taxes equal to less

[1] $(Q3-Q1) \div Q2$. Estimated from U. S. Bureau of the Census, *Census of Housing: 1960*, "Metropolitan Housing," Final Report HC (2)-1 (1963), Table B-3.

than 2 percent of income, 30 percent paid taxes equal to from 2 percent to 4 percent of income, and 33 percent paid taxes equal to more than 4 percent of income (see Table 3-7 above).

The tax also has objectionable interindustry effects. In most cases, these are conceived more readily than they are perceived in practice. However, the railroad case cited in Chapter IV is a fairly clear-cut example of the way in which differentially high taxes on the real property factor of production can have competitive ramifications which are distorting.

The adverse consequences of the tax for the spatial distribution of economic activity within urban areas, in contrast, is readily apparent. Heavy taxation of real property is a deterrent to rebuilding of the big cities, especially when it is high in relation to the prevailing rates in the suburbs. Dependence on the property tax for local finance, moreover, encourages land use planning in the developing parts of urban areas designed to maximize narrow, parochial fiscal advantage, rather than economic efficiency or broader social goals.

Alternatives to the Property Tax

When the property tax is compared on economic grounds to other revenue sources for local governments, the issue is really a twofold one depending on the following questions: First, is a tax on housing, equivalent to a very high excise on housing expenditures on the average, better or worse than the alternatives as a means of local finance? Second, is a fairly substantial ad valorem property tax on business property—substantial on the average but widely varying geographically and by industry and firm—the best way to tax business on the local level, if indeed business per se should be locally taxed?

In hypothesizing conceivable alternatives to the property tax, it is useful to commence by assuming complete revenue replacement, for this removes from the area of argument a wide range of lesser taxes, in particular the selective sales taxes, which are utterly incapable of producing adequate revenues on their own. For example, in 1963, personal consumption expenditures for alcoholic beverages and tobacco products amounted to $19.2 billion, excluding excises; excises used by all levels of government equalled about 40

TABLE 7-1. Estimated Nationwide Average Tax Rates Required for Alternative Replacements for Local Property Revenue, 1963[a]

Tax Form	Estimated 1963 Tax Base (Billions of dollars)	Rate Required to Yield $20 Billion (Percentage)
Gross receipts[b]	$981	2.0
Value added in private business[c]	373	5.4
Business profits[d]	99	20.2
Corporate profits	49	41.0
Payrolls	312	6.4
Individual income:[e]		
Federal adjusted gross income	367	5.5
Federal taxable income	204	9.8
Personal consumption expenditures:		
Money outlays for goods[f]	216	9.3
Money outlays for goods, excluding food and ethical drugs	152	13.2
Money outlays for goods plus selected consumer services[g]	247	8.1
Liquor and tobacco	19	104.2

Sources: U. S. Department of Commerce, Office of Business Economics, *Survey of Current Business*, July 1964; U. S. Treasury Department, *Statistics of Income, Individual Income Tax Returns*, 1962 (*Preliminary*), Publication No. 198 (1964).

[a] Calendar 1963 local property tax revenues estimated at $20 billion.

[b] Total retail and wholesale sales plus corporate sales in other industries.

[c] National income originating in business less net rental of owner-occupied dwellings and net imputed interest paid.

[d] Corporate profits before tax plus proprietors' income.

[e] Based on 1962 relationship of federal tax items to personal income.

[f] Expenditures for goods excluding in kind consumption and expenditures abroad.

[g] Services include utilities, admissions and amusements, and personal, clothing, appliance and auto care and repair.

percent of this total.[2] Local property tax collections in the calendar year 1963 amounted to about $20 billion; complete replacement by tobacco and liquor taxes would require sales tax rates in excess of 100 percent.

Table 7-1 suggests the level of nationwide average rates which would have been required for complete replacement of the local property tax in 1963. A gross receipts tax, uniformly despised (with good reason) by public finance analysts, would have required a 2 percent rate. A value added tax or a personal income tax without exemptions or deductions would have involved average rates in the 5 percent range. A net income tax with federal exemptions and

[2] U. S. Department of Commerce, Office of Business Economics, *Survey of Current Business*, July 1964, Tables 14, 19, and 20.

deductions or a personal consumption tax of the conventional nature (excluding most outlays for services) would have required rates in the neighborhood of 10 percent. Any narrower base—such as business profits—would produce much higher rates.

Increased Taxation of Personal Consumption

A case can be made for partial replacement of the property tax on housing by increased, across-the-board taxation of personal consumption. In 1963, property taxes on housing probably amounted to nearly $9 billion, equal to an excise on housing expenditures of 17-18 percent (see Chapter II). General retail sales tax revenues were in the neighborhood of $6 billion, implying an overall average rate of tax, including jurisdictions not using the tax, of less than 3 percent against consumption expenditures.[3] A reduction of the average housing property tax rate by about two-thirds, together with a near-doubling of average sales tax rates to replace the lost revenue, would yield a more nearly uniform consumption tax, with average rates in the 5.5-6.0 percent range.

Such a uniform tax would answer some of the main objections to the present housing tax: its lack of horizontal equity among individuals and its deterrent effects on housing construction. It is, perhaps, the best conceptual solution, on the assumption that consumption will continue to be a major basis for state-local taxation in any event. This basis can be challenged, of course: any general consumption tax is likely to be more regressive at the extreme ends of the income distribution than a proportional income tax yielding the same revenue.

This conceptual solution does raise a side issue: if a reduced property tax on housing is to be retained as the housing counterpart of a general tax on nonhousing consumption expenditures, should not the base be housing expenditures rather than property values? One argument against this is the problem of what to include. If all actual expenditures connected with housing are taxed, then differences in size of mortgages and in debt service payments on mortgages, which are determined by both the initial financial position of the purchaser and the recency of purchase, will cause differences in taxes on otherwise identical housing. The resolution

[3] The characteristic tax base includes some intermediate business purchases.

of this difficulty is to tax assessed net or gross rentals. As argued in the next chapter, if the former is taxed, the distribution of liabilities is no different from that under a tax on values, which in concept equal capitalized net rents. If gross rents are taxed, there is a real deterrent to maintenance of rental properties. And, in practice, since most American housing is owner-occupied, assessment of rents would be no easier than assessment of values.

"Social Overhead" Charges

Because of both theoretical and practical difficulties of measurement, the business component of the property tax is essentially levied on the basis of a set of proxies for the market value of the properties involved; some of the proxies are relatively close parallels, but many are not. By and large (and this is discussed further in the next chapter), this type of tax on business has no more merit than other general taxes on business as a user charge for public services consumed by business. Similarly, all general taxes on business seem equally bad considered as a form of "social diseconomy" charge—that is, as compensation for some of the external diseconomies arising from business operations, such as air pollution, congestion, and unpleasant esthetic effects. The relative volume of output, receipts, profits, and property value are all poorly correlated with consumption of public services or production of diseconomies.

Aside from pure opportunism—taxing business solely because it is a convenient source of revenue—the principal remaining argument for a general local tax on business is that business operations should contribute to "social overheads." The costs of maintaining a functioning government and a going community, without which business could not operate, are in part a justifiable component of the costs of production, to be paid as taxes by business, and to be reflected in the prices at which output is sold so that tax payments are recouped from consumers. But the notion of taxation as a contribution to social overheads is by no means a clear-cut concept. The package of local public services is a diverse one, with both collective and individual benefits and major geographic spillovers. It may be that opportunism is the only defensible argument for local business taxation. But allocational efficiency appears to demand that social overhead charges, if any, be distributed among businesses not in proportion to investment in plant, equipment, and inventories, but in proportion to the scale of business activities in the community. Indeed, if business is to be taxed to support local government in general, the most reasonable basis seems to be the value of output —that is, value added.[4] As Table 7-1 indicates, replacement of the $10 billion or so in taxes on farm and business property would have required a value added tax rate of close to 3 percent in 1963.

These strictures on the relative economic demerits of the business property tax—and, indeed, of the housing property tax—do not apply to the land component of the tax. Taxation of the bare site value of land will not deter investment in physical capital and will not change the composition of inputs, since the capitalization of site value taxes into lower land prices will maintain the cost of land as an input at its tax-free level. But the land component aside, general taxes on consumption or income and a general value added tax seem clearly preferable alternatives on economic grounds to both the housing and business property taxes.

Advantages of the Property Tax

This is not enough, however, to dispose of the case for local government reliance on the property tax. Its unique advantage is that it alone is amenable to small incremental changes in rate; other taxes seem practicable to administer only if rates are changed relatively infrequently and in relatively large discrete jumps.[5] Such flexibility is advantageous in that it reduces what has been called "tax tension"; there need not be pitched battles fought every year about tax rates, since the changes are relatively small. Of course, this is a consequence of the residual determination of property tax rates: assessments and expenditure budgets are independently determined, and the tax rate is the result. Thus, the fiscal issue in local finance is apt to be joined on the question of expenditures rather than tax rates, which seems an appropriate arrangement. To the extent that expenditures and tax rates are simultaneously determined in the local political process, citizens are consciously relating the value of

[4] This argument is fully and explicitly developed by Harvey E. Brazer in "The Value of Industrial Property As a Subject of Taxation," *Canadian Public Administration*, Vol. 55 (June 1961), pp. 137-47.

[5] But consider here the annual rate changes in unemployment insurance taxes which occur under many state experience-rating systems.

additional expenditures to their tax costs, which surely approaches the ideal prescription for the budget process with respect to the resource allocation "branch" of the public sector.

One partial rejoinder to all this is that the need for continual changes in nominal property tax rates at times has been a consequence of the sluggish response of the tax base to changes in the economy—notably in periods of rapid price level change—relative to other taxes whose responsive bases make rate changes less frequent. But, as will be seen below, this rejoinder has been of limited validity in the past fifteen years. A second rejoinder is that other taxes might be managed on the basis of small but frequent rate changes if administered in a similar manner to the property tax. These frequent rate changes in the property tax are workable in large part because tax liability is not self-assessed but determined by the tax collector who bills each taxpayer for the amount due. If businesses and individuals were to report their value added, sales, or income, and then be billed for the amounts due, small frequent rate changes would be equally practicable for nonproperty taxes. The disadvantage of such a method would be the inability to collect taxes on a reasonably current basis; they would then be subject to the same kind of deferred payment which prevails under the property tax, and which can, and does on occasion, create hardship for both governments and taxpayers.

Another advantage claimed for the property tax is that it is closely and perhaps uniquely linked to local autonomy. In part, this claim is founded on comparative and historical observations both in the United States and elsewhere: local government is most important where property taxation is heavily relied upon. There are exceptions in Scandinavia, Germany, and elsewhere. The tie between the two phenomena seems to be as much an historical accident as an unavoidable link. Another facet of the local autonomy argument is the claim that the property tax is uniquely suited to local administration, a claim critically reviewed below. Still other parts of the argument rely on the possibility for considerable local variation in rates in response to differing local needs and tastes (a situation appraised in Chapter V) and on the relative immobility of real property.

It is frequently asserted that property is a good basis for taxation by relatively small local governments simply because the tax base, at least in the short run, cannot be moved beyond the reach of the local tax collector in response to higher rates. The usual counterpart of the assertion is a comparison with sales or excise taxes: consumers can readily shift their purchases to stores in adjacent low tax or tax free jurisdictions, especially in this automobile age.

This is a valid comparison, but the comparison does not extend with equal force to other conceivable forms of local taxation. If residents are taxed heavily on their incomes, or if nonresidents are taxed heavily on their local earnings, they can escape taxation only by moving their residences or changing their employment. It is not at all obvious that a resident would move out any more readily in response to heavy income taxation than he would in response to heavy property taxes on his house; in both cases, the physical commitment produces immobility in the short run but not over time. Similarly, a differentially large value added tax (or payroll tax or profits tax) in a community is likely to produce neither more nor less flight of business than a similar adversely differential property tax.

The essential point is that, in most circumstances, large differentials in the rates of *any* major local tax among neighboring and competitive jurisdictions are likely to be bad rather than good. Over time, they are likely to yield both an inefficient spatial distribution of economic activity and an increased degree of interpersonal inequity of the fiscal system of the overall metropolitan or other geographic region. This suggests that local tax autonomy as it is now known in American metropolitan areas is neither a viable nor a worthy goal, and to the extent that the property tax is an instrument of such a policy, it is a highly questionable institution.[6]

Sophisticated defenders of the property tax are by no means also defenders of extremes in intrametropolitan tax differentials; quite the opposite. There is little argument with the proposition that, if the property tax is here to stay, as is likely, reforms directed

[6] For a good summary evaluation of this point, see Harvey E. Brazer, "Some Fiscal Implications of Metropolitanism," in *Metropolitan Issues: Social, Governmental, Fiscal,* Guthrie S. Birkhead, ed. (Maxwell Graduate School of Citizenship and Public Affairs, Syracuse University, 1962; Brookings Institution Reprint 61, July 1962), pp. 71-82; see also Wilbur R. Thompson, *A Preface to Urban Economics* (The Johns Hopkins Press for Resources for the Future, 1965), Chap. VII, for an unusual and perceptive approach to the problem.

at widening its geographic net in urban areas are essential to reduce its adverse effects on urban land use. As noted in Chapter V, one avenue in this direction is some form of "fiscal federation," under which area-wide levies underwrite large portions of local expenditure. Another is increasing the role of existing governmental units with wider geographic coverages, such as county governments. A third is an increased role for state government nonproperty taxes in those urban states, like New Jersey and Massachusetts, where property tax rates and differentials are exceedingly high. All this may be applauded, but it should be noted that area-wide property taxation will further dilute the already attenuated relation between property tax liability and level of income, a relation which the Syracuse school holds to be a major argument for the property tax.[7]

Property Tax Administration

A tax institution may be found to be meritorious on distributional and efficiency grounds, or at least less harmful than alternatives which would be equally productive of revenue, and still be a highly defective means of financing government if it cannot be administered reasonably well—that is, equitably and at moderate cost. Both those who find that the property tax has various inherent advantages and those who feel that the property tax has little to commend it in concept are highly critical of the prevailing quality of property tax administration. This unanimity of dissatisfaction is nothing new. Criticisms similar to those current today have been made, often in similar language, almost continuously for seventy-five years or more.[8] Since individuals' liabilities for property taxes for the most part are not initially determined by the taxpayers themselves (unlike sales and income taxes) but by assessors who are public officials, the heart of the property tax administrative process is assessment administration, and the criticism has been addressed to assessment practices, procedures, and organization.

[7] See Chap. I, p. 8.

[8] The best recent overviews of the administrative problems are: Frederick L. Bird, *The General Property Tax: Findings of the 1957 Census of Governments* (Public Administration Service, 1960), and Advisory Commission on Intergovernmental Relations, *The Role of the States in Strengthening the Property Tax* (1963). Bird was the principal author of the latter.

Disadvantages of Current System

The details of the indictment of assessment administration need not be reviewed here. Essentially, the criticism reduces to three salient points. First, there is conclusive evidence that, within most individual assessment jurisdictions, even the most common, least heterogeneous properties—single-family nonfarm houses—are assessed at widely varying fractions of market value. Presumably, the variation is even greater for more complicated types of property. Second, within individual jurisdictions, owners of differing types of property are treated differently by assessors, sometimes systematically, albeit extralegally, but often quite erratically. Third, assessment practices and levels differ among assessment jurisdictions within a single county or state. This matters because some property levies apply over an area larger than a single assessment jurisdiction (for example, county levies where there are separate city, town, and village assessors), and because assessed values are often used for other purposes such as determination of state aid amounts and tax rate and debt limits.

The continued volume and strident nature of the criticism for so many years suggest that the quality of assessment administration has not improved much over the years, or at least has improved at an unacceptably slow rate. This in turn suggests the possibility that the fault may not lie in the obstinacy and ignorance of public officials and legislators; instead, acceptable assessment administration simply may not be attainable, at least at costs which are at all reasonable.

Is this in fact the case? Is the pursuit of uniformity in assessments quixotic or even downright harmful? The answer would clearly be positive if it can be demonstrated that the achievement of uniformity would involve unacceptably high administrative costs. The evidence on the present cost of property tax administration is sketchy, but it appears to be quite low relative to tax collections, which is to be expected in view of the generally poor quality of the administrative job. Apparently, local assessment administration seldom costs as much as 1 percent of collections in the larger jurisdictions: in New York City, the assessment and review process involves expenditures of only about $4 million, with collections of slightly more than $1 billion.[9] But there is some indication that better quality assessment is substantially more costly. It is generally agreed that the quality of assessment is relatively high in general in California and Wisconsin, as compared to, say, New York State;[10] California and Wisconsin local and state governments appear to spend substantially more for property tax administration than those in New York State. A similar comparison can be made of the City of Milwaukee and New York City, the former having relatively high grade and high cost administration and the latter showing much poorer results for a relatively smaller administrative outlay.[11]

Cost of "Good" Administration

If the assessment quality achieved in the best performing jurisdictions currently is the target, it may be entirely possible to get "good" property tax administration in the larger jurisdictions at a cost of no more than, say, 1.5 percent of tax collections, which is probably acceptable when compared to sales and income tax administration costs. But this standard and these levels of costs raise

[9] City of New York, *Executive Budget for the Fiscal Year 1963-64* (1963).

[10] This is borne out by the evidence of the 1962 Census of Governments. See Vol. II, "Taxable Property Values" (1963), Table 19.

[11] These comparisons are based on inferences drawn from the relation of expenditures for financial administration to property and total tax revenue in U. S. Bureau of the Census, *Governmental Finances in 1962* (Series G-GF62-No. 2, October 1963) and *Compendium of City Government Finances in 1962* (Series G-SF62-No. 2, 1963). For example, New York City's property tax revenue is 34 times as great. Yet it spends only 12 times as much for financial administration. To be sure, financial administration includes much more than assessment administration, but there can be little doubt that debt management, financial control, and administration of nonproperty taxes (nonexistent in Milwaukee) are far more complicated and disproportionately expensive in New York; Milwaukee may thus spend three or four times as much for property tax administration, relative to revenue, as New York. Moreover, scale economies are not likely to be overwhelming, for this comparison: there were 156,000 properties in Milwaukee and 805,000 in New York in 1961 (see "Taxable Property Values," Table 22). Again, all local governments in California spent one-third more for financial administration than their counterparts in New York State. Although total property tax collections are similar in the two states, the number of local governments with property tax levying power is virtually the same; and California has fewer and larger primary assessment jurisdictions, which should reduce costs relative to those in New York. In addition to local administrative costs, the state equalization agency spends twice as much for property tax matters in California as in New York (*The Role of the States in Strengthening the Property Tax*, Vol. 2).

real problems for smaller jurisdictions. If the assessment function is to be handled by a full-time professional staff, as has been repeatedly recommended over the years, even a minimal size jurisdiction is likely to have an annual budget of $60,000 to $70,000.[12] This budget will be less than 1.5 percent of tax collections only in jurisdictions with revenue of $4 million or more, which implies an average minimum population size of 40,000-50,000, since per capita property tax revenue currently averages about $100. In contrast, there are currently more than 18,000 primary assessment jurisdictions in the nation,[13] with an average population of only about 10,000. The problem would not be solved by eliminating assessment districts smaller than the county in size since less than a fifth of the nation's counties have a population of 50,000 or more, and many of these appear to have total property tax revenues (including the revenues of all governments within the county) of less than $4 million. This minimum size standard appears to be met by fewer than 500 counties and cities outside counties, and suggests that multi-county or state-wide assessment districts would be necessary in many places.

This may be eminently reasonable, but does some violence to the notion that one of the main virtues of the property tax is that it is suitable for use *and administration* by even small local governments. If local self-government, autonomy, and self-respect require local administration of the major revenue source, then it is clear that the property tax is *unsuitable* on administrative grounds; local autonomy is inconsistent with acceptable standards of administration at acceptable costs of administration, except for rather large local government units. Contemporary friends of the property tax (but apparently not legislators and local officials) would answer that assessment administration can be centralized without impairing local autonomy. After all, in England and Wales, valuation for the property tax (the rates) is done by the Inland Revenue, a central government agency, and English local governments are at least as autonomous vis-à-vis the central government in Westminster as are American local governments vis-à-vis their state governments.

[12] This is the implication of the recommendation in *The Role of the States in Strengthening the Property Tax,* Vol. 1, p. 105.

[13] *Ibid.,* p. 101.

TABLE 7-2. Dispersion of Assessment Ratios for Nonfarm Houses in Selected Local Areas, 1956 and 1961[a]

	1956[b]		1961[c]	
	Number of Areas	Percentage of Total Number	Number of Areas	Percentage of Total Number
Total number of selected areas	1,263	100	1,356	100
With a coefficient of intra-area dispersion (in percent)[d] of:				
Less than 15.0	100	8	186	14
15.0–19.9	158	13	220	16
20.0–24.9	191	15	240	18
25.0–29.9	184	15	194	14
30.0–39.9	267	21	253	19
40.0 or more	363	29	263	19

Note: Detail may not add to totals in percentage columns because of rounding.

[a] Ratios of assessments to sales, based on a sample of measurable sales taking place in a 6-month period in each year. Selected areas are sample areas having five or more sample sales of previously occupied single family houses.

[b] From U.S. Bureau of the Census, *Census of Governments: 1957*, Vol. V, "Taxable Property Values in the United States" (1959), Table 19.

[c] From U.S. Bureau of the Census, *Census of Governments: 1962*, Vol. II, "Taxable Property Values" (1963), Table 19.

[d] Average deviation of assessment ratios from the median ratio, as a percent of the median value.

Standard of Excellence

A more serious problem remains, however. Just how good is the standard achieved by those jurisdictions considered outstanding today? The standard of excellence now widely accepted is that set by Bird:[14] a jurisdiction does a good job if, in the 1957 or 1962 Census assessment sales ratio studies for single-family nonfarm houses, the average deviation from the median assessment ratio in that jurisdiction for this class of property is no more than 20 percent of the median ratio. By this standard, 21 percent of the areas studied in 1957 and 30 percent in 1962 did a good job (Table 7-2). A smaller percentage, 8 percent in 1957 and 14 percent in 1962, kept the dispersion within 15 percent of the median. Apparently, there was significant improvement in the five-year period, but just as apparently most assessors are still not doing an adequate job.

But the achievement of even a 15 percent or 20 percent coefficient of dispersion does not seem an impressively good job

[14] Frederick L. Bird, *The General Property Tax*.

TABLE 7-3. Assessment Ratios for Nonfarm Houses and for Locally Assessed Realty in General (Partial Coverage), Selected Major Cities, 1961[a]

(In percentages)

City	Nonfarm Houses: Sales-Based Average Assessment Ratio[b]	Partial Coverage of All Taxable Realty: Size-Weighted Average Assessment Ratio[c]
Coefficient of dispersion for nonfarm houses of less than 20 percent:[d]		
Atlanta (Fulton County portion)	18.1	15.5
Cincinnati	43.3	42.1
Cleveland	35.4	38.0
Kansas City (Clay County portion)	26.4	24.2
Los Angeles	20.4	17.3
Milwaukee	48.4	47.7
San Diego (entire county)	11.8	18.0
Washington, D.C.	47.2	48.5
Coefficient of dispersion of 20.0–29.9 percent:		
Baltimore	66.7	67.8
Buffalo (entire county)	27.3	28.6
Dallas	18.7	17.5
Detroit	42.9	45.2
Houston (entire county)	18.5	17.8
Kansas City (Jackson County portion)	26.1	23.5
Newark	44.6	43.9
Philadelphia	57.7	58.8
Pittsburgh	35.8	40.7
Seattle	13.9	15.2
Coefficient of dispersion of 30.0 percent or more:		
Boston	34.6	34.5
Chicago	35.5	44.2
Minneapolis	10.0	11.0
New York	47.6	58.0
St. Louis	35.6	27.9
San Francisco	11.8	15.9

[a] The 23 cities of over 300,000 which are primary centers of standard metropolitan statistical areas with a 1960 population of 1 million or more.

[b] From the U. S. Bureau of the Census, *Census of Governments: 1962*, Vol. II, "Taxable Property Values" (1963), Table 22.

[c] From a special tabulation by the Governments Division, U. S. Bureau of the Census, "Partial-Coverage Assessment Ratios For Locally Assessed Taxable Real Property in Selected Major Cities: 1961" (1963). Includes all classes of locally assessed realty except for high value properties with few sales measurable for this purpose; the value size cut-off varies but in no case exceeds $300,000. The percentages of total locally assessed values of taxable realty included here vary considerably, from about 50 to 96 in one case but the variation is not related to any of the variables in this table.

[d] The coefficient of dispersion is the average deviation of assessment ratios from the median ratio, as a percent of the median value.

when measured by the standards posted for the administration of other taxes. Since the assessment of a particular property determines its tax liability,[15] a 20 percent coefficient means that the average homeowner can expect to be faced with a tax bill which is 20 percent more or less than it "should be," given a legal requirement for uniformity. It is not conceivable that sales tax administrators would be satisfied if they found that retailers, on the average, were remitting tax payments which were 20 percent greater or less than the legal requirement. Nor would income tax administrators condone such a situation. Moreover, since single-family houses are the simplest, most homogeneous class of property, the appropriate analogy in the income tax is not the accuracy of returns with regard to all income taxpayers, but with regard to taxpayers whose income is almost entirely from wages and salaries. For such taxpayers, the margin of error on unaudited returns might be in the neighborhood of 5 percent, not 20 percent, with a fourth or so of this error corrected in the normal audit program, at least at the federal level of income tax administration.[16] In the 1962 Census of Governments, only one of the 1,356 selected areas had a coefficient of dispersion as low as 5 percent, and only eight others had coefficients that ranged between 5 percent and 10 percent.

Moreover, jurisdictions which meet the Bird standard for assessment of single-family houses often assess other classes of property at levels which differ from those obtained for single-family houses.[17] Table 7-3 illustrates this by comparing average assessment ratios for single-family houses and for all locally assessed realty except the highest value properties (for which the sales evidence on which to base such computations is nonexistent) in the

[15] Assuming that the property is a small fraction of the total tax base; if it is a large fraction, then there is a significant feedback to the tax rate, if the total tax levy is given (as is the usual case).

[16] This is based on a pre-computer-age enforcement program's experience—the federal individual income tax for 1948, for which the error on Form 1040A returns was estimated at a little over 5 percent of legal liability. See Marius Farioletti, "Some Results from the First Year's Audit Control Program of the Bureau of Internal Revenue," *National Tax Journal,* Vol. 5 (March 1952), pp. 65-78.

[17] The differences may be systematic within classes of property—the coefficients of dispersion from the median ratio may be 20 percent or less within each class —but there is no evidence on this, and it is highly doubtful that such is the case.

nation's largest cities. Of the eight cities which do a "good" job in assessing single-family houses, five exhibit significant differences in the two sets of assessment ratios; in some cases, homeowners appear to be treated more favorably, but in other cases, they are not. In general, the worse the quality of single-family house assessment, the bigger the interclass differentials.

It is not at all surprising that significant intraclass and interclass nonuniformities exist even in the best administered jurisdictions. Nor would vastly increased administrative outlays in such places necessarily bring uniformity much closer. Suppose that every parcel of land in a city or county were appraised no less frequently than every other year; suppose also that each appraisal takes the time and professional personnel used in making independent appraisals for such transactions as private sales and condemnation. Then, if the cost in a large city averaged $20 per appraisal, annual costs in Milwaukee, for instance, with its 156,000 parcels, would be $3 million, or more than 6 percent of revenues. Yet, despite this expenditure, the inherent difficulty of determining the market value of assets not recently sold, each of which is unique in some respect (the actual case for all real property since no two sites are identical), is such that it is hard to believe that inequalities would be eliminated. In practice, separate, independent, simultaneous professional appraisals of the same property often differ widely. It seems likely, therefore, that increased expenditures would result in asymptotically approaching some standard of uniformity which remains highly imperfect, less so for properties like single-family houses, and more so for others.

In the real world, actual sales of properties within a short period in a large jurisdiction comprise only a small fraction of the total number of properties. For example, bona fide arm's-length sales within a year seldom amount to more than 5 percent of the number of single-family houses.[18] Thus both assessors and independent appraisers must rely on some proxy for market value (which is the conventional legal basis for taxation), and any proxy variable is likely to have a coefficient of correlation which significantly differs from $+1.0$, in a world with all sorts of market imperfections. The

[18] Measurable sales in a six-month period in 1961 were more than 3 percent of the number of properties in fewer than 50 of the 1,356 selected areas. "Taxable Property Values," Table 22.

most commonly used proxy for buildings is depreciated reproduction costs, with both depreciation and reproduction costs determined for individual properties by applying detailed formulas and tables, rules which cannot help departing from the market's evaluation in individual cases. Another common proxy used for income-producing properties is capitalized earnings. The earnings data are likely to be objectively determinable, but the capitalization rate may not coincide with that of prospective purchasers.

In their search for "true value," assessors combine the varieties of evidence: sales of similar (but not identical) properties, reproduction costs, an evaluation of the observed condition of the subject property and of its environment, and income. However objective the basic evidence, its weighting is entirely subjective and varies from case to case.[19] An extreme example of the difficulties involved is the recent and celebrated case of the Seagram Building in New York.[20] In this instance, a national corporation constructed a building as its headquarters (plus additional office space for rent) at lavish standards in a prestigious location. Capitalized net income, on the basis of rental rates in neighboring new (and also prestigious-address) buildings, amounted to only about 40 percent of construction costs. The City held that the advertising value of the structure to its owner justified an assessment substantially in excess of capitalized net income, although well below construction costs. The lower courts, in upholding the original assessment, advanced yet another approach—that at least some portion of the prestige value would be of advantage to potential purchasers. But, in the absence of an actual bona fide sale, the "true value" of the building remains an open question.

This is an extreme case, but the situation is seldom very much better for an expensive parcel of business realty. For public utility property, the valuation problem is so difficult that the Census finds "some grounds for regarding the railroad and utility category as rather widely representing a family of nominally ad valorem levies imposed in lieu of 'the' property tax . . ."[21] It would appear that the tax on business property in general can be regarded as a collection

[19] The *District of Columbia Real Property Assessment Manual* (1958) lucidly illustrates what is widely regarded as close to the best in current practice.

[20] *Joseph E. Seagram and Sons, Inc. v. The Tax Commission of the City of New York,* 14 N.Y. 2nd 314 (1964).

[21] "Taxable Property Values," p. 4.

of taxes nominally measured by market value but actually measured by a varied and changing set of evidence more or less related to market value. Nor is the situation much better in a large jurisdiction with regard to residential realty which is varied in age, type, style, and location; only where the stock of housing is homogeneous in all major respects (as in a suburban subdivision built within a brief span of time) is there any assurance that market value and its proxies will be closely correlated.

In the valuation of personal property, the achievement of uniformity is easier for certain classes and infinitely more difficult for others. Intangibles may be hard to discover or keep in one place long enough to make taxation possible but they have, for the most part, readily ascertainable values. It may be iniquitous and unrewarding to value and tax inventories as of assessment day, but the valuation problem is not serious for the bulk of the dollar value of inventories. Motor vehicles are popular objects for ad valorem taxation because they are easy to discover, due to state registration requirements, and because the existence of a well-organized second-hand market provides good guides for valuation of the well-defined categories (makes, models, etc.). In contrast, the absence of any but rudimentary second-hand markets and the extreme heterogeneity within the general class make uniform assessment of business machinery and equipment and household personalty an impossible task. Where either or both are taxed, the assessments bear an arbitrary, erratic, and rapidly changing relation to anything resembling market value.

Barriers to Improved Administration

It has been suggested up to this point that the general quality of assessment administration is poor, that even the best of current practice is not impressive, and that it is probably not possible to do much better than the best of current practice. Those who find the property tax an alternative superior to other sources of local finance might very well be satisfied if all jurisdictions did as well as the best ones do now; the more defective the property tax is held to be on conceptual grounds, the less toleration there is for an administrative performance which does not measure up to that prevailing for alternative tax measures.

Moreover, there is another serious difficulty. Poor administration, at least in the form of disparities in assessment ratios among classes of property or among subclasses of heterogeneous larger classes (which may explain some of the high coefficients of dispersion for single-family houses in large cities), may amount to a policy choice to moderate the impact of the property tax for specific types of property. That is, local governments, not just the people who happen to be their assessing officers, may conclude that uniformity will produce undesirable distributional or locational effects and they discriminate accordingly. If this is the case—if disparities are not a consequence of incompetence or inadequate resources applied to administration—then urging local governments to mend their ways on "better and cleaner government" grounds is surely quixotic. Moreover, it amounts to substituting the judgment of reform-minded tax experts for that of local governments in determining what economic impact of the property tax is desirable and tolerable in particular communities.

The surmise that "poor" assessment administration represents conscious discrimination rather than accident or incompetence is not entirely fanciful in the light of the evidence on big cities presented in Table 7-3. The big cities, after all, do have professional assessment departments and access to equipment and technical aids; at the least, they are not precluded from such access by the small size of the jurisdiction. More important, if the surmise is a valid one, then the pressure for accommodation to the tax should be greater in cities with higher effective rates, and there should be greater nonuniformity in assessments in such cities. This does appear to be the case. The cities in the top section of Table 7-3, with low coefficients of intra-area dispersion and thus considered to have "good" assessment, generally have relatively low effective tax rates. With the single exception of Milwaukee, effective rates in 1962 in these cities are estimated at 1.5 percent or less. In contrast, most of the cities with high coefficients of dispersion—cities which would win no prizes for assessment quality from any seasoned observer— have high effective rates. In 1962, for example, effective rates appear to have been well over 2 percent in Boston, Chicago, Minneapolis, and New York.[22]

---

[22] These effective rate estimates are crude ones, based on the partial-coverage assessment ratios in Table 7-3; data on gross and net assessed value (and their composition) in "Taxable Property Values," Tables 21 and 22; and U.S. Bureau

Elasticity of the Property Tax

The continued persistence of the property tax, despite its many acknowledged faults, is often explained by the thesis that "an old tax is a good tax." Individuals and the economy have so adjusted themselves to the existence of the tax that its harmful effects have long since occurred, and remedial action today would cause more loss than gain. This, however, is not sufficient basis to explain the ability of the property tax to maintain its *relative* role in the expanding state-local fisc in the past fifteen years, after years of decline. The explanation would seem to be that additional property tax revenues are relatively easy to come by.

In any event, the fact of rising property tax revenues, the availability of new estimates of national wealth, and the fashion for long-term economic projections have combined to produce a lively concern for what has been called the income elasticity of the property tax. This is more properly described as its responsiveness to changes in the level of aggregate economic activity over time. Earlier in the postwar period, when concern with state-local revenue responsiveness was conditioned by the large and rapid price level changes experienced in the Great Depression and in the initial postwar years, attention was directed by Groves and Kahn to the problem of cyclical stability.[23] Examining changes in assessed values during these periods, they concluded that the property tax was stable over the cycle, having an elasticity coefficient of only 0.22 (that is, assessed values changed by 0.22 percent for each 1 percent change in aggregate income).

More recently, the focus has been on the trend rather than on cyclical movements. The policy issue has been this: if the economy grows moderately fast over the next ten or fifteen years with only mild cyclical movements, how fast are revenues from the various

---

of the Census, *Tax Revenues of State and Local Governments in Calendar 1962* (State and Local Government Special Studies No. 46, 1963), Table 2. The crudity of the estimates stems from various assumptions and adjustments made to the published data regarding exemption, property other than locally assessed realty, special property taxes (in a few cities), and apportionment of county-area collections to the cities which do not comprehend an entire county area.

[23] Harold M. Groves and C. Harry Kahn, "The Stability of State and Local Tax Yields," *American Economic Review*, Vol. 42 (March 1952), pp. 87-102.

state and local taxes likely to increase without tax rate changes? How does this elasticity compare with likely changes in public expenditure? A fair amount of research on this has been reported in the literature.[24]

The concept of income elasticity or responsiveness is rather more ambiguous for the property tax than for most other taxes for a number of reasons. First, the nominal or legal base of the tax—assessed values—and the economic base of the tax—the market value of taxable property—do not necessarily vary proportionately with one another. Second, local government jurisdictions typically can adjust both the legal base (assessments) and nominal tax rates, an option not present with other taxes. Third, actual property tax revenues are residually determined for most local governments: the tax levy equals previously determined expenditures less revenues from other sources, notably state aid. Thus the elasticity of property tax revenue is really a reflection of the income elasticity of the demand for local government expenditure (or of residual revenue needs).

These alternative concepts have different applications. Since assessed values can be manipulated by local governments and since they do not necessarily reflect taxpaying capacity in any meaningful sense, an elasticity measure based on the responsiveness of assessments to economic change can be of use only in limited circumstances. Where local governments are operating at or near externally imposed tax rate limits (which depend on assessed rather than

[24] The whole field is reviewed and appraised by Eugene P. McLoone in "Elasticity of the Property Tax" (1963) (unpublished). The main references are: Jesse Burkhead, Chap. IV of *State and Local Taxes for Public Education* (Syracuse University Press, 1963); John D. Hogan, "Revenue Productivity of the Property Tax," *Proceedings,* National Tax Association (1960), pp. 71-77; Ernest Kurnow, "On the Elasticity of the Real Property Tax," *Journal of Finance,* Vol. 18 (March 1963), pp. 56-58; Robert J. Lampman, "How Much Government Spending in the 1960's?" *Quarterly Review of Economics and Business,* Vol. 1 (February 1961), pp. 7-17; Eugene P. McLoone, "Effects of Tax Elasticity on the Financial Support of Education" (doctoral dissertation, University of Illinois, 1961); Dick Netzer, "Financial Needs and Resources over the Next Decade: State and Local Governments," *Public Finances: Needs, Sources, and Utilization* (Princeton University Press for National Bureau of Economic Research, 1961), pp. 30-36; Selma T. Mushkin in *ibid.,* pp. 74-77; Dick Netzer, "Income Elasticity of the Property Tax: A Post Mortem Note," *National Tax Journal,* Vol. 17 (June 1964), pp. 205-07; and Benjamin Bridges, Jr., "Income Elasticity of the Property Tax Base," *National Tax Journal,* Vol. 17 (September 1964), pp. 253-64.

equalized values), the responsiveness of assessments is clearly the relevant income elasticity; this, however, is infrequent.

In a severe economic downturn, with rapid price level declines, a laggard response of assessed values may make it easier for local governments to stabilize revenues by avoiding large increases in nominal rates. If so, it is, of course, a form of "money illusion"; taxpayers and voters accept heavier tax burdens because they appear to be lower than they are. No doubt money illusions are widespread, but in the 1930's this one did not work: property taxpayers simply did not have the income flow necessary to avoid tax delinquency, regardless of assessed values.

The elasticity of the underlying tax base is the relevant measure for isolating the influence of economic forces on property tax revenues and for comparing future yields of this and other taxes. Moreover, as the evidence for the Plains states examined in Chapter V may suggest, property value may be regarded as an indicator of taxable capacity which is independent of income flows. But if the concern is to deduce from the recent past the probable ease or difficulty of gaining more revenue from the property tax in coming years; or, if one seeks to explain the recent past, the elasticity of actual revenue is the appropriate concept.

Burkhead has made an extensive analysis of the elasticity of property tax revenue in which the objective is to seek an explanation of differential rates of increase in recent years.[25] In one set of comparisons, he analyzes fifty-seven New York counties for each year in the 1949-59 period with, as the dependent variable, the ratio of annual increase in property tax collections to annual increase in county personal income.

One strong explanatory variable was the rate of population increase; apparently population increases raise local expenditure requirements faster than personal income. Also, increases in the ratio of the over-65 population were associated with higher revenue elasticity, perhaps because the outmigration of younger, higher income families reduces income more than revenue needs. Increases in the ratio of public school attendance to population were strongly associated with high elasticities, an expected relationship. Average per capita income was negatively associated with elasticity; the older

[25] *State and Local Taxes for Public Education,* pp. 53-70.

urban counties with high incomes and low elasticities (in part due to use of nonproperty taxes) occasioned this relationship. There was little relationship between full value tax rates and elasticity supporting Burkhead's emphasis "on the importance of taxes in relation to income rather than taxes in relation to the market value of property."[26]

A somewhat different picture emerged when he examined cross-section income elasticities for counties within six states in 1957. Per capita income differentials were important explanatory variables in only three states; population size had a widely differing impact on elasticity; and the full value tax rate was positively associated with elasticity in five of the six states. Thus, "property tax elasticity would appear to respond to a different pattern of influences within each state."[27]

Analysis of the elasticity of the underlying base, the market value of taxable property, has rested for the most part on Goldsmith's national wealth estimates, on other wealth estimates for particular sectors (such as Department of Agriculture estimates), and on equalized assessed value data for selected states in which adequate data of this kind are available. One projection for the 1960's, made in 1959, used a GNP elasticity coefficient of unity.[28] This was based on two observations. First, over the very long pull, capital-output ratios have been declining for the economy as a whole. According to Goldsmith's data, the value of privately owned noninstitutional realty and personalty of the kind typically subject to tax rose far less rapidly than gross national product between 1900 and 1958 (see Table 7-4). Second, in the years since 1945, the situation has been reversed. A projection based on unit elasticity represents a discounting of recent experience.

Lampman's projection for the 1960's, made in 1960, concluded that the high elasticity of the recent past might be continued; this coefficient was 1.2. Dr. Mushkin's findings, based on state equalization data, also suggest a highly responsive tax base. McLoone's much more elaborate analysis, based on Goldsmith's data and a variety of other sources but concentrating on the real property tax base, concludes that the elasticity coefficient has approached 1.0

---

[26] *Ibid.*, p. 64.
[27] *Ibid.*, p. 70.
[28] Netzer in *Public Finances.*

TABLE 7-4. Income Elasticity of Privately Owned Components of National Wealth, 1900–58 and 1945–58

(Percentage increase in wealth component divided by percentage increase in gross national product)

Wealth Component	1900–58	1945–58
Current dollars:		
(1) Land and structures	0.56	1.64
(2) (1)+Producers durables and inventories	0.60	1.75
(3) (2)+Consumer durables	0.64	1.84
Constant dollars:		
(1) Land and structures	0.32	1.38
(2) (1)+Producers durables and inventories	0.38	1.76
(3) (2)+Consumer durables	0.42	2.21

Note: Wealth data exclude holdings of nonprofit organizations.
Sources: Raymond W. Goldsmith, *The National Wealth of the United States in the Postwar Period* (Princeton University Press for National Bureau of Economic Research, 1962), Tables A-50, A-52, A-53, and A-54; *Historical Statistics of the United States*, p. 139; *Survey of Current Business*, July 1963. This table appeared in slightly different form in *National Tax Journal*, Vol. 17 (June 1964), p. 206.

over the years and that a coefficient of 0.8 is the most reasonable one to use in projections for the years immediately ahead.

McLoone examines separately each of the major classes of property subject to tax. For agricultural realty, he finds that in agricultural taxing districts, the tax base has risen a good deal faster than local income, primarily from agriculture, and that unit elasticity might be a good future projection but, for a whole state or the whole country, 0.4 is a more reasonable long-term value since agricultural income has been rising much less rapidly than other income. His long-term elasticity coefficient for residential wealth is 0.77, and his projection coefficient for the decade ahead is 0.8, which is consistent with various projections of the rate of residential construction in the 1960's. He concludes that nonfarm business realty has had a long-term elasticity of 0.57. The income and product projections of the National Planning Association suggest a projection value which is somewhat lower, but studies of the production function suggest to McLoone a projection value of 0.8 for total business capital and a much lower figure for business real property alone. He chooses 0.6 as the appropriate projection coefficient for business realty, about the magnitude of the long-term trend. For personal property, a coefficient of 1.2 seems consistent with long-term trends.

Applying these conclusions to the distribution of assessed values subject to tax in 1961 (according to the 1962 Census of Governments), McLoone estimates state-by-state elasticity coefficients. With the United States average at 0.79, the figures range from 0.47 to 1.08. The pronounced influence of the low value for agricultural property is indicated by this regional distribution of the forty-eight contiguous states:

Region	*Elasticity Coefficients of—*			
	.85+	*.75–.84*	*.65–.74*	*Less than .65*
Northeast	7	2	—	—
Midwest	—	4	3	5
West	1	3	5	2
South	—	6	5	5
All	8	15	13	12

This seems a reasonable speculation on the property tax in the decade or so ahead. The evidence of recent years, summarized in Table 7-5, is clear enough.[29] National wealth in taxable forms has risen more rapidly than GNP, but not nearly as fast as local government expenditure. Even assessed values have risen faster than GNP, as have market values of locally assessed realty. The consequence of all this has been rapidly increasing property tax revenues, with only relatively modest increases in property taxes as a fraction of property values in the market. The indications, then, are that the property tax is and will continue to be an attractively productive source of local public funds. In view of its many faults, this attractiveness of the property tax is perhaps to be deplored rather than

[29] The very high elasticity results for 1956-61 imply a substantial decline in the ratio of assessed to market values for the country as a whole in that period, a decline indicated by Census of Governments data but one not readily explainable in view of the relative stability of the price level. Moreover, the lowered rate of new private investment after the mid-1950's—especially true for investment in structures—may suggest that the longer run capital-output relationships may be reasserting themselves and that an overall property tax base elasticity figure well below unity is strongly indicated.

TABLE 7-5. Evidence on Income Elasticity of the Property Tax in the Postwar Period

Income, Wealth, or Tax Item[a]	Average Annual Percentage Increase	
	1945–58	1956–61
Gross national product	5.8	4.3
Privately owned national wealth:[b]		
Land and structures	8.2	n.a.
Realty+producer durables and inventories	8.5	n.a.
Gross assessed value of property subject to local general property taxes	n.a.	5.5
Estimated market value of locally assessed real property[c]	n.a.	7.0
Property tax revenue[d]	8.8	8.2
Local government direct general expenditure[d]	11.3	8.3

Sources: Raymond W. Goldsmith, *The National Wealth of the United States in the Postwar Period* (Princeton University Press for National Bureau of Economic Research, 1962); *Survey of Current Business*, July 1964; U. S. Bureau of the Census, *Census of Governments: 1962*, Vol. II, "Taxable Property Values" (1963), and Vol. VI, No. 4, *Historical Statistics on Governmental Finances and Employment* (1964).

n.a. Not available.

[a] All measured in current dollars.

[b] Excluding holdings of nonprofit organizations.

[c] Based on average assessment ratio weighted by type and size of property.

[d] Revenue and expenditure items are for one year later than shown by column headings, i.e., 1946–59 and 1957–62.

applauded. One of its staunchest latter-day friends, the Advisory Commission on Intergovernmental Relations, had this to say in the course of an overall view of state-local finance:

Local governments carry half of the combined State and local tax load and they continue to rely almost exclusively on the property tax. It gives us pause that most local governments' only tax source and that State and local governments' single most important source of financing is a tax which distributes its burden among the people without too much regard for either their ability to pay taxes or the benefits they derive from governmental programs. This concern has not been diminished by the property tax's unexpectedly strong revenue performance in the postwar years. That development has not only increased the urgency for improving the quality of its administration but for reappraising the compatibility of its burden distribution with national economic and social objectives as well.[30]

[30] *The Role of Equalization in Federal Grants* (1964), pp. 83-84.

CHAPTER VIII

Alternative Forms for the Property Tax

THE AMERICAN PROPERTY TAX does not fare too well in this study, but a rational case for continued heavy reliance by local governments on some type of taxation of real property can be made. If on no other grounds, such a case can be made for the lesser near-term mobility of investment in real estate compared to the mobility of other objects of local taxation. The most frequent excuse for the property tax—sheer political inertia—may be rejected as an unworthy argument, and alternative forms of local real estate taxation considered. Such alternatives have been proposed for years and are used to some extent in various other countries. They all involve fairly basic modifications of American practice and include taxation of property on an annual value rather than a capital value basis, heavier or exclusive taxation of site values, taxation of land value increments, and—most distant from current practice—taxation of property via what amounts to a "family of user charges," not all of them on an ad valorem basis.[1]

[1] The analytic portion of the argument which follows, except on the "family of user charges" notion, parallels the very lucid exposition in James Heilbrun's doctoral dissertation, "The Effects of Alternative Real Estate Taxes on the Maintenance and Rehabilitation of Urban Rental Housing," to be published by

Annual Versus Capital Values

Property tax institutions in the Western world by and large orig-
inated as money payments in lieu of in-kind feudal obligations
connected with land tenure. Since, in feudal Europe, land was not
sold, property rights were expressed in terms of annual privileges
and obligations vested in the land, and there was no meaning to the
concept, "the capital value of land." Real property taxes were thus
quite naturally assessed in terms of annual rental values, the basis
of real property taxation today in most of Western Europe,[2] Britain, and several countries with institutions in the British tradition,
including Ireland, Israel, Australia, and New Zealand. In addition,
a number of Latin American countries tax urban real estate, in part
at least, on the basis of gross rentals. The capital value basis is
much less widespread and is used mainly in the United States, Canada, South Africa, and a few European countries, notably Germany, Austria, and Denmark.

The obvious, but superficial, argument for taxation of annual
values rather than capital values is that, since taxes are paid from
income (or flows), rather than wealth (or stocks), why not tax the
net annual values of real property directly to begin with? However,
in concept and in an equilibrium situation, there should be no real
difference in the distribution of real estate tax liability among individual property owners whether the basis is net annual income or
capital value. In concept, capital value is equal to net annual income capitalized at the relevant market interest rate, and in an
equilibrium situation property owners are assumed to be using their
properties so as to maximize net income. The argument for taxing
annual values must have a different basis, then, if it is to be taken
seriously.

And in fact it does, for in the countries which tax real property
on an annual value basis, the tax is *not* one on normal, maximized
net income. Instead, the tax is levied on annual values which are
much closer (if not actually equal) to gross rentals: gross rentals not

---

the Columbia University Press. The Heilbrun study presents a close and careful
analysis of some major alternatives and is by far the best available treatment
of this aspect of the property tax; see Chap. 10 of the book for a summary of
its conclusions.

[2] See Table 1-4.

from the most profitable possible use of the sites involved but from actual existing uses of the property. The British "rates," the most important of the annual value property taxes, are taxes on the annual rental value of occupied real property, with statutory percentage deductions for maintenance and insurance costs.[3] These are not net rent taxes, since actual costs are not deducted but, instead, a statutory formula is provided. The deductions decline as gross rents rise, from 40 percent in the lowest bracket to one-sixth in the highest —amounting, in fact, to a graduated tax on gross rents rather than a net rents tax.[4] Rateable values are based on actual use of the property, not potential use, and since the tax is legally on the tenant or occupier rather than the owner, vacant properties bear no tax. Rateable values are assessed centrally for England and Wales by the Inland Revenue, a national government agency; revaluations have been infrequent, and the standard of value is not the current year's rental (as adjusted), but an average for several years.

Thus, even aside from the administrative problems of actually determining values, the distribution of tax liability under the American and British systems is quite different. Properties in suboptimal uses are taxed at much lower levels under the British system. Also, properties with an above-average ratio of net profits to gross rents are taxed at higher levels in the American system, since in general the higher profitability can be expected to be capitalized into higher prices.

This rather different distribution of liabilities is the rationale for the case for taxation on the basis of annual values. During the 1930's, there was active discussion in the United States of proposals for switching to a British-type system of property taxation. The proponents were usually real estate industry representatives acutely conscious of the height of property taxes, based on slowly changing ratios of assessed capital values to gross rents in depression conditions with high vacancy rates.[5] In the circumstances, a tax on tenants

[3] There are numerous descriptions of the British system in the literature. The most authoritative is that found in the Annual Reports of the Commissioners of Her Majesty's Inland Revenue; see, for example, the *Report for the Year Ended 31 March 1963*, Cmnd. 2283 (London), pp. 210-13.

[4] If, as is likely, there are significant economies of scale in property operating costs, the net effects of the graduation are likely to be rather small.

[5] A capsule summary of the Tax Institute forum on the subject appears in Mabel Walker, "Fiscal Aspects of Land Use," Part III of Series on "Land Use and Local Finance," *Tax Policy*, Vol. 29 (July-August-September 1962), pp. 29-30.

based on gross rentals was enormously appealing: if there were vacancies, there would be no tax; as rents declined, so would tax liability; and equally important, tax delinquency would not lead to foreclosure since the tenant, not the owner, would be legally liable. Apparently, low vacancy rates in the past twenty years have caused this kind of interest in a British-type tax to evaporate.

An entirely different reason for advocating the taxing of property on the basis of earnings rather than capital value is put forward by the many individuals and organizations eager to "tax the profits out of slums." It is demonstrably true that overcrowded slum buildings with high gross rent receipts and high net returns bear low property taxes, relative to nonslum residential properties, in most large cities. Occasionally this is due to faulty assessment practice, but the more general source of the difficulty is that the market values of slum properties are low relative to gross and net earnings. Clearly, this in turn is a consequence of the market's evaluation of the riskiness of investment in slum property and the life expectancy of the presently large income stream: prospective investors in slum properties evidently demand a high and quick profit, relative to investors in other types of rental housing.

A tax based on capital values cannot possibly be a deterrent to investors in slum property under these conditions, unless there is some sort of penalty built into the system, say, via differentially high assessment ratios—a practice which presumably would not stand up very well in most courts. A tax on gross rents, or on net earnings, would indeed fall more heavily on "excess profits from slums," but whether this would help solve the underlying social problem—that of slums—is rather more questionable.

In concept, any tax on improvements, whether on a capital value or on an annual value basis, is likely to have an adverse impact, relative to no tax at all, on investment in new construction and remodelling of old structures. If the tax is borne by tenants, the quantity and quality of building demanded is reduced; if borne by owners, the quantity and quality offered is reduced.[6] In concept, the British and American taxes do not significantly differ on this score, but they may well differ in actual application.

In theory, a tax on capital values will not affect decisions on

[6] See Chap. III.

operation, maintenance, and replacement of worn elements of structure. This is because capital value tends to be equated with capitalized returns net of all costs; and operation, repairs, and maintenance are cost items which rational prospective purchasers take into account. A gross rents tax, on the other hand, will act as an inducement to lower standards of operation and maintenance, falling as it does on receipts inclusive of costs. Since the demand for housing *quality* seems to be a good deal more elastic than the demand for housing *space,* the reduction in quality offered in response to a gross rents tax could be appreciable.[7] Thus, switching from the prevailing American practice to the British system or some other gross rents tax is likely to worsen rather than alleviate the problem of slums.

Certain other resource allocation effects of a gross rents tax are also objectionable. The American system in theory presents the site owner with a lump-sum charge; land is supposedly valued on the basis of its capitalized net return in the most profitable possible use. But a gross rents basis, related to actual use, encourages withholding of sites from use entirely (rental value and tax equal zero) and more generally favors low return uses over high return uses.[8] Further, if vacant improvements are not taxed, owners of rental property have an incentive to reduce their costs in cyclically difficult times by withholding rental property from the market. This is a real misallocation, since buyers of the services of this property would be willing to pay the marginal costs of producing such services but the services may not be produced due to the tax. And, if vacant properties are not taxed, the tax rate on occupied properties must be higher than in an alternative system of taxation (to yield equivalent revenues), thus further discouraging new investment and high standards of operation and maintenance.[9]

It has been argued on occasion that a real property tax based on annual rents or rental values is administratively less difficult than one on capital values.[10] The argument runs this way: it is easier to

---

[7] See Heilbrun, "The Effects of Alternative Real Estate Taxes," Chap. 7, for a much more adequate discussion of this.

[8] A net income tax on real estate is even worse on this score; *ibid.,* p. 194.

[9] *Ibid.,* pp. 198-99.

[10] It is important here to abstract from differences in assessment organization in Britain and the United States: rateable values for all England and Wales,

assess rented property on the basis of rents than of capital value because there is some objective evidence in existence, even if it is not very readily available to the assessor. It is, of course, easier to use the capital value basis for owner-occupied property, rather than going through the elaborate process of imputing rents; here, the objective evidence to use as a check on assessment validity consists of the small sample of sales in any one year. However, far more properties are rented than sold in a given year. If rental value is the basis of assessment, there is a large body of potentially available evidence on rents on rented property to use as a basis for assessing owner-occupied property. On the other hand, the sales evidence is much more limited in quantity.

There are a number of flaws in the argument. First, and most general, while there are some property classes for which comparable rented and owner-occupied properties exist within the same real estate market area, such a situation occurs infrequently. For example, rented steel mills and power plants are nonexistent, and in many areas rented single-family houses are rarities. In such cases, rental evidence is useless; on the other hand, sales evidence, such as it is, applies to both rented and owner-occupied properties. Second, contract rent is not an unambiguous concept: the distribution of expenses between landlord and tenant differs greatly among properties. To take one instance, surely data on rents paid for furnished single-family houses (which may be the only rented houses in some suburbs) are not clear evidence as to the rental value of owner-occupied houses.

Third, information on sales prices under practices prevailing in much of the United States is more or less in the public domain, but information on rents is not. There may be many rented properties, but an assessor would not have ready access to the information short of access to income tax returns (with huge problems of matching income taxpayers with parcels of property). Moreover, a sizeable proportion of personal ownership of rental property involves

---

as noted earlier, are centrally assessed by the highly professional national government tax collection agency, the Inland Revenue. Obviously this produces better results than assessment by amateur, elected township assessors, the practice in many parts of the United States. This makes a case for changing assessment organization, not necessarily the basis of assessment.

individuals with modest holdings and low incomes, where record-keeping can be expected to be least adequate; this dispersion of ownership itself adds to the sheer physical magnitude of the information problem.[11]

The much larger proportion of owner-occupied properties in the United States (and also Canada) than in Britain is a decisive factor in the argument. Unlike Britain, in the United States only a minor proportion of farm real estate parcels are leased rather than held on a freehold basis, and the great bulk of nonfarm residential properties are owner-occupied.[12] Moreover, building owners in this country usually own their sites as well, and most nonfarm business realty is owner-occupied rather than rented. Thus, in general, an annual value basis would appear to be administratively more, rather than less, difficult than current American practice. A few large cities might be exceptions to the rule but, even here, the case is a doubtful one and in any case would not outweigh the resource allocation disadvantages of a British-type tax.

Site Value Taxation

The ancient case for taxation of site values, either exclusively or at a rate substantially higher than that applicable to the value of improvements, is far less of a straw man than the case for taxation on an annual value basis. However, from Henry George in 1879 right down to the present, the extravagant arguments of passionate advocates of site value taxation appear to be designed to repel rather than persuade, to disarm (or even negatively convert) dispassionate sympathizers and to convince opponents that this was and is a crank cause. Site value taxation has been presented not only as a panacea for urban land use but also as a cure for unemployment, a preventative for inflation, and a guarantor of perpetual industrial

[11] A study of personal income in Milwaukee County, Wisconsin, in 1955, based on state income tax returns, showed that individuals' rental income from Wisconsin real estate was more concentrated at the lower end of the income scale than any other source of income, *including* wages and salaries. Federal Reserve Bank of Chicago, "Personal Income in Milwaukee County, 1955," (1957) (mimeo).

[12] About 35.6 million properties were covered by the Residential Finance Survey in 1959-60; 27.9 million of these were homeowner properties and 7.7 million were rental and vacant properties. U.S. Bureau of the Census, *Census of Housing, 1960*, Vol. V, "Residential Finance," Parts 1 and 2 (1963).

and international peace.[13] Despite the utopian tone of this argument, the renewed interest in problems of urban economies and urban land use in the face of high property taxes compels a serious examination of the case, and there are signs that this is increasingly being done, with results favorable to site value taxation.[14]

Administrative Feasibility

It is perhaps best to start out by disposing of the administrative feasibility argument. One strand of this argument is not merely unfavorable to site value taxation, but utterly devastating. This is the claim that there is no meaningful way, in theory as well as in practice, of separating the value of the site from the value of improvements if the site is not a vacant one. This view was advanced by anti-Georgists as far back as Richard T. Ely; more contemporary protagonists include Fisher and Turvey.[15] The Fisher argument does not rely on the superficial analogy with a chemical reaction, sometimes used by appraisers—that the construction of the improvement permanently changes the character of the site. Since buildings are impermanent and destructible, the only *permanent* change to a particular site resulting from an improvement on it is to add demolition costs as a factor in actual appraisal.

Rather, the Fisher argument states that the demand for urban land is derived from the intensity and character of the demand for structures in general and that the character of improvements on particular sites shapes the demand for the sites themselves. This may be illustrated by a simple, but topical case—the value of land immediately adjacent to an interchange on an interstate highway in

[13] Citations for this statement can be provided in abundance, but would serve no purpose other than to ridicule and humiliate.

[14] Examples include the celebrated August 1960 issue of *House and Home*, Vol. 17, pp. 98-164, devoted entirely to the question of urban land and involving major contributions by Ernest Fisher and Mason Gaffney; Ralph Turvey in *The Economics of Real Property* (London: George Allen & Unwin, 1957), pp. 76-92, an analytical appraisal of site value taxation; an empirical investigation in a suburb of Vancouver, British Columbia, was made by Mary Rawson in *Property Taxation and Urban Development* (Urban Land Institute, 1961); a review article by Clyde E. Browning, "Land Value Taxation: Promises and Problems," *Journal of the American Institute of Planners*, Vol. 29 (November 1963), pp. 301-309; and Heilbrun, "The Effects of Alternative Real Estate Taxes."

[15] Ernest M. and Robert M. Fisher, *Urban Real Estate* (Holt, 1954), pp. 54-57; Turvey, *The Economics of Real Property*, pp. 22-24.

a rural area. The land can be used either for farming or for motels, gas stations, and the like. Initially, very high bids will be submitted for sites to be used for such highway services, since the first establishments to start in business can recoup the high profits of an innovator. But as new establishments are developed, the returns on motels and other services will fall and the prices bid for sites will decline, eventually perhaps to the level of pure farmland. In the extreme case, when so many establishments exist that none is profitable, the market price of a site cleared, say, by a fire, might be the farmland price. It thus appears that it is the improvements that determine site value and that the notion of a bare site value for land on which a motel exists is nonsense.

However, this conclusion rests on a rather elementary fallacy, a failure to distinguish between the value of land in general—which is surely derived from the demand for improvements—and the value of one specific site.[16] If property value (whether it is site value or some other property value) is to be used as a basis for taxation, the key point is not the total value of all property taxed but the value of each taxable property vis-à-vis the others. If a given amount of revenue is to be raised from alternative tax devices, the first concern is the distribution of tax liability among taxpayers. Thus the valuation process does not ask what properties could be sold for if *all* were offered simultaneously, but what each would bring in a bona fide sale when added to whatever properties are being transferred as of the date on which the appraisal is being made.

To deny that there is a distinguishable site value for a specific improved site, independent of the nature of the actual improvements on it, is to deny that there is any such thing as location rents —that is, differential returns available from the use of one urban site rather than another in an environment in which every site is unique in some respect. Individual entrepreneurial decisions surely do not deny this.

Consider this simplified example. Suppose there are a number of vacant sites in and near the central business district of a large city on which it is physically and legally possible to construct a large office building, and that there are investors considering this decision. Location rents will be negative for this use for any site at

[16] The classical economists had no trouble in avoiding this fallacy, however.

which the proposed building fails to yield the minimum return necessary to elicit the investment in the building itself (assuming that there is, in fact, some site at which the necessary return will be realized). This minimum return is determined by the returns available from other forms of investment, adjusted for the risk and illiquidity premiums required for real estate investment and including all the appropriate items in costs.[17] The differentials above and beyond this minimum, which arise in alternative locations, constitute location rents and will presumably be shared in some proportion by entrepreneurs and site owners, the proportion depending on the usual variety of demand and supply factors. Clearly, in this situation, the capitalized value of the location rent of the site which actually wins out is its site value in the market, and the capitalized value of the net return on the building, after deduction of location rent, is the market value of the building.

It will be helpful to clothe this example with some hypothetical figures. Assume that the minimum return required on the equity portion of real estate investment of this type (giving effect to risk and illiquidity premiums) is 9 percent and that mortgage financing equal to two-thirds of the total investment in the building is available at 6 percent; then the required return on the total investment is 7 percent. If the investment in the building totals $20 million, then the minimum required return on the building will be $1.4 million. Suppose, in one particular site, the net rents that can be realized from the building, before return on the investment and before ground rents, but after all other costs (including depreciation), are $1.5 million. Location rent in this case—the excess over the minimum return required to elicit the investment which can be realized by putting up this particular building on this particular site—will be $100,000; if capitalized at 5 percent, the value of the site will be $2 million.

In concept, changes in the demand for office space can be handled by going through the same kind of appraisal at the new point in time. If an increased demand is simply for office space anywhere in or near the central business district, sites which previously had location rents lower than that of the favored site will now be brought into use for new office buildings. If, however, such an increased demand is focused entirely on this particular building

<hr>

[17] In this discussion, it is convenient to speak as though the income tax did not exist.

already standing (perhaps because of some improvement in transport service which uniquely favors it), then the net rents which it can yield will be higher; if there has been no change in the supply price of real estate investment capital, an independent phenomenon, that particular site's location rent and market value are enhanced.

But to return to the original illustration, assume now that this valuable site is *not* in its most profitable use, but instead has a smaller, older structure on it, owned separately from the site under a ground lease with an annual ground rental of $20,000; the structure yields $100,000 before ground rents. The value of the existing building to a prospective buyer therefore presumably would be the $80,000 net return (after ground rent) capitalized at the appropriate rate.[18]

Now, the extent to which the site owner could realize the value of $2 million in the most profitable possible use depends upon the length of the encumbrance—the ground lease. If the lease has a very short time to run, then the site owner can come quite close to this value, the principal deduction being demolition costs. If the lease is a very long one (say, longer than the useful life of the new building under consideration), the site owner is out of luck. The premium price for the location can be realized by the leaseholder if he is willing and able to rebuild, or willing and able to assign his leasehold interest. Assuming normal reversionary provisions in the lease, any intermediate term will result in an intermediate situation: the potential return from rebuilding to the most profitable possible use must be discounted on the basis of the length of time the lease has to run.

All this suggests that there is no fundamental conceptual problem in valuing sites for taxation, but that there would be formidable difficulties in practice, related to problems such as encumbrances. Moreover, the market evidence—sales of unimproved sites comparable to improved sites—is rather scarce, which makes assessment even more difficult, and would make testing of assessment levels and quality virtually impossible in many circumstances. A further difficulty in valuation which is hard to surmount is the problem of distinguishing the value contributed by old improvements to land, such as grading and fertilization, from the bare site value.

[18] The new buyer, of course, may have a different depreciation schedule, and thus may make his calculations on the basis of a different net return figure, ordinarily a lower one.

However, site value taxation can be ruled out on administrative grounds only if these difficulties are held to be far greater than the problems of administration under the existing property tax. Here, it should be noted that some similar problems do exist with the present form of real property taxation. Sales evidence is very thin for all types of properties which are relatively expensive and/or which are highly specialized in nature. The encumbrance problem for sites is a special case of the more general problem of distinguishing between the value of property, whether land or buildings, as presently used and value in the most profitable possible use.

Moreover, separate valuation of improved sites is hardly an unheard of practice. As Browning points out, depreciation allowances for income tax purposes require separate valuations of land and depreciable improvements.[19] This demands at least as high a standard of accuracy (relatively, among taxpayers) as valuation for property taxation. And, as Heilbrun points out, the existence of land value taxation in various parts of the world is at least a presumption in favor of the view that it is administratively feasible.[20]

Experience with Site Value Taxation

Differentially heavy taxation of land, or complete exemption of improvements from a general ad valorem tax on real estate, is practiced in the United States only in Pennsylvania (notably in Pittsburgh), but is widespread in Australia, New Zealand, Canada, and South Africa. Some of the European real property taxes have differential rates for land and buildings, but the rate on land is not always higher.[21] In addition, differentially heavy taxation of land recently has been instituted in Hawaii.

In 1913, Pennsylvania authorized the cities of Pittsburgh and Scranton to shift, over a period of twelve years, to a "graded tax," under which land is taxed at twice the rate on improvements; since 1925, this has been the practice. However, the "graded tax" applied only to city levies, not to county and school levies, which are large for both these cities. Consequently, in 1960, improvements in Pittsburgh were taxed at 71 percent of the rate on land, not 50 percent.

---

[19] In *Journal of the American Institute of Planners*, p. 303.

[20] "The Effects of Alternative Real Estate Taxes," p. 206. The abandonment of the Australian land tax, in part because of administrative difficulties, does not refute this point (see below).

[21] See Table 1-4, above.

Legislation in 1951 and 1959 extended authorization for differential taxation of land to forty-eight other Pennsylvania cities (not including Philadelphia) without limit on the ratio of tax rates on land to tax rates on improvements, but few cities have taken advantage of this.[22]

Since the 1890's in the Australian states and in New Zealand, local taxing units have been either permitted or required to exempt all improvements from local taxation; in both countries, the majority of taxing units do so.[23] Moreover, New Zealand has had a national land tax since 1891 and Australia had a federal land tax from 1910 until 1952; both of these were taxes with exemptions, graduated rates, and major nonfiscal purposes.[24] In Canada, the four western provinces, beginning with British Columbia in 1892, provided for partial or complete untaxing of improvements by local governments. However, at present, improvements are not wholly exempted anywhere in Canada. In British Columbia, improvements are taxed at 75 percent of the land rate for school purposes, but at rates ranging from 30 percent to 75 percent for municipal purposes. In Saskatchewan and Alberta, the improvements rate is in the 45 percent to 60 percent range, and in Manitoba, it ranges from 30 percent to 100 percent of the land rate.[25]

The South African provinces, beginning in 1916, have allowed local governments wide latitude in differential taxation of land. As

[22] Based on sources cited in Heilbrun, "The Effects of Alternative Real Estate Taxes," pp. 170-72; and Browning, in the *Journal of the American Institute of Planners*, p. 305.

[23] Chapters on Australia and New Zealand in Harry Gunnison Brown and others, eds., *Land-Value Taxation Around the World* (Robert Schalkenbach Foundation, New York, 1955).

[24] See Richard M. Bird, "A National Tax on the Unimproved Value of Land: The Australian Experience, 1910-1952," *National Tax Journal*, Vol. 13 (December 1960), pp. 386-92. The Australian land tax, according to Bird, was abandoned because its minor revenues seemed no longer worth the administrative problems. One major class of these problems related to the exemptions and progressive rates, which stimulated efforts to utilize dummy devices to split land ownership and reduce tax liability. The second class of problems was inherent in land value taxation, distinguishing land values from improvement values. The principal difficulty in Australia apparently related to excluding the value of site improvements such as clearing and drainage, especially with regard to rather old improvements of this type. The Australian experience hardly suggests that land value taxation is truly administratively infeasible.

[25] Dominion Bureau of Canada, Statistics Bureau, *Principal Taxes and Rates—Federal, Provincial, and Selected Municipal Governments, 1963*, Catalog No. 68-201 (Ottawa, 1964), pp. 19-29.

of 1960-61, 52 of 362 local authorities taxed land only and another 131 had differential taxation of land and buildings. Of the twenty-nine largest cities, only four taxed land and buildings equally; eleven exempted improvements; and fourteen had differential rates as high as 14:1, although frequently lower.[26]

Thus site value taxation is a well-established practice in a number of developed countries in which there is relatively heavy reliance on local property taxation. Although the single-tax literature is replete with extravagant claims as to the benefits which have stemmed from these tax institutions, the rigorous evidence adduced is almost nonexistent.[27] A field investigation of land value taxation in Australia and New Zealand in 1964 by A. M. Woodruff and L. L. Ecker-Racz found that the social and economic impact of site value taxation in these countries has been minor, in part because of the low level of local property taxes in general and because of exemption from the land tax. They observed little visible evidence of differences between communities which use site value taxation and those which use more conventional forms of property taxation.[28]

Experience with site value taxation perhaps does no more than prove that it is a conceivable alternative.

Differential taxation of land is also not uncommon in underdeveloped countries, at times for fiscal purposes and at times for nonfiscal ends.[29] But neither the resource allocation setting nor the level of administrative performance suggests that this experience has much relevance for the United States.

Resource Allocation Effects

The essence of the argument for site value taxation is simple enough. There *is* such a phenomenon as location rents—that is, differential returns in particular sites which are entirely independent of the nature of improvements (including not only structures but also grading, site preparation, and soil conditioning for farm uses). Location rents constitute a surplus, and taxing them will not reduce

[26] O. D. Gorven, *Local Government Taxation in Durban* (City of Durban, South Africa, 1963), pp. 70-72.

[27] Rawson, in *Property Taxation and Urban Development*, does produce some interesting evidence.

[28] Study financed by the Lincoln Foundation (not published to date).

[29] Perhaps the first nonfiscal use of this device was in 1658 when New Netherlands enacted a special tax on vacant land to encourage building. James Ford, *Slums and Housing* (Harvard University Press, 1936), Vol. I, p. 32.

the supply of sites offered; instead, the site value tax will be entirely neutral with regard to landowners' decisions, since no possible response to the tax can improve the situation, assuming that landowners have been making maximum use of their sites prior to imposition of the tax. Thus a change from the present property tax, which tends to discourage investment in new construction and rehabilitation, to the site value tax, which is neutral, will encourage building and rehabilitation.

The site value tax is also neutral with regard to the intensity of use of particular sites: it is a lump-sum charge to the owner. While the land component of the present American property tax is similarly neutral in concept, the part of the tax on improvements, by discouraging development, tends to foster low return land uses. Moreover, although the site value tax itself has no bearing on choices among land uses in theory, switching over to heavy taxation of land values would increase substantially the holding costs of land and thus encourage more intensive utilization: this will not reduce the site value tax, but will make it a smaller fraction of total gross receipts from the site and its improvements.

Finally, increased taxes on site values will be capitalized into land prices, which will decline since the net after-tax return on land is now lower. Conceivably, this might be mitigated if untaxing improvements, by stimulating new construction, led to a general rise in the demand for sites. Also, the tax might reduce the interest rate used for capitalization of land rents, although this seems unlikely in view of the small segment of the overall capital market represented by land itself. On balance, land prices should be reduced by heavier taxation of land.

The argument suggests, therefore, an increased rate of investment in new and better structures, less speculative withholding of land from development, and reduced "urban sprawl": checkerboard, discontinuous development at low densities on the fringes of urban areas. As for the older parts of cities, one contemporary proponent claims: "To exempt improvements and at the same time to tax land more heavily would provide a double incentive to the owners of derelict buildings to demolish them and to use the land more intensively. Here surely is a golden key to urban renewal, to the automatic regeneration of the city—and not at the public expense."[30]

[30] Rawson, in *Property Taxation and Urban Development*, p. 28.

To be sure, heavier taxation of site values combined with lower taxation of improvements may not by itself produce all the salutory results often claimed, but it is difficult to find any flaws in the argument that this tax change will tend to work in this direction and therefore have favorable resource allocation effects. The few arguments against site value taxation on resource allocation grounds do not seem very substantial.

One of these arguments questions the basic notion that location rents are, in the long run, a true surplus, without relation to variations in supply. A major attribute of location rents is differences in accessibility and, in the long run, accessibility can be varied by changes in transportation technology and by increased investment in transport facilities of a conventional nature, as well as by other actions involving reproducible capital. A tax affecting investment decisions which change accessibility would hardly be neutral in its resource allocation effects. However, most investment decisions which affect accessibility are large-scale public decisions, in regard to transport facilities, water supply, and the like, rather than those of individual landowners; they consequently would not be affected by site value tax considerations.[31] Moreover, transport improvements tend to change accessibility in large discrete steps, often widely separated in time. Between such improvements, the supply of locations is once again invariant and location rents are true surpluses.

A second argument against site value taxation hinges on its tendency to foster more intensive development. It is often claimed that raising the holding costs of land in low return uses ("discouraging speculation") would tend to force "premature development" and make it difficult to preserve open space in and around the large urban concentrations. Farmland on the fringes of urban areas, privately owned golf courses, and similar developable sites would bear very much higher taxes than at present and would quickly be transformed into sites for housing, shopping centers, and the like. It is also said to foster unwanted additional congestion in central areas by increasing the intensity of use.

The first thing to be said about this argument is that it presumes

[31] If public utility companies were subjected to the site value tax rather than the present forms of property taxation, their tax liability would almost certainly be very substantially reduced, and the property tax would be an even more minor consideration in their investment decisions affecting accessibility.

that an unneutral rather than a neutral tax is sound social policy—that the property tax *should* be unneutral in the direction of favoring low return uses, as it now tends to be. The conventional wisdom in the study of public finance is that it is usually more sensible to try to effect desirable nonfiscal ends by direct measures—for example, to reserve open space by actual public acquisition of property rights in the desired land—rather than by manipulating major general taxes for this purpose, with attendant administrative difficulties and, frequently, unanticipated toxic side-effects. A tax which is neutral with respect to land use decisions, as is the site value tax, therefore has a presumption in its favor.

In addition, it is open to question whether the untoward consequences are severe enough to merit elimination. In view of the fragmented nature of local government in most urban areas, land on the rural-urban fringe, which is the land at issue in the "premature development" argument, is generally within local taxing units with little urbanization which thus have the characteristically low nonurban expenditure and tax levels. Moreover, there are few structures in these jurisdictions; hence, a shift to site value taxation is not likely to produce overwhelming tax incentives to "premature development."[32] And if the goal is the preservation of open spaces, then an unneutral property tax is a clumsy instrument indeed to guarantee this in the event of urbanization. It cannot assure that the appropriate types and locations of open space are preserved, only an entirely accidental selection.[33]

Furthermore, an unneutral tax favoring low-intensity development has social costs as well as gains. It encourages discontinuous development, with higher transport costs and higher costs of infrastructure in general. Vacant land within cities is also highly wasteful of public services. To be sure, heavier taxation of land is likely to foster more intensive development within cities, which may result in private and social congestion costs, but the "congestion" problem can be overdrawn, as Heilbrun shows.[34] For one thing, it may mean

[32] A metropolitan area-wide system of site value taxation at a higher rate would be a rather different story.

[33] This, incidentally, casts considerable doubt on the case for preferential assessment of agricultural land in urbanizing areas, usually in the form of provision for taxation of agricultural land in its present rather than potential use. Since 1960, constitutional amendments providing for this have been adopted in Maryland and New Jersey; statutory provisions exist in five other states.

[34] "The Effects of Alternative Real Estate Taxes," p. 193.

no more than a shifting of activity within the city, which is not necessarily worse. Moreover, if more buildings are constructed but in
some sense less intensively used (for example, the construction of
taller office buildings with much more floor space per employee)
"congestion" is not increased.

Most empirical studies of the impact of land value taxation on
the distribution of tax payments by type of property have indicated
that the most noticeable effect would be to increase taxes on centrally located urban properties and reduce those on peripheral
properties.[35] This gives rise to another source of concern. Although
heavier taxation of centrally located land would tend to encourage
its redevelopment, it may be that the extent of redevelopment possible is very limited.[36] The point is that urban economic activity has
been decentralizing, and the attraction of central locations has become quite limited. If there were a shift to heavier taxation of land,
eventually this change in the opportunities for central city land
would show up in assessed values.

However, initially, there would be many individual sites, examined vis-à-vis all others, which would appear to have location rents
very disproportionate to their present state of development. Very
large increases in taxes on these properties might encourage present
owners to sell out and shift their operations to peripheral locations;
while the purchasers would have paid a lower price for the sites,
reflecting the capitalized new tax, redevelopment would not be in-
stantaneous. Note, however, that this argument against site value
taxation rests on institutional imperfections—sluggishness of the
valuation process and of investment decisions, and some irrational-
ity among investors. These may very well be factors, but the site
value tax should *tend* to produce positive effects on urban redevelopment.

Equity and Adequacy

The equity argument for site value taxation has a very simple
ethical basis. A major share of the value of land, other than that
used in extractive industries, is not the consequence of actions by
individual landowners, but instead stems from population growth

[35] See, for example, the Haig study cited by Heilbrun, in *ibid.*, pp. 120-21;
Rawson, in *Property Taxation and Urban Development*, Part II.
[36] See Walker, in *Tax Policy*, pp. 23-24.

and general community improvements—some publicly financed and some, such as utility services, privately financed but paid for by the community at large. The community therefore has every right to recapture as much of this "unearned increment" as it chooses; happily, as indicated earlier, taxing this surplus has no adverse economic consequences, in theory.

Seligman and others objected that our society abounds with "unearned increments" and that there was no equity in singling this particular one out. This was Seligman's objection to site value taxation as a single tax, and the land value tax would be less inequitable today simply because of the existence of substantial federal and state income taxes which tax capital gains on land very lightly, relative to many other types of monetary enhancement. Moveover, land value taxation is surely more satisfactory on equity grounds than the existing property tax.

There is one fundamental equity problem, however: the equity effects of shifting from the present system to site value taxation. This, too, is an old argument. Whatever the "unearned component" of the present value of land, land is not necessarily in the hands of those who have received the "unearned increments"; many present owners have paid full value for their investments. Thus, heavy taxation of site values, which appropriates a large part of the value of land, is, in part at least, an unjustifiable discrimination against investors who happen to have put their funds in land rather than in other forms of wealth.

How serious this inequity is depends on the longevity of land ownership in particular cases, but unquestionably there would be a large number of highly inequitable situations stemming from a change to site value taxation. Offsets might occur through a rise in construction activity spilling over into a rise in the demand for land and gross land rents; also, property owners whose land-to-building value ratio is at or near the average ratio for all property in a taxing jurisdiction would experience no inequity, no matter what purchase price they paid.

Any really radical change in the distribution of a major tax involves windfall gains and losses, although perhaps not to the extent that some landowners would experience in this instance. Radical tax changes, consequently, usually take effect in stages, over a period of time. This is a possible resolution of the equity problem:

inequities would result from a shift from the present property tax to a site value tax, but they would perhaps be more bearable if the change takes place over some years (it was twelve years in Pittsburgh), and they would be reduced if the shift was not a complete one; that is, if the new system involved partial rather than total untaxing of improvements.

The equity problem is a serious drawback to a complete shift to site value taxation; an equally serious drawback relates to the adequacy of revenues. Heilbrun, by means of ingenious use of the very sketchy data which are relevant to the problem, suggests that the present yield of the real estate tax in the United States may exceed the whole rent of land, which is the theoretical maximum revenue potential, since a land tax which equals more than the before-tax rent of the land will result in negative land values.[37]

Heilbrun shows algebraically that the rent of land will exceed the present real estate tax yield only if, after capitalization or shifting of present taxes, the ratio of the interest rate for capitalization of land rents to the average effective real estate tax rate is greater than the ratio of the capital value of buildings to the capital value of land.[38] Goldsmith's estimates for 1956 for private noninstitutional property, excluding farm and forest property, provide a ratio of buildings to land of 4.4:1. In 1957, the effective property tax rate on nonfarm realty was about 1.4 percent.[39] Thus, unless the interest rate

[37] Heilbrun deals with adequacy in "The Effects of Alternative Real Estate Taxes," pp. 234-45.

[38] *Ibid.*, p. 236.

  Let N_L = rent of land
  R = the yield of the present realty tax
  r_a = the rate of the present realty tax
  C_L = capital value of land after capitalization of the present land tax
  C_B = capital value of buildings after capitalization or shifting of the present tax
  i_L = rate of capitalization of the rent of land
  $N_L = C_L(i_L + r_a)$
  R = $r_a (C_L + C_B)$
Therefore, $N_L > R$ can be written as
  $C_L(i_L + r_a) > r_a(C_L + C_B)$
or, $i_L C_L + r_a C_L > r_a C_L + r_a C_B$
which reduces to
  $i_L C_L > r_a C_B$
or, by rearranging terms, to
  $i_L/r_a > C_B/C_L$

[39] This figure differs slightly from that used by Heilbrun. It is based on the

for capitalization of land was well over 6 percent in 1957, the yield of the real estate tax equalled all, or nearly all, of the rent of land.[40]

The underlying data are open to question, however. Goldsmith, for example, does not estimate land values directly, but assumes that they equal specified fractions of structure value, for each of the classes of structure he deals with. The Goldsmith method is likely to produce somewhat lower estimates for the land component than alternative approaches, but it is highly unlikely that any estimate would result in a fundamentally different conclusion than that reached by Heilbrun: "Unless we are prepared virtually to end private ownership of rights in land by taking almost its whole rent it is no longer feasible to substitute a land tax for the real estate tax at the present level of yield."[41]

It is entirely possible, of course, that this is not true for particular places, at least not to the same extent. Ronald Welch's calculations for California as of 1962 suggest that the ratio of total improvements value to total land value is 1.35:1, rather than Goldsmith's 4.4:1; this results in a required return of only about 2.2 percent on land to produce enough rent to replace the entire yield of the existing property tax.[42]

Assessed value data which show land and improvements separately, however, are entirely inadequate for testing this proposition in most places since the quality of the separation is highly questionable: neither assessors nor taxpayers have any need to be greatly concerned about accuracy of anything except the total assessment. Isolated examples from abroad do suggest the possibility of revenue adequacy in particular places, relative to the existing property tax. For example, a pilot survey of Whitstable in England, released in early 1964, indicated that existing rateable values exceeded site values by only 13 percent.[43] But English rateable values, as noted earlier, are on the basis of existing rather than potential uses.

It is also possible, if not probable, that untaxing buildings might lead to a rise in gross land rents, thus providing somewhat more

---

estimated distribution of property tax payments in Table 2-3 and the Goldsmith wealth data.

[40] $6.16/1.4 = 4.4$, the ratio of building to land values.

[41] "The Effects of Alternative Real Estate Taxes," p. 235.

[42] Letter to author, Dec. 29, 1964.

[43] *The Economist* (London), Feb. 29, 1964.

leeway for site value taxation. Nevertheless, the general conclusion must be that 100 percent revenue replacement through exclusive taxation of land is not a practicable alternative: either improvements must continue to be partially taxable or some nonproperty tax source must substitute for part of the present real property tax yield. The conclusions of the earlier portions of this study would support the latter course of action: reducing reliance on property taxation overall sufficiently to permit exclusive taxation of land values.[44]

Land Value Increment Taxation

The taxation of land value increments for many years has been something of an aside in public finance. The tax is used in various guises in a number of countries (for example, Denmark and Spain, among the countries covered by Table 1-4), but in none is it a major tax nor are lofty claims made for it. The American public finance literature has contained over the years scattered and usually favorable references to it.[45] Here, too, the claims are limited.

The basic justification for the land increment tax is the existence of "unearned increments"—rising land values as a social rather than individual product. However, by taxing only increments (and, in some American proposals, only at time of transfer), it would avoid the equity problem entailed in shifting to the site value tax—the expropriation of past increases in land values which may have been paid for in full by new owners, prior to the tax shift. While equity problems may be much less severe than with the site value tax, the economic advantages are correspondingly less significant. Revenue from the tax, if levied only at the time of transfer of ownership, cannot be large enough to form a complete replacement for the present property tax: if the rate is low, the yield will be minor and if high it will encourage owners to postpone realization.

Thus the neutrality of the increment tax with respect to new

[44] Substantially reduced reliance on property taxation overall combined with exclusive taxation of site values implies an equity problem of importance: owners of existing buildings would receive major windfall gains in this case.

[45] See those in Walker, *Tax Policy*, pp. 26-27; Edwin Spengler, "The Taxation of Urban Land-Value Increments," *Journal of Land and Public Utility Economics*, Vol. 17 (1941), pp. 54-58; C. Lowell Harriss, "Alternative Bases for Real Estate Taxation," in *Property Taxes*, Tax Policy League (1940), pp. 219-25.

construction is not likely to prove much of an advantage. As a supplement to other local taxes, it would tend to encourage more intensive uses of land by reducing the net after-tax return available from withholding land from use for speculative resale. Also, by taxing prospective capital gains on investment in land more heavily than gains on investment in other assets, it would tend to marginally depress land prices, which has positive effects on development. Another advantage of the tax is that it is not cyclically destabilizing from the standpoint of the economy, or more burdensome in periods of declining asset prices from the standpoint of the individual.

Essentially, then, this is a supplementary capital gains tax on land which could provide at best only limited revenues. It has the unusual advantage of being highly acceptable on equity grounds while having generally beneficent, if not overwhelmingly powerful, allocation effects. Perhaps the strongest case can be made for it either as a substitute means of financing certain kinds of capital improvements frequently handled through special assessments, or at least as a means of recouping part of such costs.

The special assessment is a halfway house between the property tax and a user charge, with physical extent (or, in some cases, value) of property used as the basis for distributing the cost of a capital improvement, typically sewers or streets, among abutting property owners who are presumably the principal beneficiaries. If the costs can be apportioned on a basis more closely related to actual use and the benefits are really quite confined, then an out-and-out user charge is much to be preferred. If the benefits are very generalized, then a general tax is to be preferred. But there is surely an in-between area, in which cost apportionment is difficult but benefits are highly unevenly distributed, with some land values rising sharply as a result of a public improvement and others hardly affected at all. One example is the extension of subway lines in various parts of New York City in the past, which made it possible to use land near the stations for apartment house sites, thus greatly increasing its value. A land value increment tax would seem superior to the special assessment as a device to recoup part of the costs of the improvement in such cases: the tax payment is made only when and if land values do actually rise in response to the improvement, not in the cheerful expectation or desperate hope that land values may rise some time in the future.

A "Family of User Charges"

The benefit argument for the real property tax is not a new one. The rationale that possession of property is the best objective measure of ability to pay has long since been undermined by the changing nature of the economy, the narrowing of the general property tax itself, and the wide variations in rates and coverage among jurisdictions in large urban areas. An attractive substitute was long ago found in the benefit argument. Essentially, the case is that, through local government, "property is afforded services or given special advantages which make it so attractive to owners, tenants and speculators that, directly or indirectly, they are willing to pay a premium for its use or possession."[46]

Obviously, this has limited validity, for most local public services financed from property tax revenues are designed to yield their benefits to residents primarily in some other capacity than as users of real property—as parents of schoolchildren, as welfare recipients (and philanthropically inclined, more affluent citizens), as users of transport facilities, and so on. But these services do enhance the usefulness and value of real property, as do more obviously property-oriented public services, notably police and fire protection, water supply and sewerage, refuse removal, and transportation services (some of which are amenable to direct user charges on bases which are independent of property characteristics). The problem is that there is no real way of distinguishing between services to property as such and services to residents.

But the existing property tax is a crude instrument for financing even these services, since the distribution of tax liabilities is proportionate neither to the benefits received nor to the costs of providing the services. If the benefit rationale is to have appeal on equity grounds, it is not enough to say that property in general benefits from public services; individual tax obligations must bear some relation to the specific public services which justify the tax. Moreover, the present property tax as a benefit tax is deficient on efficiency grounds as well. As Harriss has said:

[46] Edwin H. Spengler, "The Property Tax as a Benefit Tax," in *Property Taxes,* Tax Policy League (1940), p. 170.

. . . the cost of the services which the community renders or which it makes because of the existence and nature of property bears no necessary relationship to either the value or the income of the property.

Consequently, allocating the total cost on the basis of value means that some property owners or users of property will bear less than their economic share of the total costs and others will bear more. The result will be a less than optimum economic utilization of resources. Improvements whose costs to the community are greater than their costs to their owners continue in existence while new investments are not made even when the social advantages would warrant because the money costs are too great.[47]

The failure of the present tax on efficiency grounds in this connection is not merely a consequence of its imperfections or of tax-rate differentials within economically meaningful geographic areas. Even a tax on pure net rents is not satisfactory to finance public services which are provided "because of the existence and nature of property"; such a tax would be satisfactory only if the schedules of individuals' liabilities were identical under the pure rent tax and under a system of direct user charges. Neither the benefits conferred by public services to property nor the cost of providing such public services are likely to be extremely closely correlated with net rents.[48]

This argues for use of a "family of user charges" or of benefit taxes to finance services to property, revenue forms which are clearly linked to the nature of the public services themselves rather than tenuously linked like the present property tax. Such revenue forms might very well have some property characteristics as the measure of liability, but not necessarily the market value of site plus improvements.

Vickrey has pointed out a number of these alternatives.[49] For example, the benefits from fire protection are roughly correlated with the value of improvements, but with many striking exceptions. However, the costs of the service are largely determined by area:

[47] Harriss in *Property Taxes*, p. 228.

[48] This distinction was pointed out by Lynn A. Stiles of the Federal Reserve Bank of Chicago in his discussion of my paper at the Regional Science Associa tion meetings in December 1961.

[49] William Vickrey, "General and Specific Financing of Urban Services," in *Public Expenditure Decisions in the Urban Community*, Howard G. Schaller, ed., (Resources for the Future, 1963), pp. 64-86.

the principal operational guide for providing the service is to have the equipment located within a specific number of minutes travel time to all protected property. Vickrey's conclusion is that the chief criterion for an economic revenue device for financing fire protection should be either land area or land value exclusive of improvements, probably the latter.

For water distribution facilities, he concludes that the best simple rule is to tax on the basis of front footage since, due to economies of scale in water main size, "the cost of the mains is proportional to their length and relatively independent of the required volume of flow."[50] A municipal frontage tax, to defray the basic traversal costs of a variety of other public utility services, ranging from electricity supply to mail delivery, whether or not provided by the municipality itself, is an analogous Vickrey proposal.[51] In regard to transportation services, Vickrey argues for a comprehensive system of marginal cost pricing related to transport use rather than property characteristics. This, however, would leave a sizeable intermarginal residue to be financed elsewhere, and here he argues that taxes on the value of outlying land rather than taxes on property value in general are called for.

This or some similar "family of user charges" amounts to a radical transformation, but not outright abolition, of the property tax on real property. For one thing, administration of this type of revenue system would seem to call for a single assessment organization, since assessing of the various measures of tax liability—area, frontage, site value, improvements value—can and should be done by a single administrative agency. In addition, this system calls for a huge amount of decision-making on cost and benefit connections and preferences for individual services. Individual voter-taxpayers are not likely to relish or participate heavily in such a time-consuming process, and thus the decision-making can justifiably be left to general-purpose local government authorities, which render single tax bills built up from a variety of measures.[52]

Moreover, such proposals as these do not deal with the major portion of property tax revenues today—the revenues used to finance services to persons rather than property. The propriety of

[50] *Ibid.,* p. 67.
[51] *Ibid.,* pp. 85-86.
[52] Lynn Stiles, in unpublished materials, has elegantly elaborated this approach.

reliance on the property tax for such purposes depends on the considerations discussed throughout this study: the income redistributing effects of the property tax; the case for and against giving so much income redistributing authority to thousands of small local governments; the effects on investment in real property; and the locational effects among competing jurisdictions of taxes which do *not* represent a payment for services to property.

Conclusion

Some of the proposed alternative forms of real property taxation appear to rank a good deal higher on efficiency and equity grounds than the existing American property tax system. There is a strong economic argument for taxing location rents via the site value tax, but considerations of both equity and revenue adequacy indicate that such a tax cannot be a complete replacement of the existing tax on real property, save in rare instances. There is also a good case for supplemental capital gains taxation of land value increments.

Land and improvements taxes specifically levied as benefit taxes or "a family of user charges," on bases which relate more closely to the public services they finance, also earn high marks on economic grounds. Here, however, there is no case for metropolitan area-wide uniformity of rates. Instead, there is a case for uniformity of rates only within the optimal service area for each function so financed. The definition of service areas involves consideration of both economies of scale and spillovers. Where large-scale operations are substantially more efficient and/or where there would be major spillovers of costs and benefits if the geographic unit is small, the service area would be a large one. However, some services to property, such as fire protection, obviously do not require large geographic units. If the service area is a sensible one, differences in rates among adjacent jurisdictions do not have adverse locational effects, since a higher rate is a quid pro quo for better quality public services

Relative to these alternatives, the economic case for a property tax on business property which is neither a tax on location rents nor a user charge is weak indeed. On the other hand, there is a much stronger case for a continued property tax on housing, above and beyond site value, land value increment, and user charge taxation. In the American tax system, consumer expenditures for housing are treated very lightly under the major nonproperty taxes and very harshly under the property tax. State and local sales taxes universally reach only a very minor fraction of total housing outlays—expenditures for fuel and utility services and goods used for housing maintenance and repair.[53] Owner-occupied housing is also notoriously favored by the federal income tax. Thus, in the absence of a property tax on housing, the tax system in the aggregate would be markedly unneutral, in favor of housing vis-à-vis all other forms of consumption. There is, therefore, an argument for continuing the property tax as a form of excise on housing expenditures, although perhaps only at rates analogous to those which generally apply to other taxed items of consumer expenditures—say, 5 percent instead of 15 percent or more.

The above discussion states the economic case for new forms of real property taxation, assuming that local taxation of real property in some form is to be continued, and continued at something like its present importance. Obviously, under this assumption, the case collapses if these alternatives cannot possibly yield sufficient revenues. Can they? Consider the evidence for 1957. In that year, the total property tax yield was $12.9 billion; approximately $9.2 billion was derived from taxes on nonfarm land and structures.[54] According to the Goldsmith estimates, the current value, at year-end 1956, of all privately owned nonfarm and noninstitutional land was roughly $120 billion.[55] A 3 percent tax on this value—more than double the indicated effective rate on nonfarm land and buildings combined—would probably come close to appropriating one-half the rent of land after present taxes and would yield $3.6 billion.

[53] Often these are taxable only if purchased at retail by consumers themselves, and not taxable when supplied via contract services.

[54] See Chap. II. This assumes that 80 percent of state assessed public utility property took the form of land and structures. As indicated earlier in this study, this is an artificial distinction; in effect, the assumption here is that if there were no personal property taxation, property taxes paid by utilities in the states where personalty is taxed would have been 20 percent lower than they were in 1957, which is probably an invalid assumption.

[55] Raymond W. Goldsmith, *The National Wealth of the United States in the Postwar Period* (Princeton University Press for National Bureau of Economic Research, 1962), Tables A-40 and A-41.

Presumably, the equity considerations discussed in the section on site value taxation above would preclude taxation which absorbs very much more than half the rent of land. However, the yield of a possible site value tax should be related to land rents before existing taxes, if these are to be replaced. On the assumption that the appropriate capitalization rate for land is 6 percent—which may be too high—the rent of land worth $120 billion, which is an after-tax valuation, was $7.2 billion in 1956-57. To this, the present tax must be added: $120 billion times an average effective rate in 1957 of 1.4 percent, or $1.68 billion. This amounts to a before-tax annual rent of $8.88 billion. Therefore, a tax equal to one-half the gross rent of land in 1957 would have yielded $4.44 billion.

During the 1950-58 period, land values in current prices rose at an annual rate in the $7.5-$8 billion range, considering again only private nonfarm and noninstitutional land, according to the Goldsmith data. Most of these capital gains, of course, were not realized by transfer in any one year but, assuming that a land increment tax was imposed with very little room for escape at death or by gift, the average annual tax base over a long period might be in this range. A tax at a rate of, say, 20 percent would therefore yield about $1.5 billion. But if a site value tax equal to 50 percent of land rent were also imposed, land value increments would be reduced significantly. Net land rents after tax would be reduced from $7.2 billion, in the 1957 example, to $4.44 billion, a reduction of 38 percent. If the rate of capitalization were not affected, land value increments would be correspondingly reduced, and the yield of a 20 percent land value increment tax would be $0.93 billion.

Revenues from the user charge types of property tax will depend on the extent to which this method of financing is considered appropriate. For this illustrative calculation, it has been assumed that sewerage, other sanitation, and fire protection are indisputably services to property and candidates for financing by these special types of property tax to the extent not now financed by direct user charges. Local government expenditure for highways not covered by user taxes and charges and state aid is included as well. In addition, it has been arbitrarily assumed that one-third of police costs and of general overheads (general control, general public buildings, other and unallocable) represent services to property. In 1957, local government current operating and estimated debt service outlays for these functions, less applicable state aid, user charges, and special assessments, amounted to about $3.5 billion.[56] This would be another element of the revenue potential of the alternatives.

As Tables 2-3 and 2-8 indicate, 1957 property taxes on non-farm residential property amounted to nearly $5.3 billion, representing on the average about 17 percent of housing costs or gross rents. Therefore, the property tax on housing at a rate which averages no more than 5 percent or so—to make it closer to the more common range of consumption taxes—would have yielded about one-third as much as housing property taxes did yield, or about $1.7 billion.

The four alternatives in this example add to $10.6 billion:

	Billions of Dollars
Site value tax at half the rent of land	4.44
Land value increment tax at 20 percent	.93
User-charge-type property taxes	3.50
Housing tax at not more than 5 percent of housing costs	1.70
Total	10.57

This is in excess of the actual 1957 yield of nonfarm realty taxes, $9.2 billion. It suggests that the problem of revenue yield does not preclude this form of radical reform of the property tax, in the direction of a system which has greater attractiveness on efficiency and equity grounds.

Aside from the inertia inherent in the existing tax, there are some serious drawbacks to this, however. For one thing, there would be real equity problems in the transition, with substantial windfall losses and gains as the tax burden was redistributed. For another, the administration of such a system would be much more complicated than that of the present system.

Radical reform of the property tax requires the weighing of advantages and disadvantages—a hard and unpleasant choice among alternatives none of which is desirable on all counts. It is in the nature of life to present societies and individuals with hard choices. The essential message of this study is that the decision to continue with the property tax we do have is just such a choice and that it is not at all obvious that it is the best—or the worst—of all possible choices.

[56] U.S. Bureau of the Census, *Census of Governments, 1957,* Vol. III, No. 5, "Compendium of Government Finances" (1959).

APPENDIXES

Derivation of Estimates
for Tables 2-1, 2-2, and 2-3

Table 2-1

BETWEEN DECEMBER 1962 AND MARCH 1963 (and again in December 1963), the Governments Division of the Bureau of the Census made special tabulations of data from the 1957 Census of Governments. This was done under a special contract with the Brookings Institution. The tabulations have been used to estimate the distribution of the 1957 state and local government general property tax revenue by the property use class employed in that Census.

Volume V of the 1957 Census, "Taxable Property Values in the United States," contains, in Tables 2, 3, and 4, estimates of assessed values for local general property taxation in 1956, by major use class and by state. If these assessed value distribution data are applied to the totals of property tax collections in 1957 for the country as a whole (or by states separately and then cumulated), crude national totals of the distribution of revenue by use class can then be derived. However, this procedure has a major defect; it ignores the very considerable range of variation in property tax *rates* among jurisdictions. Consider the following highly simplified example. Suppose that there are only two jurisdictions, with equal total assessed values composed of two use classes, but having very different distributions of property and very different tax rates:

222

	Jurisdiction A	Jurisdiction B	A+B
Total assessed value:	$100.00	$100.00	$200.00
Use Class 1	20.00	80.00	100.00
Use Class 2	80.00	20.00	100.00
Tax rate	*2%*	*4%*	*3%* (average)
Tax revenues:			
Total	$2.00	$4.00	$6.00
Use Class 1	0.40	3.20	3.60
Use Class 2	1.60	0.80	2.40

On the basis of a simple averaging of both jurisdictions, it would appear that cach use class provides 50 percent of the revenues, since each accounts for 50 percent of total assessed values. But if the tax revenue distribution is computed separately for the two jurisdictions and then added, it is clear that the distribution of revenues is 60-40, not 50-50.

In practice, the problems stemming from tax rate variation are closely related to urbanization. In heavily urbanized areas property tax rates tend to be relatively high, and such areas tend to contain higher proportions of nonfarm residences, commercial property, and vacant lots; and lower proportions of farm real estate, state assessed utility property, and taxable personal property.[1] Therefore, in this special tabulation, nation-wide totals were built up on the basis of separate computations for a sample of counties and county areas.

The sample used (see Appendix Table A-1) consisted of 516 of the nation's 3,096 counties and county areas. This is a sample which has been developed by the Governments Division in connection with its new nationwide quarterly series on local government tax collections.[2] Total general property tax revenue estimated on the basis of the sample came within 0.6 percent of the actual national total which appears in Volume V, Table 1, of the 1957 Census of Governments.

[1] The last point may sound surprising in view of the concentration of business personalty in cities. However, in the Census sample (see below), locally assessed personalty provided nearly 22 percent of general property tax revenues for county areas with populations of less than 25,000, but only 14 percent for county areas over 250,000 in population and 19 percent for county areas between 50,000 and 250,000.

[2] The actual sample for the new quarterly series differs slightly from that used in this special tabulation; a few county areas were substituted because data on the distribution of assessed values by use class for 1956 were unavailable. County areas include, in addition to counties, independent cities outside any county government and merged city-county governments.

TABLE A-1. Sample of County Areas Used for Estimated Distribution of General Property Tax Revenue by Type of Property, 1957

(Dollar amounts in thousands)

Sample Strata—Population Size (1960)	County Areas		Local Property Tax Revenue		Ratio of Sample to U. S. Total
	Number in U. S.ᵃ	Number in Sample	U. S.	Sample	
I 250,000 or more	121	121	$ 7,467,237	$7,467,237	1/1
II 100,000–249,999	176	109	1,648,460	1,001,139	1/1.65
III 50,000– 99,999	291	73	1,016,699	263,921	1/3.85
IV 25,000– 49,999	586	92	983,564	158,168	1/6.22
V 15,000– 24,999	631	57	590,513	49,411	1/11.95
VI 10,000– 14,999	463	31	314,310	20,836	1/15.08
VII Less than 10,000	828	33	343,454	13,188	1/26.04
Total	3,096	516	$12,364,237	$8,973,900	—

ᵃ In terms of 1957 status, that is, excluding Alaska and Hawaii.

The procedure used was, first, to multiply total general property tax revenue for each county area by the percentage distribution of net taxable assessed values for that county area; second, to cumulate the resulting revenue by use class figures within sample classes; and third, to blow up the sample classes by the appropriate factors. Net taxable assessed value equals gross assessed value of property subject to local general property taxation less the tax-exempt portions of locally assessed valuations. These partial tax exemptions applied in twenty-four states in 1956-57, and consisted largely of homestead and veterans' exemptions; they amounted to $8 billion, less than 3 percent of total gross assessed values in the United States. The Governments Division itself had developed in the 1957 Census a procedure for estimating the portions of these exemptions applicable to real and personal property, respectively. For this tabulation, I supplied the Governments Division with formulas for the distribution of the exemptions applicable to real property by realty use class for each county area. The formulas were largely the result of an examination of legal provisions governing the exemptions in each state.

In eight states—the six New England states, plus Michigan and Wisconsin—assessed value data by Census use class are available only for cities and towns (or townships), not by county. I supplied the Governments Division with county estimates, based on available Census data for major local units, fragmentary state data, and related economic series. A further modification was made by the Governments Division to take into account state general property tax revenues in those states which collect significant amounts from the tax (the adjustment is necessary because state government revenues do not, of course, appear in the data for property tax revenue by county area).

A major adjustment was required for the acreage and farm category. Since counties and county areas were the primary units for this tabulation, the procedure described above implicitly assumes that the county-wide distribution of assessed values is an appropriate allocator for the property tax revenues of all local governments within the county. This is, of course, not a valid assumption but for the most part the resulting distortions probably are small and to some extent offsetting. One distortion, however, is serious: there is virtually no acreage and farmland within city limits, and spreading city property tax revenues over acreage and farms beyond city limits very substantially overstates the acreage and farm share of property tax revenue (especially in view of the high proportion of total property tax revenue accounted for by the cities). Therefore, the tabulation was devised so that city property tax revenue does not apply to acreage and farms, while all other property tax amounts are spread among all classes of taxable property in the sample counties. This adjustment reduced the acreage and farm share by about one-sixth, from 9.7 percent to 8.2 percent.

Limitations

There are a number of possible sources of significant error in the resulting estimates, stemming from the procedure employed:

1. Most fundamental (except for the farm and acreage adjustment), this procedure ignores the significant intra-county tax rate variations. Such variations are likely to be most important in the case of counties in the larger metropolitan areas which do not consist wholly, or largely, of the central cities themselves and which contain large numbers of taxing jurisdictions performing major governmental functions. It is not entirely clear what the effects are, but in general it seems likely that the final results overstate slightly the share of property tax revenues derived from industrial and agricultural property, probably at the expense of residential and commercial property.

2. There is some sampling error, probably quite small, inherent in the 516 county area sample as a whole.

3. The underlying Census data on assessed values are partly sample-based and thus are subject to sampling error.

4. There are definitional problems in converting data based on

use classes prescribed by state law into the Census use classes.

    5.   The distribution of partial exemptions by use classes is a relatively crude one.

    6.   Similarly, estimates for the eight "city-and-town" states are rough.

The Results

The results appear in Table 2-1, which presents the national totals, and shows a distribution estimated from the sample and adjusted to account for the full amount actually collected by state and local governments in 1957. The final column shows, for comparative purposes, the results of a crude estimate based on the national totals in Tables 2 and 4 of Volume V of the 1957 Census.

The differences in the relative shares of general property tax revenue provided by the various use classes among counties grouped by population size (the sample classes) are major ones; they reflect differences in the composition of the stock of private wealth in places with varying degrees of urbanization, and presumably also differences in state law and assessment practice between the more densely and less densely populated states (although this is not nearly so apparent).

As the population size of areas declines, there is a striking decline in the importance of nonfarm residential property, of commercial property, and of industrial property. For the entire country, residential property accounts for 42 percent of the tax revenue. For the group of counties with populations of over 250,000 the proportion is over 50 percent, but for the below-25,000 group, the proportion is less than 20 percent. Commercial and industrial realty (especially the former) and vacant lots exhibit similar population-related characteristics. The significant offset to this is the increasing importance of agricultural realty in the tax base as area population size declines. In addition, the importance of state assessed property, largely consisting of public utility property, rises appreciably as area size declines. The importance of locally assessed personal property rises slightly as area size declines, presumably because of taxes on farm inventories and machinery and the greater relative importance of motor vehicles in general in the stock of wealth in less urbanized places.

Table 2-2

The special tabulation underlying Table 2-1 refers only to revenue from *general* property taxation. In addition to the $12.4 billion collected in 1957 from the general property tax, state governments in thirty-three states and local governments in twenty states had revenue totaling $442 million from *special* property taxes in 1957. These taxes, mostly on personal property, are levies on an ad valorem basis, but for which "a rate applies which is not directly governed by the rate of general property taxation in particular local areas. Usually, this is a uniform state-wide rate, either specified by law or representing the average of general property tax rates for the entire state."[3]

Tables 1 and 23 of Volume V of the 1957 Census provide the basis for an estimate of the distribution of these revenues:

	Millions of Dollars
Total	$421.6
Intangibles	170.5
Motor vehicles	200.3
Transportation and public utility property	48.6
Machinery and inventories	2.1

It is fairly simple to refine some of the data from the special tabulation further, especially in regard to state assessed property (which is estimated to have produced $953 million of general property tax revenue in 1957) and in regard to locally assessed personalty. Some crude indications can be drawn from assessed value data. The following is the apparent distribution of the assessed value of state assessed property in 1956, based on Table 2 of Volume V:

	Millions of Dollars
Total state assessed property	$22,540
Railroads	6,546
Other public utilities	13,354
Estimated intangibles	484
Estimated tangible personal property	922
All other (largely real property used in mining and oil and gas production)	1,233

As a rough approximation, it is perhaps permissible to assume that revenues from state assessed property are distributed in proportion to these assessed values. The error originating in tax rate variations would appear to be in the direction of understating the public utility share, since state assessed property other than railroads and public utility property appears to be concentrated in places where tax rates tend to be low. To make an adjustment in the right direction, in Table 2-2 it is assumed

[3] U.S. Bureau of the Census, *Census of Governments: 1957*, Vol. V, "Taxable Property Values in the United States," p. 2.

that 90 percent of the revenue from state assessed property comes from railroads and other public utilities, rather than the 88 percent indicated by the assessed value distribution.[4]

Table 2-2 also involves one other rough approximation on the basis of assessed value data: the distinction of revenue from locally assessed personal property between tangibles and intangibles. It is estimated that $1,515 million of the total of $47,978 million of locally assessed personal property in 1956 (before exemptions) represents intangibles, and that all of the partial exemptions applicable to personal property apply to tangible personalty.[5] Thus, 3.2 percent of the locally assessed personalty tax base consists of intangibles. This percentage has been applied to the total revenue figure for personalty from Table 2-1.

Table 2-3

This table incorporates, in addition to the data in Table 2-2, a refinement of the treatment of acreage and farms, a detailed breakdown of tangible personal property taxes (based on material in Chapter VI), and a rough breakdown of the nonfarm business sector.

Acreage and Farms

"Acreage and farm realty" includes a significant but unknown proportion of real property described on local tax rolls in terms of acreage, rather than lots, which is not agricultural at all—unimproved timber land, mineral land (in some places), waste land, rural nonfarm residences. Since the market and assessed values of most of this nonfarm acreage are markedly below those of farm acreage, the proportion is not likely to be high for the country as a whole. However, near urban areas, the proportion may be much higher, because of nonfarm residential property. Regional Plan Association data for the twenty-two county New York-New Jersey-Connecticut metropolitan region, for example,

[4] When state data for the classes of state assessed property detailed in Table 2, Volume V, of the 1957 Census of Governments (railroads, other public utilities, other), are multiplied by a computed state-wide average tax rate (general property tax revenue divided by assessed value subject to tax) and then cumulated, thus giving effect to interstate tax rate variation, railroad and public utility property appears to have accounted for 88.9 percent of revenue from state assessed property.

[5] 1956 data shown in Table 2, *ibid.*, have been adjusted here (and in the preceding text table) to take account of the corrected data for South Carolina and Texas shown in *Census of Governments: 1962*, Vol. II, "Taxable Property Values" (1963), p. 19.

suggest that the assessed value of nonfarm residential real estate in blocks of four acres or more (which are likely to be listed on tax rolls as acreage) may be in the $175-$200 million range, assuming assessment at one-third of market value. Even in this metropolitan region, where very large residential lots are unusually common, this represents much less than 1 percent of locally assessed realty valuations; however, it is a very large share of the estimated $300 million in total assessed value of "acreage and farms" in the region.

These nonagricultural elements of the category have been estimated as follows. In 1961, 21.6 percent of the gross assessed value of acreage and farms was located within standard metropolitan statistical areas (SMSA). Here it is estimated that one-fourth of this amount represents nonfarm residences and residential sites described on tax rolls as acreage. As indicated, the proportion in the New York area seems to be much higher than this, but probably is lower elsewhere. On a purely arbitrary basis, it is assumed that a nominal 3 percent of non-SMSA farm and acreage assessments is nonagricultural (timber land, etc.). Applying the percentages and weighting to account for the fact that nominal tax rates in metropolitan areas in 1957 averaged about 1.4 times those in nonmetropolitan territory, the following results:

$1,015 million $(.216 \times .25 \times 1.4) = $77 million, assigned to nonfarm residential realty

$1,015 million $(.784 \times .03 \times 1.0) = $24 million, assigned to nonfarm business realty.

Tangible Personal Property

Based on the data and analysis in Chapter VI, estimated revenues from taxes on tangible personal property have been distributed as follows, in Table 2-3:

	Millions of Dollars	*Percentage Distribution*
Commercial and industrial	$1,505	*66%*
Agricultural	205	*9*
Household	114	*5*
Motor vehicles	455	*20*
Total	$2,279	*100%*

These estimates include general property tax revenue from state assessed as well as locally assessed personalty (which are distinguished in Table

2-3 in order to make the transition from Table 2-2 more apparent), plus special property tax revenue.

The motor vehicle category has been further subdivided into property taxes on motor vehicles paid by farmers, nonfarm households, and nonfarm business. U.S. Department of Agriculture estimates indicate that in 1957 farmers paid more than 10 percent of total state motor vehicle registration fees. The states which subject motor vehicles to some form of property taxation account for most of the country's farm population and income; it therefore seems justifiable to apply this 10 percent relationship to motor vehicle property taxes. Leonard G. Rosenberg[6] obtained data for California and Illinois indicating that the personal/business motor vehicle property tax split in those states (which accounts for about one-third of all motor vehicle property tax revenue in the United States) was roughly 70/30. This proportion has been used here. Thus:

	Millions of Dollars
Total property taxes on motor vehicles	$455
Estimated farm share	45
Nonfarm share	410
Personal	287
Business	123

Nonfarm Business/Industry Breakdown

TRANSPORTATION AND PUBLIC UTILITY PROPERTY. There are two sources of information here. First, there is the Census of Governments data, indicating that property taxes paid by this industry group include an estimated 90 percent ($858 million) of the revenue from state assessed property (Table 2-2), $49 million from special property taxes, plus an unknown share of locally assessed industrial realty (and a small amount of locally assessed commercial and industrial personalty and motor vehicles). Second, there are estimates by industry and data on tax payments from company and industry sources.

The first step is to isolate the industry classifications to be included in this category, that is, those which are frequently treated in a distinctive fashion in property tax administration. The following is the 1957 assessment status of the various groupings, indicating the number of states in which the treatment shown is predominant:

[6] See Appendix B.

Industry	General Property Taxes		Special Property Taxes	No Property Tax
	Locally Assessed	*State Assessed*		
Railroads	6	33	6	4
Gas and electric	18	29	1	1
Telephone and telegraph	10	31	2	6
Carlines	12	*7	17	1
Motor carriers	16	*	6	1
Pipelines	15	*	—	1
Airlines	14	*	7	1

It seems appropriate to single out all the listed industries for special treatment. The following are some reasonable estimates of tax payments on an industry and firm basis, including special property taxes:

	Millions of Dollars
Electric and gas utilities	$ 789
Telephone and telegraph	331
Railroads	365
Pipelines	22
Air transportation	4
Motor carriers; carlines	30
Total	$1,541

The data on electric and gas utilities and telecommunications are from industry sources.[8] The railroad estimate is based on an unpublished estimate of the Advisory Commission on Intergovernmental Relations. State assessed railroad property amounted to 29 percent of all state assessed property in 1956 and one-third of state assessed utility property of all types, which would suggest tax revenues of about $280 million in the majority of states which use state assessment for railroads. Special property taxes amounted to about $12 million in six other states. The states with all or some local assessment of railroads for general property taxation include some with high property tax rates (Massachusetts, New

[7] Asterisk indicates that this item is state assessed in most of the remaining states.

[8] Supplied by Edison Electric Institute, American Gas Association, American Telephone and Telegraph Company (AT&T), Western Union Telegraph Company, and United States Independent Telephone Association.

Jersey, and New York) and/or heavy concentrations of railroad property (Texas). In 1957, railroad property taxes on locally assessed properties probably amounted to nearly $50 million in New York and New Jersey.

The estimates for pipelines and air carriers are those used by Rosenberg.[9] For pipelines, Rosenberg estimated property tax payments at the same percentage of net physical assets (1.8 percent) that applies to electric and gas utilities, using industry-supplied tax payment data for the latter. This seems appropriate, since pipelines have some of the same physical characteristics that electric and gas utilities do (space-using, highly visible fixed assets) as well as similar legal and economic characteristics. The air carrier figure is based on data compiled from carrier reports to the Civil Aeronautics Board.

The motor carrier and carline figure is an educated guess. Regulated motor carriers owned less than 5 percent of total truck and bus registrations in 1960, and a negligible share of autos, and thus probably accounted for no more than 10 percent of $123 million in motor vehicle property taxes assigned to nonfarm business. Their real property assets are very minor in the aggregate. As for carlines, special property taxes in the seventeen states using such taxes on carlines totalled only about $4 million in 1957.

The Advisory Commission on Intergovernmental Relations estimated property tax payments by the utility group in 1960 at $1,523 million.[10] Between 1957 and 1960, tax payments by electric and gas utilities rose by $229 million and those by telecommunications companies by $130 million. On the other hand, railroad tax payments apparently declined, by perhaps $50-$60 million. Thus, the estimate here seems well above that of the Advisory Commission, but the data support it.

The estimate also appears high in the light of the Census of Governments data. In Table 2-2, $907 million in utility property taxes is identified, leaving the substantial sum of $634 million to be accounted for by utility property included in other locally assessed categories, if the two estimates are to be reconciled. Some of this is to be found in locally assessed "industrial" realty. The 1962 Census of Governments estimate is that, in the nine states where locally assessed utility property is relatively important, its assessed value amounted in 1961 to $5.2 billion, or 17 percent of industrial real property assessments.[11] If the same percentage

[9] See Appendix B.
[10] *Measures of State and Local Fiscal Capacity* (1962), Table 37.
[11] "Taxable Property Values" (1963), p. 3.

of 1961 assessments applied to 1957 revenue amounts, some $170 million of taxes on industrial realty would actually represent taxes on utility property.

However, these nine states, in which large amounts of utility property are assessed locally, are high tax rate states, and the figure could be much higher. It is estimated on the following basis, for the nine states noted in the 1962 Census:

	1961—Utility Property as Percentage of Locally Assessed Realty	*1956 Locally Assessed Realty×(1) (Millions of Dollars)*	*1957—Average State-Wide General Property Tax Rate in Percentages*	*(2)×(3) (Millions of Dollars)*
	(1)	*(2)*	*(3)*	*(4)*
Arizona	*8.0%*	$ *44.3*	*6.2%*	$ *2.7*
Delaware	*5.4*	*50.1*	*1.5*	*0.8*
Maine	*7.3*	*67.7*	*5.7*	*3.4*
New Hampshire	*6.5*	*60.2*	*5.1*	*3.1*
New York	*9.3*	*3,223.6*	*5.0*	*161.2*
North Carolina	*5.2*	*209.9*	*2.0*	*4.2*
Rhode Island	*4.3*	*75.3*	*2.9*	*2.2*
Texas	*4.4*	*339.2*	*5.5*	*18.7*
Vermont	*9.2*	*33.0*	*6.7*	*2.2*
Total, nine states				*198.5*

This may be an understatement for two reasons: first, between 1956 and 1961, state assessed utility property declined as a proportion of total assessed values (from 7.3 percent to 7.0 percent), and it is possible that this also applied to locally assessed utility property; and second, there are minor amounts of locally assessed utility property in other states. On balance, therefore, a reasonable figure for utility property in the industrial category appears to be *$220 million.*

In addition to this, utilities do own office buildings, frequently high value parcels in downtown areas. At least some of these are likely to have escaped the net in the 1962 Census estimate just noted: for example, AT&T corporate headquarters in New York, which would not appear as operating utility property in any New York State tabulations since AT&T is not an operating utility from the State's point of view. To reflect utility property in the commercial category, the best that can be done is to make an arbitrary estimate of, say, *$20 million.*

Another reconciliation item involves commercial and industrial personalty. In the states which both tax personalty and locally assess utilities for general property taxation, some utility property (other than motor vehicles, treated below) is likely to be classed as personalty. For example, in New Jersey in 1962, $19 million was paid in taxes on telephone company personalty, amounting to a fifth of all taxes on commercial and industrial personalty. In 1957, forty-six states (including the District of Columbia) taxed business personalty; eight of these locally assessed telephone and telegraph companies and sixteen of these locally assessed most other nonrailroad utilities. Combining this, it is a reasonable guess that perhaps 20 percent of utility-owned personalty in the nation was locally assessed for general property tax purposes. If the New Jersey 1962 relationship, where 20 percent of business personalty is represented by utility-owned personalty, is applied to this, then about 4 percent of all general property taxes on locally assessed business personalty is on utilities: $1,469 million $\times$ .04 = *$59 million*.

Finally, utilities (not only motor carriers) are significant owners of motor vehicles. Of the twenty-one states which in 1957 locally assessed motor vehicles for general property taxes, four also assessed telephone and telegraph companies locally, and six also assessed most other nonrailroad utilities locally. This suggests that perhaps one-fourth of utility-owned motor vehicles in the twenty-one states is locally assessed for general property taxation. Based on general measures of economic activity, a reasonable guess is that about one-tenth of all motor vehicles owned by nonfarm businesses is utility-owned. Combining all this, it is estimated that of the $123 million allocated to general and special property taxes on nonfarm business motor vehicles, *$10 million* came from motor carriers, and *$5 million* came from other utilities.

To recapitulate, therefore, the estimated utility taxes included in other categories are divided as follows:

	Millions of Dollars
Industrial realty	$220
Commercial realty	20
Business personalty	59
Motor vehicles	15
Total	$314

This falls far short of the $634 million gap noted above. Possible explanations include: gross underestimates in these reconciliation estimates, gross overestimates of ad valorem tax payments in industry and company data (for example, if there is a timing problem, a one-year difference would amount to nearly $100 million), and very high rates of taxation on locally assessed utility property. The latter is probable, but it is hard to imagine that it could account for more than $100 million of the gap, at the extreme. A minor gap-filler would be the utility share of taxes on intangibles and vacant lots, but this is hardly likely to be more than $25 million or so. Thus, there remains an unreconciled difference.

MANUFACTURING. There is some independent evidence on property tax payments by manufacturing industry from the 1958 Census of Manufactures.[12] A sample survey of 50,000 manufacturing establishments in 1957 yielded data on real and personal property tax payments (a combined figure) by four-digit industry for the nation and by two-digit industry by state. The total for the United States amounted to $1,450 million.

This figure, however, does not cover taxes on property used for manufacturing paid by the owners of rented assets (who pay the tax themselves initially) rather than by the manufacturers. Such indirect property tax payments have been estimated on the basis of rental payments reported in the Census of Manufactures release just cited. An overall average percentage figure was selected to apply to rental payments. In selecting such a percentage, conflicting considerations have to be taken into account. First, since rented real property used in manufacturing appears to be concentrated in central portions of urban areas, particularly in the Northeast, property taxes are apt to contribute a high proportion of the rents. An aggravating factor in this connection is the poor competitive position of much of this realty because of high vacancy rates and low rents per square foot. (The implication of this is that the incidence of taxes on rented industrial realty is likely to rest heavily on the owners rather than on the renters of this realty.)

Rented equipment, on the other hand, is likely to have a much lower ratio of property tax liabilities to rental payments, in view of assessment practices and in view of the exemption of personalty in two leading industrial states—New York and Pennsylvania. In Chapter VI, it is estimated that, in 1961, the aggregate assessed value of commercial and industrial personalty was 20 percent of legally taxable wealth in that form. In contrast, the Census of Governments found that, in 1961, realty assessments were about 30 percent of market values. In the ten leading

[12] "Supplementary Employee Costs, Costs of Maintenance and Repair, Insurance, Rent, Taxes, and Depreciation and Book Value of Depreciable Assets: 1957," Subject Report MC58(1)-9 (1961).

industrial states, the following is the distribution of average size-weighted assessment/sales ratios for commercial and industrial realty in 1961:

Percentage	Number of States
15%–25%	3
25 –35	2
35 –40	3
55 –60	2
Total	10

Put another way, if rents on industrial realty average 12 percent of market value, if this realty is assessed at 35 percent of value and taxed at a nominal rate of 5 percent (the national average), then realty property taxes equal about 15 percent of rents. For equipment, if rents average 25 percent of market value and if equipment is assessed at, say, 18 percent of market value (giving effect here to exemption in a few states) and taxed at 5 percent, then personal property taxes equal only about 4 percent of rents. Putting all this together, it is here assumed that property taxes on rented property used in manufacturing in 1957 equal *12 percent* of rents, or *$170 million.*

Reconciliation of these estimates based on Census of Manufactures data with Census of Governments data is complicated since the relevant assessed value categories include both public utility and mining property, as well as manufacturing property. At any rate, the evidence suggests that a good share of $1,620 million estimated to have been paid in respect of real and personal property used in manufacturing industry—perhaps more than half—was for personal rather than real property, which is in keeping with the evidence on the distribution of manufacturing investment (see Table 2-4). The following are the relevant estimates:

	Millions of Dollars
Taxes on locally assessed industrial realty	$1,010
Taxes on state assessed industrial and mining realty	44
	$1,054
Less: Included taxes on utilities (perhaps 220) and on mining property, which is unknown but not negligible	300*
Equals: Taxes on manufacturing realty	800*
Plus: Taxes on manufacturing personalty	800*
Total property taxes on manufacturing	$1,620

* Approximate figures.

ALL OTHER NONFARM BUSINESS. This is simply the the residual, subtracting the rather differently based utility and manufacturing estimates from the estimated total for all nonfarm business based on Census of Governments data. It should be noted that the 2 percent of total property tax revenues, derived from what the Governments Division calls "other and unallocable" locally assessed real property, is here assigned to the nonfarm business sector. It is dominated by separately assessed mineral, oil, and timber rights, which are, in an economic sense, nonfarm business property. Moreover, much of the truly unallocable residual is believed to be business property not described adequately for classification elsewhere.

VACANT LOTS AND INTANGIBLES. These have not been allocated by sector in Table 2-3. For vacant lots, it is not clear what the relevant purposes of such an allocation might be. One type of allocation would be to split vacant lots into those designed mainly for ultimate residential use and those for business use. Presumably, the former would be much the largest share of the acreage and number of lots, and a somewhat smaller share of assessed value and tax revenues. For example, if allocated on the basis of tax revenue (from locally assessed realty) from housing versus revenue from commercial property, three-fourths of the amount would be assigned to housing. However, this clearly would exaggerate property tax payments relative to housing expenditures, since consumer expenditures in any year are not incurred for building lots held by builders and others. An alternative would be to assign to housing consumers (and particular industries) only estimated tax payments on those vacant lots held by prospective owner occupiers and by builders in the process of construction. All other taxes on vacant land would be assigned to some kind of catchall real estate industry, meaning here speculators and investors. However, there is no basis at all for such an estimate.

In concept, intangibles could also be split, for example, on the basis of Federal Reserve Flow of Funds data on the ownership by sector of financial assets which are taxable under the property tax. However, since the taxation of intangibles is so partial and erratic, this procedure does not inspire confidence. Furthermore, personal property taxes on some types of financial assets, especially bank deposits, are absorbed by financial institutions, rather than the beneficial owners of the assets. While it may make some sense in an analysis of incidence to allocate the tax on intangibles on the basis of, say, ownership of bank deposits, this would be largely for the sake of completeness.

Alternative Estimates of Property Tax Impact

Rosenberg Estimates

A COMPREHENSIVE SET OF ESTIMATES of property taxes paid by nonfinancial industry for the 1953-59 period was incorporated in a doctoral dissertation by Leonard G. Rosenberg of the University of Chicago.[1] The research for this was done as part of the study of taxation of income from capital, under the direction of Professors Arnold C. Harberger and Martin J. Bailey. It was one of the Studies of Government Finance conducted by the Brookings Institution. A summary comparison of the Rosenberg results and those in Table 2-3 is presented in Appendix Table B-1.

In broad outline, the results rather closely coincide. This is hardly surprising since Rosenberg relied on the 1957 estimates I have used in this study for nonfarm residential realty, intangibles, household personalty, and telecommunications and electric and gas utilities; these categories account for 52 percent of the total tax revenue in Rosenberg's tabulation.[2] However, the detailed industry estimates made by Rosenberg do not readily reconcile with Census of Governments data, on which I have had to rely heavily. Moreover, they are based, of necessity, on simplified estimating procedures which do not actually shed much

[1] July 1963 version, pp. 51-73.
[2] The two studies also use what is essentially the same railroad estimate, accounting for 3 percent of total tax revenues.

TABLE B-1. Two Distributions of Property Tax Revenue by Type of Property Compared

Sector and Type of Property	Percentage Distribution	
	This Study 1957[a]	Rosenberg 1953–59[b]
Nonfarm household property	44.1%	43.6%
Residential realty	40.4	40.5
Household personalty	0.9	0.8
Nonfarm personal motor vehicles	2.2	2.3
Residential realty acreage	0.6	—
Agricultural property	9.0	10.1
Nonfarm business property	43.1	44.3
Manufacturing	12.6	16.0
Utilities	12.0	12.6
Other	18.5	15.7
Trade	—	8.4
Services	—	3.1
Finance	—	0.9
Mining	—	1.5
Construction	—	0.9
Miscellaneous	—	0.8
Not allocated by sector	3.8	2.0
Intangibles	2.0	2.0
Vacant lots	1.8	—

Note: Because of rounding, details may not add to totals.

[a] From Table 2–3.

[b] Unpublished doctoral dissertation by Leonard G. Rosenberg, University of Chicago, July 1963. Research for this dissertation was conducted as part of the study of taxation of income from capital, in progress at the University of Chicago under the direction of Arnold C. Harberger and Martin J. Bailey, for the Brookings Institution Program of Studies of Government Finance.

light on the property tax per se. They may, nonetheless, be entirely adequate for a study of taxes on income from capital, which is a rather different matter.

Most of the difference in the two sets of estimates for *manufacturing* as a whole, and also for the "all other nonfarm business" group taken as a unit, relates to Rosenberg's use of a company rather than the establishment industrial classification. He did this because his detailed industry breakdown relied on *Statistics of Income* data, which are of course on a company basis. Consequently, his estimate for total property taxes paid by manufacturing industry is more than $300 million higher than the Census of Manufactures figure, since companies primarily in the manufacturing business (and so classed in tax returns) may have extensive nonmanufacturing activities.

The Rosenberg methodology for detailed industry estimates begins with relatively firm property tax data or estimates for a few major business sectors—agriculture, manufacturing, and major types of utilities. The tax payments figures are then compared to net physical assets of the industry groups, based on Internal Revenue Service book value data and depreciation materials (to supplement IRS data, for unincorporated businesses). A computed effective property tax rate is then determined, and applied to physical asset data for other industries; for example, the manufacturing rate is used for mining, construction, trade, and finance.

This implicit assumption that property tax payments bear a uniform relation to the book value of an industry's physical assets is a somewhat doubtful one. Differences in asset composition, assessment practices, and geographic location patterns among industries all have an immense effect. High assessment ratios for office buildings combined with central business district locations, for instance, suggest that realty involved in financial business is likely to be far more heavily taxed on the average than manufacturing realty. Mining property, on the other hand, is likely to be far *less* heavily taxed.

Another aspect of the Rosenberg method is indicated in his handling of property taxes paid indirectly through rents—taxes on land, structures, equipment, and mineral rights owned by persons and firms in the business of holding assets for rent or lease to others. Rosenberg deals with this as a residual, after distributing direct payments to other industries, and reduces it to a very modest figure—about a $400-million average for the years 1953-59. He then distributes this by industry on the basis of the percentage distribution of rent payments shown on 1959 business income tax returns.

However, property taxes paid through rent probably bear no consistent relationship to total rent payments by industry for the nation as a whole. For one thing, data on rental payments include leases of mineral rights and of equipment, as well as realty, and these are differentially taxed. Moreover, business realty leases themselves have all sorts of peculiar features with respect to real estate taxes. Ground leases net of taxes on the site are not uncommon; in such cases, the rental data are useless for estimating indirect property tax payments. Furthermore, the property rented may be tax-exempt to the owners, such as publicly owned airport property leased to common carriers. Therefore, in Table

2-3, this study deals with indirect property tax payments by singling out only manufacturing, and assuming that tax payments equal some overall average percentage of rental payments selected arbitrarily (see Appendix A).

There are two other lesser differences between the Rosenberg methodology and that used in this study. Rosenberg relies on U. S. Department of Agriculture estimates for taxes paid on agricultural real and personal property. The USDA real estate tax figure is about $100 million higher than the one I have used here (see below). Second, taxes on vacant lots are not shown separately in Rosenberg and thus, under his approach, they are implicitly allocated among nonfarm businesses; this largely explains the difference in the two estimates for all nonfarm business combined in Appendix Table B-1.

Estimates of Taxes on Nonfarm Housing

The National Income accounts, the 1960 Census of Housing, and 1960 *Statistics of Income* data all provide alternative estimates of all or part of the property taxes paid on housing. Appendix Table B-2 provides a summary comparison of some of these data. They are discussed somewhat more fully below.

The Office of Business Economics (OBE) makes annual estimates of property taxes paid on owner-occupied farm and nonfarm housing, in connection with the National Income tables on personal consumption expenditures and imputed personal income. Prior to the 1965 benchmark revisions of the National Income accounts, the OBE estimates were substantially higher than the Census of Governments data used here suggest. However, the revised series is consistent with the estimates in this study.

The alternative estimates presented in Appendix Table B-2 generally support the Census of Governments based estimates, notably the estimates constructed from the real estate tax information in the Residential Finance volume of the 1960 Census of Housing (Appendix Table B-4). These estimates suggest, for example, that in 1959-60, taxes on owner-occupied nonfarm housing were about 31 percent of total property tax revenue; the estimate based on the 1957 Census of Governments data (in Appendix Table B-3) amounted to 27.4 percent. However, the Residential Finance estimate for taxes on all nonfarm housing equalled 45.8 percent, somewhat above the 1962 estimate from Census of Governments data.

TABLE B-2. Alternative Estimates of Property Taxes on Nonfarm Housing

(In millions of dollars)

Source of Estimate and Year	Comparable Total Property Tax Revenue Figure	Property Taxes on Nonfarm Housing						Total Owner Occupied	Total Renter Occupied	Total All Housing
		Single-Family Houses			Multi-Family Housing					
		Total	Owner Occupied	Rented	Total	Owner Occupied	Rented			
Census of Governments, 1957 (Table 2–3)	$12,864	$4,391	n.a.	n.a.	$ 804	n.a.	n.a.	n.a.	n.a.	$5,195
Census of Governments, 1962[a]	19,054	7,056	n.a.	n.a.	1,364	n.a.	n.a.	n.a.	n.a.	8,420
1960 Census of Housing, Residential Finance Survey, 1959–1960[b]	15,500[c]	5,110	$4,480	$630	1,993	$365	$1,628	$4,845	$2,258	7,103
Statistics of Income 1960—Real estate taxes itemized on U.S. individual income tax returns[d]	17,000[e]	n.a.	n.a.	n.a.	n.a.	n.a.	n.a.	4,134	n.a.	n.a.

n. a. Not available.

[a] This represents an updating of the 1957 estimates, based on the changes in the housing share of assessed values subject to tax between 1956 and 1961, as follows:

	Single-Family Houses	Apartments
Estimated 1956 Share of Assessed Values (Percentage)	31.8%	6.2%
Increase in Share, 1956–61 (Percentage Points)	2.7	0.9
Percentage Increase in Share	8.49	14.52
Share of 1957 Revenue (Table 2–3)	34.13	6.25
Estimated Share of 1962 Revenue	37.03	7.16

[b] See Appendix Table B–4.

[c] Estimated calendar 1959 property tax revenue.

[d] U. S. Treasury Department, *Statistics of Income, Individual Income Tax Returns, 1960*, Table O, p. 14. Includes all real estate taxes claimed as deductions on individual income tax returns with itemized deductions.

[e] Estimated calendar 1960 property tax revenue.

The Residential Finance data on real estate taxes on nonfarm housing are tabulated in the form of frequency distribution of properties by real estate tax paid per dwelling unit, real estate tax per $1,000 of property value, and real estate tax as a percentage of owners' income, and as a percentage of housing costs (the latter two only for homeowner properties). The data are tabulated separately for homeowner and rental properties, within each of these by dwelling-unit size of structure, and within each of these categories by mortgage status. Total property taxes paid are not shown in the data but must be inferred from the basic frequency distributions, with some filling of gaps by crude techniques. Nonetheless, this is the only set of estimates available by both occupancy status and type of structure, and fortunately does appear to be reasonable in the aggregate.

Another fragment of evidence is found in *Statistics of Income* data for 1960. As Appendix Table B-2 shows, United States individual income tax payers who filed itemized deduction returns for 1960 claimed $4,134 million as personal deductions for real estate taxes paid. A total of 16.4 million returns claimed some deduction for real estate taxes; this compares with approximately 26.8 million owner-occupied properties covered in the Residential Finance Survey data for 1959-60. Real estate taxes paid by nonfilers and by taxpayers using the standard deduction are thus excluded. Even for itemized deduction taxpayers, this may not be an entirely satisfactory statistic, since the amounts claimed as personal deductions may include some taxes on property held for business purposes; on the other hand, some real estate taxes on owner-occupied residential property may be claimed as business expense deductions, rather than personal deductions. Moreover, the term "real estate tax" is not in all cases the familiar term for the local property tax, and the instructions to the taxpayer for 1960 returns did not clarify this.[3]

The *Statistics of Income* evidence, however, does seem consistent with the Residential Finance Survey data, and also with the Census of Governments data used here. That is, recognizing that taxpayers filing itemized returns on balance have higher incomes (a greater proportion owning their own homes thus paying higher real estate taxes than standard deduction taxpayers), and assuming, moreover, that high real estate taxes themselves provide an incentive to itemize deductions, it seems entirely reasonable that the deductions claimed should involve about 60 percent of owner-occupied properties and about 80 percent of

[3] Actually, there was no revenue reason to do so; the Internal Revenue Service was not concerned with the title of the tax, or the taxpayers' classification of it, as long as all state and local taxes paid by individuals were deductible.

TABLE B-3. Estimated Distribution of Property Tax Revenue Derived from Nonfarm Housing, 1957[a]

(Amounts in millions of dollars)

Occupancy Status	Percentage Distribution			Amount of Tax Revenue
	Housing Units[b]	Assessed Values[c]	Tax Revenue[d]	
Nonfarm single-family:				
Owner-occupied	75.6%	76.8%	77.3%	$3,394
Tenant-occupied	24.4	23.2	22.7	997
Total	100.0	100.0	100.0	4,391
Nonfarm apartments:				
Owner-occupied	17.2	16.7	16.6	133
Tenant-occupied	82.8	83.3	83.4	671
Total	100.0	100.0	100.0	804
Nonfarm totals:				
Owner-occupied	60.6	66.7	67.8	3,527
Tenant-occupied	39.4	33.3	32.2	1,668
Total	100.0	100.0	100.0	5,195

Sources: Special tabulation from 1957 Census of Governments of property tax collections by use class of property (Table 2–1); U. S. Bureau of the Census, *Census of Housing: 1960*, Advance Reports, "Housing Characteristics," HC(A2)-1 (June 1962); *Census of Governments: 1962*, Vol. II, "Taxable Property Values" (1963); *Census of Governments: 1957*, Vol. III, No. 6, "Local Government Finances in Standard Metropolitan Areas" (1959); and *Census of Governments: 1957*, Vol. V, "Taxable Property Values in the United States" (1959).

[a] Based on occupied year-round units only.

[b] Occupied nonfarm housing units as reported in 1960 Census of Housing.

[c] Based on: (1) assessed value data for 1961, from the 1962 Census of Governments, for single-family houses and for apartments, within and outside standard metropolitan statistical areas (SMSA), were divided by the numbers of occupied housing units in the 1960 Census of Housing, to produce these assessed values per unit figures:

	Inside SMSA's	Outside SMSA's
Single-family houses	$4,605	$2,383
Apartments	2,426	708

(2) these weights were applied to the Housing Census data on tenure status of units, within the four classes indicated in (1) above, and the totals by tenure status combined to yield the percentages shown in the table.

[d] The value data in column 2 were weighted on the basis of metropolitan location, on the assumption that nominal tax rates in metropolitan areas are 40 percent higher than in non-metropolitan territory, on the average. This, in turn, was based on calculations from the 1957 Census of Governments, for areas *then defined* as metropolitan. Local property tax revenue in 1957 divided by total assessed value subject to tax after exemptions yielded the following nominal rates:

Within 1957 standard metropolitan areas	5.10%
Outside	3.65%

the Residential Finance estimate of aggregate taxes paid on these properties.[4] Mean real estate tax per return in the *Statistics of Income* data was $257 while mean real estate tax per owner-occupied property in the Residential Finance data was $180.

[4] The 80 percent figure is the ratio of the *Statistics of Income* deductions for 1960 to estimated calendar 1960 real estate taxes on owner-occupied housing; the latter is the Residential Finance figure updated to calendar 1960 on the basis of the increase in aggregate property tax revenue from 1959 to 1960.

TABLE B-4. Estimated Real Estate Taxes on Nonfarm Housing, 1959–60, Based on 1960 Census of Housing Data[a]

Type of Property	Estimated Real Estate Taxes (Millions of dollars)
Homeowner properties[b]:	
1 Housing unit	$4,480
2–4 Housing units[c]	730
Subtotal	5,210
Rental and vacant properties:	
1 Housing unit	630
2–4 Housing units	406
5–49 Housing units	500
50 or more housing units	357
Subtotal	1,893
Total, all properties covered	7,103
Exhibit:	
Owner-occupied units[d]	4,845
Renter-occupied and vacant units[d]	2,258

[a] Except for 2–4 unit homeowner properties, based on frequency distributions of properties by real estate tax per dwelling unit, in U. S. Bureau of the Census, *Census of Housing: 1960*, Vol. V, "Residential Finance," Parts 1 and 2 (1963). For properties acquired before 1959, the number of units within each cell of the frequency distributions was multiplied by an estimated mean figure for the real estate tax class, and the cumulated total multiplied by the average number of dwelling units in each property in that size-class—(for example, 2.4 for 2–4 unit rental properties, 9.6 for 5–49 unit rental properties). Taxes on previously occupied properties acquired in 1959 and 1960 were estimated from the median figures for all properties in the class. Properties built in 1959 and 1960 were ignored, on the assumption that the taxes paid on these properties in the survey period (1959 to early 1960) covered only the site in its prior condition, not the new improvements.

[b] Owner-occupied housing in the form of cooperative apartments in buildings with more than four units is not covered in this table at all. The number of units involved is extremely small, less than 1 percent of all housing units covered by this table.

[c] Based on data from a special tabulation done by the Housing Division of the Census Bureau from the Residential Finance Survey responses (the Homeowner "Y" Tables); the raw material in this case was a cross-tabulation of properties by value of property and real estate tax per $1,000 of value.

[d] Assumes that one-half of taxes on 2–4 unit homeowner properties are attributed to owner-occupied units (the estimated average number of units per property is 2.1), and that there is one owner-occupied unit per property.

Taxes on Agriculture

The U. S. Department of Agriculture produces annual estimates of taxes paid by farmers. For 1957, the USDA estimate of taxes on farm personal property—$233 million—is, for all practical purposes, no different from the $250 million estimate (including motor vehicles) used in Table 2-3, given the tenuous procedures employed in allocating personal property taxes. The estimate for farm real estate taxes, however, is substantially higher than the one in Table 2-3—$1,032 million as against $914 million.[5] The USDA annual series is tied to the Census of Agriculture which employs a very inclusive definition of a "farm." Numerous properties which are defined as farms in the Census of Agriculture may not even be reported as "acreage and farms" in the Census of Governments assessed value tabulations. On the other hand, farms occupied by individuals not actually farmers (for example, "exurban" estates worked partly as farms) will be included in the USDA figures, but hopefully are excluded in Table 2-3, by means of the adjustments used. In general, the USDA compilers of the series are of the opinion that the discrepancy between the two estimates is a surprisingly small one.[6]

[5] Revised estimate from U. S. Department of Agriculture, Economic Research Service, *Farm Real Estate Taxes, Recent Trends and Developments* (September 1963).

[6] Frederick D. Stocker, U. S. Department of Agriculture, letter to author, January 6, 1964.

APPENDIX C

Nonresidential Property Taxes and Expenditure Benefits: Derivation

THE APPROACHES INVOLVED in this analysis, and the statistical evidence used to develop the estimates of incidence by income class, parallel those used in some of the major state tax studies completed in the last decade, particularly those of Minnesota, Michigan, and Wisconsin.[1] All these studies are essentially elaborations of the approach originally developed by Musgrave and his associates at the University of Michigan for the country as a whole for 1948.[2]

Basically, the approach involves making assumptions as to the incidence of each type of tax or expenditure by economic sector or group. The amounts thus assumed to be borne or received by each group are distributed among income classes on the basis of a relevant economic series which forms a proxy allocator. Thus, for example, taxes which are assumed to fall on corporate profits are distributed among income classes on the basis of the distribution of dividend income; expenditures which are assumed to benefit nonbusiness highway users are distributed

[1] The best discussions of the incidence portions of these studies are: O. H. Brownlee, *Estimated Distribution of Minnesota Taxes and Public Expenditure Benefits* (University of Minnesota Press, 1960); Richard A. Musgrave and Darwin W. Daicoff, "Who Pays the Michigan Taxes?" Chap. 4 of *Michigan Tax Study Staff Papers* (1958); University of Wisconsin Tax Study Committee, *Wisconsin's State and Local Tax Burden* (1959), Chap. II, together with background material prepared by the Wisconsin Department of Taxation, John A. Gronouski, and Maynard S. Comiez.

[2] "Distribution of Tax Payments by Income Groups: A Case Study for 1948," *National Tax Journal*, Vol. 4 (March 1951), pp. 1-53.

on the basis of consumer expenditure for automobile transportation or gasoline and oil purchases.

Since the shifting assumptions are central to the analysis and since there is so little agreement about the shifting of some types of taxes (with obvious parallels for expenditure benefits), usually the results under alternative shifting assumptions are presented. Also, the convention requires analysis on the basis of more than one income concept: money income, the broader personal income concept used in the national income accounts, income after taxes, and in one case, permanent income. The complexity of the analysis also depends on how refined the tax and expenditure categories are. In this study, eight classes of nonresidential property taxes, based on the impact analysis in Chapter II, and a six-way breakdown of local government expenditure financed by the property tax, corresponding to the Musgrave-Daicoff breakdown, are used.

Few of the available statistical series used as proxy allocators are entirely satisfactory. In all such studies, the investigators have to make do with some allocators which are admittedly poor ones. Where resources are available, it is possible to do considerable refinement on this score. For example, the Wisconsin study developed income data from a special sample of Wisconsin state income tax returns; the Michigan study used Survey Research Center materials to a greater extent than the other studies. In this study, it has not seemed worthwhile to go to great lengths in developing highly refined allocators, largely because inspection of alternative allocators suggested that some possible refinements would produce only minor differences in the final results overall. However, the reader should be cautioned that the relatively crude approach followed may very well have produced some striking anomalies for particular income brackets and for particular tax and expenditure categories.

There is a wide range of choice among alternative allocators connected with income distribution, that is, amounts of income and numbers of families by income class. The three annual series providing the greatest detail are: (1) *Statistics of Income* data on adjusted gross income on federal individual income tax returns; (2) the Census *Current Population Survey* data, in Series P-60 releases, on total money income of families and unrelated individuals, a broader concept than adjusted gross income in that it includes social insurance, pension, public assistance and similar transfer payments; and (3) the Office of Business Economics data, appearing periodically in the *Survey of Current Business,* on the size distribution of personal income, a broader concept still, including imputed and in-kind income. Other income distribution data available include those from the Survey Research Center and various one-time or infrequent series, such as the Bureau of Labor Statistics data for 1950 and 1960-61 included in the *Survey of Consumer Expenditures* for those years. The income tax data for adjusted gross income include, in the definition of income, a part of realized capital gains and losses, while the other two series do not include any capital gains and losses.

It would be desirable to show the widest possible range of differences in incidence resulting from the choice of income concepts, by using two or more income series here. However, consumption data by income class, with income defined as Commerce personal income, are not available. Therefore, the comparisons in this study are based on the narrower *Statistics of Income* data for 1957. Actually, the SOI data do not differ greatly from the Census series on total money income.

The most comprehensive consumption data, by income class, are available on two quite different bases. In 1950-51 and again in 1960-61, the Bureau of Labor Statistics surveyed the consumption patterns of the urban population, with the primary purpose of providing the basis for revising the expenditure weights in the Consumer Price Index.[3] The BLS data present three difficulties for this study. First, the dates do not correspond to the 1957 property tax impact data used. Second, the BLS surveys were confined to the urban population (about 70 percent of total U. S. consumer units in 1960-61). Third, in both BLS studies, the results are presented on the basis of money income *after* personal taxes, not before taxes, as in all other income data available.

The second source of consumption data is the *LIFE Study of Consumer Expenditures* (1957), a survey of 1956 expenditure patterns, with an income classification based on total money income in 1955. Here the dates and geographic coverage present no problems, but there is a somewhat unusual definition of households, and in addition, some downward bias in reporting of incomes. Despite the difficulties, there is little choice but to rely on these sources.

An examination of the LIFE data indicates that the income distribution is reasonably consistent with that of adjusted gross income in the SOI data. Therefore, LIFE consumption series are used in most of the tabulations.

[3] The sources are: 1950—*Study of Consumer Expenditures, Incomes, and Savings,* Vol. XVIII, *Summary* (Wharton School of Finance and Commerce, University of Pennsylvania, 1957); U. S. Bureau of Labor Statistics, *Consumer Expenditures and Income, Urban United States, 1960-1961,* BLS Report No. 237-38 (April 1964).

The income brackets used in the various series are not entirely con-- sistent. For income classes between $5,000 and $10,000 the BLS series employs a break at $7,500; these data have been adjusted to present a uniform $7,000 class limit. Second, the LIFE study has no breakdown above $10,000; a $15,000 class limit was used and the LIFE data were adjusted, on the basis of various pieces of evidence, to yield this.

The decision to compare property tax burdens and benefits from property tax financed services required the exclusion of the small amounts of state government property tax revenues from both sides of the computations. State property tax revenues are so small a fraction of total state revenues that it is meaningless to speak of any particular set of state expenditures as being "financed from the property tax." The bulk of state revenues from the property tax are from special, rather than general, property taxes; the impact of these can be readily ascer- tained from Census of Governments data.[4] For state general property taxes, the deductions from the tax impact amounts shown in Table 2-3 are based on the state-wide distribution of assessed values in the 1957 Census of Governments. The distortions involved are small, in view of the minor amounts of tax revenue.

Nonresidential Property Taxes

Agricultural Property

In theory, of course, taxes on the value of farmland (exclusive of reproducible components of this value—fertilizer, irrigation systems, etc.) are borne by the owner of the land. A general tax, imposed throughout a closed economy, on improvements and personal property, can be expected to be shifted forward to consumers when imposed on a competitive sector of the economy confronting relatively inelastic de- mand like agriculture. Musgrave and Daicoff essentially follow this rea- soning in assuming that three-fourths of the tax is shifted to consumers and one-fourth is borne by recipients of farm income. Brownlee, for Minnesota, in contrast, assumes that the taxes are borne entirely by farmers.

His reasoning is not spelled out, but there are a number of reasons for expecting somewhat less shifting than the Musgrave-Daicoff assump- tion suggests. First, taxes on land constitute a large element of farm property taxes. Second, the wide geographic variations in effective tax rates on reproducible assets used in agriculture should limit the extent of

[4] See Chap. VI, especially Table 6-7.

shifting. Third, the shifting process in competitive industry requires that supply be reduced by transfer of resources to other uses; despite substantial reductions in the farm population, low farm incomes evidently are insufficient to overcome much immobility of resources in agriculture; it may be argued that, to some extent, low farm incomes impede as well as induce mobility. Fourth, the determination of farm prices, and hence the extent of shifting, is heavily influenced by federal policy actions; federal support prices in recent years (in contrast to earlier postwar years) have not automatically been increased to reflect higher costs of production, including higher property taxes.

The Wisconsin study uses a more refined set of shifting assumptions for agriculture, which seem a better reflection of the probable realities of the situation. Taxes on farmland are assumed to be 75 percent borne by the owner and 25 percent shifted forward to food consumers, the latter an allowance for applications of capital to improving the land itself. Taxes on farm structures and personalty are assumed to be half shifted and half borne by farmers. For the country as a whole, according to the Goldsmith national wealth estimates, agricultural land recently has amounted to roughly 52 percent of the net stock of land, structures, producer durables, and inventories of agriculture.[5] On this basis, the Wisconsin shifting assumptions would suggest that not more than 37 percent of property taxes on agriculture are shifted forward.

In this study, the two more extreme assumptions—Musgrave-Daicoff on the one hand and Brownlee on the other—are used, to indicate the extent to which the shifting assumptions alter the distribution of the tax burden by income class (Appendix Table D-2). The shifted portion is distributed on the basis of total consumer expenditure (not only food, as in Wisconsin, since on a national basis nonfood products of agriculture are of importance), and the unshifted portion is distributed on the basis of the distribution of farm income.[6]

Nonfarm Business

MANUFACTURING. Musgrave and Daicoff divide property taxes on manufacturing property into two classes: the automobile industry and all other manufacturing. For the former, there are two cases, one with no forward shifting, and a second with half of the tax assumed to be shifted forward to purchasers of automobiles. Non-automotive manufacturing

---

[5] Raymond W. Goldsmith, *The National Wealth of the United States in the Postwar Period* (Princeton University Press, 1962), Table A-53.

[6] The Commerce Department farm income concept is used here, because of its ready availability.

property taxes are assumed not to be shifted at all. Brownlee similarly assumes no forward shifting.

The case for no forward shifting of taxes on manufacturing property stems from examination of one state's tax system in isolation. Manufacturers in a single state—with the possible exception of the automobile industry in Michigan—do not dominate the markets for their products, but compete in national markets with manufacturers located in other states, with different tax systems. Therefore, manufacturers in the given state will be unable to shift local taxes (or indeed any other costs peculiar to that one state) forward to consumers; any effort to raise prices to do so will result in a loss of sales to out-of-state competitors.

The Wisconsin study, in contrast, assumes that only taxes on land used in manufacturing are not shifted. Substantially all the remaining taxes are assumed to be shifted. Here, too, the Wisconsin study seems to have the best of the argument. As Gronouski points out,[7] the property tax on manufacturing is to a considerable degree a general tax. Manufacturing realty is taxed to some extent everywhere in the United States, even in the lowest tax-rate areas, and industrial personalty is widely taxed as well. Although effective tax rates do vary widely among regions, most manufacturers in direct competition with one another tend to be located within the same part of the country, where rate differentials are not nearly as large, on balance. Therefore, at least part of the property tax is a common cost item, which can be expected to be shifted forward. Moreover, some manufacturers do not operate in national markets but only in local markets, with all competitors subject to rather similar local taxes.

Two alternative shifting assumptions are used here. Case I assumes that only one-half of the tax is shifted forward to consumers, recognizing that rate differentials might inhibit shifting. In Case II, following the Wisconsin study, it is assumed that 90 percent of the tax is shifted forward. The unshifted 10 percent reflects, crudely, the land component. Since manufacturing is overwhelmingly done in the corporate form, in both cases the unshifted portion is distributed on the basis of dividend income. The results of the alternative assumptions are shown in Appendix Table D-3.

UTILITIES. Taxes on regulated public utilities are business costs taken into account for rate-making purposes. Since the demand for most utility services is relatively price-inelastic, complete forward shifting is generally assumed for utility taxes. However, this may not have been equally

[7] In the background material to the Wisconsin study, Appendix IX-A.

true in recent years for railroad property taxes. Declining demand for rail transport service may have prevented increases in rates from fully reflecting increased costs, including taxes; at any rate, this is suggested by the very low (or negative) net income figures for railroads in recent years. Therefore, it is assumed here that one-fourth of property taxes on railroads (an arbitrarily selected fraction) is not shifted and distributed in proportion to dividend income. It may be that a larger proportion is not shifted, but alternative assumptions here make little difference in the overall results.

It is further assumed that one-half of the shifted portion relates to direct consumer expenditure for utility services and the other half to business purchases of utility services, distributed on the basis of total consumer expenditure.

OTHER NONFARM BUSINESS. Musgrave and Daicoff assume that 75 percent of these taxes are shifted forward. The Wisconsin study makes the same assumption for taxes on structures and personalty, with land taxes not shifted. In this study, an across-the-board 75/25 split is similarly assumed.

This split is probably reasonably satisfactory, as least for the large proportion of this class which represents businesses operating only in local markets—trade, services, much of the finance group—where tax-rate differentials are limited. These limited differentials are reflected in the fraction assumed not to be shifted. However, for mining property and for commercial property of firms operating in national markets, shifting may be somewhat more inhibited. Rate differentials are larger, and, for mining property, land is a larger component.

On the basis of U. S. business tax data, it is assumed that 62.5 percent of the unshifted portion represents taxes on unincorporated enterprises, distributed on the basis of this source of adjusted gross income. The remaining corporate portion is distributed on the basis of dividend income.

Other Nonresidential Property Taxes

INTANGIBLES. These taxes are assumed to rest on individual owners of the assets, and are distributed in proportion to individuals' property income in adjusted gross income.

VACANT LOTS. Here the incidence is clearly on the owners of the sites, but there is no obvious way of approximating the distribution of site ownership. It is arbitrarily assumed that one-third of the taxes are on corporate-owned sites, distributed according to dividend income. The remainder is distributed on the basis of individuals' rental income in adjusted gross income.

PERSONAL MOTOR VEHICLES AND HOUSEHOLD PERSONALTY. These taxes are assumed to rest on the owners and are distributed according to consumer expenditures for automobiles and for home furnishings, respectively.

"Exporting" of the Property Tax

In the state tax studies, an allowance is made for shifted taxes paid by people resident in other states. Although there is no doubt some analogous "exporting" of taxes to other countries, for the United States taken as a whole, this is minor and no allowance is made here.

Another form of tax "exporting" for an individual state stems from reductions in federal tax liability due to the deductibility of state and local taxes. The underlying assumption is that federal tax rates are unaffected by the deductibility of one state's taxes, since this makes so little difference in aggregate federal tax revenues. However, the conceptual problem is somewhat more difficult when taxes imposed throughout the country are taken into consideration. Unshifted nonresidential property taxes in 1957 amounted to $3.3 billion and $1.8 billion under the two shifting assumptions, respectively—a tax loss, at a marginal rate of only 20 percent, in the $350-$650 million range, which is surely on the low side. In addition, unshifted residential property taxes claimed on federal individual income tax returns in 1960 amounted to approximately $4 billion, indicating a probable revenue loss of more than $800 million three years earlier, in 1957.

Thus, in the absence of business and personal deductions for property taxes, federal individual income tax rates might have been three to four percent lower across the board in 1957, to yield the same total federal revenues. This is on the assumption that the individual income tax is the residual, accounts-balancing tax in the federal revenue system. A comprehensive picture of the effect of the federal tax offset on the income distribution, therefore, should include both a tabulation of the extent to which the property tax burden is reduced, for each income class, by the federal offset and a tabulation of the increase in federal income tax liabilities resulting from tax rates higher than those possible without property tax deductibility. The latter has not been attempted here, largely because it requires unprofitable speculation on the likely structure of rates with and without property tax deductibility. It does seem likely, however, that the combination of deductibility and higher across-the-board income tax rates has a generally regressive effect: that higher income groups gain on balance.

The effect of deductibility has been computed on a number of bases. First, for the unshifted portions of property taxes paid by corporations, the tax amounts are reduced by 46 percent before distribution among income classes according to the distribution of dividend income. The 46 percent figure is the ratio of U. S. corporation income tax payments in 1957 to profits before taxes in the national income accounts. Second, an estimated marginal tax rate is applied to each bracket, against unshifted property taxes on agriculture, the unincorporated business sector of "other nonfarm business," intangibles, and personal holdings of vacant lots, on the assumption that virtually all of these taxes appear on federal tax returns as business expense or personal deductions. Third, for household personalty and personal motor vehicles, an estimated effective rate for each bracket has been constructed, on the basis of 1960 data on deductions for state-local taxes.[8] Here it is assumed that some of these taxes are paid by individuals who do not itemize on federal income tax returns. The effective rate for each bracket for all taxes has been multiplied by the proportion of taxpayers in that bracket claiming real estate taxes as personal deductions in 1960. These new computed rates in turn have been multiplied by 0.35, on the assumption that roughly 35 percent of household personalty and motor vehicles are located in states in which these are legally taxable.[9] The results are shown in Appendix Table D-4.

Benefits from Property Tax Financed Expenditures

The methods used for allocating expenditure benefits by income class essentially duplicate those used by Musgrave and Daicoff.[10] In Appendix Table D-5, local government expenditures financed from the property tax in 1957 are estimated, by major functional groupings. In that table, debt-financed expenditures are handled by a short-cut method. It is assumed that the property tax and other current revenues must finance current operating costs, debt service, and some capital outlays. Therefore, debt retired and interest expense are added to the relevant functional expenditure items, and debt issued is subtracted. The result-

[8] U. S. Treasury Department, *Statistics of Income, Individual Income Tax Returns, 1960,* Table 0.
[9] See Table 6-3.
[10] *Op. cit.,* pp. 152 ff.

ing figures equal estimated general expenditure financed from current revenue sources.

Some current revenues are earmarked for specific functions, implicitly or explicitly—most state and federal aids and user taxes and charges. These then are deducted from the expenditure figures; the remainder must be financed from non-earmarked local revenue sources, including the property tax. A small proportion of these general funds can be ascribed to specific functions, on the basis of the nature of the governmental units receiving the revenues: for example, nonproperty tax revenues of school districts can be used only for education, by definition. But most non-earmarked local revenues are distributed, in Appendix Table D-5, in proportion to expenditures not covered by earmarked sources of funds. A few adjustments are necessary for balancing the accounts, including an allowance for changes in cash balances, and for certain intra-governmental transactions netted out in the Census data. These include local government contributions to their own employee retirement funds and net payments by publicly owned utility operations to the parent governments.

The Musgrave-Daicoff analysis separates public expenditures into two groups—those conferring benefits to specific parts of the population and those conferring general benefits to the entire population. Two cases are used. In the first, it is assumed that a relatively large share of expenditures is specific in benefit. All outlays for education, highways, health and hospitals, sanitation, and welfare are assigned to specific beneficiaries. In addition, it is assumed that 20 percent of all other expenditures confer specific benefits, in that they are provided to businesses, as intermediate consumers of the service. These are treated as, in effect, a negative sales tax on business output, and apportioned among income classes on the basis of total consumer expenditure. In Case I, specific benefit expenditures amount to $9.3 billion of the $12.4 billion distributed.

In Case II, the assumption is that benefits are much more generally spread. One-third of the expenditures for education, highways, health and hospitals, sanitation, and welfare are treated as general benefit outlays, as are all expenditures for other functions. In this case, only $5.7 billion are treated as specific benefit expenditures.

Specific Benefit Expenditures

EDUCATION. These benefits are allocated on the basis of the distribution of the number of children under eighteen by family income classes. Both the BLS surveys and the Census *Current Population Surveys* provide data on the average number of children per family by income class; the two sets of data are quite similar. These data have been applied to the numbers of families in each class.

HIGHWAYS. It is assumed that 30 percent of the benefits from highways are business inputs, amounting to a negative sales tax distributed on the basis of total consumer expenditure. The remaining 70 percent—the personal share—is distributed on the basis of consumer expenditures for gasoline and oil.

HEALTH AND HOSPITALS. In the Musgrave-Daicoff treatment, these expenditures are distributed on the basis of the estimated income distribution of the recipients of state-local hospital and medical care in Michigan. This seems an appropriate treatment, but there is no assurance that the Michigan recipients' income distribution applies on a national basis. The Michigan data suggest that the use of public hospital and medical facilities is inversely proportional to family income, however, and this is the approach followed by Brownlee for Minnesota. Here benefits are distributed in proportion to the reciprocal of the average income within each class.

SANITATION. Musgrave and Daicoff distribute these benefits on the basis of residential property tax payments. This assumes that this element of the property tax is a reasonably good user charge. It may be, but it seems preferable to avoid circular reasoning. Here, the benefits are distributed on the basis of consumer expenditures for utility services, which seem a better measure of the use of sanitation services.

WELFARE. Musgrave and Daicoff assign 95 percent of the specific benefits to the income class under $2,000 and 5 percent to the $2,000-$3,000 class. This is based on Michigan information about welfare recipients, but appears to be of general application and is used here.

General Benefit Expenditures

There is no uniquely "correct" manner of distributing expenditures whose benefits are general in nature by income class. Musgrave and Daicoff use three alternative methods, which are followed here. The first distributes general benefits in proportion to aggregate family income within brackets, presumably on the basis of the assumption that the truly general benefits of government are valued more highly by richer people. The second uses property income as an allocator, assuming that these general benefits are realized largely by enhancing and protecting the value of property. The third uses numbers of families (a per capita basis is a reasonable substitute), an approach which is possibly the most rigorous in that it eschews any assumption about the incidence of general benefits which implies that they are something less than truly general.

Summary

The alternative assumptions and concepts used have resulted in a large number of cases. For nonresidential property taxes, there are calculations for two differing incidence assumptions, both before and after federal tax offsets—a total of four cases. For expenditure benefits, there are two sets of incidence assumptions, under each of which general benefits are distributed on three alternative bases, for a total of six cases. The reader therefore may use the tables to combine sets of assumptions about tax and expenditure incidence other than those referred to in Chapter III.

Selected Tables

TABLE D-1. Shifting Assumptions and Allocators for Local Property Taxes on Nonresidential Property, 1957

(Amounts in millions of dollars)

Class of Property	Amount of Tax Distributed[a]	Shifting Assumptions	Allocators Used
Agricultural	$1,106		
Case I		None shifted	Farm income
Case II		$\frac{3}{4}$ shifted forward	All consumer expenditures
		$\frac{1}{4}$ not shifted	Farm income
Manufacturing	1,583		
Case I		$\frac{1}{2}$ shifted forward	All consumer expenditures
		$\frac{1}{2}$ not shifted	Dividend income
Case II		$\frac{9}{10}$ shifted forward	All consumer expenditures
		$\frac{1}{10}$ not shifted	Dividend income
Utilities	1,460	$\frac{1}{4}$ of railroad taxes not shifted	Dividend income
		$\frac{1}{2}$ of remainder shifted forward to domestic consumers	Consumer expenditures for utility services
		$\frac{1}{2}$ of remainder shifted forward via intermediate business purchases	All consumer expenditures
Other nonfarm business	2,317	$\frac{3}{4}$ shifted forward	All consumer expenditures
		$\frac{1}{4}$ not shifted	Dividend income and unincorporated business income
Intangibles	162	Not shifted	Property income
Vacant lots	225	Not shifted	Dividend income and personal rental income
Personal motor vehicles	204	Not shifted	Consumer expenditures for automobiles
Household personalty	113	Not shifted	Consumer expenditures for home furnishings and equipment

[a] Adapted from Table 2–3; state government property tax revenue excluded and reapportioned among property classes on the basis of assessed value data, for general property taxes, and on the basis of Table 6–7, for special property taxes.

TABLE D-2. Distribution of Taxes on Agricultural Property by Income Class, 1957, Under Alternative Shifting Assumptions[a]

(Amounts in millions of dollars)

Money Income Class	Shifting Assumption	
	Case I[b]	Case II[c]
Less than $2,000	$ 100	$ 100
$ 2,000–$ 3,000	125	114
3,000– 4,000	142	152
4,000– 5,000	131	199
5,000– 7,000	216	253
7,000– 10,000	155	155
10,000– 15,000	108	60
Over $15,000	130	74
Total	$1,106	$1,106

Note: Because of rounding, details may not add to totals.
[a] Before adjustment for any federal tax offset.
[b] Assumes no forward shifting.
[c] Assumes three-fourths of the tax shifted forward to consumers.

TABLE D-3. Distribution of Taxes on Manufacturing Property by Income Class, 1957, Under Alternative Shifting Assumptions[a]

(Amounts in millions of dollars)

Money Income Class	Shifting Assumption	
	Case I[b]	Case II[c]
Less than $2,000	$ 95	$ 133
$2,000–$3,000	100	147
3,000– 4,000	132	204
4,000– 5,000	180	289
5,000– 7,000	234	351
7,000–10,000	171	212
10,000–15,000	110	73
Over $15,000	560	175
Total	$1,583	$1,583

Note: Because of rounding, details may not add to totals.
[a] Before adjustment for any federal tax offset.
[b] Assumes one-half shifted forward, one-half on dividend income.
[c] Assumes 90 percent shifted forward, 10 percent on dividend income.

TABLE D-4. Marginal Federal Income Tax Rates Used in Computation of Federal Tax Offsets

(In percentages)

Income Class	Estimated Marginal Rate[a]	Proportion of Returns with Real Estate Tax Deductions 1960[b]	Column 1 × Column 2[c]	Column 3 × .35[d]
	(1)	(2)	(3)	(4)
Less than $2,000	0	3.6%	0	0
$2,000–$3,000	20%	11.4	2.3%	0.8%
3,000– 4,000	20	17.0	3.4	1.2
4,000– 5,000	20	24.2	4.8	1.7
5,000– 7,000	20	39.9	8.0	2.8
7,000–10,000	22	49.9	11.0	3.9
10,000–15,000	22	57.7	12.7	4.4
Over $15,000	38	69.3	26.3	9.2

[a] Used for unshifted property taxes on agriculture, unincorporated nonfarm business, intangibles, and personal holdings of vacant lots.
[b] From U. S. Treasury Department, *Statistics of Income, Individual Income Tax Returns, 1960*, Table O and 1.
[c] Used for owner-occupied residential property taxes.
[d] Used for taxes on household personalty and personal motor vehicles.

TABLE D-5. Estimated Local Government General Expenditure Financed from Property Taxes, 1957

(Amounts in millions of dollars)

Function	General Expenditure	Estimated General Expenditure from Current Revenue[a]	Estimated Property Tax Financed Portion	
			Amount[b]	Percentage of Current Revenue
All general expenditure	$26,148	$24,381	$12,385	50.8%
Education	11,674	10,953	5,948	54.3
Highways	2,971	2,754	862	31.3
Health and hospitals	1,601	1,557	632	40.6
Sanitation	1,443	1,222	582	47.6
Welfare	1,688	1,688	500	29.6
Other	6,770	6,206	3,859	62.2
Police and fire	2,100	2,100	1,557	74.1
General control	1,195	1,195	882	73.8
Miscellaneous	3,475	2,911	1,419	48.7

Source: Estimated mainly from U. S. Bureau of the Census, *Census of Governments: 1957*, Vol. III, No. 5, "Compendium of Government Finances" (1959).
Note: Because of rounding, details may not add to totals.
[a] Column (1) plus estimated interest on general debt applicable to function less estimated net increase in general debt applicable; based on distribution of debt outstanding in 1957.
[b] Column (2) less state and federal aid and user taxes and charges applicable to specific programs and proportionate shares of other nonproperty tax revenues. Adjustments have been made for changes in balances and for intragovernmental transactions netted out of Census data but relevant here.

TABLE D-6. Real Estate Taxes on U. S. Individual Income Tax Returns for 1960

Adjusted Gross Income Class	Returns Claiming Real Estate Tax Deductions as Percentage of All Returns with Itemized Deductions	Returns with Itemized Deductions as Percentage of All Taxable and Nontaxable Returns
$3,000–$4,000	49%	34%
4,000– 5,000	57	42
5,000– 6,000ᵃ	68	54
6,000– 7,000	75	58
7,000– 8,000	79	61
8,000– 9,000	82	63
9,000–10,000	85	63
10,000–15,000	85	68
15,000–20,000	83	79
20,000–25,000	81	86
25,000–50,000	80	91
50,000 and over	80	97
All returns, $3,000 and over	72	53

Source: U. S. Treasury Department, *Statistics of Income, Individual Income Tax Returns,* 1960, Tables 0, 4, and 7.
ᵃ Includes all nontaxable returns with adjusted gross income of $5,000 or over.

TABLE D-7. Percentage Distribution of Homeowner Properties by Value, 1960ᵃ

Single-Family Houses		Two-to-Four-Family Structures	
Value of Property	Percentage of Properties	Value of Property	Percentage of Properties
Less than $5,000	11.1%	Less than $10,000	24.1%
$5,000– $7,400	12.7	$10,000–$14,900	30.7
7,500– 9,900	12.7	15,000– 19,900	22.0
10,000– 12,400	17.2	20,000– 24,900	11.1
12,500– 17,400	23.5	25,000– 34,900	8.1
17,500 and over	22.8	35,000 and over	4.0

ᵃ From special tabulation by U. S. Bureau of the Census, Housing Division, from responses to Residential Finance Survey, *Census of Housing: 1960.*

262

TABLE D-8. Income of Households in Owner-Occupied Housing within Standard Metropolitan Statistical Areas, 1959[a]

	Percentage Distribution of Households	
Household Income in 1959	In Single-Family Nonfarm Owner-Occupied Units	In Other Owner-Occupied Units
Less than $2,000	9.4%	17.2%
$2,000–$2,999	4.8	8.1
3,000– 3,999	5.7	8.6
4,000– 4,999	8.2	9.9
5,000– 6,999	23.4	21.0
7,000– 9,999	25.5	21.2
10,000–14,999	15.5	9.7
$15,000 or more	7.6	4.2
All classes	100.0	100.0

Note: Because of rounding, details may not add to totals.
[a] From U. S. Bureau of the Census, *Census of Housing: 1960*, "Metropolitan Housing," Final Report HC(2)-1 (1963), Table B-3. The first column comprises 17.3 million units; the second, 2.8 million units. Approximately 600,000 of the latter appear to be farm units, in the Census definition, although within the confines of metropolitan areas.

TABLE D-9. Income and Rent for Nonfarm Renter-Occupied Housing in the United States, 1960[a]

Income Characteristic	Median Gross Monthly Rent	Median Income
Household income in 1959:		
Less than $2,000	$ 52	—
$2,000–$2,999	60	—
3,000– 3,999	66	—
4,000– 4,999	72	—
5,000– 5,999	76	—
6,000– 6,999	81	—
7,000– 7,999	85	—
8,000– 9,999	90	—
10,000–14,999	99	—
15,000 or more	more than $120	—
All classes	71	—
Gross rent as percentage of income:		
All classes	$ 71	$4,200
Less than 10%	55	8,500
10–14	68	6,500
15–19	75	5,200
20–24	78	4,300
25–34	76	3,200
35 or more	68	less than $2,000

[a] U. S. Bureau of the Census, *Census of Housing: 1960*, "Metropolitan Housing," Final Report HC(2)-1 (1963), Tables A-2 and A-3.

TABLE D-10. Income and Value Relationships, Owner-Occupiers of Single-Family Nonfarm Houses, 1960

Value of House, by Income Classes[a]		Family Income, by House Value Classes[b]	
Income Class[c]	Indicated Median House Value	House Value Class	Median Family Income[c]
Less than $2,000	$ 6,400	Less than $5,000	$ 2,800
$2,000–$2,999	8,200	$5,000–$7,400	4,500
3,000– 3,999	8,600	7,500– 9,900	5,400
4,000– 4,999	9,800	10,000–12,400	6,100
5,000– 5,999	11,400	12,500–14,900	6,800
6,000– 6,999	12,800	15,000–19,900	7,700
7,000– 7,999	14,600	20,000–24,900	9,200
8,000– 8,999	15,600	25,000 or more	12,700
9,000– 9,999	15,900	All classes	6,200
10,000–11,999	17,500		
12,000–14,999	19,900		
15,000 or more	27,500		
All classes	12,000		

[a] Based on special tabulations by the Census Bureau of responses to the Residential Finance Survey, *Census of Housing: 1960*. Covers 25.0 million of the 26.2 million single-family nonfarm owner-occupied houses. Median home value for the 26.2 million units was $11,900, versus the $12,000 figure here.

[b] From U. S. Bureau of the Census, *Census of Housing: 1960*, "Metropolitan Housing," Final Report HC(2)-1 (1963), Table A-3.

[c] Income in 1959.

Residential Property Tax Incidence in Northern New Jersey*

Scope of Study

THIS APPENDIX SUMMARIZES the results of a study of the incidence of the residential real property tax on households residing within the eight counties which together make up the New Jersey portion of the New York-Northeastern New Jersey Standard Consolidated Area.[1] One of the objectives of this study was to examine the effects, on the incidence pattern of the tax, of shifting from a current income basis, that is, income received by the average household within a one-year period, to a longer time period, that is (following Friedman, and others) to a "normal" or "permanent" income basis.

The principal stigma, though not the only one, usually associated with the functioning of the real property tax within given housing markets is the tax's celebrated regressivity. On a current income basis, at least in this particular eight-county area, the tax shows up, quite clearly, as a regressive one. However, its regressivity is considerably modified by the introduction of a longer run income-receiving perspective. For, it seems to be the case, that the tax's extreme regressivity on a current income basis is, in good part, a function of the (relatively) short-term income inelasticity of housing consumption expenditures.

* This Appendix was prepared by Emanuel Tobier.
[1] These are Bergen, Essex, Hudson, Middlesex, Morris, Passaic, Somerset, and Union counties.

If housing outlays are income-inelastic in the short run, this, naturally, leads to a regressive tax pattern on a current income basis since the
tax is levied on property values at a uniform rate. But, when the entire
life cycle of the average household or some reasonable semblance
thereof is taken into account, housing outlays become roughly proportional to long-run income. Thus, if there is a proportional relationship
between housing outlays, averaged out over the family cycle, and lifetime family income, expressed, say, in average annual terms, the earlier
pattern of regressivity is transformed into one of proportionality.

Characteristics of Study Area

The New Jersey counties which serve as the focus for this particular
study—Bergen, Essex, Hudson, Middlesex, Morris, Passaic, Somerset,
and Union—were chosen principally because: (1) they generate the
kinds of data without which such a study could not easily be conducted;
(2) the role of the property tax in New Jersey's combined state-local tax
structure is of overwhelming importance; that is, the functioning of the
property tax should make a difference here if it makes a difference
anywhere.[2]

The eight counties in question had, in 1960, a combined population
of approximately 4.1 million persons, consisting of close to 1.3 million
households. Approximately 53 percent of these households owned their
own homes, of which the overwhelming proportion were single-family
structures. The remaining 47 percent occupied rented quarters, of which
only a minor proportion was accounted for by single-family structures.
However, considerable differences exist between the counties involved
with regards to the distribution of form of tenure. These differences, together with population and household data as of 1960, are summarized
in Appendix Table E-1. (All tables for Appendix E are at the end of the
Appendix.)

The weighted median income of families and unrelated individuals
for the study area as a whole came to just under $6,350 in 1960. How-
ever, once again, considerable differences existed between the counties,
with the median income of families and unrelated individuals ranging, as
Table E-2 shows, from Bergen County's $7,417 to Hudson's $5,476.

The weighted average sales value of all occupied units (combining

---

[2] New Jersey's combined state-local finance structure is clearly dominated
by the property tax. In 1962, 65 percent of New Jersey's total state and local
tax revenue was derived from the property tax, compared to 44 percent in New
York, 35 percent in Pennsylvania, and 46 percent in the entire United States (see
Table 5-1).

owner and renter units) came to $14,300 for the area as a whole, rang-ing from a high of $18,100 in Bergen County to a low of $9,100 in Hudson County. Higher values, of course, reflect higher incomes, al-though part of the variation in values between counties results from differences in the relative proportions of owner and renter housing (ren-ter housing tending to have a much lower average value per unit than sales housing).

The basis for real property taxation is, of course, assessed values. Theoretically, assessed values should bear a uniform relationship to market or sales value. Between counties, they definitely do not (not to speak of within counties). As shown in Appendix Table E-5, the ratio be-tween assessed and sales values, on the average, varied from 87 percent in Essex County to Somerset County's 17 percent.

The size of the average property tax levy per household is shown for each county in Table E-2. When the average property tax burden, medi-an family income, and the average sales value per occupied unit are sys-tematically related to each other, on a county-by-county basis, the fol-lowing conclusion emerges: there is no evident tendency for the value-income ratio to decline as income rises. That is, to the extent that the value-income ratio can be considered as a meaningful proxy for the con-sumption of housing services, the latter increases with income, treating counties as the unit of observation.

The remainder of this Appendix is divided into two parts. The first part discusses the methodology, data, and assumptions used in develop-ing estimates of property tax burdens by income class for each of the counties in the study area. The second part traverses similar ground in regard to property tax burden on a permanent income basis.

Tax Burdens: The View from Current Income

Any current examination of a particular housing market in a given metropolitan region, or substantial portions of a given region, will yield a remarkable variety and range of relationships between house value, monthly rentals, and income. Much of this diversity is real, that is, in-herent in consumer behavior.

Within this apparent diversity, however, there is a clear tendency, at any point in time, for the relationship between housing consumption and current income to be a declining one. Households with higher incomes, on the average, spend more for housing services, but marginal differences, between higher and lower income households for this partic-ular component of consumption are only a fraction of the differences in their respective incomes.

That this occurs should hardly be surprising since it has long been the conventional wisdom, at least since the enunciation of Engel's Law. Similarly, as regards the incidence of the property tax, it has also long been the conventional wisdom that the levy is a regressive one—that its exactions relative to income decrease as household incomes rise. This regressivity is a quite dramatic aspect of the tax's functioning in New Jersey. Indeed, outside of a flat-rate poll tax or a particularly maladroitly designed sales tax, it is hard to conceive of a tax whose incidence pattern would be more regressive than the incidence of the State's property tax at present.

Of course, it is inevitable that this should be so since: (1) housing consumption is income inelastic; and (2) the residential real property tax is levied as a uniform rate on the basis of property values. Moreover, since the tax is levied on the basis of assessed values rather than sales prices, and since there is some tendency for assessors to overvalue low value homes and undervalue high value homes, the tax turns out, in practice, to be more regressive in its incidence than one would expect to be the case simply from the combined effects of the first two factors cited. This last point, however, is easy to exaggerate. The greatest impetus to regressivity arising from the tax is due not to regressive assessment practices but to the income-inelasticity of housing consumption expenditures. In the eight-county study area, it is estimated that less than 5 percent of the regressivity was due to regressive assessment practices, with the remaining 95 percent attributable to the income-inelasticity of the demand for housing.

Estimates were made of the percent share of income the residential property tax represented for the following income classes in each of the counties in the study area: under $3,000, $3,000-$4,999, $5,000-$6,999, $7,000-$9,999, $10,000-$14,999, $15,000-$24,999, $25,000 and over.

For each income class (in each county) estimates were made separately for the average assessed value per unit of owner- and renter-occupied units.

In the case of owner-occupied units, the average sales value for each of the sales size classes shown in Appendix Table E-4 was calculated separately for each county. Assessment-sales ratios by sales value class (see Appendix Table E-5) were applied to the relevant average sales figure in order to obtain the average assessed value for each sales size class. The resulting average sales and average assessed values by sales size class are summarized by county in Appendix Table E-4. These sales-size specific average assessed value figures were then weighted by the income distribution which characterized the owner-occupied households in each category to derive the average assessed value for the entire income class.

To illustrate the computation process which was followed, the derivation of the average sales value and average assessed value for owner-occupied households in Bergen County whose 1960 income was less than $3,000 is given below.

Sales Size Class	*Number of Households*[a]	*Average Assessed Value*[b]	*Average Sales Value*[b]
(1)	*(2)*	*(3)*	*(4)*
Under $5,000	115	$ 1,100	$ 3,800
$5,000–$9,000	587	2,700	7,900
10,000–14,900	3,013	4,200	13,400
15,000–19,900	3,207	5,200	17,900
20,000–24,900	1,956	6,000	21,400
25,000–34,900	739	8,000	28,600
35,000 and over	535	11,300	41,200
Total	10,152	$ 5,400	$18,500

[a] From S. J. Tesauro & Co., *People and Homes in the American Market*, Cross-Tabulations of Population and Housing Characteristics from the 1960 Decennial Census, New Jersey (1961).

[b] See Appendix Table E-4.

Column (2) provides the distribution of households whose current income is below $3,000 according to the value of the single-family house which they occupy. Columns (3) and (4) present the average assessed value and average sales value, respectively, for each sales size class. Thus, the weighted average sales value for the group of owner households who occupy-own single-family homes and whose income was below $3,000 in 1960 comes to $18,500; the weighted average assessed value, to $5,400.

In order to estimate the income-class-specific weighted average assessed and average sales value for renter-occupied housing units it was necessary to (1) determine total gross annual rents by income class; (2) reduce these to net annual rents; (3) translate net annual rents into sales and assessed value per renter-occupied housing units.

Available data cross-classifying income and rent employ the following monthly rent breaks: under $50; $50 to $99; $100 to $149; $150 and over. Average rents were computed in each county for each of these rent classes. These are summarized in Appendix Table E-6. The resulting average rents were then applied to the number of households, adjusted for income, in each rent class to obtain the average gross monthly rent, and then, multiplying by twelve, the gross annual rent. Gross rent is the contract rent plus the average monthly cost of utilities (water, electricity, and gas) and fuels such as wood, coal, and oil if these items are paid by the renter. In order to isolate the average contract rent— which is rent agreed upon regardless of any furnishings, utilities, or services that may be included—the gross monthly rent was reduced by the percentage relationship between the median contract rent and median gross monthly rent (see Appendix Table E-7).

In order to convert average net annual rental receipts into a value figure (per occupied unit), a capitalization rate was applied which, theoretically, represents the relationship between rental receipts and value. The rate chosen for this purpose was derived from the 1960 Census of Housing, Volume V, "Residential Finance," Part 2, "Rental and Vacant Properties." In that volume the median figures for rental receipts as a percent of value were given for the following classes of rental properties for the United States as a whole: single-dwelling unit properties (8 percent); properties with 1-4 dwelling units (9 percent); properties with 5-49 dwelling units (12 percent); 50-or-more dwelling unit properties (14 percent). By applying these relationships to renter units distributed by number of units per structure in the particular county, estimates were obtained for the individual counties expressing the percent relationship between rental receipts and property value. This procedure together with the underlying data is summarized in Appendix Table E-8.

The resulting figure was then divided into the average net annual rental amount (previously computed) to produce the average sales value in the particular income class. Finally, the weighted average assessed value was computed by multiplying the resulting average sales value by the assessment-sales ratio for properties with five or more dwelling units (shown in the last item of Appendix Table E-5).

To illustrate the process just described, the computation for determining the average assessed and sales values of renter units occupied by households in Bergen County whose 1960 income was less than $3,000 is tabulated below.

Column (2) distributes this particular set of households according to its gross monthly rentals. Column (3) gives the estimated average rent for each gross monthly rent class. The weighted average annual gross rent, Line 1, is the sum of the products of columns (2) and (3) multiplied by the number of months in the year. The weighted average annual net monthly rent, Line 2, is the result of multiplying Line 1 by the percentage relationship between the median contract and gross rent prevailing on a county-wide basis (Appendix Table E-7). Line 3 is obtained by

Amount of Rental	Number of Households[a]	Estimated Average Rent[b]
(1)	(2)	(3)
Less than $50	1,553	$ 41
$50–$99	5,661	80
$100–$149	2,180	120
$150 and over	277	187
Total	9,671	$ 86

Line 1, weighted average annual gross monthly rental	$1,032
Line 2, weighted average annual net monthly rental	929
Line 3, weighted average sales value	9,290
Line 4, weighted average assessed value	2,759

[a] From S. J. Tesauro & Co., *op. cit.*
[b] See Appendix Table E-6.

dividing Line 2 by the percent relationship between rents and value of renter-occupied units and gives, in effect, the weighted average sales value for renter-occupied dwelling units (Appendix Table E-8). Finally, Line 4 gives the weighted average assessed value for renter-occupied dwelling units in this particular income class and is the result of multiplying Line 3 by the relevant assessment-sales ratio for Bergen County (Appendix Table E-5).

The necessary data for computing comparable value data for each income class in Bergen County are provided in Appendix Table E-9. With one exception, identical calculations were made for the owner- and renter-components by income class for each county in the study area. The exception was that of the group of renters whose 1960 incomes were reported as being $25,000 and over. Due to a defect in the underlying sample data, the original estimate of the weighted average gross monthly rental in the $25,000-and-over income group produced by following the procedure outlined above drastically underestimated the average rent applicable to this class. To compensate for this, the weighted average annual gross rental for $25,000-and-over households in each county was set at a figure 33 percent greater than the weighted average annual gross monthly figure for households whose annual incomes were between $15,000 and $24,999. The 33 percent factor was based on an extrapolation of the declining percent relationships found to exist between marginal changes in average rents and average incomes for selected Standard Metropolitan Statistical Areas in the New Jersey portion of the Standard Consolidated Area.

Thus far, average assessed and average sales values have been computed by income class and by county for owner- and renter-occupied housing separately. The owner and renter sectors within each income class can now be combined in order to produce a composite value figure both in regards to sales and assessment values. The results of the merger of the owner and renter sectors are summarized in Appendix Table E-10. The weights used in effecting this merger represent the percentage distribution between owning and renting within each income class. In this case, owning refers as well to owner-occupants of other than single-family units, that is, it also refers to households occupying one unit of a two-or-more unit structure which they own. However, in computing the average sales and assessed figures of owner units, the only units taken into account were single-family owner-occupied units. Thus, by using the overall owner-renter weights for purposes of combining the assessment and sales figures for owner and renter units, it is implicitly assumed that the value-income ratios of owner-occupants, adjusted for income, of other than single-family homes are identical with those of owner-occupants of single-family units. Given what is known of the income characteristics of owner households who occupy units in other than single-family houses, this seems, on the whole, to be a reasonable assumption.

We are now in a position to provide a measure of the (current) income elasticity of housing consumption—via the sales value-income ratio—as well as one of the incidence pattern of the real property tax—via the assessed value-income ratio. As can be seen in Appendix Table E-11, the relationship between house value and current income declines precipitately as income rises with the decline extending through the highest income class taken into consideration. This phenomenon occurs in each of the study area's counties. Interestingly enough, however, there is a noticeable tendency for the individual income classes in the higher income counties to have higher value-income ratios than their income class counterparts in lower income counties. This tendency serves to indicate that housing consumption's income inelasticity might be exaggerated by the use of cross-sectional data such as those employed in this section.

Table 3-11 summarizes the results of an estimate of the relationship between the residential real property tax and average household income by income class for each county in the eight-county study area. A first-round property tax calculation was made by applying the property tax rate, computed for the county as a whole, to the average assessed value for each income class. This produced a figure for the average property tax burden by household which was uniformly higher than the actual reported average tax burden per household as shown in Appendix Table E-3. This initial result was accordingly modified by the percent relationship between the first-round average estimate and the actual amount. The adjusted or second-round estimate of the percent relationship between tax burden and income by income class for each county is that shown in Table 3-11. As can be seen, the resulting pattern is, indeed, a very regressive one.

Tax Burdens: The Permanent Income Hypothesis

The measurement problem this section is addressed to is the determination of the long-term relationship between income and the related consumption of housing services. As has been shown, the consumption of housing services as evidenced by the value-income ratio is, in the short run, income-inelastic. As a result, the residential real property tax which is applied at a uniform rate is, naturally, a regressive one. But if the long-run relationship between income and housing consumption is less inelastic than is shown by current income data, the property tax would, other things equal, be less regressive than it is generally assumed to be.

Numerous studies, using cross-section data, have, in examining the relationship between current income and housing consumption, concluded that the consumption of housing services is income-inelastic—that is, housing outlays as a relative share of income decline as incomes rise. However, other, more recent, investigations, using Friedman's permanent income hypothesis as a point of departure, have concluded that the results of the earlier studies were biased in a downward direction because of their use of cross-sectional data. As a result of lengthening the time period during which income is received and housing outlays are made, these later researchers, notably Reid and Muth,[3] conclude that housing consumption is income-elastic—that is, as income rises the percentage share of income devoted to housing increases.

While cross-section data clearly show that the aggregate value-income ratio declines as income rises, within any given income class a considerable dispersion exists so far as house value is concerned. The large variance implicit in housing expenditure-income relationships results partly from adjustment lags and partly from the wide range in individual preferences.[4]

The irregular behavior of housing consumption outlays within in-

[3] Margaret Reid, *Housing and Income* (University of Chicago Press, 1962); Richard F. Muth, "The Demand for Non-Farm Housing," in *The Demand for Durable Goods*, Arnold Harberger, ed. (University of Chicago Press, 1960).

[4] S. J. Maisel and Louis Winnick, "Family Housing Expenditures—Elusive Laws and Intrusive Variances," in *Consumption and Saving* (University of Pennsylvania, Wharton School), Vol. 1, pp. 359-436.

come classes at a given point of time does cast some doubt on the adequacy of current income as the most appropriate determinant of current housing expenditures. It seems reasonable to assume that for many categories of goods and services current consumption is related not to current income, but is geared to average actual and anticipated income over a number of periods as well as to income received in the current period. It seems reasonable to assume, moreover, that for especially long-lived purchases, such as housing, and particularly single-family homes, the time perspective might indeed be quite lengthy.

Housing expenditures thus can be thought of as a function of permanent income. However, the permanent income hypothesis itself, which is a specific formulation of the relationship between expected values of income and consumption, tells us nothing at all about what the expected shape of the permanent housing consumption function should look like for different permanent income groups.

From the point of view of the permanent income hypothesis, true income elasticities can only be obtained when the transitory component of income is eliminated from measured (*i.e.,* current) income. For this purpose, one has to identify, and combine into groups, consumer units which may be expected to have more or less the same level of normal income. Since transitory income for a group of families homogeneous in normal income is, by definition, composed of erratic or more or less random elements, this combination procedure serves to reduce greatly the relative importance of transitory income. Regressions of housing expenditure on permanent income are much more likely to yield true long-run income elasticities than are the usual regressions based on cross-sectional data with the individual family as the unit of observation.

Thus, the first requirement of any attempt to estimate income elasticities of housing consumption expenditures, using the permanent income hypothesis as a framework for ordering the results, is to identify homogeneous elements with relation to normal income and compare their income elasticities with respect to housing consumption. If, as normal income rises, the value-income ratio declines, then housing consumption is income inelastic. If it rises as normal income rises, then the opposite situation is true.

What has to be done to develop permanent income estimates for current income classes? Permanent income, roughly, is the annual equivalent of the revenues which a person expects to get over a long period of time. A consumer unit, such as a household, is assumed to determine its standard of living on the basis of expected returns from its resources over a lifetime. Clearly, from an empirical point of view, this is a very difficult hypothesis to test, because of the difficulty of measuring permanent income and permanent consumption. How long should the period be? The period will differ among consumer units, depending upon the unit's horizon. While the period is longer than a year, it might be only a few years or even a lifetime. The time span which is relevant for permanent income is the minimum period over which income influences must persist before the consumer unit regards them as permanent. Certainly in the case of housing consumption a strong case can be made for the use of a very long-run enabling measure for income—lifetime income or average annual lifetime income.

One of the most useful of available measures for estimating the lifetime income of current income classes is occupation of head of household. Households, classified by current income class, can be stratified by occupation of the head of the household to gain some insight into their expectable lifetime or "permanent" behavior as regards major categories of consumption such as housing. For example, over 4,000 family households in the study area whose head was currently engaged in one of the occupations represented within the professional, technical, and kindred worker category earned less than $3,000 in 1960. This seems hardly to be indicative of the average annual earning power of a head of household in this particular occupation over the span of his entire working career. His low current earnings probably reflect a temporary setback, or the low starting salaries of the young, and hence, relatively inexperienced, or the curtailed income opportunities of more senior members of the labor force. Also, the 20,000 or so family households headed by professional, technical, and kindred workers whose 1960 income was in excess of $15,000 indicated largely high current earnings for professionals at the peak of their earning power, rather than sustained average annual lifetime earning power. In other words, the current distribution of income within occupationally homogeneous income groups (broadly speaking) reflects, very importantly, the distribution by age of head of household currently prevailing within that income group as well as numerous other factors.

To facilitate testing, assume that the age distribution characterizing each major occupation group within a particular area is a normal one, that is, it contains a proportionate distribution of persons at the various stages of the worklife cycle. The average income figure implicit in this distribution could be considered as representative of the average annual lifetime income for that occupation.

While the best available proxy for approaching the question of permanent income is occupation, within the broad occupational categories for which statistical data are presented,[5] it is clear that there exist wide disparities in income, current and lifetime, among each major class's individual components. That is, teachers and self-employed doctors are both considered part of the professional, technical, and kindred worker category. However, the median income of the teacher in 1960 for the United States as a whole was $8,800, while for the self-employed doctor it was closer to $12,000. However, if we take relatively limited geographical areas, such as are provided by counties, it is possible to hypothesize that the mix in each county within a given broad occupational category is a relatively homogeneous one. That is, the median income of Hudson County's professional, technical, and kindred worker households at $8,560 is quite a bit below that of its Bergen County counterpart whose median income is closer to $10,000. This is presumably due to the fact that Hudson County's professional category is heavily weighted with teachers whose lifetime income prospects are relatively low, while in Bergen County the mix favors such sub-groups as self-employed physicians, whose lifetime income prospects are notably high.

The county-wide current income distributions by occupations of head of household were weighted to produce a figure which, theoretically, serves as a proxy for average annual lifetime income. For illustrative purposes take the group of 32,400 households in Bergen County whose head in 1960 was employed in one of the occupations included in the professional, technical, and kindred worker class. In 1959 the income distribution characterizing these 32,400 households was as follows:

Income Class (1)	Number of Households[a] (2)	Average Income[b] (3)
Under $3000	778	$ 1,500
$3,000–$4,999	1,426	4,000
5,000– 6,999	4,601	5,900
7,000– 9,999	9,979	8,300
10,000–14,999	9,882	12,000
15,000–24,999	3,920	18,700
25,000 and over	1,814	42,400
Total	32,400	$11,900

[a] From S. J. Tesauro & Co., *op. cit.*
[b] See footnote, Appendix Table E-11.

---

[5] Professional, technical, and kindred workers; farmers and farm managers; managers, officials, and proprietors; clerical and kindred workers; sales workers; craftsmen and kindred workers; operatives; private household workers; other service workers; and laborers (including farm labor).

By multiplying the number of households in each income class (Column 2) by the appropriate average income figure for that class (Column 3), a figure is produced—close to $12,000 in this case—which represents the weighted average income of Bergen County households whose heads are classified occupationally as being one sort or another of professional, technical, or kindred worker. If we assume that this group of households headed by professional, technical, and kindred workers represents, in a proportionate manner, all stages of the family or household life cycle, then we can go on to say that this weighted average current income figure could also be used to denote this group's average annual lifetime income.

Employing similar reasoning, we can go on to investigate the weighted average current consumption of housing services associated with each occupation class and characterize the result as equivalent to its average annual lifetime housing consumption. Thus, to continue the previous illustration, in 1960, 75 percent of Bergen County's professional, technical, and kindred worker households resided in owner-occupied housing units and only 25 percent were renters. The 24,200 owner households were distributed according to value of property in the following manner:

Value of Property	*Number of Households*[a]	*Average Sales Value*[b]
(1)	*(2)*	*(3)*
Under $5,000	97	$ 3,800
$5,000–$9,900	218	7,900
10,000–14,900	1,258	13,400
15,000–19,900	7,986	17,900
20,000–24,900	7,163	21,400
25,000–34,900	5,469	28,500
35,000 and over	2,009	41,200
Total	24,200	22,900

[a] From S. J. Tesauro & Co., *op. cit.*
[b] See Appendix Table E-4.

The result of multiplying the number of households in each property value class share by the appropriate average sales value figure for that class is $22,900, which can be taken to represent the weighted average sales value of all owner units occupied by households headed by professional, technical, and kindred workers.

The 8,200 professional, technical, and kindred worker households in Bergen County who were renters in 1960 were distributed by amount of gross monthly rental, in the following manner:

Amount of Rental (1)	Number of Households[a] (2)	Average Gross Monthly Rent[b] (3)
Under $50	410	$ 41
$50–$99	2,936	80
$100–$149	3,739	120
$150 and over	1,115	187
Total	8,200	$111

[a] From S. J. Tesauro, *op. cit.*
[b] See Appendix Table E-6.

Translated into value terms (by the procedure described in the preceding section), the weighted average sales value of the rental units occupied by such households amounts to $12,100. The combined weighted average sales value of all housing units occupied by professional, technical and kindred worker households in Bergen County, weighted by the relative proportions of owner and renter households, comes to $20,200.

The latter figure can also be taken to represent the average annual lifetime value of housing services consumed by professional, technical, and kindred worker households. We now have, for this particular occupational category, both the average annual lifetime income as well as the average annual lifetime consumption of housing services. The underlying data necessary for carrying out a similar calculation for each major occupational category in Bergen County are given in Appendix Tables E-13 and E-14.

Similar computations were carried out for the ten major occupational categories in each of the eight counties in the study area, a total of 80 observations in all. The results are summarized in Appendix Table E-15, which gives for each county and occupation the following information: average annual lifetime income, average value of occupied housing units, and the value-income ratio on a lifetime basis.

What has been the significance of using the county as the basic geographical unit of observation? That is, first of all, is there any difference in the lifetime income prospects of, say, professional worker households in Bergen County compared to their Hudson County counterparts? That there are such differences is the clear implication of the results summarized in Appendix Table E-15. The potential significance of the difference can be deduced from the percent size of the difference—close to 30 percent on the average in the case of this particular comparison.

That such inter-county differences exist and that they are considerable is hardly surprising in view of the substantial differences between the two counties in the internal composition of their respective professional, technical and kindred worker groups. Between the same nominal occupations in both counties, differences in current income probably reflect not so much differences in age but rather differences in status and in income-earning abilities, hence differences in lifetime income.

Thus, by using the county as our unit of observation, we implicitly assume that real differences in the composition of each major occupational category between the individual counties are captured in some manner. Earlier attempts to measure the effect of permanent or normal income upon the elasticity of housing consumption relied on family median income figures either by census tract or municipality as a proxy for long-term income.[6] However, the use of median income figures for all families in a particular census tract as a proxy for normal income hardly seems a realistic procedure, since it more or less ignores the life cycle process common to all household units. Over the life cycle, income and housing requirements change as the family or household unit ages, changes its size and varies (or has varied for it) its income. These complex and persistent changes are hardly likely to be negotiated within the relatively narrow confines of a given census tract or of a municipality.

One might make a case for saying that the underlying forces of residential segregation which operate within any housing market area tend to bring together into particular subareas groups whose lifetime income prospects are more or less alike. However, in the nature of things, this foregathering of households with roughly comparable lifetime income prospects is only likely to take place at a unique point in their individual family life cycles. For example, young households (and old ones as well) are likely to rent rather than own and units available for rental are not likely to be found in the same municipality, much less the same census tract, as are owner-occupied housing units. Among households with *identical* lifetime income prospects but at different stages of the family cycle and, hence, with differences in current income, there are bound to be differences in the geographic area of settlement. If we characterize these separate areas of settlement by their prevailing value-income ratios the result is, naturally, greatly influenced by current income considerations and not by those long-term forces which presumably are being tested for their effect.

It seems quite plausible to assume that this difficulty is at least partially overcome when one uses the county as the geographic unit of ob-

[6] For one such investigation see Reid, *op. cit.*

servation and occupation as the means of classifying households by life-time income. That is, it is more likely to be the case that the typical or average Bergen County professional, technical and kindred worker household currently residing in Bergen County is (1) likely to satisfy its lifetime housing needs at various locations within Bergen County but not necessarily within a specific municipality or census tract, and (2) is likely to have different lifetime income prospects than its Hudson County counterpart even though both households are nominally classified, according to the occupation of their head, as falling into the professional, technical, and kindred worker category. If lifetime permanent housing consumption is a function principally of lifetime permanent income, then being able to provide a methodological basis for establishing the differences in lifetime income between different groups of households is indispensable for testing the relationship between lifetime income and lifetime housing consumption in a quantitative sense.

Unfortunately, related current income and housing consumption distributions from which one could compute lifetime value-income ratios are available only for the major occupation groups mentioned earlier. These broad groupings, in turn, are composed of detailed occupational listings characterized by greatly differing lifetime income prospects. According to one recent study, the lifetime earnings prospects in 1960 for the United States as a whole of males aged 24 to 64 currently employed in the major occupation category, professional, technical, and kindred workers, ranged from $175,000 for clergymen to $717,000 for physicians and surgeons.[7]

Ideally then in order to be able to determine the relationship between lifetime housing consumption and different levels of lifetime income, the major occupational categories would have to be further disaggregated into detailed occupations characterized by different lifetime income prospects. Needless to say, such data, encompassing both income and housing consumption patterns, do not exist. To some extent, however, the differences between counties in the internal structure of each major occupational category produce an effect comparable to that which would have been produced by further disaggregation.

The results summarized in Appendix Table E-15 have been plotted in Figure 6, Chapter III. The X axis represents average annual lifetime income, the Y axis, the value-income ratio associated with each average annual lifetime income observation. Additional scatter diagrams (not

[7] Statement of Herman P. Miller, Special Assistant, Office of the Director, Bureau of the Census, before Subcommittee on Employment and Manpower, U. S. Senate Committee on Labor and Public Welfare, July 31, 1962.

reproduced here) have been plotted, separating the so-called suburban counties from the so-called old counties. The differences between the suburban and the old counties revolve principally about the relative dominance in the latter of old central cities where renting is the characteristic form of tenure. In addition, three more scatter diagrams were drawn which omit households headed by domestic workers since it was felt that the inclusion of the latter unnecessarily distorts the long-term value-income ratio due to their atypical family composition. The slopes of the straight line regression equations fitted to the various diagrams are very much alike. However, their Y-intercept is quite a bit different. The value-income ratio, roughly speaking, expresses the percentage of income spent on housing. The slope of the line thus represents the income elasticity of housing consumption expenditures. In all cases, as long-term income rises there is a very slight decline in the percentage of income which is spent for housing. However, in the case of the old counties, where renting dominates as a form of tenure, the level of the line is lower than it is in the case of the newer counties. Principally this seems to reflect the fact that the average value of renter-occupied units is substantially lower than that of owner-occupied units.

The regression of long-term housing consumption against "lifetime" income shows that the income elasticity of the former is, at least for this particular area, suspiciously close to unity. This finding, of course, runs counter to the quite pronounced income-inelasticity of housing consumption which has often been observed in studies using cross-section data (including the one summarized here). In fact, it lends support to the thesis of those who maintain, with Muth, that the relation of consumption to current income as between income classes at a given point in time yields misleading results when attention is focused upon the income elasticity of demand as between different years. This is because the income a consumer receives in a given year may differ from his expectations about his normal (or permanent) income level and it is the latter which is the more important determinant of consumption. Current income fluctuates around its permanent income level for many causes. In addition to the accidents of timing, there are factors such as windfalls, losses, etc. Similarly the expected level of consumption differs from current outlay because of lumpy purchase of durables, the impact of accidents, illness, etc.

But perhaps more importantly, the finding of a more or less proportional response of housing consumption to rising income, both conceptually conceived of in lifetime terms, seems to indicate a reversal in the secular trend in housing consumption. Grebler, Blank, and Winnick found that the per capita value of residential capital in constant prices fluctuated within narrow margins and in 1950 was only slightly larger than in 1890.[8]

This almost imperceptible rise in real housing consumption occurred during a period in which real incomes rose quite considerably, indicating that in the long run as well as in the short, housing consumption in regard to income was highly inelastic. Part of this pronounced long-run inelasticity could, of course, be attributed to adverse price movements, since, relatively speaking, residential construction costs rose more rapidly than all other consumer prices. However, given the state of the indexes involved one can hardly say with any but the most feeble show of certainty what the relative rates of price increase were in drawing comparisons between residential construction costs and all other prices.[9] Moreover, empirical studies of the price elasticity of housing consumption between two periods of time are notable principally for their absence. The one extant specimen of this scarce genus, however, that of Duesenberry and Kistin,[10] estimated a price elasticity of −0.08, which is hardly enough to account for the virtually static level of real housing consumption in the face of rapidly rising real incomes.

However, whatever the forces accounting for the slow secular increase in pre-1950 real per capita housing consumption, they seem to have been reversed in the period since then. In extending the Grebler-Winnick-Blank data to 1958, Maisel and Grebler have found a tendency for the constant-dollar value of the stock of residential wealth in the form of structures to increase at a faster rate than real disposable income, the reverse of the pre-1950 experience. The resulting increase in the value-income ratio, moreover, cannot easily be attributed to the effects of differential price changes since for the post-1950 period residential construction cost indexes seem to have been advancing at more or less the same rate as all other consumer prices.

[8] Leo Grebler, David M. Blank, and Louis Winnick, *Capital Formation in Residential Real Estate* (Princeton University Press, 1956), Table 73 and pp. 252-60.

[9] For an elucidation of the difficulties involved see Leo Grebler and Sherman J. Maisel, "Determinants of Residential Construction: A Review of Present Knowledge," in *Impacts of Monetary Policy,* A Series of Research Studies Prepared for the Commission on Money and Credit (1963), pp. 543-50.

[10] James S. Duesenberry and Helen Kistin, "The Role of Demand in the Economic Structure," in *Studies in the Structure of the American Economy,* Wassily Leontieff, ed. (Oxford University Press, 1953), pp. 451-82.

In addition, a preliminary investigation of 1950-60 changes in the aggregate value-income ratios for 16 major metropolitan areas in the United States indicates that, in general, housing consumption has in the postwar period begun to represent an increasing share of household income.

Tables

TABLE E-1. Population, Number of Households, and Form of Tenure by County in Study Area, 1960

County	Population[a] (Thousands) (1)	Households		
		Total Number[a] (Thousands) (2)	Percentage Owner- Occupied[b] (3)	Percentage Renter- Occupied[b] (4)
Bergen	780.3	230.6	71.9%	28.1%
Essex	923.5	289.0	41.9	58.1
Hudson	610.7	198.0	29.4	70.6
Middlesex	433.9	120.4	74.8	25.2
Morris	261.6	72.0	77.5	22.5
Passaic	406.6	125.9	53.6	46.4
Somerset	143.9	40.1	74.2	25.8
Union	504.3	150.2	66.2	33.8
All counties	4,064.8	1,226.2	56.1	43.9

[a] U. S. Bureau of the Census, *U. S. Census of Population: 1960, General Population Characteristics, New Jersey.* Final Report PC(1)-32B (1961), Table 13.

[b] *U. S. Census of Housing: 1960,* Vol. I, "States and Small Areas, New Jersey." Final Report HC(1)-32 (1962), Tables 14 and 28.

TABLE E-2. Family Income, Property Values, and Property Taxes in Study Area, 1960

County	Median Income, Families and Unrelated Individuals[a] (1)	Average Sales Value Per Occupied Housing Unit[b] (2)	Sales Value-Income Ratio (3)	Average Assessed Value Per Occupied Housing Unit[b] (4)	Average Residential Real Property Tax Per Occupied Housing Unit[c] (5)
Bergen	$7,417	$18,100	2.44	$ 5,200	$314
Essex	5,675	13,200	2.32	11,400	326
Hudson	5,476	9,100	1.65	3,700	195
Middlesex	6,525	14,100	2.17	3,200	227
Morris	6,962	17,300	2.47	4,700	329
Passaic	5,768	13,200	2.28	3,900	220
Somerset	6,815	16,600	2.44	3,200	251
Union	7,067	16,100	2.27	4,700	300
All counties	6,350	14,300	2.22	5,933	276

[a] From U. S. Bureau of the Census, *U. S. Census of Population: 1960, General Social and Economic Characteristics, New Jersey.* Final Report PC(1) -32C (1962), Table 86.
[b] For computation, consult Appendix Tables E-4 to E-10.
[c] For computation, see Appendix Table E-3.

TABLE E-3. Actual Real Property Tax Per Occupied Housing Unit by County

County	Real Property Taxes on Occupied Housing Units[a] (Millions of dollars)	Number of Occupied Housing Units[b] (Thousands)	Real Property Taxes Per Occupied Unit
Bergen	$ 72.3	230.6	$314
Essex	94.5	289.0	326
Hudson	38.6	198.0	195
Middlesex	27.3	120.4	227
Morris	23.7	72.0	329
Passaic	27.7	125.9	220
Somerset	10.1	40.1	251
Union	45.0	150.2	300
All counties	339.2	1,226.2	276

Note: Figures in column 3 have been rounded.
[a] Total real property tax levy for each county taken from State of New Jersey, *Annual Report of the Division of Taxation in the Department of Treasury for the Year 1960;* percentage distribution of total levy by type of property (e.g., nonfarm residential) derived from interpolation of 1956–61 trends in the percentage distribution of gross assessed value of locally assessed real property by county shown in U. S. Bureau of the Census, *Census of Governments: 1957 and 1962,* Vol. II, "Taxable Property Values" (1958 and 1963), Table 22; percentage distribution of resulting nonfarm residential real property tax levy between occupied and all other housing units developed by comparing relative median values and contract rents of occupied owner and renter housing with comparable items for available vacant housing as shown in U. S. Bureau of the Census, *U. S. Census of Housing: 1960,* Vol. 1, "States and Small Areas, New Jersey." Final Report HC (1)-32 (1962), Tables 17 and 30.
[b] U. S. Bureau of the Census, *U. S. Census of Housing: 1960,* Vol. I, "States and Small Areas, New Jersey." Final Report HC (1)-32 (1962), Tables 12 and 28.

284

TABLE E-4. Average Sales[a] and Average Assessed[b] Value by Sales Price Interval for Residential Properties with Four Housing Units or Less, 1963

				Sales Price Interval			
	Under $5,000	$5,000–$9,900	$10,000–$14,900	$15,000–$19,900	$20,000–$24,900	$25,000–$34,900	$35,000 and Over
Bergen County							
Average sales value	$3,800	$7,861	$13,385	$17,914	$21,375	$28,500	$41,225
Average assessed value	1,113	2,743	4,170	5,213	6,006	7,952	11,254
Essex County							
Average sales value	3,913	7,960	12,742	17,572	21,150	28,200	40,800
Average assessed value	5,740	7,713	10,729	14,532	18,126	24,421	37,332
Hudson County							
Average sales value	3,722	7,790	12,612	17,396	20,925	27,900	39,950
Average assessed value	2,453	3,085	3,985	4,836	5,336	7,115	10,267
Middlesex County							
Average sales value	3,714	8,059	13,328	17,091	20,475	27,300	40,375
Average assessed value	1,266	2,071	2,892	3,709	4,402	5,897	8,640
Morris County							
Average sales value	3,623	7,736	12,877	17,369	21,375	28,500	41,225
Average assessed value	1,145	2,158	3,412	4,898	6,049	7,952	10,801
Passaic County							
Average sales value	3,510	7,686	12,909	17,487	21,150	28,200	40,800
Average assessed value	1,551	2,613	3,576	4,669	5,859	7,840	11,465
Somerset County							
Average sales value	2,824	7,824	13,005	17,540	21,150	28,500	41,225
Average assessed value	717	1,471	2,263	3,192	3,617	4,817	6,344
Union County							
Average sales value	3,733	7,738	13,061	17,517	21,600	28,800	40,800
Average assessed value	1,419	2,492	3,383	4,800	6,372	8,611	13,178

[a] From unpublished data provided by the State of New Jersey, Department of the Treasury, Division of Taxation, Local Property Tax Bureau.
[b] Derived by applying appropriate assessment-sales ratio (see Appendix Table E-5) to average sales value.

TABLE E-5. Weighted Assessment-Sales Ratios by Sales Price Interval and Type of Residential Property for Counties in the Study Area, 1963[a]

Sales Price Interval and Type of Property	Weighted Assessment-Sales Ratios							
	Bergen	Essex	Hudson	Middlesex	Morris	Passaic	Somerset[ ]	Union
Residential properties with four housing units or less								
Under $5,000	29.3%	146.7%	65.9%	34.1%	31.6%	44.2%	25.4%	38.0%
$ 5,000 to $ 9,900	34.9	96.9	39.6	25.7	27.9	34.0	18.8	32.2
$10,000 to $14,900	32.1	84.2	31.6	21.7	26.5	27.7	17.4	25.9
$15,000 to $19,900	29.1	82.7	27.8	21.7	28.2	26.7	18.2	27.4
$20,000 to $24,900	28.1	85.7	25.5	21.5	28.3	27.7	17.1	29.5
$25,000 to $34,900	27.9	86.6	25.5	21.6	27.9	27.8	16.9	29.9
$35,000 and over	27.3	91.5	25.7	21.4	26.2	28.1	15.4	32.3
All units	28.3	86.6	28.3	21.7	27.6	27.7	17.3	29.3
Residential properties with five or more housing units								
All units	29.7	88.6	50.1	26.9	25.5	34.2	b	30.6

[a] Based upon unpublished data provided by the State of New Jersey, Department of the Treasury, Division of Taxation, Local Property Tax Bureau.
b No applicable sales for this category in 1963.

TABLE E-6. Estimated Average Gross Monthly Rental by Rental Class for Counties in Study Area, 1960

Rent Class[a]	Bergen	Essex	Hudson	Middlesex	Morris	Passaic	Somerset	Union
				Number of Units				
Less than $50								
Less than $20	55	186	255	89	36	121	32	42
$20 to $29	164	2,253	1,559	423	86	639	69	176
$30 to $39	665	4,356	5,283	1,003	187	1,997	136	1,095
$40 to $49	1,755	8,654	11,729	1,882	407	4,250	312	1,750
$50 to $99								
$50 to $59	3,186	13,800	19,474	2,699	748	6,554	578	3,423
$60 to $69	5,180	19,606	24,834	3,700	1,116	8,537	819	4,882
$70 to $79	6,998	24,356	26,495	4,142	1,641	9,480	1,335	6,513
$80 to $99	18,223	50,292	32,701	7,963	3,899	15,266	3,266	14,242
$100 to $149								
$100 to $119	12,646	23,842	9,159	3,957	3,147	6,664	1,485	8,088
$120 to $149	8,927	11,547	3,907	2,834 }	2,334	2,314	1,304 }	5,515
$150 and over								
$150 to $199	3,460	3,967	1,022		854	621		2,666
$200 or more	1,038	1,504	233		273	175		947
				Average Gross Monthly Rent				
Estimated midpoints[b]								
Less than $50	$ 41	$ 39	$ 40	$ 40	$ 38	$ 40	$ 38	$ 40
$50 to $99	80	78	74	81	79	75	80	78
$100 to $149	120	118	117	120[c]	121	116	121[c]	120
$150 and over	187	189	184	187[c]	187	186	187[c]	188

[a] From U. S. Bureau of the Census, U. S. Census of Housing: 1960, Vol. I, "States and Small Areas, New Jersey." Final Report HC(1)-32 (1962), Tables 17 and 30. This item includes only those units which are rented and for which rents are paid. As a result, occupied units for which no rent is paid are not included. The amount of rent tabulated is the "gross rent." Gross rent is the amount of rent plus the cost of all utilities and/or heat which are paid for by the tenant.

[b] Estimated midpoints in the rent classes cited (less than $50, $50 to $99, $100 to $149, $150 and over) represent the weighted averages of the narrower components presented in the upper portion of the table. The weights are the number in each of these narrower components multiplied by the class midpoint. In the open-end categories—less than $20 and $200 or more, $10 and $225, respectively, were employed as the class average.

[c] Calculated as an extrapolation based on the relationship between estimated midpoints in successive rent classes in the other counties in the study area.

TABLE E-7. Relationship Between Median Monthly Contract Rent and Median Monthly Gross Rent by County in Study Area, 1960[a]

County	Contract Rent (1)	Gross Rent (2)	Contract Rent as Percentage of Gross Rent (3)
Bergen	$85	$94	90%
Essex	72	83	87
Hudson	61	72	85
Middlesex	67	81	83
Morris	78	96	81
Passaic	63	77	82
Somerset	75	88	85
Union	76	89	85

[a] From the U. S. Bureau of the Census, *U. S. Census of Housing: 1960*, Vol. I, "States and Small Areas, New Jersey." Final Report HC(1'-32 (1962), Tables 17 and 30.

TABLE E-8. Derivation of Relationship Between Net Rental Receipts and Value of Renter-Occupied Housing Units, 1960

	Bergen	Essex	Hudson	Middlesex	Morris	Passaic	Somerset[b]	Union
Units in structure[a]								
1	14,253	13,137	8,138	10,905	9,117	6,691	5,464	10,010
2 to 4	27,452	77,639	56,036	14,722	5,072	33,635	3,925	25,536
5 to 49	17,489	58,249	69,289	} 4,665	1,813	15,980	} 940	11,374
50 or more	5,534	18,806	6,308		209	2,193		3,856
Total number of units	64,728	167,831	139,771	30,292	16,211	58,499	10,329	50,776
Annual rental receipts as a percentage of value by number of dwelling units on property[c]								
1	8%	8%	8%	8%	8%	8%	8%	8%
2 to 4	12	12	12	12	12	12	12	12
5 to 49	12	12	12	12	12	12	12	12
50 or more	14	14	14	14	14	14	14	14
Weighted average percentage relationship between net rental receipts and value of renter-occupied units	11.3	11.9	11.9	10.6	9.8	11.6	9.9	11.4

[a] From U. S. Bureau of the Census, U. S. Census of Housing: 1960, Vol. I, "States and Small Areas, New Jersey." Final Report HC(2)-32 (1962), Tables 14 and 28.
[b] Partly estimated.
[c] From U. S. Bureau of the Census, U. S. Census of Housing: 1960, Vol. V, "Residential Finance," Part 2, "Rental and Vacant Properties" (1963), Table 1 of Chaps. 1–4, respectively.

TABLE E-9. Value of Single-Family Owner-Occupied Units and Gross Monthly Rents by Income of Household in Bergen County, 1960[a]

	Total Number of Households[c]	Total Income of Household[b]						
		Under $3,000	$3,000–$4,999	$5,000–$6,999	$7,000–$9,999	$10,000–$14,999	$15,000–$24,999	$25,000 and Over
Value of property								
Under $5,000	1,000	11.5%	22.0%	26.9%	35.5%	2.0%	0.0%	2.1%
$5,000–$7,400	1,000	20.0	25.7	15.4	28.0	7.4	3.6	0.0
7,500– 9,900	2,200	17.6	16.3	24.4	19.5	15.9	3.6	2.7
10,000–12,400	6,700	19.6	14.4	23.3	25.8	13.4	1.5	2.1
12,500–14,900	13,600	12.5	13.1	25.7	26.9	18.0	2.3	1.5
15,000–17,400	24,000	7.4	9.8	29.3	30.8	17.7	4.0	1.0
17,500–19,900	31,100	4.6	8.0	21.4	36.6	22.6	5.9	0.8
20,000–24,900	36,900	5.3	4.5	16.0	30.0	30.8	10.3	2.0
25,000–34,900	23,100	3.2	3.2	10.9	20.6	33.2	21.7	7.3
35,000 and over	9,900	5.4	4.1	5.4	10.7	17.7	27.5	29.3
Amount of rental								
Less than $50	45	34.5	21.2	18.7	15.3	6.4	1.7	2.3
$50 to $99	339	16.7	21.8	28.0	22.5	8.2	1.0	1.8
$100 to $149	218	10.0	12.8	23.3	30.9	18.2	3.5	1.2
$150 and over	44	6.3	4.6	9.6	24.9	30.5	15.2	8.8

[a] Based on data from S. J. Tesauro & Co., People and Homes in the American Market, New Jersey (1961).
[b] Percentage of total number of households in value or rental class.
[c] To nearest hundred.

TABLE E-10. Summary of Estimates of Composite Average Assessed and Average Sales Values for All Occupied (Owner and Renter) Housing Units by Total Income of Household, 1960[a]

	Total Income of Household						
	Under $3,000	$3,000–$4,999	$5,000–$6,999	$7,000–$9,999	$10,000–$14,999	$15,000–$24,999	$25,000 and Over
Bergen County							
Average assessed value	$4,268	$4,169	$4,652	$5,082	$5,769	$7,081	$8,299
Average sales value	14,883	14,515	16,274	17,821	20,276	24,949	30,478
Essex County							
Average assessed value	8,643	8,772	9,963	11,622	14,392	19,096	22,343
Average sales value	9,855	9,989	11,381	13,315	16,537	21,991	30,469
Hudson County							
Average assessed value	3,280	3,523	3,663	3,938	4,358	4,901	6,254
Average sales value	7,969	8,278	8,974	10,186	14,150	14,517	18,865
Middlesex County							
Average assessed value							
Average sales value	11,524	11,838	13,571	15,010	16,625	19,750	20,811
Morris County							
Average assessed value	3,674	3,623	4,011	4,488	5,651	6,763	8,222
Average sales value	13,545	13,415	14,751	16,429	20,575	24,615	31,569
Passaic County							
Average assessed value	3,009	3,162	3,643	4,178	4,831	6,047	6,353
Average sales value	9,911	10,263	12,267	14,367	16,873	20,332	24,220
Somerset County							
Average assessed value	2,622	2,772	2,904	3,245	3,535	4,436	5,105
Average sales value	12,721	12,852	14,582	16,895	19,147	24,950	27,243
Union County							
Average assessed value	3,592	3,524	3,953	4,544	5,532	7,109	8,687
Average value	13,735	13,281	15,318	17,894	22,177	28,781	38,799

[a] Based on data from S. J. Tesauro & Co., *People and Homes in the American Market, New Jersey* (1961), and Appendix Tables E-5, E-6, E-7, and E-8. See text for description of derivation.

TABLE E-11. House Value-Income Ratio by Current Income Class for Counties in Study Area[a]

County	Total Income of Household						
	Under $3,000	$3,000– $4,999	$5,000– $6,999	$7,000– $9,999	$10,000– $14,999	$15,000– $24,999	$25,000 and Over
Bergen	9.90	3.62	2.76	2.14	1.69	1.32	0.72
Essex	6.60	2.56	1.90	1.60	1.40	1.18	0.65
Hudson	5.00	2.02	1.50	1.26	1.21	0.78	0.36
Middlesex	7.67	2.95	2.27	1.83	1.39	1.06	0.44
Morris	9.00	3.44	2.47	1.98	1.75	1.32	0.67
Passaic	6.60	2.58	2.08	1.73	1.40	1.09	0.57
Somerset	8.47	3.23	2.43	2.06	1.62	1.34	0.58
Union	9.13	3.41	2.55	2.16	1.88	1.55	0.83

[a] The income figure used as the denominator of the value-income ratio is that for 1961 average adjusted gross income as shown in Table E-12. For Bergen and Passaic Counties, respectively, the average adjusted gross income figure used is that for the Paterson-Clifton-Passaic Standard Metropolitan Statistical Area; for Essex, Morris, and Union Counties, respectively, the relevant SMSA is Newark; for Hudson County, it is the Jersey City SMSA. For Somerset and Middlesex Counties, due to the absence of comparable data, it was assumed that income class averages were equal to the weighted averages of the Jersey City SMSA, the Newark SMSA, and the Paterson-Clifton-Passaic SMSA.
The value figure used as the numerator of the value-income ratio is that for 1960 average sale value of single-family, owner-occupied houses, as shown in Appendix Table E-9.

TABLE E-12. Average Adjusted Gross Income by Income Class in Standard Metropolitan Statistical Areas Within Study Area, 1961[a]

SMSA and Subject Category	Income Class						
	Under $3,000	$3,000–$4,999	$5,000–$6,999	$7,000–$9,999	$10,000–$14,999	$15,000–$24,999	$25,000 and Over
Newark SMSA[b]							
Adjusted gross income (millions of $)	287	551	769	922	733	465	564
Number of returns (thousands)	191	140	129	111	62	25	12
Average adjusted gross income ($)	1,502	3,936	5,961	8,306	11,823	18,600	47,000
Jersey City SMSA[c]							
Adjusted gross income (millions of $)	108	279	312	322	152	50	52
Number of returns (thousands)	67	68	52	40	13	3	1
Average adjusted gross income ($)	1,612	4,103	6,000	8,050	11,692	18,740	52,791
Paterson-Clifton-Passaic SMSA[d]							
Adjusted gross income (millions of $)	167	308	481	678	563	299	316
Number of returns (thousands)	115	77	81	82	47	16	7
Average adjusted gross income ($)	1,452	4,000	5,938	8,268	11,978	18,688	42,399

[a] From U. S. Treasury Department, Statistics of Income, Individual Income Tax Returns, 1961, Table 20. AGI figures are rounded in millions of dollars and number of returns are rounded in thousands for presentation purposes. As a result, average adjusted gross income, which is calculated from the unrounded data, may differ from the results produced by use of the rounded figures.
[b] Includes Essex, Morris, and Union Counties.
[c] Coextensive with Hudson County.
[d] Includes Bergen and Passaic Counties.

TABLE E-13. Income Distribution Among Households in Bergen County by Occupation of Head of Household, 1960[a]

Occupation of Head	Total Number of Households	Total Income of Household[b]						
		Under $3,000	$3,000–$4,999	$5,000–$6,999	$7,000–$9,999	$10,000–$14,999	$15,000–$24,999	$25,000 and Over
Professional, technical, and kindred	32,400	2.4%	4.4%	14.2%	30.8%	30.5%	12.1%	5.6%
Farmers and farm managers	400	15.6	15.1	24.6	20.0	24.6	0.0	—
Managers, officials, and proprietors	34,000	2.4	4.7	13.0	23.2	30.3	18.0	8.4
Clerical and kindred	19,300	6.4	17.2	24.4	29.9	17.2	4.9	—
Sales workers	18,800	3.8	8.8	19.6	26.1	26.0	12.3	3.5
Craftsmen and kindred	41,400	2.3	9.1	27.2	36.9	20.1	3.9	0.5
Operatives	32,100	5.7	14.2	30.3	33.1	14.1	2.6	—
Private household workers	700	76.6	5.3	6.2	6.5	2.9	2.5	—
Other service workers	9,900	13.0	22.6	27.1	21.1	14.3	1.4	0.5
Laborers (all)	5,200	6.7	19.1	32.2	31.7	8.0	2.3	—
Armed forces	400	0.0	22.3	36.0	26.9	10.4	4.4	—
Not in labor force and not reported	35,900	44.4	14.4	14.1	13.3	9.5	3.3	0.9

[a] Based on data from S. J. Tesauro & Co., People and Homes in the American Market, Cross-Tabulations of Population and Housing Characteristics from the 1960 Decennial Census New Jersey (1961).
[b] Percentage of total households in occupation class.

TABLE E-14. Value of Single-Family Owner-Occupied Units and Gross Monthly Rentals by Occupation of Head of Household in Bergen County, 1960[a]

	Total Number of Households[c]	Occupation of Head[b]									
		Professional, Technical, and Kindred	Managers, Officials, and Proprietors	Clerical and Kindred	Sales Workers	Craftsmen and Kindred	Opera-tives	Private Household Workers	Other Service Workers	Laborers	All Other Workers[d]
Value of property[e]											
Under $5,000	1,000	14.6%	3.8%	3.8%	0.0%	30.8%	15.1%	0.0%	3.8%	0.0%	28.1%
$5,000–$7,400	1,000	7.5	5.9	4.9	5.3	11.2	20.5	4.7	1.8	8.3	29.9
7,500– 9,900	2,200	2.7	3.8	4.7	2.8	21.9	15.6	0.0	7.9	4.5	36.1
10,000–12,400	6,700	5.5	5.4	9.7	1.5	18.7	17.4	1.3	8.2	2.5	29.8
12,500–14,900	13,600	6.1	6.6	9.8	4.1	22.4	18.7	0.6	7.1	3.2	21.4
15,000–17,400	24,000	11.6	8.5	8.9	5.7	23.3	18.2	0.2	5.2	1.9	16.5
17,500–19,900	31,100	15.6	12.7	9.1	8.3	23.9	13.4	0.1	3.8	1.4	11.7
20,000–24,900	36,900	18.5	21.7	7.2	11.2	17.9	7.5	0.0	3.6	0.9	11.5
25,000–34,900	23,100	22.4	28.0	6.1	13.4	12.0	4.1	0.1	1.8	1.3	10.8
35,000 or over	9,900	19.3	42.3	2.2	11.0	7.4	1.7	0.0	1.0	0.2	14.9
Amount of rental[f]											
Less than $50	4,500	8.9	6.1	5.7	2.3	14.6	20.7	2.2	7.0	4.2	28.3
$50 to $99	33,900	8.7	6.2	12.4	6.2	16.7	22.2	0.8	5.3	5.0	16.5
$100 to $149	21,800	16.9	14.6	10.4	10.8	14.1	13.0	0.0	3.5	1.6	15.1
$150 and over	4,400	26.0	23.9	4.7	12.3	6.7	7.5	0.0	1.8	0.5	16.6

[a] S. J. Tesauro & Co., People and Homes in the American Market; Cross-Tabulations of Population and Housing Characteristics, from the 1960 Decennial Census, New Jersey (1961).

[b] Percentage of total number of households in each value or rental class.

[c] Rounded to nearest hundred.

[d] Includes the following groups of households classified according to occupation of head of household: "Farmers and Farm Managers," "Armed Forces," and "Not in Labor Force and Not Reported."

[e] This item includes: only units on less than 10 acres owned or being bought and, in addition, consist of only one unit with no business on the property. The term business means only a clearly recognizable business establishment such as a restaurant, store, or filling station.

[f] This item includes only those units which are rented. However, occupied units for which no rent is paid are included in these tabulations as rental units paying less than $50 per month. The amount of rental tabulated is the "gross rent." "Gross rent is the amount of rent plus the costs of all utilities and/or heat which are paid for by the tenant.

TABLE E-15. Weighted Average Value of All Occupied Units, Average Annual Lifetime Income, and Value-Income Ratio, by Occupation of Head of Household and by County, for Counties in Study Area

Occupation of Head	Bergen	Essex	Hudson	Middlesex	Morris	Passaic	Somerset	Union
	Weighted Average Value of Occupied Units							
Professional, technical, and kindred	$20,200	$17,400	$11,100	$16,000	$19,400	$16,700	$19,500	$19,900
Managers, officials, and proprietors	22,600	19,500	11,900	16,200	22,700	18,300	22,500	21,500
Clerical and kindred workers	16,100	11,300	8,700	14,000	15,900	12,900	15,300	13,900
Sales workers	20,100	16,200	10,900	15,600	21,300	14,800	18,300	18,900
Craftsmen and kindred	17,200	12,600	9,500	14,400	15,700	13,100	16,400	15,700
Operatives	14,900	10,300	8,300	13,100	13,200	11,500	13,600	13,000
Domestics	9,900	8,500	6,700	7,600	8,100	7,000	9,500	12,100
Other service workers	16,000	10,500	8,400	13,200	14,000	11,700	13,700	13,200
Laborers	13,600	9,300	7,900	11,300	14,000	9,200	13,700	12,100
	Average Annual Lifetime Income							
Professional, technical, and kindred	$11,900	$12,400	$9,400	$9,400	$11,400	$10,000	$11,300	$12,600
Managers, officials, and proprietors	13,500	13,500	9,000	9,700	13,600	10,100	12,000	13,000
Clerical and kindred workers	7,700	6,500	6,300	7,700	7,500	6,800	7,400	7,000
Sales workers	10,600	9,700	7,300	8,500	10,900	8,200	11,100	10,100
Craftsmen and kindred	8,400	7,700	7,500	8,000	7,900	7,500	8,200	8,600
Operatives	7,400	6,200	6,000	6,500	7,000	6,200	7,200	7,100
Domestics	3,100	3,000	2,400	2,400	3,200	2,600	3,300	3,100
Other service workers	6,600	5,600	5,800	6,500	5,800	6,000	6,100	7,000
Laborers	6,800	5,500	5,900	6,200	6,100	5,700	6,400	6,500
	Value-Income Ratio							
Professional, technical, and kindred	1.70	1.40	1.18	1.70	1.70	1.67	1.73	1.58
Managers, officials, and proprietors	1.67	1.44	1.32	1.67	1.67	1.81	1.88	1.65
Clerical and kindred workers	2.09	1.74	1.38	1.82	2.12	1.90	2.07	1.99
Sales workers	1.90	1.67	1.49	1.84	1.95	1.80	1.65	1.87
Craftsmen and kindred	2.05	1.64	1.27	1.80	1.99	1.75	2.00	1.83
Operatives	2.01	1.66	1.38	1.93	1.89	1.85	1.89	1.83
Domestics	3.19	2.83	2.80	3.17	2.53	2.69	2.88	4.03
Other service workers	2.42	1.88	1.45	2.03	2.41	1.95	2.25	1.89
Laborers	2.00	1.69	1.34	1.82	2.30	1.61	2.14	1.86

Evidence from the 1960 Census of Housing on Property Tax Rate Differentials by Type of Property

THE RESIDENTIAL FINANCE Survey of the 1960 Census of Housing included questions on property values, rental receipts, and real estate tax payments, as well as mortgage information. This material (Volume V of the Census, in two parts, Part 1 for homeowner properties and Part 2 for rental and vacant properties) offers some indirect evidence on the application of the property tax by dwelling unit size classes, that is, properties classified by the number of dwelling units in the structure. The evidence is by no means conclusive, but deserves mention.

The survey of rental and vacant properties covered 7.7 million properties with approximately 16.4 million dwelling units. Since the data are presented in the form of national aggregates, and since property tax rates differ so widely, it is worthwhile trying to refine them somewhat. The goal of the refinement is to focus on urban conditions as far as possible. The major distinction made in the Census volume, between mortgaged and nonmortgaged properties, does help in this regard, as Appendix Table F-1 indicates. Only 43 percent of all single-family rental properties are located in metropolitan areas, in contrast to 70 percent or more for larger properties. But nearly 2.5 million of the 3.1 million single-family properties located outside metropolitan areas are not mortgaged, and thus 60 percent of all mortgaged single-family properties are within metropolitan areas. Therefore, this note will focus on the 2.6 million mortgaged properties, containing 7.9 million dwelling units. This

**TABLE F-1. Composition of Rental and Vacant Nonfarm
Residential Properties, United States, 1960**

	Total[a]	1-Family Houses	2-4 Family Houses[a]	5-49 Unit Properties	Properties with 50 or More Units
All properties					
Number of properties (thousands)	7,713	5,539	1,626	533	15.1
Percentage in SMSA's	52%	43%	70%	81%	97%
Estimated number of dwelling units (millions)[b]	16.4	5.5	4.0	5.1	1.8
Mortgaged properties					
Number of properties (thousands)	2,551	1,643	596	299	13.6
Percentage in SMSA's	67%	60%	79%	86%	98%
Estimated number of dwelling units (millions)[b]	7.9	1.6	1.5	3.1	1.6
Nonmortgaged properties					
Number of properties (thousands)	5,162	3,896	1,030	234	1.5
Percentage in SMSA's	44%	37%	64%	75%	95%
Estimated number of dwelling units (millions)[b]	8.5	3.9	2.5	2.0	0.2

SMSA—Standard Metropolitan Statistical Area.
Source: U. S. Bureau of the Census, *Census of Housing: 1960*, Vol. V, "Residential Finance," Part 2, "Rental and Vacant Properties" (1963).
[a] Two-to-four family houses with one unit owner-occupied are not included.
[b] Estimated from data on average number of dwelling units in Table A of source.

reduces the problem of a nonurban bias for the smaller properties (with presumably lower tax rates outside metropolitan areas), but does not eliminate it: 98 percent of mortgaged properties with fifty units or more are within metropolitan areas.

The striking feature of Appendix Table F-2, on mortgaged properties, is the rapid increase in reported effective tax rates, as size of property rises, from 1.4 percent for single-family houses to 2.7 percent for fifty-unit-plus apartment houses. The increase is a steady one: the data imply (although they do not show this directly) that the median effective tax rate for two-to-four family houses is 1.8 percent, substantially above that for single-family houses.

How significant is this? One way to examine the significance of these results is to attempt crudely to standardize for metropolitan location.

For this purpose it is assumed that effective property tax rates are uniformly 40 percent higher in metropolitan areas than outside metropolitan areas. This was the nominal rate relationship for the United States as a whole for 1957 and is almost surely an understatement, since assessment ratios in metropolitan areas appear in most cases to exceed those for their respective states. However, there is no satisfactory alternative to the 40 percent factor. On this assumption, the implicit metropolitan area effective rates would be:

1-family	1.6%
2–4 family	2.0
(1–4 family combined)	(1.6)
5–49 units	2.1
50 units or more	2.7

Another factor is indicated by Appendix Table F-3: the heavy concentration of the larger properties in the relatively high property tax rate Northeast. Now, regional tax rate differentials are in part related to differences in the relative degree of urbanization; a cross-classification of metropolitan status and regional location, which would permit sorting out of this effect, is not provided by the Residential Finance Survey. Nonetheless, there is some evidence that there are broad regional differences in effective tax rates, even when the analysis is confined to metropolitan areas, related to overall tax structures and expenditure levels.

In *Measures of Fiscal Capacity,* the Advisory Commission on Intergovernmental Relations presents some estimates of effective tax rates by states for 1960. If we confine the comparison to states with a sizeable proportion of assessed values located in SMSA's in 1961 (more than 60 percent), and adjust for homestead exemptions in Florida and Georgia, which presumably do not apply to rental property, the following figures roughly indicate the relative regional rankings in effective tax rates (the absolute magnitudes are not important here):

Northeast	1.9%
North Central	1.5
South	1.3
West	1.4

TABLE F-2. Median Values, Rents, and Real Estate Taxes, Mortgaged Rental and Vacant Nonfarm Residential Properties, United States, 1960

	All Properties[a]	1-Family Houses	1–4 Family Houses[a]	5–49 Unit Properties	Properties with 50 or More Units
Median value of properties	$11,500	$9,700	$10,700	$42,000	$540,000
Median value per dwelling unit	$ 8,200	$9,700	$ 8,700	less than $ 5,000	$ 6,300
Median monthly rent per dwelling unit[b]	n.a.	$ 61	$ 55	$ 45	$ 67
Rental receipts as percentage of value, median[b]	n.a.	8%	8%	12%	14%
Median real estate tax per dwelling unit[c]	$ 111	$ 122	$ 114	$ 94	$ 157
Real estate tax per $1,000 of value, median[c]	15	14	15	20	27
Real estate tax as percentage of rental receipts, median[b]	n.a.	17%	17%	17%	20%

n.a.—Not available.

Source: U. S. Bureau of the Census, *Census of Housing: 1960*, Vol. V. "Residential Finance," Part 2, "Rental and Vacant Properties" (1963).

[a] Two-to-four family houses with one unit owner occupied are not included. The Census tables do not show two-to-four family properties separately.

[b] Rental data are adjusted to exclude owner expenditures for utilities and fuel, for properties with two or more units. Covers only properties acquired before 1959 and having rental receipts.

[c] Includes all properties acquired before 1959.

TABLE F-3. Regional Distribution of Mortgaged Rental and Vacant Nonfarm Residential Properties, 1960

(In percentages)

	All Properties[a]	1–4 Family Houses[a]	5–49 Unit Properties	Properties with 50 or More Units
United States	100.0	100.0	100.0	100.0
Northeast	21.5	19.6	33.5	61.8
North Central	20.5	20.3	22.3	11.7
South	33.5	36.0	15.8	14.5
West	24.5	24.0	28.4	11.9

Source: U. S. Bureau of the Census, *Census of Housing: 1960*, Vol. V, "Residential Finance," Part 2, "Rental and Vacant Properties" (1963).

Note: Because of rounding, details may not add to totals.

[a] Two-to-four family houses with one unit owner-occupied are not included.

To correct for broad regional differences, the following steps can now be taken:

1.   Assume that the North Central region rate is approximately the national average for metropolitan areas, and express the other regions' rates as relatives of the North Central rate.

2.   Multiply the regional distribution of properties by size class in Appendix Table F-3 by these relatives to produce a correction factor for each size group.

3.   Divide the implicit metropolitan area effective rates shown above by the correction factors.

The results are these:

1–4 family properties	1.6%
5–49 units	2.0
50 units or more	2.4

Thus, the spread is narrowed, but not closed. The conclusion, therefore, is that there is some evidence that, in general, effective property tax rates tend to rise with the size of residential structure (measured by the number of units) within metropolitan areas. Presumably, this is due to assessment practices. One other possibility, that central city effective tax rates are generally higher than rates in suburban areas of the same SMSA, is not true for some of the largest metropolitan areas (including New York). A second alternative explanation might be that the crude correction for regional differences in effective tax rates is inadequate; for example, large apartment houses might be concentrated, *within* regions, in those cities with the very highest overall effective tax rates. This does not seem to be the case; in the Midwest, Chicago is the city of big apartment houses but has an overall effective tax rate below those in Detroit and Milwaukee, and New York City is by no means the highest tax-rate big city in the Northeast.

Derivation of Data in Tables to Chapter V

Table 5-2

THE DATA in this table have been computed, estimated, or taken directly from U. S. Bureau of the Census, *Census of Governments: 1962,* Vol. II, "Taxable Property Values," Tables 2, 4, and 24. Estimation was required to allocate exemptions applicable to real property (shown in Table 2 of the source) by class of property, for the twenty-one states where such exemptions exist, including four states included in Table 24 of the Census document, in which table no allocation has been made. The allocation was based on an examination of the character of the exemptions from statute law (veterans, homestead, middle-income housing in New York, etc.) and on the character of the real property tax base in numerous counties within each state. In general, the exemptions were divided only between residental and farm property. For most of the states involved, the resulting allocation is approximated by this formula:

$$\frac{\text{residential}}{\text{share}} = \frac{\text{gross assessed value of residential property}}{\text{gross assessed value of residential plus } \frac{1}{2} \text{ acreage and farms}}$$

Data on assessed values for New York State are based on corrections made by the Census Bureau after publication of Volume II.

The first four columns of the table, shown for all states, are based on the Census assessed-value categories, with no subdivision of personal property. The "acreage and farms" category is not entirely agricultural but includes a small (and unknown) proportion of nonagricultural realty described on tax rolls as acreage. The "other" category includes vacant lots, commercial and industrial realty, other and unallocable locally assessed realty (mostly separately assessed mineral rights), and nearly all state-assessed property.

The last three columns are shown only for the twenty states (included in Tables 23 and 24 of the Census volume) for which the Census presents detail on types of personalty, plus the four states which do not tax personal property, plus four other states (Louisiana, Mississippi, West Virginia, and the District of Columbia) for which the nature of the legal provisions and fragmentary data in the Census of Governments permit an estimate of the character of assessed personalty. For four of these states, the figures differ slightly from those in Table 24, because of the handling of the exemptions.

In the final three columns, "residential" includes nonfarm residential realty; household personalty where taxed (twelve of the twenty-eight states shown); a share of motor vehicles where taxed (ten states); and a share of intangibles where taxed (Arkansas, Illinois, Louisiana, and West Virginia only, of the states shown). Goldsmith's data for 1958[1] indicate that 73 percent of the total wealth in the form of motor vehicles was owned by nonfarm individuals, 10 percent by farmers, and 17 percent by nonfarm businesses. The farm percentage no doubt varies considerably among the states. In the absence of other data, it has been estimated for these ten states from data on the farm share of personal income (relative to the U. S. average) and the median income of farm males over 14 with income (relative to the U. S. median). The nonfarm business/individuals split (individuals included under "residential") is estimated at 20 percent/80 percent of the nonfarm total, following the Goldsmith data, except for Illinois, where direct evidence suggests a 30/70 split. The results are tabulated below.

	Farm	*Nonfarm Business*	*Individuals*
Arkansas	25%	15%	60%
Illinois	8	28	64
Kentucky	15	17	68
Mississippi	14	17	68
Missouri	12	18	70
Nebraska	40	12	48
North Carolina	16	17	67
South Carolina	9	18	73
Utah	14	17	69
West Virginia	4	19	77

[1] Raymond W. Goldsmith, *The National Wealth of the United States in the Postwar Period* (Princeton University Press, 1962), Tables B-36, B-82, B-86, B-119, and B-129.

For the four relevant states, intangibles have been allocated half to individuals (residential) and half to nonfarm business. Flow of Funds data would suggest a larger share for individuals, but the marked biases in coverage dilute this conclusion. Most of the value which does not avoid the assessor in Illinois, for example, consists of bank deposits, and much of that is owned by corporations; a significant proportion of the tax is absorbed, in effect, by banks themselves.

"Farm" includes acreage and farm realty; agricultural personalty where taxed (twenty of the twenty-eight states shown); and a share of motor vehicles in ten states (see above). The "Other" category includes other locally assessed realty; nearly all state-assessed property; commercial and industrial personalty where taxed (twenty-four of twenty-eight states shown); a share of motor vehicles in ten states; a share of intangibles in four states; and all other personalty where taxed (eighteen of twenty-eight states).

Table 5-3

These estimates were made by the Advisory Commission on Intergovernmental Relations.[2] The derivation is explained in Appendix B of the report, pp. 107-12. It includes privately owned (except for tax-exempt organizations) land and structures and farm and business equipment and inventories, except motor vehicles. The relative value of public utility property was assumed to be proportional to the distribution of gross receipts or payrolls (for railroads). Other value estimates were in the main based on the 1957 Census of Governments and on the federal economic censuses.

Table 5-4

The Advisory Commission estimates for all taxable property equal total property tax revenue excluding estimated property taxes on public utilities and motor vehicles divided by the estimated market value of privately owned (excluding tax-exempt organizations) land and structures, and business and farm equipment and inventories (excluding public utilities and motor vehicles). For single-family dwellings, the value information is based on 1957 Census of Governments: 1956 gross assessed

[2] In *Measures of State and Local Fiscal Capacity* (1962), Table 17.

values of single-family houses divided by weighted average assessment ratios based on measurable sales. Revenue data take account of exemptions applicable to single-family houses.

The final column is based upon the estimated market value of all taxable locally assessed real property before partial exemptions in 1956 and 1961, divided into general property tax revenue from locally assessed realty in 1957 and 1962. These estimates were computed by the Census Bureau.

Table 5-7

The thirty-two areas included in this table have been selected from the forty-three cities with a 1960 population in excess of 300,000. The criterion for selection in most cases has been the availability of taxable property value data usable in this comparison. Thus Dallas and Houston are omitted because "Taxable Property Values" contains no assessed value data for the central cities; five other cities are omitted because they are located in states in which the primary assessment unit is the municipality rather than the county, and equalized value data are not readily available for these areas. Four other cities are omitted for various reasons. Similarly, the selection of outlying areas (with which to compare the central cities) has been governed by the availability of comparable value data; the entire SMSA is not covered, for most multi-county SMSA's. The central cities of Atlanta, Kansas City, Oklahoma City, and Portland spill over county lines; the value data for these central cities apply only to the portion of the cities located in the principal county, but the revenue data apply to the entire central city, of necessity.

Twenty of the central cities shown comprise less than the counties in which they are located, and county-wide assessment prevails; thus cities and suburbs are in a single assessment jurisdiction and assessed values can be directly compared. For these areas, the figures shown were computed by dividing the assessed value subject to tax for 1961, from Table 21 of "Taxable Property Values," by the 1960 population. For Denver, Philadelphia, St. Louis, San Francisco, and Washington, which require comparisons across county lines, a similar procedure was employed, except that the assessed value data were divided by indicated assessment ratios: for single-family houses, for suburban areas, from Table 22 of "Taxable Property Values," and for all locally assessed realty types (except highest value properties), from a special Census tabulation, "Partial-Coverage Assessment Ratios for Locally Assessed Taxable Real Property in Selected Major Cities: 1961" (1963). For the remaining seven areas, the computation is based on these local sources:

Baltimore—*Final Report of the Baltimore Metropolitan Area Study Commission to the Governor* (September 1963), Table 1; 1960 "adjusted value" and 1960 population.

Buffalo, New York, and Rochester—New York State Department of Audit and Control, *Comparison of Revenues, Expenditures and Debt: 1949-1959* (Comptroller's Studies in Local Finance, No. 1, 1961); 1959 "full value" and 1960 population.

Newark—New Jersey Taxpayers Association, *Financial Statistics of New Jersey Local Government, 1960 Edition* (Trenton, 1961) and Morris Beck, *Property Taxation and Urban Land Use in Northeastern New Jersey* (Urban Land Institute, 1963), Appendixes A and C; 1960 "equalized value" and 1960 population.

Detroit—Karl D. Gregory, "The Property Tax in Detroit" (mimeo.), a Staff Memorandum Prepared for the Citizens Income Tax Study Committee of the City of Detroit (December 1960), Table 6; 1960 "county equalized values" and 1960 population.

Milwaukee—Father Donald J. Curran, S. J., kindly provided his worksheets underlying his article, "The Metropolitan Problem: Solution from Within?" *National Tax Journal*, Vol. 16 (September 1963), pp. 213-23. The data are from Wisconsin Department of Taxation records; 1960 values and 1960 population.

For the seven areas which involve comparisons of whole counties or independent cities outside counties (Baltimore, Denver, New York, Philadelphia, St. Louis, San Francisco, and Washington), the data are 1957 per capita property tax revenue comparisons as shown in U. S. Bureau of the Census, *Local Government Finances and Employment in Relation to Population: 1957* (1961). For twenty-one other areas—cities within counties—a much more shaky procedure was used to derive 1957 data. First, 1957 population estimates were derived by straight-line interpolation from 1950 and 1960 Census data, and combined with the county estimates used in the Census publication just cited (which were similarly derived). Second, 1957 property tax revenue data for the governments overlying the central city and for local governments in the remainder of the county—excluding the county government and county-wide special districts—were obtained from U. S. Bureau of the Census, *Census of Governments: 1957*, Vol. III, No. 6, "Local Government Finances in Standard Metropolitan Areas" (1959), Table 4, and from the individual state bulletins which comprise Vol. VI of the *Census of Governments:*

1957. Thus, the exclusion of county-wide tax revenues overstates the differentials, and the distortion is greater where county government is more important, especially noticeable for Fort Worth, Memphis, and San Antonio. For the four other areas, the following sources were used:

Cleveland—Seymour Sacks and William F. Hellmuth, Jr., *Financing Government in a Metropolitan Area: The Cleveland Experience* (1961), Tables III-6 through III-9; 1956 population and revenue data.

Newark—New Jersey Taxpayers Association, cited above; 1960 population and revenue data.

Buffalo and Rochester—New York State source cited above and also the same author's *1959 Tax Atlas of New York State* (Comptroller's Studies in Local Finance, No. 2, 1961).

The effective tax rate data were computed by dividing the per capita revenue relatives in column 2 by the per capita tax base relatives in column 1. Where the data in the first two columns are relatively reliable and where they apply to dates which are nearly coincident, the figures in column 3 should be a rather good indicator of effective rate relationships. However, in most cases, there is a gap of several years between the two sets of data. Moreover, the revenue data are generally less reliable; where these are good, as in the cases of whole-county comparisons, the tax base data may be suspect. Thus, these figures should be regarded with some suspicion; they are presented here because alternative effective rate data are very rare, and having derived the two per capita series in the first two columns, the marginal effort required to present this series is nominal.

Figures in parentheses, in contrast, are direct computations from the local sources cited above; the figure shown for Newark is for a somewhat different area—the 22 core communities in the nine-county northeastern New Jersey area versus the 257 other taxing jurisdictions in this area. It applies only to real property. These data are rather accurate descriptions of the situation, subject only to the inherent inaccuracy of the equalization process.

The following special geographic definitions apply to outlying areas:

Philadelphia includes only Pennsylvania counties.

St. Louis includes only Missouri counties.

San Francisco excludes Alameda County, treated in conjunction with Oakland.

Baltimore includes Harford County, in addition to the official SMSA counties.

Washington excludes the city of Falls Church.

Table 5-9

Sources and Definitions for Each Area

CHICAGO. "Corporate" (municipal general purpose) tax rates, per capita municipal expenditures, and assessed values per capita standardizing for intercounty differences in assessment ratios for single-family houses in 1956. Computed from: Northeastern Illinois Metropolitan Area Planning Commission, *Suburban Factbook, 1950-60* (June 1960), Table 10; U. S. Bureau of the Census, *Census of Governments: 1957,* Vol. VI, No. 11, "Government in Illinois" (1959), Table 40, and Vol. V, "Taxable Property Values in the United States" (1959) Table 22.

NEW YORK STATE. Municipal full-value tax rates, per capita operating expenditures for common municipal functions, and per capita full valuation (N = 61, 55, and 185, respectively). Sources: New York State Department of Audit and Control, *The State and Local Government—The Role of State Aid* (Comptroller's Studies in Local Finance, No. 3, 1963), Table VII-4; John J. Carroll and Seymour Sacks, "The Property Tax Base and the Pattern of Local Government Expenditures: The Influence of Industry," *Papers and Proceedings,* Regional Science Association, Vol. 9 (1962), Tables 3, 4, and 6.

WESTCHESTER COUNTY. Village full-value tax rates and per capita general operating expenditures (N = 22). Computed from: New York State Department of Audit and Control, *Comparison of Revenues, Expenditures and Debt: 1949-1959* (Comptroller's Studies in Local Finance, No. 1, 1961) and *1959 Tax Atlas of New York State* (Comptroller's Studies in Local Finance, No. 2, 1961).

CUYAHOGA COUNTY. All Cuyahoga County data computed from various tables in Seymour Sacks and William F. Hellmuth, Jr., *Financing Government in a Metropolitan Area: The Cleveland Experience* (The Free Press, 1961). The school district data are school tax rates, school operating expenditures per average daily membership (ADM), and assessed values per ADM (N = 32). The municipal data are municipal tax rates, operating expenditures per capita, and assessed values per capita (N = 20 and 38 for cities and villages, respectively). The first column figures are Spearman rank correlation coefficients.

BERGEN COUNTY. Equalized school tax rates, per pupil school operating expenditures (including pro rata share of regional high school districts), and equalized assessed value per pupil. Figures in parentheses are the results when school tax levy per pupil—an indicator of total school expenditures which are locally financed—is substituted for per pupil operating expenditures. (N = 69, excluding an extreme low-tax industrial enclave). Computed from: New Jersey Taxpayers Association, *Financial Statistics of New Jersey Local Government,* 1960 and 1962 editions; New Jersey State Chamber of Commerce, *The Local Property Tax in New Jersey in 1960,* Parts I and II (1960).

HARTFORD. Full valuation tax rates (for municipal plus school), expenditures relative to full valuation (proxies for separate school and municipal tax rates), expenditures per capita and per average daily membership, and full valuation per capita (N = 26). Source: Capital Region Planning Agency, *Municipal Taxation and Regional Development* (East Hartford, Connecticut, March 1963), Appendixes (prepared by Seymour Sacks).

CONNECTICUT AND MASSACHUSETTS. Equalized tax rates, per capita current expenditures, and equalized property values per capita, both school and nonschool (N = 163 for Connecticut, 351 for Massachusetts tax rates and property values, and 161 for Massachusetts expenditures and property values). Source: George A. Bishop, "Notes and Statistical Materials on Equalized Property Tax Rates in New England," supplement to article, "The Property Tax and Local Government Spending in New England," *New England Business Review,* December 1962 (Federal Reserve Bank of Boston).

Derivation of Table 6-3

THE ESTIMATES in Table 6-3 are designed to reflect the portions of national wealth in the form of privately owned tangible personal property which are located in states in which the various types of personalty are legally taxable. The Goldsmith estimates in Table 6-2 have been reduced to account not only for complete exemption, but also for partial exemptions, which are important for agricultural and household personalty. The figures in Table 6-3 thus are very crude ones, developed mostly to provide some rough approximation of the *legal* tax base; Table 6-2 indicates the wealth potentially taxable, while Tables 6-1 and 6-5 indicate the wealth on assessment rolls.

Commercial and Industrial Personalty

Legally taxable amounts are estimated at 80 percent of the net equipment figure in Table 6-2 and 75 percent of inventories. The five states with virtually complete exemption of commercial and industrial personalty account for 17 to 20 percent of manufacturing activity (depending on the measure used) and 17 to 25 percent of trade activity. Other states allow a variety of special exemptions as well, which would reduce the percentages used. The equipment estimate is essentially based on the share of manufacturing activity, adjusted roughly for special exemptions and for partial coverage in Pennsylvania (done by defining some equipment as realty). The inventory estimate is based on the percentage shares of activity of various types in the exemption states, weighted by the size of manufacturing, retail, wholesale, and service industry inventories and adjusted roughly for special exemptions.

Agricultural Personalty

This is estimated at 80 percent of the figure in Table 6-2. In eight states accounting for 10 to 11 percent of most farm income and output measures, agricultural personalty is virtually completely exempted. For the remaining states, partial and special exemptions are assumed arbitrarily to equal 10 percent of total agricultural personalty, per Table 6-2.

Household Personalty

This is estimated at 35 percent of the figure in Table 6-2. This is the approximate share of U. S. personal income received by residents of the twelve states in which household personalty is fully taxable, together with fractions of state personal income (one-half or two-thirds) of an additional nine states where significant portions of household personalty appear to be legally subject to tax. This latter is also a crude adjustment.

Motor Vehicles

Motor vehicles are generally included in the legal tax base in twenty-one states with about 37 percent of U. S. motor vehicle registrations. This percentage was revised downwards, to 35 percent, to reflect (1) the mobility, and hence ease of tax avoidance, of trucks and buses; and (2) the generally lower per capita income characteristics of the states subjecting motor vehicles to the general property tax, which suggest that the average market value of registered motor vehicles is lower than the national average in such states.

INDEX

Index

Ability to pay related to tax, 5, 29, 56, 214

Accessibility, effect of: On land values, 35-36, 39; on location rents, 206

Acreage, tax on (*see also* Land; Farms), 18-21, 98, 225, 228-29, 303

Administration: Annual value property tax, 193, 195-97; "family of user charges," 216, 220; income tax, 179; property tax, 5-8, 173-83; site value taxation, 198-202, 203n; standard of excellence of, 177-79, 183

Ad valorem taxation, 11, 12a, 13, 34, 202; applied to apartments, 82; business property, 166; motor vehicles, 182; personalty, 138; utilities, 21n, 140n, 181

Advisory Commission on Intergovernmental Relations, 7, 97, 101-03, 107, 189-90, 231-32, 299, 304

Agricultural property (*see also* Farms): Personalty, 143-49, 151-52, 157, 207n, 229, 311; realty, 188-89, 226, 251-52; taxes on, 20-21, 28, 44, 110-11, 239, 245-46, 259-60

Agriculture, Department of, 107, 152n, 187, 241

Air transportation, 26, 73, 231-32

Alabama, 91, 99, 100, 103

Alaska, 91, 99, 100, 103, 141

Allocative efficiency, 109-16, 123-24, 135, 162-63, 169, 217

Annual vs. capital property values, 192-97

Antipodes, 11

Apartments: Assessment of, 78, 80; effective tax rates, 298-301; income tax treatment, 74; location, 120; property tax, 18-19, 53, 75, 77-79, 81-83, 108, 244-45; tax abatement, 85

Appraisal costs, 180

Arizona; Property tax, 90, 95n, 100; property tax rates, 103-105, 233; property values, 98

Arkansas: Property tax, 91, 100; property tax rates, 103, 109; property values, 99, 303-04

Assessment, 6, 18, 165, 173-83; of agricultural land, 207n; "family of user charges," 216; in Great Britain, 176, 195n; increases in, 7, 21n, 189; local, 23, 25, 76-80, 83-84, 183, 185-86; personalty, 95, 98-99, 114, 139-43, 145-50, 153-54, 162, 182, 303-04; regressivity in, 56-57, 268; of rents, 169, 196; site value, 201, 211; slum property, 194; special, 213; by states, 23, 95, 150-51

Atlanta, Ga., 76, 106, 107, 118, 178, 305

Australia, 12, 192, 202-04

Austria, 12, 14, 192

Automobiles (*see also* Motor vehicles), 39, 251-52

Back, Kenneth, 80n

Bailey, Martin J., 238

Baltimore, Md., 106, 118, 119, 122, 178, 306-07

Bank deposits, 141-42, 237, 303

Banks, tax on realty owned by, 23, 27

315

Beck, Morris, 119*n*, 125*n*, 133*n*, 134, 306
Belgium, 12, 14
Benefits (*see also* Public services): Correlation with property tax, 5, 29, 41-42, 59-62, 110, 213; financed by property tax, 65, 70-71, 74, 214-16, 247, 255-58, 261; tax, 81-82
Bergen County, N.J., 130, 137, 265-96, 308-09
Bird, Frederick, L., 139*n*, 173*n*, 177, 179
Bird, Richard M., 203*n*
Birkhead, Guthrie S., 135*n*, 172*n*
Birmingham, Ala., 118
Bishop, George A., 309
Blank, David M., 281-82
Boston, Mass., 31, 75, 106, 107, 178, 183
Brazer, Harvey E., 47*n* (table), 55*n*, 110*n*, 115*n*, 135*n*, 170*n*, 172*n*
Break, George F., 87
Bridges, Benjamin, Jr., 185*n*
Brown, H. G., 32*n*, 203*n*
Browning, Clyde E., 198*n*, 202, 203*n*
Brownlee, O. H., 43*n* (table), 46*n* (table), 247*n*, 250-52, 257
Buehler, Alfred G., 139*n*
Buffalo, N.Y., 31, 106, 118, 178, 306-07
Burkhead, Jesse, 8, 133-35, 185*n*, 186-87
Business: Costs (nontax), 113; equipment (*see* Equipment, business); expenditures benefiting, 61, 256; public services used by, 38, 115-16, 169
Business property (*see also* Commercial property; Industrial property): Alternative to property tax on, 169-70; as tax base component, 95-96; assessment of (*see also* Assessment), 80, 95; external diseconomies, 115; immobility of, 81; opportunism in taxing, 169; personalty, 6, 147*n*, 152-53, 156-62, 234-36; realty, 158-60, 181, 188, 197; revenues from, 20-27, 110, 239; shifting of taxes, 38-40, 43-44, 251-53, 259; tax rates, 108-10, 167; taxes on, 42-44, 71-72, 111-16, 166, 169-70, 217; urban areas, 117, 120, 122, 125, 127, 130, 155

California: Assessment in, 149*n*, 175; housing, 97; property tax, 91, 93*n*, 100, 103, 230; property values, 96, 99, 211
Campbell, Alan K., 8, 133*n*, 161
Canada, 1, 11, 12, 192, 197, 202-03
Cannon, Edwin, 32*n*
Capital: Definition of, 9*n*; demand for, 36-37; gains, 69, 74, 209, 213, 217; improvements, 213; regions short in, 93, 108; reproducible, 33; shifting of investment in, 68, 72
Capital-output ratios, 23, 26
Capital *vs.* annual property values, 192-97
Capitalization: Of earnings (income), 181, 192-93, 195, 200; of land rents, 210-11, 219; of property tax, 33-36, 52, 59, 83, 130, 170, 205
Carroll, John J., 308
Census Bureau, 18, 77, 140*n*, 149-50, 222
Census of Housing, 40*n*, 42, 78, 105-06, 165, 297-301
Census of Manufactures, 108
Central Cities. *See* Cities
Chicago, Ill.: Assessment in, 76, 178; housing in, 78, 83; per capita property values, 118-19, 126, 308; property tax, 81, 106-07; shift of bank deposits, 141; tax rates, 128-30, 183, 301; taxing units, 124
Chow, Gregory C., 39*n*
Cincinnati, Ohio: 118-19, 178
Cities (*see also* Metropolitan areas; Urban areas): Decentralization, 123, 208; nonproperty tax in, 93; property tax in, 9-10, 39, 74-85, 89, 134, 166, 301; versus suburbs, 117-24, 155
Cleveland, Ohio: Assessment in, 76, 178; per capita property values, 118, 126, 307; property tax, 81, 106; tax rates, 129, 134
Cohen, Wilbur J., 47*n* (table), 55*n*
Colorado, 90, 98, 100, 103-05
Columbus, Ohio, 118, 122
Comiez, Maynard S., 247*n*

Commerce, Department of, 251*n*

Commercial property, 81, 117, 120; assessment of, 76, 78-80, 109; personalty, 143-49, 154-55, 160, 229, 234-35, 310; realty, 160, 226, 235-36; revenue from tax on, 18-20, 152

Commodity taxes, 4-5, 37

Connecticut: Hartford area, 126, 129, 137, 309; property tax, 90, 100, 102; property values, 98, 228-29; sales tax, 94; tax rates, 125-27, 133, 309

Consumer durables (*see also* Households: Personalty), 188

Consumers: Behavior of, 62; effect of property tax on, 36, 39; shifting of property tax to, 112, 156-59, 162-63

Consumption: Data, 249; expenditures, 42-43, 166-67; tax, 6, 27*n*, 40, 68-69, 87, 109, 168-70

Counties, 173, 176, 278-80; assessment in, 174; New Jersey, 265-96; personalty in, 155; property tax in, 9, 186-87, 223-36; tax rates in, 150

Curran, Donald J., 119*n*, 135, 306

Daicoff, Darwin W., 34, 43*n* (table), 46*n* (table), 247*n*, 248, 250-51, 253, 255-57

Dallas, Tex., 76, 106, 107, 178

David, Martin H., 47*n* (table), 55*n*

Delaware, 91, 99, 100, 103, 233

Denmark, 12-14, 192, 212

Denver, Col., 118, 305-06

Depreciation (real estate), 74, 79-80

Depression (*1930's*), 6, 184, 186, 193

Detroit, Mich., 106, 118, 178, 301, 306

Differentials in property tax, 79-82, 85; geographic, 86-137, 153-55, 172

District of Columbia (Washington): Assessment in, 80, 178; property tax, 91, 100, 106, 118, 143, 154; property tax rates, 103; property values, 99, 305-07

Due, John F., 13*n*, 109*n*, 112*n*, 114

Duesenberry, James S., 282

Dye, Thomas R., 135*n*

Ecker-Racz, L. L., 204

Economic effects of property tax, 67-85

Economic neutrality of property tax, 26-29

Economic sectors, impact of property tax on, 17-31

Edgeworth, F. Y., 32*n*, 35

Education: As property tax benefit, 29, 60*n*, 67, 115, 257-58, 261; expenditures for, 10, 65, 116; income elastic demand for, 105, 122, 135; investment in, 68

Elasticity: Income (*see* Income elasticity); price, 156, 158

Ely, Richard T., 198

England, 176, 193, 195*n*, 211

Equalization, 80, 115, 119

Equilibrium analysis, 33, 36, 37, 45

Equipment, business, 161-62; assessment of, 149, 182; property tax on, 3, 67, 95, 143-44, 310

Equity: In property tax incidence, 66, 164-65, 168, 214; in site value taxation, 208-10, 212-13, 217-18; interpersonal, 66, 135, 136; transitional problems, 209-10, 220

Europe, 14-15, 192

Excise taxes, 27*n*, 30, 68, 166

Exemptions from property tax: Homestead, 92-93, 96, 109, 224, 302; personalty, 95-96, 139-40, 142-46, 154, 310-11

Expenditures, public: Benefits of (*see* Benefits); correlation with tax rates, 126-29, 133, 135, 155, 164-65, 170, 186; increase in, 7

Farioletti, Marius, 179*n*

Farms: Personalty, 147*n*, 149, 152*n*, 157-58, 245; realty, 34, 96, 98-103, 107-09, 158-59, 197, 245-46, 303; revenue from property tax on, 18-21, 28, 225, 228-29

Federal aid, 108, 121

Federal Housing Administration, 53

Ferber, Robert, 65

Finland, 13, 14

Fire protection, 67, 105, 116, 214-17, 219, 261

Fiscal federation, 136-37, 173

Fiscal mercantilism, 131-32

Fisher, Ernest M., 198

Fisher, Robert M., 198n
Florida: Housing, 97; property tax, 7, 91, 100; property tax rates, 103, 105; property values, 99
Ford, James, 204n
Fort Worth, Tex., 118, 307
France, 12, 14
Friedman, Milton, 62n, 265, 273
Frontage tax, 216

Gaffney, Mason, 198n
Geographical differentials in property taxation, 86-137, 153-55, 172; by choice, 87, 95; interstate, 88-116; urban areas, 116-37
George, Henry, 5n, 197
Georgia, 91, 99, 100, 103
Germany, 12-14, 171, 192
Goldsmith, Raymond W., 2, 24n, 25, 28n (table), 29n (table), 53, 140n, 143n, 144n (table), 145-48, 187, 188n (table), 190n (table), 210-11, 218-19, 251, 303, 310
Goode, Richard, 69, 70n
Gorven, O. D., 82n, 204n
Great Britain (United Kingdom), 11, 12, 192-95, 197; England, 176, 193, 195n, 211; Wales, 176, 193, 195n
Great Lakes states, 89, 94, 96, 107, 109, 153
Grebler, Leo, 281-82
Greece, 14
Gregory, Karl D., 306
Gronouski, John A., 247n, 252
Gross national product (GNP), 2, 8-9, 187, 189, 190
Gross receipts tax, 167
Groves, Harold M., 7n, 184

Hady, Thomas F., 156n, 158-59, 163
Harberger, Arnold C., 39n, 63n, 73n, 238, 273n
Harriss, C. Lowell, 7n, 212n, 214-15
Hartford, Conn., 126, 129, 137, 309
Hawaii: Property tax, 89, 91, 100, 202; property tax rates, 103; property values, 99
Health benefits: For lower income groups, 61, 116, 121, 257; property tax revenue for, 10, 60n, 67, 261

Heer, Clarence, 7n
Heilbrun, James, 191n, 195n, 198n, 202, 203n, 207, 208n, 210-11
Hellmuth, William F., Jr., 80n, 125n, 132-33, 137, 307, 308
Herman, Harold, 135n
Highway user tax, 6
Highways, 10, 60n, 257, 261
Hogan, John D., 185n
Homestead exemptions, 92-93, 96, 109, 224, 302
Hospitals, expenditures for, 10, 60n, 257, 261
Hotels, tax on, 23, 27
Households: In northern New Jersey, 283; income of, 263; occupation of head of, 275-77, 294-96; personalty, 144-49, 152, 156, 182, 254, 259, 311; property tax revenue from, 20, 229, 239
Housing (see also Residential property): Assessment of (see also Assessment), 76-80, 177-78, 182; correlation with income, 291-92, 296; effect of taxes on, 5, 36, 69-70, 163n, 165, 168-69, 218, 220; high-value, 122-23; income elasticity of demand for, 42, 63-65, 188; low-value, 121; multi-family (see Apartments); nonfarm, alternative estimates of taxes on, 241-45; owner-occupied, taxing of, 38, 45, 46, 47, 48, 50-55, 71-72, 79, 242-45; percentage distribution by value, 262; property tax revenue from, 18-21, 29-31, 67, 158-59, 220; rehabilitation of, 84-85, 205; single-family (see Single-family housing); slum, 194; taxes on, 40, 45-59, 68-70, 73, 81-82, 284
Houston, 178
Human capital, investment in, 68

Iceland, 12, 13
Idaho, 90, 98, 100, 101, 103
Illinois: Cook County, 141; personalty assessment, 148, 153n; property tax, 90, 93n, 100, 113, 154, 230; property tax rates, 102; property values, 98, 303-04
Improved sites, property tax on, 35-36

Improvements: Assessment of, 211; capital, 213; taxes on, 194, 202-05, 210, 212; value of, 198-202

Incidence of property taxes, 5, 32-66, 193, 208, 238-50, 265-96

Income: Classes, incidence of property tax and benefits, 40-56, 60-62, 70, 247-58; concept of, 55-56, 61; correlation with housing, 291-92; current, 42, 57, 62-66, 267-73; in New Jersey, 64, 284, 293-94, 296; permanent, 42, 58, 62-66, 265, 273-83; personal (*see* Personal income); redistribution of, 42, 62, 87-89, 95, 136, 162, 164-65, 217

Income elasticity: Demand for education, 105, 122, 135; demand for housing, 42, 57, 63-65, 268, 272-74, 281-82; of property tax, 7-9, 184-90

Income tax: Administration of, 179; as alternative to property tax, 167, 170; corporate, 113n, 114, 161-63, 255; effect of deduction provisions in, 41-51, 61, 156n, 158, 254-55; effect on real estate investment (housing), 69-70, 74, 75, 195n, 218; property tax deductions in, 56, 243, 262; rates, 255, 261; state, 6, 94, 163, 209

Increment tax, 212-13, 217, 219-20

Increments, unearned, 209, 212

Indiana, 90, 98, 100, 102, 113

Industrial enclaves, 124-25, 127, 130, 131

Industrial property: Assessment, 76, 78, 80, 109; effect of property tax on, 68, 72; personalty, 143-49, 155, 160, 229, 234, 310; realty, 120, 160, 226, 232-33, 235-36; revenue from property tax on, 18-27, 71, 81, 152

Industry, property tax estimates, 238-41

Insurance companies, 23, 27, 84

Intangible personal property, 140-43, 146, 150-51, 182; assessment, 303; property tax on, 6, 21n, 39-40, 142, 237, 253; revenue from tax on, 19-20, 227-28, 239; shifting of tax on, 259

Interarea differentials in property tax, 89-116

Interest: Deductibility of, 69; effect of property tax on rates, 36-37

Internal Revenue Service, 42, 240, 243n

Inventories, 3, 6, 95, 161-62, 310; assessment of, 182; growth of, 139; income elasticity of, 188, 190; revenue from tax on, 151, 227; subject to tax, 143-44, 149, 158

Investment: Correlation with property tax, 36-37, 69, 87-88, 165, 194; in cities, 75, 83-84, 199-200, 205-06; in farm property, 28, 100; in housing, 5, 74; in intangibles, 141; in land, 213; shifting of, 68

Iowa, 90, 98, 100-02

Ireland, 11, 12, 192

Israel, 192

Italy, 15

Japan, 11, 12, 138n

Jensen, Jens P., *vii, ix,* 2n, 3, 4n, 5n, 32n, 34, 39, 40n

Kahn, C. Harry, 184

Kansas, 46, 90, 98, 100, 102

Kansas City, Mo., 76, 118, 178, 305

Kentucky: Personalty assessment, 153n; property tax, 91, 100; property tax rates, 103, 109; property values, 99, 304

Kistin, Helen, 282

Kurnow, Ernest, 185n

Labor, substitution for capital, 72

Lampman, Robert J., 185n, 187

Land: As property tax component, 45, 71, 170, 211; as tax base in financing public services, 216; income elasticity of, 188, 190; bare land component of tax base, 33-36, 52, 53; rental values of, 192; site value taxation, 197-212, 219; use planning, 39, 132, 135, 136, 166; value increment taxation, 212-13, 217, 219-20

Latin America, 192

Leland, Simeon E., 6n

Leontieff, Wassily, 282n

Liebman, Charles S., 135n

LIFE Study of Consumer Expenditures, 249-50

Local governments (*see also* Cities; Metropolitan areas; Urban areas): Alternatives to property tax, 166-70; assessment practices, 23, 25, 76-80, 83-84, 183, 185-86; differentials in property tax, 88, 116-37; expenditures, 6, 185, 189; nonproperty taxes, 87, 93-94, 121, 171; personalty assessment, 142, 146-47, 150-51, 153-55; property tax rates, 105-07, 170-71, 185-86; property taxes and expenditure benefits, 59-62, 247-58; revenue from property tax, 1-3, 9-13, 18-21, 89-92, 104, 222-37; use of property tax, 86, 170-73, 176, 190; user charges, 71, 216, 219

Location rents, 81, 115-16, 123, 199-201, 204, 206, 208, 217

Locational effects of taxation, 109-16, 123-24, 135, 162-63, 169, 217

Los Angeles, Calif., 76, 106, 118, 124, 178

Louisiana, 91, 99, 100, 103

Louisville, Ky., 118

Luxembourg, 12, 15

Mace, Ruth L., 131n

Maine, 90, 98, 100, 102, 233

Maisel, Sherman J., 273n, 282

Manufacturing: Location, 44, 117, 123; revenue from property tax on, 20, 22-27, 72, 108, 160-62, 235-36, 239-41; shifting of tax on, 251-52, 259-60

Market value: As tax base, 8, 97, 101, 185; elasticity of, 187, 189; use in assessment, 109, 180, 182, 201

Marshall, Alfred, 33n

Maryland: Assessment in, 153n, 207n; property tax, 91, 100; property tax rates, 103; property values, 99

Massachusetts: Assessment in, 80, 231; nonproperty taxes, 173; property tax, 90, 94, 100; property tax rates, 102, 126-27, 309; property values, 98

McLoone, Eugene P., 185n, 187-89

Memphis, 118, 307

Metropolitan areas (*see also* Cities;

Urban areas): Acreage in, 229; assessment ratios in, 77, 96; investment in, 75; property tax in, 30-31, 155, 165, 228-29; tax autonomy, 172; tax differentials, 106, 116-37; tax rates, 58-59, 88, 297-301

Michigan: Automobile industry, 252; hospital expenditures, 257; property tax, 43, 46-47, 90, 100, 109-10, 112, 247-48; property tax rates, 102, 104; property values, 34, 98, 224

Middle Atlantic states, 92, 105, 108

Miller, Herman P., 280n

Milwaukee, Wis., 120n; assessment in, 178, 180; property tax, 118-19, 175, 306; tax rates, 75, 122, 135, 183, 301

Mining, 20, 23-27, 160, 236, 239-40, 253

Minneapolis, Minn., 106, 178, 183

Minnesota: Personalty tax, 156-58; property tax, 43, 46-47, 90, 94, 100, 109, 113; property tax rates, 102, 104; property values, 98; tax study, 247, 257

Mississippi, 91, 99, 100, 103, 304

Missouri, 90, 98, 100, 102, 148, 304

Mitchell, George, 6, 7n

Monopoly, 112, 116

Montana, 90, 98, 100-02

Morgan, James N., 47n (table), 55n, 56

Mortgaged properties, 297-300

Morton, Walter, 47n

Motor carriers, tax on, 73, 231-32

Motor vehicles: Incidence of tax on, 254, 259; ownership of, 303; property tax on, 39, 155n, 156, 182, 311; revenue from tax on, 20, 151-52, 227, 229-30, 234, 239; value of, 144-49

Mountain states, 92, 96, 98, 100, 102, 153

Municipalities. *See* Cities.

Musgrave, Richard A., 32n, 43n (table), 46n (table), 247-48, 250-51, 253, 255-57

Mushkin, Selma J., 185, 187

Muth, Richard, 63, 73n, 273, 281

National Planning Association, 188

National Tax Association, 6*n*

Nebraska: Property tax, 89, 90, 94, 100; property tax rates, 102, 104; property values, 98, 101, 304

Net wealth taxes, 13-15

Netherlands, 12, 13, 15

Netzer, Dick, 131*n*, 137*n*, 185*n*, 187*n*

Neutrality: Economic, 26-29; increment tax, 212-13; property tax (*see* Unneutrality)

Nevada, 90, 98, 100, 103

New England: Property tax, 89-90, 100; property tax rates, 102, 105, 125; property values, 98, 108, 224

New Hampshire: Property tax, 90, 94, 100; property tax rates, 102, 233; property values, 98

New Jersey, 63-64, 265-96; assessments in, 148, 207*n*, 228, 231-32; Bergen County, 130, 137, 308-09; nonproperty taxes, 173; personalty tax, 156-61, 234; property tax, 58-59, 62, 87, 90, 94, 100, 116, 266*n;* property tax rates, 102, 122, 125-26, 128, 133-35; property values, 98, 119; residential property tax incidence, 265-96

New Mexico, 90, 95*n*, 98, 100, 103

New York (state): Counties, 186; nonproperty taxes, 87, 93; property tax, 87, 90, 100, 108, 143, 175, 235; property tax rates, 102, 125-26, 232-33, 308; property value, 98, 302; tax abatement, 85

New York City: Assessment in, 76, 78, 80, 174-75, 178, 181; land values, 213; Manhattan, 112, 116; metropolitan area, 31, 132-33, 161, 228-29; nonproperty tax, 93; property tax, 81, 82*n*, 83, 106-07, 118-19, 306; property tax rates, 122, 124, 183, 301; tax abatement, 85

New Zealand, 12, 192, 202-04

Newark, N.J., 75, 118-19, 120*n*, 178, 306-07

Nichols, Dorothy M., 141*n*

Nonproperty taxes, 87, 93-94, 121, 171, 173

North Carolina: Property tax, 91, 100, 148; property tax rates, 103, 109, 233; property values, 99, 304

North Dakota, 90, 98, 100-02

Northeast: Property tax, 106, 120, 153, 189; property tax rates, 101, 105, 107-08, 299; property values, 97-99; residential properties, 300

Norway, 12, 13, 15

Oakland, Calif., 118

Occupation, as factor in permanent income, 63-64, 275-77, 294-96

Office of Business Economics, 241, 248

Ohio: Cuyahoga County, 80, 124-26, 132-34, 137, 308; personalty tax, 156; property tax, 90, 96, 100, 113; property tax rates, 102, 104; property values, 98

Oklahoma, 91, 99, 100, 103

Oklahoma City, 118, 120*n*, 305

Omaha, Neb., 118, 120*n*

Oregon: Personalty tax, 157; property tax, 87, 91, 94, 100; property tax rates, 103-04; property values, 99

Pacific Coast states, 99, 103, 108, 153

Partial-coverage assessment ratios, 76-78

Payroll taxes, 69, 72, 167, 172

Pealey, Robert H., 46*n* (table)

Pennsylvania: Property tax, 87, 90, 100, 108, 116, 143, 235; property tax rates, 102; property values, 98; realty tax, 160, 202-03

Per capita: Economic base of property tax, 100; income, 97, 101, 186-87; property tax revenue, 90-91; property values, 97, 100-01, 117-18, 124-30, 133, 135

Personal income: Distribution of, 99, 248-49; per capita, 97, 101, 186-87; property tax on percentage of, 90-92, 94, 104-05, 186; school taxes on, 122*n;* tax on (*see* Income tax); versus capital as tax base, 192

Personal property: As tax base component, 138-63; assessment of, 98-99, 139-43, 145-50, 153-54, 162, 182, 303-04; defined, 140*n;* exemptions of, 95-96, 139-40, 142-46, 154; farm,

147n, 149, 152n, 157-58, 245; household, 144-49, 152, 156, 182, 254, 259, 311; income elasticity of, 188; industrial, 143-49, 155, 160, 229, 234, 310; intangible (see Intangible personal property); tangible, 139, 142, 143-50, 227-30, 310-11

Personal property tax, 138-63; Canada and Japan, 11; coverage by, 140-49; criticism of, 4-6; geographic differences, 153-55; incidence, 155-63; on business, 95, 114, 120, 147n, 234-36; rates, 25-26; revenue from, 18-21, 149-53, 223n, 227-30; shifting of, 36, 39, 44; versus heavier realty taxes, 156-61

Philadelphia, 106, 107, 118-19, 124, 135, 178, 305-07

Phoenix, Ariz., 118

Pittsburgh, Pa., 76, 106, 178, 202, 210

Plains states: Personalty, 153; property tax, 92, 94, 96; property tax rates, 107; property values, 97, 101, 186

Police protection, 105, 116, 121, 214, 219, 261

Pollution, from business operations, 115, 169

Population, correlation with property tax revenue, 186-87

Portland, Ore., 118, 305

Portugal, 15

Price elasticity, 156, 158

Producer durables, 36, 38, 68, 143-44, 188, 190

Progressivity in property tax, 54, 58, 60-61, 63, 66

Property. See Business property; Personal property; Real property; Residential property.

Property tax: Ability to pay, 5, 29, 214; administration of, 5-8, 173-83; advantages of, 164-65, 170-73, 176, 218; alternatives, 166-70, 191-220; assessment of (see Assessment); as income tax deduction, 41-51, 56, 61, 156n, 158, 243, 254-55, 262; business component of (see also Business property), 95-96; base of (see Tax base); benefits (see Benefits);

capitalization of, 33-36, 52, 59, 83, 130, 170, 205; characteristics, 1, 3, 5, 38; criticism of, 3-8, 165-66; differentials in, 79-82, 85, 86-137, 153-55, 172; economic effects of, 67-85; elasticity of, 7-9, 184-90; exemptions from (see Exemptions); incidence of, 5, 32-66, 155-63, 193, 208, 238-50, 265-96; land component of, 45, 71, 170, 211; nonresidential (see also Business property; Personal property), 42-45, 247-58, 259; personal (see Personal property tax); progressivity of, 54, 58, 60-61, 63, 66; proportionality of, 48, 51, 56, 61-62, 65-66, 74, 164, 266; rates (see Tax rates, property); redistribution effect of, 42, 62, 87-89, 95, 136, 162, 164-65, 217; reform proposals, 136-37, 172-73; regressivity of (see Regressivity, property tax); residential (see also Housing), 20, 45-59, 110, 156, 226, 239, 254, 265-96; revenue from (see Revenue from property tax); shifting of, 36-40, 43-45, 112, 156-58, 161-62, 248, 250-55, 259-60; United States, 1, 7-12, 192-97; unneutrality of, 26, 67-72, 88, 207

Property values: Annual vs. capital, 192-97; effect of capitalization of, 34-35; in northern New Jersey, 284; per capita, 97, 100-01, 117-18, 124-30, 133, 135; percentage distribution, 98-99; relative changes in, 119-22; use as tax base, 168, 186, 199

Proportionality in property tax, 48, 51, 56, 61-62, 65-66, 74, 164, 266

Public services (see also Benefits): Business use of, 38, 115-16, 169; financing of, 29, 34, 67, 88-89, 94-95, 214-17; relationship of tax revenues to, 59-60, 70, 130-31; suburbs, 117; urban areas, 105, 107, 116, 121, 127, 129, 136

Railroads: Revenue from tax on, 227-28, 231-32; shifting of tax on, 253; tax on, 21n, 26, 72-73, 166, 181

Rawson, Mary, 198n, 204n, 208n

Real property: Business, 158-60, 181, 188, 197, 226, 235-36; farm, 34, 96, 98-103, 107-09, 158-59, 197, 245-46, 303; industrial, 120, 160, 226, 232-33, 235-36

Real property tax (*see also* Property tax; Residential property), 3, 6, 23, 97, 190; ad valorem, 11-13, 21n, 34, 82, 140n, 166, 181, 202; alternative forms of, 166-70, 191-221; as proportion of income, 165; assessed value of property subject to, 98-99; assessment of, 76-80, 139, 178-81; correlation with personalty tax, 156-61; effective rates, 102-03, 114, 210; in cities, 9-10, 39, 74-85, 89, 134, 166; on land, 33-36, 39, 52, 53; on structures, 38-39, 53; reported on income tax returns, 47-51; revenue from, 18-21, 210-11

Redistribution effect of property tax, 42, 62, 87-89, 95, 136, 162, 164-65, 217

Regional Plan Association, 132n, 223

Regressivity, consumption tax, 40, 168

Regressivity, property tax, 40-51, 265-66, 268; incidence of, 5, 55, 61, 66, 136, 165; on personalty, 158, 163; on renters, 53-54; on residential property, 56-57, 59, 65, 273

Rehabilitation of property, 83-85

Reid, Margaret G., 63, 65n, 73, 163n, 273, 279n

Renewal, urban, 83-85, 205, 208

Rental values, as tax base, 192-96

Rented property, 297-98; in big cities, 75, 79, 85; in manufacturing, 108, 235-36; in northern New Jersey, 283; income from, 263; tax on, 40, 45, 51-54, 59, 240-42; urban areas, 38, 75, 79, 85

Renters, 47, 53-54, 57, 70, 73

Rents: Assessment of, 169, 196; imputed, 55, 69; land, 33-34, 218-19; location, 81, 115-16, 123, 199-201, 204, 206, 208, 217; median, 300; New Jersey, 269-71, 278, 287-90, 295; revenue from, 37-38, 210-11; tax on, 169, 215

Reproducible assets, property tax on, 35

Reproduction costs, 181

Residential Finance Survey (1960), 51, 53, 241-45, 297, 299

Residential property (*see also* Housing): Choice of, 127-29; dispersion of ownership, 197; distribution of assessed value, 98-99, 303; effect of tax differentials, 110; effect of tax exemptions, 96; in metropolitan areas, 125, 161, 297-301; in northern New Jersey, 285-86; in suburbs, 117, 119-21, 130, 132; regressivity of property tax on, 56-57, 59, 65, 273; taxes on, 20, 45-59, 156, 226, 239, 254, 265-96

Resort communities, 124

Resource allocation, 67, 71, 171, 195, 197, 204-08, 213

Resources, national, use of, 114-16, 135

Revenue: Land value increment tax, 212-13; nonproperty taxes, 121, 212; personalty tax, 149-53; property tax alternatives, 166-70; site value land tax, 210-12

Revenue from property tax, 4, 6-8, 10, 158, 184-90, 216-20; by property use class, 222-26; by type of property, 239, 241-46; local governments, 1-3, 9-13, 18-21, 89-92, 104, 222-37; personalty, 18-21, 149-53, 223n, 227-30; realty, 18-21, 210-11; sources of, 17-31; state governments, 1-3, 9, 18-21, 87, 90-92, 104, 222-37; utilities, 19-24, 26, 151, 227-28, 230-35, 239

Rhode Island, 90, 98, 100, 102, 233

Richman, Raymond L., 39n

Riew, John, 134

Robertson, Jack E., 46n (table)

Rochester, N.Y., 118, 306-07

Rolph, Earl R., 37

Rosenberg, Leonard G., 230, 232, 238-41

Sacks, Seymour, 80n, 125n, 132-33, 137, 307-09

St. Louis, Mo., 76, 78-79, 106, 118, 122, 178, 305-07

Sales taxes, 74, 94, 156, 163, 166-68, 172, 179, 218
San Antonio, Tex., 118, 307
San Diego, Calif., 76, 118, 178
San Francisco, Calif.: Assessment in, 76, 78, 178; property tax, 81, 106, 118, 124, 305-07
Sanitation, expenditures for, 10, 60n, 67, 257, 261
Scandinavia, 171
Schaller, Howard G., 215n
School districts, 9-10, 125-26, 130
School taxes, 122, 132, 135-37
Schools. See Education.
Schultz, Theodore W., 68n
Scranton, Pa., 202
Seagram Building, New York, 181
Seattle, Wash., 76, 118, 178
Seligman, Edwin R. A., 5n, 139, 209
Sestric, Joseph P., 80
Sewers, expenditures for, 71, 116, 213, 214, 219
Shopping centers, 130, 131
Shoup, Carl S., 13n, 32n, 34n
Simon, Herbert A., 32n, 35-36
Simpson, Herbert D., 119n
Single-family housing: Assessment of, 56, 76-80, 174, 177-80; Bergen County, 290, 295; income and value relationships, 264; median value, 82, 165; mortgaged, 297-300; percentage distribution by value, 262; property tax on, 50-51, 54, 105-07, 242, 244-45; rented, 37-38, 45, 196, 297-98; revenue from, 18-19; suburbs, 120, 132; tax rates, 102-03
Single-tax movement, 4
Site value taxation, 197-212, 217, 219-20; adequacy, 210-12; administrative feasibility, 198-202; encumbrance problem in, 201-02; equity, 208-10; experience with, 202-04; resource allocation effects, 204-08
Slums, taxes on, 194-95
Social overhead charges, 169-70
South Africa, 11, 12, 82n, 192, 202-04
South Carolina: Property tax, 91, 95n, 100; property tax rates, 103; property values, 99, 304
South Dakota, 90, 98, 100-02

Southern states: Elasticity coefficient for, 189; personalty tax in, 120, 153; property tax, 92, 96; property tax rates in, 101, 106-11, 152, 299-300; property values, 99; residential properties, 300
Spain, 15, 212
Spengler, Edwin H., 7n, 212n, 214n
Springfield, Mass., 80
Standard metropolitan statistical areas (SMSA): Acreage in, 229; assessment ratios in, 77, 96; regional differences, 106, 118; use of property tax, 121, 124, 155
State governments: Assessment in, 23, 95, 150-51; corporate income tax, 161-63; interstate differentials, 88-116, 153-55; revenue from property tax, 1-3, 9, 18-21, 87, 90-92, 104, 222-37; use of nonproperty taxes, 5-7, 59, 93, 173; use of property tax, 86, 89, 112, 190, 250
Stiles, Lynn A., 131n, 136n, 215n, 216n
Stocker, Frederick D., 246n
Stolper, Wolfgang F., 109n, 110n, 111n
Suburbs: Fiscal mercantilism, 131-32; industry in, 116; migration to, 82; personalty tax in, 155; property tax in, 30, 58-59, 74-75, 130, 165; school tax rates, 135; versus central cities, 117-24
Sweden, 12n, 13, 15
Switzerland, 15

Tax abatement, 83, 85
Tax base, property, 7-9, 86, 100, 168, 185-86, 199, 216; business property component of, 95-96; character of, 95-101; elasticity of, 186-88; personal property component of, 138-63; relationship to tax rates, 125-27, 129, 171
Tax rates, income, 255, 261
Tax rates, property, 101-09; correlation with land rents, 210-11; differentials in, 23, 152, 183, 297-301; effect of increase in, 33-35, 83, 114; local governments, 105-07, 170-71, 185-86; personalty, 25-26; suburbs, 30, 58-59; trend toward uniformity

in, 132-37; urban areas, 19, 21, 23, 70n, 105-07, 122-29, 223; variation in, 38, 150, 222-24, 228n
Tax rates required to replace property tax revenue, 167-68
Taxable capacity, metropolitan areas, 117-22
Tenants. See Renters.
Tennessee, 91, 99, 100, 103
Texas: Property tax, 91, 100; property tax rates, 103, 109, 232-33; property values, 99
Thompson, Wilbur R., 172n
Tiebout, Charles M., 127; hypothesis, 127, 129-31
Tobier, Emanuel, 58n, 265n
Toledo, Ohio, 118-19, 122
Trade activities, property tax on, 162, 239
Transportation services (see also Railroads): Financing of, 214, 216; revenue from property tax on, 19-21, 24, 26, 227, 230-32
Turvey, Ralph, 198

Unearned increments, 209, 212
United Kingdom. See Great Britain.
United States, role of property tax in, 1, 7-12, 192-97
Unneutrality (property tax), 26, 67-72, 88, 207
Urban areas (see also Cities; Metropolitan areas): Assessment in (see also Assessment), 56; differentials within, 116-37; industrial rental property, 38; open space in, 206-07; personalty, 155; property tax, 35, 88, 116-37, 166, 173; property tax rates in, 19, 21, 23, 70n, 105-07, 122-29, 223; public services in, 105, 107, 116, 121, 127, 129, 136; renewal in, 83-85, 205, 208; site value taxation, 198-99
Urban sprawl, 205
User charges, 71, 115-16, 169, 191, 213-17, 219-20
Utah: Property tax, 90, 95n, 100; property tax rates, 103, property values, 98, 304
Utilities: Assessment of, 140n, 181;

immobility, 81; property tax on, 67, 72, 111, 218n; revenue from property tax on, 19-24, 26, 151, 227-28, 230-35, 239; shifting of tax on, 44, 252-53, 259; site value tax on, 206n; user charges for, 216

Vacant lots, 199, 207, 226, 237; assessment of, 78; incidence of tax on, 253-54; revenue from tax on, 18-20, 21n, 158-59, 239; shifting of tax on, 259
Vacant properties, 193, 297-98, 300
Value added: In manufacturing industries, 27; increment tax on land, 212-13, 217, 219-20; tax on, 71, 167, 170, 172
Van Peski, Neva, 141n
Vancouver, B.C., 198n
Venezuela, 13
Vermont, 90, 98, 100, 102, 233
Vernon, Raymond, 117n, 123n
Vickrey, William, 215-16
Virginia, 91, 99, 100, 103, 109

Wales, 176, 193, 195n
Walker, Mabel L., 85n, 193n, 208n, 212n
Washington (state): Property tax, 87, 91, 94, 100; property tax rates, 103-04; property values, 99
Washington, D.C. See District of Columbia
Water supply, 116, 214, 216
Welch, Ronald, 211
Welfare benefits: Income groups, 61, 116, 121, 257; property tax revenue for, 10, 60n, 67, 137, 261
West Virginia: Property tax, 91, 100, 141; property tax rates, 103; property values, 99, 304
Westchester County, N.Y., 126, 308
Western states, 90-92, 97-99, 108, 120, 189, 299-300
Weston, J. Fred, 27n
Williams, Oliver P., 135n
Winnick, Louis, 273n, 281-82
Wisconsin: Assessment in, 53n, 175; Milwaukee County, 197n; personalty tax, 156-57; property tax, 43, 46,

90, 94, 100, 109, 114; property tax rates, 102; property value, 98, 224; tax study, 247-48, 251-53

Wonnacott, Ronald J., 110*n*, 113

Woodruff, A. M., 204

Wueller, Paul, 7*n*

Wyoming: Property tax, 90, 95*n*, 100; property tax rates, 102, 104; property values, 98

Zoning, effect on land use, 130-32, 135